CONSTRUCTION CONTRACT POLICY

Improved Procedures and Practice

Editors

John Uff
Director

Phillip Capper
Masons' Visiting Professor

Centre of Construction Law and Management,
King's College, London

1989

Published in Great Britain by
Centre of Construction Law and Management,
King's College, University of London,
The Old Watch House, Strand,
London WC2R 2LS.
01 873 2446
01 872 0210 (Fax)

Printed by The Eastern Press, London and Reading.

ISBN 0-9514866-0-8

Preface

The Centre of Construction Law and Project Management was established in King's College, London University, two years ago. It is an independent, self-financed Centre which maintains close links within the College with the Faculties of Laws and Engineering and the Department of Management. It comprises, and has direct connections with, construction industry professionals, like civil engineers, architects and surveyors, and practising lawyers, whether judges, arbitrators, barristers or solicitors. Their enthusiastic participation in the Centre's activities led to the Centre's first major Conference on Construction Contract Policy on 14th, 15th and 16th September 1988.

This unique book is the product of that exceptionally successful Conference which concentrated on the forms of contract used in the construction industry with a view to improved procedures and practice. After all, the obscurity and pitfalls present in standard forms are at the core of the construction industry's problems. These papers by leading experts identify and develop various heads of policy to be taken into account in drawing up improved, standard forms of contract so as to avoid costly and lengthy disputes. They represent a most valuable aid for anyone drawing up construction contracts and they demonstrate to the European Community that the United Kingdom can fully accommodate the demands of the modern construction industry through new and rationalised forms of contract.

The Centre is deeply indebted to the busy experts who so generously contributed their time and labour in preparing their papers and to all those who assisted in the demanding tasks of preparing the papers for publication. Special thanks are due to Baker & McKenzie, solicitors, who sponsored the Conference.

I am delighted that the profits of the Conference have contributed to the establishment of a joint law lectureship for the Centre and for the Faculty of Laws. This will greatly assist the Centre in its activities, including the MSc course in Construction Law and Arbitration. The Centre is putting on its second annual conference on 21st and 22nd September 1989 entitled "International Chamber of Commerce Arbitration in Action" and the proceedings should also be published in due course. These annual conferences will be significant ventures, as one might expect when the UK construction industry accounts for nearly 10% of the entire Gross Domestic Product and produces major export earnings.

David Hayton
Professor, Dean of Faculty of Laws,
King's College, London
July 1989

Contents

Working Party Papers

Part V - Developments outside the Terms of Contract

Part VI - Conclusions

General Introduction

This Conference took place over three days, 14, 15, 16 September 1988 at King's College, London. It represents the first major public event organized by the new Centre of Construction Law and Management. This volume contains the papers presented at the Conference, updated where appropriate and edited, together with collated and edited reports of the discussion and debate at the Conference, and overall conclusions from the proceedings.

The Conference and the proceedings presented here were divided into four main sessions covering the following subject areas:

— Risk assessment and allocation

— Project management and quality control

— Control of programme and payment

— Developments outside the terms of contract

The papers and the Conference proceedings were arranged in the following pattern. In each of the first three principal sessions, two major papers were commissioned to cover the whole subject area. These were presented and debated in plenary session. The Conference then divided into three working parties, each of which had a separate paper presented on a specific topic within the overall framework of the session. In order to provide continuity between the plenary session papers and the working party groups, the two presenters of the papers and the chairman of the Plenary session acted as chairmen of the three working party groups. These working parties were intended to stimulate a relatively free exchange of view and debate, with the intention of seeking to reach conclusions or defined positions on the various subjects debated.

The working party discussion and debate was noted and the results presented at the conclusion of the Conference, so that those attending one working party session could know the outcome of the other sessions. Those reports have now been further collated and edited and are presented, together with a note of the plenary session discussion, at the end of each of the first three sessions.

The fourth session of the Conference presented four papers on contrasting subjects within the overall theme. These were introduced in plenary session and the debate there offered an opportunity to bring together other themes touched on during earier sessions of the Conference. This volume contains the four papers presented, followed by a review of the papers and of the debate. Finally, this volume contains a review and suggested conclusions from the Conference overall.

The Conference was opened with a keynote speech given by the Solicitor General, Sir Nicholas Lyell, QC, MP. An overview of the printed conference papers was then presented by the Director of the Centre, Professor John Uff. These two contributions appear in the opening sections of this volume.

Throughout the Conference proceedings, the discussion and debate were assiduously noted and the notes transcribed and edited by the three Conference rapporteurs, Kate Morton, Christopher Dering and Paul Stafford. The organisers and the whole conference expressed their gratitude for the work carried out, the fruits of which now appear in the discussion and debate section of this volume.

The Centre of Construction Law expresses its gratitude to all those who contributed to the success of the Conference: to those who contributed papers, to the delegates, and to the many organisers who gave tirelessly of their time and effort. The full list of Conference contributors, including the chairmen and rapporteurs is set out at the front of this volume. In addition to those whose contribtutions are formally recognised, the Centre would like to express its particular thanks to Hazel Webb and Dr RK Dixon, respectively the Secretary and Manager of the Centre up to September 1988, and Pauline Gale who joined the Centre just before this Conference and has now assumed these roles. In addition, the principal organisers of the conference were Brigadier Dennis Begbie, Lady Otton and Jackie Bausch of Legal Studies and Services Limited, to each of whom we are greatly indebted.

After the conclusion of the Conference the considerable task of collating the material and preparing it for publication was undertaken by the General Editors who have been greatly assisted by Mr. Charles Manzoni, Pauline Gale and Kate Morton. The Centre is also greatly indebted to Jane Belford and Andrew Prideaux for providing the expertise and advice necessary to allow the Centre itself to publish this first record of its work.

Finally, the Centre of Construction Law and Management owes its existence to the encouragement and support received from colleagues at King's College, London. We remain grateful for the particular support we have received from the Principal, Professor Stewart Sutherland.

1st August 1989

JFU
PNC

Centre of Construction Law and Management
King's College, London

List of Contributors

Session Chairmen

Sir Philip Otton, Judge of High Court of Justice

The Lord Hacking, MA, FCIArb, Solicitor, Partner, Richards Butler

Sir William Stabb, QC, former Senior Official Referee

Peter Stott, CBE, MA, FICE, FEng., Nash Professor of Civil Engineering, King's College London

Participants

Sir Nicholas Lyell, QC, MP, Solicitor General for England & Wales

John Uff, QC, PhD, FICE, FCIArb, Visiting Professor and Director, Centre of Construction Law, King's College London

Max W. Abrahamson, BA, LLB, FCIArb, Visiting Professor, Centre of Construction Law; Consultant, Baker & McKenzie

Humphrey LLoyd, QC, MA, LLD. Former President of the Society of Construction Law, practising barrister and arbitrator.

John Barber, MA, LLB, MICE, Barrister and Consulting Engineer

David Cornes, BSc(Eng), AKC, MICE, Solicitor, Partner Winward Fearon & Co.

Chris Chapman, BASc, MSc, PhD, PEng, Professor of Management Science, Department of Accounting & Management Science, University of Southampton

Stephen C. Ward, BSc, MSc, ACIB, MBIM, Lecturer in Business Economics, Department of Accounting & Management Science, University of Southampton

Bernard Curtis, BSc, ACGI, MICE, Research Fellow in Construction Management, University of Southampton

Martin Barnes, BSc(Eng), PhD, FICE, FEng., Management Consultancy Division, Deloitte Haskins & Sells

Donald Keating, QC, BA, FCIArb, Barrister and Arbitrator

Michael Stanger, BSc(Eng), ACGI, Solicitor, Partner Lovell White Durrant

Jeremy Winter, LLB, Solicitor, Partner Baker & McKenzie

Michael Pepper, FICE, FIStructE, Partner Harris & Sutherland

Sir Patrick Garland, Judge of High Court of Justice

Ian Duncan Wallace, QC, MA, Visiting Professor, Centre of Construction Law, King's College London

John Bishop, LLB, Solicitor, Partner Masons

Philip Naughton, QC, LLB, Barrister

John Bellhouse, BA, Solicitor, Partner McKenna & Co.

Phillip Capper, MA, BA, Masons' Visiting Professor, Centre of Construction Law, King's College London

Michael Furmston, MA, BCL, LLM, Professor of Law, Pro-Vice Chancellor, University of Bristol

Anthony May, QC, MA, Barrister, Recorder and Arbitrator

George Stringer, LLB, Solicitor, Partner Rowe & Maw

Conference Rapporteurs

Katharine Morton, BA, BCL, Barrister
Paul Stafford, MA, DPhil, Barrister
Christopher J. Dering, BA, Barrister

Part I : Introduction

Session Chairman : Sir Philip Otton

Speakers :

Sir Nicholas Lyell

Professor John Uff

Part II : Risk Assessment and Allocation

Session Chairman : Sir Philip Otton

Speakers :

Professor Max Abrahamson

Humphrey LLoyd

Working Parties :

John Barber

Chairman : Sir Philip Otton

David Cornes

Chairman : Humphrey LLoyd

Professor Chris Chapman

Chairman : Professor Max Abrahamson

Part III : Project Management & Quality Control

Session Chairman : Lord Hacking

Speakers :

Dr. Martin Barnes

Donald Keating

Working Parties :

Michael Stanger

Chairman : Donald Keating

Jeremy Winter

Chairman : Dr. Martin Barnes

Michael Pepper

Chairman : Lord Hacking

Part IV : Control of Programme and Payment

Session Chairman : Sir William Stabb

Speakers :

Sir Patrick Garland

Professor Ian Duncan Wallace

Working Parties :

John Bishop

Chairman : Sir William Stabb

Philip Naughton

Chairman : Sir Patrick Garland

John Bellhouse

Chairman : Professor Ian Duncan Wallace

Part V : Developments outside the Terms of Contract

Session Chairman : Professor Peter Stott

Speakers :

Professor Philip Capper

Professor Michael Furmston

Anthony May

George Stringer

Table of Statutes

Table of Cases

Part I

Introduction

Construction Contract Policy Keynote Address 1

Sir Nicholas Lyell

The construction industry is one of the power houses of our national economy. It accounts for nearly 10 percent of the entire Gross Domestic Product, some £35 billion. The value of new work started in 1987 alone was $19.1 billion. The industry employs directly over 1.5 million people. It also accounts for major export earnings. The value of contract works undertaken abroad in 1986 was nearly 1.9 billion and architects, consulting engineers, surveyors and other professional experts earned a further 0.6 billion.

The subject of this Conference is Construction Contract Policy. It is apt that this is so. The widely used FIDIC form of contract produced by the International Federation of Consulting Engineers is United Kingdom inspired and largely based on our own Institution of Civil Engineers form of contract. English is the universal language of contract and dispute and United Kingdom professionals including lawyers enjoy an unrivalled confidence world-wide for skill, probity and independence. This is highlighted by the frequency with which the International Chamber of Commerce appoints lawyers from London as the independent chairmen of tribunals where Britain has no other connection with the dispute; and the number of disputes brought to London for hearing which represents valuable export of services.

The availability of appropriate and efficient forms of contract is a necessary part of the British contribution to international construction. But we must not be complacent. Other countries, perhaps France in particular, may seek to challenge us. The European Commission has been carrying out work on liability, insurance and indemnity, and harmonization in different areas has been under discussion by Commission Working Groups. The question of a standard form of construction contract within the European Community has been raised. This Conference represents a timely opportunity to demonstrate to the world at large that the United Kingdom industry is able to accommodate the demands of the modern construction industry in drawing up new and rationalized forms of contract.

The keynote of this Conference is to identify and develop various heads of policy for drawing up standard forms of contract which will be an improvement on the present forms. The Government in recent years has in relation to its own public investment, made increasing emphasis on the importance of ensuring performance to time, quality, and budget. The concept of lane rental in motorway repair is an example much appreciated by the public. The spectacle of long running disputes has rightly caused public concern. Some disputes about hospital construction come to mind, many of which seem to have run for longer than the original construction programme incurring costs which could have built several more hospitals. Many of these disputes turn ultimately on the provisions of the standard form of contract. It is the view of distinguished practitioners that the types of dispute which arise are not inevitable - indeed I would endorse that view from my own modest experience of building contract work. The recent line of cases such as *F.G. Minter* v. *Welsh Heath Technical Organisation*[1] where Humphrey LLoyd QC blazed the trail both in argument and academic critique, and *Rees and Kirby* v. *Swansea City Council*[2], in which I appeared, are good examples. An unequivocal statement as to who bore the financing costs involved in variations and additions could, in such cases, have saved years of costly argument. There is a powerful case for designing standard contracts in a way which reflects not merely the sectional interests as viewed by the drafting institution; or the ad hoc resolution of the particular commercial forces applying at the moment of contract; but which seek to draw a proper balance between the interests of the different parties and the wider interest of the industry and the public at large.

There have in the past been a number of Government inquiries into the subject such as the Banwell Committee in 1964 and the Harris Committee in 1968. Recommendations were made but nothing in fact came of them. The problem facing the Ideal Draftsman, to introduce an 18th century concept, has been to communicate with all the necessary parties involved including the construction industry professionals, civil engineers, architects, surveyors and the various categories of lawyer.

The unique contribution of the Centre of Construction Law here at King's College is that it is composed of and maintains direct links with all these professionals. What is more it does so in a way that is entirely self-financing through generous donations from business and the professions and through fees charged for courses. This Conference in particular represents a unique forum in which to consider and debate the types of construction contract which are needed for the future. Government, not only as a major client of the construction industry, but in its wider responsibility to create the conditions in which fair dealing prevails and business can flourish will take a close interest in your deliberations.

But as you embark you will be mindful of the words of the prayer of Sir Francis Drake that "it is not the beginning of any great venture, but the continuing of the same until it be thoroughly finished which yieldeth the true glory."

If this Conference and the work which flows from it can bring this venture to a practical conclusion in the form of improved contracts - best of all a model form of contract - for future use here and overseas your efforts will deserve the gratitude of both employers and contractors for generations to come.

1 (1981) 13 Build LR 1.
2 (1985) 5 Const LR 34.

Origin and Development of Construction Contracts 2

Professor John Uff

Synopsis

This paper examines the origin, importance and current relevance of standard (or common) forms of contract used in construction. Consideration is given to the proper role of standard forms and whether they should follow or lead the development of contract practices. The role of the courts is discussed in relation to the interpretation of standard forms and the reaction of the initiating bodies.Particular issues of current interest are considered and the question is addressed- how may a policy be defined. A review of other papers is then given with discussion of some of the main themes emerging.

Introduction

The development of construction contract forms stands at a watershed: the old forms are losing their influence; instead of orderly change, the existing institutions are being outflanked by the introduction of new forms and new systems; and the institutions are tending to respond by promoting more and more diverse forms of their own. The volume of activity in the production of standard forms is unprecedented. These facts demonstrate a clear need for a collective body of learning on the subject of construction contracts which is accessible and relevant; and an equally clear need for a considered appraisal of the policies which might govern change.

There is no generally accepted definition of a construction contract. To describe it as a contract for the supply of work and materials is to miss most of the crucial factors which give rise to its importance and difficulties. A more practical view would be to regard a construction contract as a commercial venture in which both parties anticipate some level of profit, but recognise the possibility of much greater losses; a venture in which most of the material facts which will dictate whether profit becomes loss are unkown; and where those facts which are known may later prove inaccurate or may be changed at the behest of one of the parties. In these terms some of the difficulties regularly encountered in construction may be appreciated.

Some argue that construction contracts are irrelevant unless and until a dispute arises. Only then need the wording be considered, and by lawyers and not by those involved in the construction. This view may go some way to explaining the strange fact that much of the content of a so-called modern construction contract would have been familiar to Victorian engineers, in the days when the motive power on construction sites was the steam engine and the horse. By way of example, many current contracts still provide that the contractor "is deemed to have examined the site", even though he has not and even though the employer today has at his disposal the most sophisticated means of determining the actual site and subsoil conditions, which could not have been dreamed of by the Victorians who first invented the phrase. The continued use of this type of provision (and there are many other examples in the common forms) is a triumph of legal caution over technical advance.

Origin

Standard forms of contract used in construction work were well known during the 19th century when the outlines of modern construction law were beginning to emerge. Their history could be linked to the ebb and flow of economic power, first of the employers, then of the trade associations, the professions and even the Government itself. Their development and use could also be linked to the means of printing and dissemination such that there could be identified an initial period in which powerful public bodies printed their own forms; a period of unification in which most construction work was performed under a small number of standardized printed forms; and the current position in which there appears to exist a conflict between the promoters of proliferating numbers of standard forms and consumers or producers who offer their own individual forms specially tailored with the aid of electronic processing.

By way of detail, many of the building and civil engineering cases from the 19th century law reports record the use of standard forms of contract[1]. Many of these appear to be of a type familiar to the courts. For example, in a case tried in 1888 the Lord Chief Justice observed: "Now, the contract is a contract substantially in the terms which are very common in cases of this sort, whereby the contractor is, if the literal terms of the contract be adhered to, handed over, bound hand and foot to the other party to the contract or to the engineer of that other party..."[2]. In the building field there was, apparently, already in existence by 1878, a standard form sponsored by the RIBA and certain trade bodies[3]. Successive versions of what became known as the RIBA Form were issued between 1909 and 1957[4]. The further development of this form was taken over by the Joint Contracts Tribunal (JCT) who produced editions in 1963 and 1980 with a number of significant revisions particularly to the former.

Conversely, civil engineering work continued to be carried out under individual forms well into the present century, no doubt in part because the great bulk of this work was commissioned by public bodies. The first

1 See *Hudson's Building Contracts*, 4th Ed. (HBC 4) Vol. 2.
2 *Bush* v. *Whitehaven Trustees*, HBC 4, Vol.2 pp 122, 124.
3 See HBC 4, Vol.2. p. 54.
4 See Keating, *RIBA Forms of Contract*, (1959) Sweet & Maxwell.

standardized form was produced by the Institution of Civil Engineers in 1945. Successive editions of the ICE General Conditions of Contract were produced in 1950, 1951, 1955 and 1973. By the year 1964 it was apparent that most construction work was being carried out under one or other of the standard forms just mentioned and the problems appeared to lie in the proliferation of sub-contract forms. This prompted the Banwell Committee to recommend that the development of a single standard form of contract for the whole construction industry was both desirable and practicable and that standardization of sub-contract conditions should follow[5]. Subsequent events showed that, however desirable, this aim soon ceased to be practicable.

The last 20 years has shown an unprecedented expansion in the numbers of standard forms available, such that the term almost requires redefinition. Her Majesty's Government produces its own standard form for certain categories of construction work[6]. Trade and professional bodies have produced their own standard forms[7] and there are numerous forms available for use in particular circumstances[8]. The United Kingdom civil engineering industry has also inspired forms of contract for international use[9], the current version being recommended also for domestic use. In addition to these, there are a number of private forms or contract systems whose existence and sometimes details are well-known[10].

Importance and Relevance of Forms

Compared to other standard commercial documents, the growth and proliferation of construction contract forms is notable and suggests an intention to achieve some object. That object is, however, rarely defined other than in generality[11], usually consisting of a desire to "improve" the operation of the form. There is also, when new forms or editions are drawn up between parties representing different sectors of the industry, an element of negotiation, each "side" seeking to maintain or improve its position. It is suggested that both these elements, namely general improvement and the gaining of supposed advantage are, on analysis, largely irrelevant to the real interests of those involved. As to the former, the operation and control of construction work is now sufficiently appreciated that drafting should not be a serious impediment, given an adequate brief. As to the latter, if contracts are properly drafted, the person taking on the work must price for what is being undertaken. It may be that a commercial "advantage" may exist in relation to administrative procedures, for example, the ability to challenge decisions.

5 Banwell Report HMSO 1964.
6 General Conditions of Government Contracts for Building and Civil Engineering Works, GC/Works/1 and /2.
7 See Forms issued by Association of Consultant Architects (ACA), National Federation of Building Trades and Employers (NFBTE) and system proposed by British Property Federation (BPF) etc.
8 See *e.g.* Model Form of General Conditions of Contract for Mechanical and Electrical Works (Model Form A) and JCT Standard Form of Management Contract.
9 Fédération Internationale des Ingénieurs - Conseils (FIDIC) Form, 4th. Ed. 1987.
10 A number of forms created by the Bovis Group have appeared in reported cases.
11 See discussion on ICE 5th Ed., reported in *New Civil Engineer*, July 5, November 1 and December 20, 1973.

While this may be a matter of legitimate concern, it is unlikely to affect the operation of the contract in terms of efficiency and economy.

It is suggested that the importance and relevance of standard forms lie in their ability to regulate and modify the position of the parties, primarily the contractor, and thereby to influence the performance of the work itself. It is suggested that this is the aspect of standard forms which is least developed yet most capable of creating beneficial impact on a project. The arrangement of control, sanctions and incentives should, it is suggested, be seen as elements in the achievement of these aims.

Proper role of standard forms

Two aspects of this question are considered. First, what are perceived as the proper objectives to be attained by a construction contract; and secondly, should contracts themselves attempt to dictate or lead practice or conversely, should they follow procedures already established to be commercially viable.

Considering the first aspect, it is suggested that the following (which are not in any order of priority) are or should be among the proper objectives of any construction contract:

- Providing necessary machinery for the efficient administration of the work;
- Providing an apportionment of risk arising out of the performance of the work and the end product of the work;
- Providing for possible contingencies regarding price, time and other variables;
- Providing for the coverage of any risks which are not to be borne ultimately by the parties (usually by insurance);
- Facilitating proper management of the works being carried out;
- Achieving proper economy in regard to performance of the works and the finished product;
- Maintaining sufficient flexibility to attain the proper objectives of the contract;
- Dealing appropriately with disputes which may arise out of the contract.

The first four of these objectives are matters for debate as to what provision ought to be made and by what means. The existing standard forms provide a variety of answers and there will be debate on many of these particular questions. It is proposed to comment here primarily on the remaining items which may be regarded as contentious in the wider sense that views may be held as to whether these are proper objectives at all, or as to whether they are achievable through contract.

Management

In construction, this is usually taken to connote a form of direction imposed on behalf of the employer involving more than mere supervision, or control. It may be applied separately or in conjunction with the traditional supervising and certifying roles of the architect or engineer. The term may also include planning and direction by the contractor. The question who is to provide management will clearly have a fundamental effect on the drafting of the contract. Management is discussed further below in relation to the particular conference topics.

Economy

The achievement of economy occurs at a variety of stages, initially through the selection of appropriate designs and the tender proposals submitted by the contractor. After the contract is entered into, the concept of economy usually becomes unilateral *i.e.* under most standard forms the contractor is entitled to perform the works in the most economic manner and using the most economic materials that will comply with the contract, but the employer is not entitled to change the works without incurring financial penalty[12]. The inclusion of prime cost or provisional sums to be expended as directed gives some scope for economy on behalf of the employer, but this is rarely the primary reason or motive for use of these devices. There is no reason why a contract should not include obligations as to the achievement of economy for the employer's benefit, suitably backed by incentives, particularly where a management role is to be built in. Economy may also be considered in a broader sense of ensuring that each party can obtain its rights under the contract economically (or efficiently), for example, so that the contractor is paid without undue dispute or delay and the employer can obtain the appropriate quality without unduly expensive enforcement.

Flexibility

This is used here to mean the ability to change the contract without incurring financial penalty, for the purpose of achieving some other objective, such as economy. There are many devices available, for example, giving the employer power to add or remove items of work, or requiring the contractor to sub-let or to bring in other direct contractors.

Disputes

The process of pursuing disputes is rightly regarded as wasteful of resources and unproductive if allowed unduly to proliferate in number or size. It is suggested, however, that the view that all disputes should be avoided is not necessarily well founded. The existence of opposed interests under the contract is not in itself detrimental to proper performance. Further, it is arguable that the proper price for work is unlikely to be arrived at except in the context of competing interests which may amount to a dispute. It is suggested, therefore, that the potential development of a dispute is one element in the proper operation of any price fixing under the contract. The proper objective of the contract is not to avoid disputes, but adequately and efficiently to manage such disputes as must inevitably and properly arise.

12 See, typically, ICE 5th Ed., cl.11. 13, 14, 51(1).

Should standard forms lead or follow?

The process of developing an adequate framework for new contracting systems should ideally be iterative and progressive. Most of the significant developments of contractual practice have been driven by economic forces and it is clearly desirable for contracts to follow close on the heels of such development and to seek to create necessary refinements as need becomes apparent.

Unfortunately, the history of contract developments is far from smooth. Standard forms acquire a degree of inertia which often results in them continuing to be used in circumstances where they are no longer appropriate. The process of producing new forms is long and tortuous, and examples could be given of negotiated forms being already out of date or otherwise inappropriate by the time that they have been approved and printed. Conversely, some commercially produced forms are kept regularly under review and can quickly reflect changing commercial needs.

Where standard forms seek to create new practices, it is clearly desirable that this should be achieved in conjunction with informed opinion. However, the extent to which any new form or system is adopted is dependent on many factors, some of which are subjective. It should be recognized that one of these factors will inevitably be perceived commercial advantage.

Role of the Courts

It is curious and paradoxical that those who draft standard forms of contract should, on the one hand refrain from expressing views on what they intend the contract to mean[13] and on the other, accept what the courts decree the contracts to mean, whether or not the particular matter has ever been considered by those drafting the form. This attitude seems to evidence a curious and misplaced subservience to the courts. This should not be confused with respect for the law, which is undoubted. It is not, however, any part of the function of the law or of the courts to write contracts. It would be appropriate for draughtsmen to bear in mind that their function is to achieve the stated objective or brief through appropriate drafting and not to achieve any other objective. The law, or the rules of construction, are merely the tools by which the proper objectives of the contract are achieved.

The point is well illustrated by the celebrated *Bickerton* case[14]. This was a test case brought to establish whether, under the 1963 edition of the JCT form of contract, there existed a duty to renominate at the employer's expense after the failure of a properly appointed nominated sub-contractor[15]. The point having arisen, there was no evidence that it had ever been considered or decided by the draftsmen. Clearly the contract could have provided expressly what was to be done. Instead, the High Court, the Court of Appeal and finally the House of Lords were asked to construe the contract, no easy matter in regard to this particular question. The fact that the various decisions of the

13 See practice notes issued by JCT and ICE (Conditions of Contract Standing Joint Committee) on their respective forms.

14 *N W Regional Hosp. Bd.* v. *T A Bickerton* [1970] 1 WLR 607; and see also *Gloucester CC* v. *Richardson* [1969] 1 AC 480.

15 See JCT Form 1963 Ed. 11(3) and 27.

Judges who heard the case (nine in total together with an arbitrator) were neither consistent nor unanimous is legally irrelevant. What is paradoxical is that the decision in *Bickerton* thereafter became treated as though it were a proposition of law. The JCT form of contract was not then amended and in 1973 the ICE quite inexplicably adopted this supposed principle of law when redrafting the equivalent clauses of the ICE Conditions of Contract[16].

It is suggested that this experience (which is by no means unique) is the antithesis of the proper role of the court. A distinction needs to be drawn between *(a)* questions of pure construction where the draftsmen must be taken to have considered the point, and to have had some intention which was then not clearly set down and *(b)* questions of inference where the matter was not or may not have been considered at all. In the latter event, when the point arises, there is a plain duty on the draftsmen to consider and decide it as clearly as they are able to. While the courts have jurisdiction to decide either type of point, in practice they will usually come first before an arbitrator, and the distinction might be of relevance when the court is deciding whether to allow leave to appeal against the arbitrator's decision[17].

One matter which is clear is that the court has no proper function in settling the term of any contract. In litigation or arbitration the dispute is private between the particular parties concerned. It is a convention and not a rule of law that decisions of the Courts in other cases on standard forms of contract are treated as binding. Contracts should be drafted and reviewed by those to whom the task is given, and not by the Judges.

Particular Issues

Papers presented and debated at this Conference include detailed consideration of particular matters arising within four broad issues.

Risk Assessment and Allocation

One of the fundamental characteristics of all construction work is its uncertainty. Risks can be manipulated statistically over a sufficiently large sample, but on an individual project, and particularly to a party who engages infrequently in construction or development, uncertainty is fundamental and must be provided for. Particular areas of risk arise in relation to the means and methods of performance (particularly in civil engineering construction) and also in regard to the design of the works which may affect construction as well as the completed project. Current forms of contract deal with such risks in a crude and often unsatisfactory manner which may produce serious financial anomalies when the risks eventuate[18]. Risk has been the subject of considerable academic attention[19]. Sophisticated means of analysis are available where

16 See ICE 5th. Ed. cl.11. 58, 59A and B.
17 See *BTP Tioxide* v. *Pioneer Shipping* (*The Nema*) [1981] 2 Lloyd's Rep 239.
18 See ICE 5th Ed. cl. 12.
19 See *e.g.* Abrahamson, "Risk Management" ICLR V.l. pt. 3; Ashley, "Construction Project Risks" Proc. PMI/Internet, Boston 1981; Perry, "Dealing with risk in contracts", *Building Technology and Management* April 1986.

alternative courses of action require the identification and analysis of risks. It must be recognized that construction contracting involves also substantial commercial and entrepreneurial elements which may be seen as militating against undue sophistication. Nevertheless, there exists considerable room for improvement through a proper understanding and appreciation of risk.

Project Management and Quality Control

These topics are linked by the common theme of imposed direction or control of the work on behalf of the employer, whether through an agent or direct. Questions of economy and efficiency arise: how far should the contractor be permitted to operate to his own methods and at his own pace; should the intervention on behalf of the employer be restricted to securing the employer's own narrow interests; or can the overall benefit to the project be brought into account? In relation to efficiency of the construction operation itself, has this to be judged separately for each party, or is there an overall concept of efficiency which would allow assessment of the project overall?

In regard to the means of direction or control, it is a common feature of standard forms to provide over-wide powers which are then rarely used[20]. In regard to project management, however, the problems involved in incorporating new methods and concepts into standard forms remain largely unsolved. One of the particular problems appears to be the provision of workable sanctions or incentives to achieve the objectives of management. The view exists that project management can be operated under existing forms of contract without the need of additional powers. If this is so, then it indicates a significant gap between the wording of contracts and their performance.

Management in its broad sense is an example of practice leading the development of new forms of contract. There are presently a variety of new contract systems available. These include variants on the prime cost contract, in which all the work is sub-contracted, but one principal contractor remains in overall control, although not usually in a position of full legal responsibility; and other systems whereby the role of the main contractor disappears and is replaced by a hybrid body, part-contractor part-professional, who directs the work, physical performance being undertaken through a series of direct contracts made with the employer. The full import and consequences of these systems is yet to be worked out, and the pace of development is such that it is unlikely that relevant standard forms will evolve for the present. In consequence of these changes, the role of the employer's agent must undergo serious reconsideration, as must the role of the professional bodies. The climate of change, at least within the United Kingdom, is presently such as to make such re-appraisal a serious possibility.

In regard to control of quality and performance by contractors, traditional sanctions and methods have proved far from effective, as evidenced by the huge volume of latent defect litigation and reported escalation in insurance costs[21]. New methods involving various forms of quality assurance have evolved quite independent of the contracting systems[22]. The immediate task is

20 See *MOT* v. *Farr* [1960] 1 WLR 956 at 964.
21 BUILD: Insurance Feasibility Steering Committee report, 1988.
22 See BS 5750 and the extensive literature on QA.

to identify appropriate contract mechanisms to incorporate these new systems, and subsequently to modify contractual arrangements so as to obtain the greatest advantage in terms of efficiency and economy.

Control of Programme and Payment

These two concepts embody many of the traditional and perennial problems of construction. Delivery to time and price has at times seemed an unattainable goal. Yet changing commercial pressures have produced surprising results: some areas of construction have demonstrated the ability to avoid commercially unacceptable delay[23]; while in other areas the industry has been compelled to accept prices not subject to later adjustment[24]. In terms of cost recovery, there is considerable experience in contract models of varying degrees of sophistication, aimed at producing suitable incentives[25]. Again, the point needs to be made that construction contracting embodies a serious entrepreneurial element which tends to militate towards certainty and against over-complexity. The optimum level of incentive is a debatable issue.

Conversely, the element of time has not been subject to anything approaching the same degree of attention. This may in part be due to the strangely anachronistic approach of the English courts towards devices aimed at controlling time[26]. In principle, there is no reason why time should not be manipulated in the same way as cost recovery so as to optimize performance. Equally, there is a strong argument for adopting simplicity and certainty. The contract which provides for a variable quantity of work within a pre-fixed time is by no means commercially unreal.

Policy for Construction Contracts

There is little evidence of policy having played a significant part in drafting of standard forms of construction contract, other than in the most general terms. Indeed, the reason for embarking on a new edition or revision of a standard form has usually been the existence or emergence of specific problems requiring solution. The example discussed above of liability for nominated sub-contractors is one area in which the promoters of standard forms, through an absence of policy or debate have fallen into a situation giving the appearance of policy, but in fact having occurred through the accident of litigation. Such a situation, once established, becomes the more difficult to change, as evidenced by the continual accretion of standard forms embodying the same supposed policy[27]. The whole subject of sub-contracting is strewn with ad hoc solutions to particular problems which then become established as normal practice with little or no consideration being given to their overall

23 See *e.g.* "the Lane Rental" contracts used in highway repair.
24 Contracts excluding most or all of the traditional heads of claim as well as excluding the certifying powers of the engineer or architect are found in various parts of the world, including the Middle East and Far East.
25 CIRIA: Target and Cost - Reimburseable Contracts, rep. R. 85.
26 See *Peak Construction* v. *McKinney* [1971] 1 Build LR 114.
27 See *e.g.* JCT Management Form 1987 cl. 3.21.

effect. For example, the undertaking of design responsibility by nominated sub-contractors leads to the use of direct contractual warranties enforceable by the employer. These warranties, however, pose serious problems where (as frequently is the case) there is a division of responsibility between various parties, some of whom have agreements containing arbitration clauses[28]. The procedural problems involved in seeking to enforce obligations arising out of design defects (where claims and cross claims may arise between different parties under several different contracts) are such that any consideration of policy would be bound to lead to the conclusion that some more workable system was imperative. A system where effective enforcement is defeated by complexity is unacceptable on any view.

There is no reason why an appropriate policy cannot be identified in any particular area of construction contracting. One difficulty may be in identifying the appropriate authority to draw up policy. This should normally not be the same body as that which undertakes the drafting exercise: the drafting team should be appointed to carry out the policy. A question which arises is to what extent any policy should be settled by negotiation between the competing interests within the industry and to what extent it may be derived analytically. For the purposes of this Conference it is appropriate to assume that statements or conclusions as to policy will be reviewed and reconsidered as necessary whenever they are to be applied in practice. One of the principle aims of the Conference is to establish the concept of policy as an essential ingredient in drafting and to seek appropriate guidelines to the identification of policy in any particular area.

In approaching and formulating policy it is suggested that the following matters need to be considered:

- What is the policy subject; which parties are affected by it and in what degree?
- Is there an element of public interest and/or global interest within the construction industry and if so what is it?
- What are the elements which make up the policy subject?
- Are there any relevant principles which should affect the policy?
- What are the objectives to be achieved by the policy and what is their priority?

No attempt is made to define individual policy subjects. For the purposes of this Conference a particular division of areas has been adopted. Identification of particular policy subjects, however, is a matter for debate.

Review of Conference Papers

This paper now turns to examine some of the themes which emerge from the papers printed later in this volume. The papers were delivered and are now printed in groups dealing with particular aspects of construction. This review starts with a theme common to all aspects of construction and contracts.

28 Multi-party arbitration is notoriously difficult, often approaching the point of procedural impossibility.

Change

Several papers refer to the pace at which forms are developing. Changes include new forms and also new procedures, such as the Management Contract (in which there is still a Main Contractor, but with limited responsibility) and more recently the Project Management Contract (in which there is no Main Contractor and traditional sub-contractors become Direct Contractors). Winter (Paper 12) observes that all change is not necessarily new, the Management Contract having apparently been reintroduced via the United States. In regard to the pace of change, Stringer (Paper 24) comments that one of the well-known drafting bodies has failed to realise that the industry cannot wait for its forms to catch up. Hence the recent explosion of one-off forms and "standard amendments" to the standard forms. While most contributors are agreed that changes are occurring, the extent of penetration and the impetus for change give rise to a number of questions. Winter (Paper 12) comments that it is strange that management contracting is not more used abroad. Perhaps the explanation is, as observed by several writers, that the impetus for change is from the construction industry itself and not from employers. For example Barnes (Paper 9) refers to the ICE initiative for the New Style Contract. Much of the impetus for Prime Cost and Management Contracts has come from those traditionally working as contractors. The British Property Federation as an Employer's body is a notable exception in promoting change. Her Majesty's Government has also shown interest in change in standard forms. But the recent decision of DTp, without debate, to remove the independent role of the Engineer appears to be motivated more by administrative convenience rather than desire for planned improvement.

Nowhere is it more important to respond constructively to change in contract practices than in overseas work. Bellhouse (Paper 19) charts the movements in overseas construction work. He records that the United Kingdom has behind it a distinguished but declining share of work in the developing world and presently an increase in work in North America and Australia. And in 1992 the European Community will present an open market representing one quarter of construction activity in the whole world. In this context the European Commission has considered the feasibility of a common standard form. If such a form were to be attempted, it would be vital for the United Kingdom to present a strong case for its forms to be adopted. If the nations within the European Community are to continue to offer their own forms in competition, it is equally vital for UK forms to command respect abroad.

What is wrong with standard forms?

The desire for change implies that there is something wrong in the construction industry. It may be said that this is manifested in:

- Cost and time overruns
- Problems of quality and fitness
- Costly disputes

A number of views are expressed on what is the underlying cause of these matters. Barnes (Paper 9) observes that allocation of risks is a principal factor governing the influence achieved by different forms of contract. Keating

(Paper 10) offers the view that it is the quality, quantity and method of management which distinguishes one contract from another. Winter (Paper 12) also comments on the need for better management. Professor Duncan Wallace (Paper 16) argues that incentive is a principal factor. We therefore have an initial pointer towards possible improvement of contract practices.

The impact of these three factors (risk, management and incentive) is illustrated by the example given earlier concerning responsibility for nominated sub-contractors. The Main Contractor is effectively relieved of responsibility for time, cost and quality as regards work by the nominated sub-contractor. While one could regard this as the very negation of a contract, it has nevertheless paved the way for the prime cost contract and latterly the management contract in which the "Main Contractor" is expressly relieved of these responsibilities, on the footing that he does at least provide management. The important question remains whether this additional input of management to the project is regarded as of such value as to offset the loss of recourse regarding time, quality and cost.

The papers contain a number of observations on the abilities of architects and engineers to provide effective management. It is to no point creating new responsibilities unless there are going to be personnel able to fulfil them. Another aspect of management is the role of the employer's agent. Stanger (Paper 11) points to the important inconsistency between the traditional independent role of certifier and the demands of management and control. But whoever is to manage, the question arises what are the appropriate tools? Keating (Paper 10) examines the role of Quality Assurance - the new panacea for improving quality without increasing cost. Pepper (Paper 13) makes some practical observations regarding Quality Assurance and goes on to examine the alternative role of insurance. Reference should also be made, in this regard, to the recently published Report of the Bishop Committee into BUILD (Building Users' Insurance against Latent Defects).

Time and Cost

Professor Duncan Wallace in his comprehensive review (Paper 16) argues cogently and at length for radical recasting of financial risk with the aim of encouraging better building rather than better claims. Provisions for payment appear to offer limitless opportunity to create more balanced incentives within a spectrum ranging from the crude lump sum entire contract (the whole payment being due on final completion) to sophisticated forms of target adjustable contract in which different risks can be shared in a variety of ways.

This is to be contrasted with the question of time where it appears the rule of freedom of contract, during the 19th century, came up against the doctrine of prevention. Sir Patrick Garland (Paper 15) examines the historical origin of the peculiar common law rules regarding time. Their effect is to make time-related sanctions of doubtful enforceability. This is indeed curious when one considers that the Courts are prepared to allow a contractor to be paid nothing if he fails to complete an entire contract; prepared to hold a contractor to have assumed fully a risk which he could not possibly have known of or ascertained; and prepared to enforce a demand for payment of a first-call bond where the sum payable is patently not matched by any comparable loss. There are many similar examples of obvious "unfairness" which are disregarded by the Courts when enforcing contracts. But for reasons of historical precedent, the Courts are not prepared to enforce a time penalty when there exists a possibility that the result might be unfair. If it is correct, then draftsmen are deprived of the opportunity to use time and time-related sanctions as means of managing and regulating performance. This is an area where fresh thought and policy is needed. Sir Patrick Garland also queries whether oil industry contracts can be called construction contracts. These forms, often originating from the United States, tend to take a robust view of many of the matters regarded as of the highest sensitivity in United Kingdom contracts, for example, extensions of time.

Risk

The assessment and allocation of risk is the subject of the first group of papers. In one sense, it is the theme that underlies all the papers. Professor Abrahamson's paper covers risk and risk sharing (Paper 3) as it bears on the work of construction. The question of risk to the product is dealt with by LLoyd (Paper 4) who examines the difficult issues involved in the concept of fitness for purpose. This is an area where, in the world of real contracts and litigation, the question of whether and to what extent a particular risk is assumed is often finely balanced and in many cases finally decided only after litigation in which both sides are able to present a strong argument. Another aspect of risk, infrequently addressed in the legal context and imperfectly understood outside specialized circles is the theory of risk and risk analysis. The paper by Chapman, Ward and Curtis (Paper 7) gives an analytical basis for testing assertions about who should bear risk, and the consequences. This work is based on analysis applied in non-contentious decision making and illustrates the complexity involved in analysing the effect of contract provisions.

Conclusions

Standard forms of construction contract have historically played an important role in the management and economics of construction. That role has not diminished and standard forms continue in widespread use although considerable diversification is currently evident.

Little attention appears to have been paid to the potentials which exist through the medium of construction contracts for achieving reform and rationalization, as well as optimizing performance and efficiency. One of the reasons for this is a conspicuous lack of identified policy in drawing up or amending standard forms. It is now appropriate to consider whether elements can be identified which may form the basis of policy to be adopted when drawing up forms for particular use.

The initial conclusion from the conference papers is that improvements are feasible in construction contracts in the areas of risk placing and in ensuring the provision of adequate management. In both areas, changes to the traditional roles played by parties to construction projects will need to be kept under review. Any question of improvement must be measured ultimately by performance, in terms of quality, time and cost. These elements may need to approached both directly through the provision of contractual sanctions and safeguards, as well as indirectly through providing the incentives to proper performance. The aim of any improved contract must be to achieve better and more efficient use of resources, measured in terms of performance to time and quality.

Part II

Risk Assessment and Allocation

Risk Problems relating to Construction 3

Professor Max Abrahamson

Synopsis

This paper (which has been revised with the benefit of the Conference) examines risk planning in construction by setting out and discussing a number of distinctions, in the light of recent court decisions and in the context of particular construction problems. The effect on claims is considered; comment is then made on recent changes in the law of negligence and their effects on the risks taken by parties to projects.

Introduction

There is no purpose in duplicated raids into such a complex, chaotic battlefield as risk. All discussion of theory could be suspended until practice has caught up, if pragmatists (as commanding at the Conference as in court[1]) were pragmatic enough to notice the casualties of their pragmatism . At least, theory up to date must be summarized shortly: a risk should be placed on insurers or other professional gamblers where practicable; otherwise it should be placed on whoever gains the main economic benefit of running it; that is, unless the risk should be moved elsewhere for efficiency or safety, on to one who carelessly or wilfully creates it, or can best control the events that may lead to it occuring or best manage it when it does occur. If it is not known how to move a risk effectively, without excess trouble or alternative risks (including risk of abuse), leave it where it falls.[2]

The following Table 1 draws a number of distinctions which may be a further step forward in risk planning. These distinctions are then used in numerical order to examine different aspects of risk in respect of a range of topics chosen because they happen to be currently in the law reports or, in the case of claims, because they are always newsworthy.

1 See the recent decisions on negligence, under Distinction No. 8 below.
2 The above principles are an amalgamation of Abrahamson: "Contractual Risks in Tunnelling," *Tunnels and Tunnelling* (1973-1974), reproduced in CIRIA Report '79, Tunnelling (1978) and Hayes, Perry, Thompson & Willmer: *Risk Management in Engineering* Construction, an SERC Project Report of UMIST (1986). Professor Chapman's paper and workshop at the Conference was also very valuable on the actual assessment of risk. See also footnote 15 below.

Table 1

	Distinguish -	From -
1.	Risk engineering	Forensic engineering
2.	Contracts	Reality
3.	Liability	Construction
4.	Construction	Payment
5.	Communication	Construction/legal jargon
6.	Primary performer	Checker/guarantor
7.	Insurance	Counter-insurance
8.	Floodgates	Various designs
	Strict logic	
	Natural risks	State of the art
	Casual negligence	Systematic abuse
	Construction risks	Risk of insolvency

1. Risk/forensic engineering

In *Glenlion Construction Ltd.* v. *The Guinness Trust*[3] it was said: "Mr. Ramsey (counsel) for the contractors...readily conceded that a relevant fact is that both parties at the time of entering into the contract would have been well aware that contractors frequently produce programmes that were over-optimistic."[4]

Some of the most dangerous risks lie covered up behind this first distinction between real problems of risk management and those constructed by forensic engineering, as glimpsed in that judgment. That is one reason for trying to open up risk management for examination down to its foundations.

2. Contracts/reality

In *Mitsui* v. *A-G of Hong Kong*[5] the specification provided: "Whilst tunnel driving is in progress the Engineer will order the type of permanent lining to be subsequently installed and separate items for excavation are provided according to the type of lining ordered." Consequently, the contract drawings showed only six "Typical Cross Sections" of an unlined tunnel and of a tunnel lined and supported by five alternative combinations of concrete, sprayed concrete, and heavy steel ribs. The bill of quantities included a separate item for each alternative. The contractors needed twice the original contract period to install the ribs eventually ordered, 70 times the billed quantity. The Government failed with its denial that the Engineer had power to change bill rates to cover all the contractors' extra time- related costs.

The Contract Conditions included a reinforced version of the usual clause by which the contractors were "deemed" to know all about the sub-soil, irrespective of "any allegation or fact that incorrect or insufficient information was given" to them by the Government. According to one of the judgments, it was:

3 (1988) 11 Con. LR 26
4 *Per* Judge Fox-Andrews QC.
5 (1986) 33 Build LR 1

> "hard to suppress the thought that a great deal of trouble and uncertainty all around would have been saved if the Government had gone for a straight Schedule of Rates style of contract other than what has been devised here"[6].

It has been suggested[7] that although that would have avoided a great deal of trouble and uncertainty in terms of contract drafting, and to courts and lawyers, it would not have changed the ground through which the tunnel passed, made it visible from the surface, or stopped it falling in if the wrong lining was chosen. A contract may make its own reality, but only in its own world. Draftsmen cannot change the natural order by their drafting; or avoid causing practical problems if they forget whether it is their own or the Almighty's order they are using, or do not notice when moving from one creation to the other.

3. Liability/Construction

The further suggestion has been made that it was those considerations that caused the Hong Kong Government to give control of the choice of lining during excavation to its own engineer who had been considering the design for years. With that control went responsibility not only for the physical success of the supports eventually decided on, but to pay for them. Only if the contractors had been given the time and adequate payment to use the required specialised design and constructions skills and resources, could they have evaluated and with confidence taken responsibility for the supports, and priced them at tender as far as practicable. So the primary issues were about physical construction and their solution rightly decided the kind of contract and detailed terms chosen to regulate payment and liability, not vice versa.

4. Construction/Payment

The Mitsui contractors used this distinction to defeat the argument that there had been no variation to the works because the contract said that billed quantities were not guaranteed, and everyone knows they change. For the purpose only of payment the works included in the contract sum were defined as exactly those quantified in the bill. It is immaterial to the success of such contractual "deeming" that an owner may not realise that for this reason (and others less justified) the "price" he is quoted is not for the works he wants, but for phantom works in a risk-reduced world specially created for fixing the price.

5. Communications/Construction Jargon

In the case of *Yorkshire Water Authority* v. *McAlpine Ltd*[8] the specification provided that the contractors were to "supply with ... tender a programme in

6 *Mitsui*, *per* Rhind J. in the Hong Kong High Court (unreported).
7 (1986) 5 ICLR 431.
8 (1985) 32 Build LR 114.

bar chart form"; the bar chart and method statement were submitted and approved at a meeting; the formal agreement then incorporated the minutes of that meeting and the approved statement; according to the statement the works were to be constructed upstream; but during construction the contractors maintained that was impossible; after delay the works proceeded downstream. It was held that the contractors were entitled to a variation order and valuation for a change in a "specified method of construction" that was "necessary for completion of the Works" under Clauses 51 and 52 of the ICE conditions, because the incorporated method statement was "physically impossible" within the meaning of Clause 13(1).

A fancy cardboard cover is a contract document to protect the rest (consider also the limited contractual effect of ubiquitous Methods of Measurement, and codes (below)). The following extracts from the judgment show how the *McAlpine* decision recognised that a simple "yes" or "no" answer to the question whether or not a document is part of the contract has little meaning:

> "This question turned solely on the construction of this particular contract. It does not involve any general question of construction of the I.C.E. standard conditions ... it would be wholly artificial and unrealistic to regard [this] method statement as a document provided under clause 14. It is a document expressly provided under clause 107 of the specification 'in addition to the requirements of clause 14'. It was incorporated in the contract in the same way as was the programme in bar chart form ... in a valuable and important contract like this the applicants wanted to tie the contractor to a particular programme and method of working before the contract was signed and as a contractual obligation."[9]

It may meet the parties' intention to specify in the contract that the contractor's actual programme and method will be "no less favourable" to the employer than those "proposed" (the word in ICE Clauses 14(1) and 14(3)) in his tender. That is usually what is intended when any other expert - doctor, dentist, or even lawyer - proposes and explains in advance how he intends to do his job in order to gain the confidence of his client, who wants to satisfy himself that he will not be harmed even though entitled to compensation if he is.

The irresistable temptation to refer to the communication level of JCT'80 may trespass on areas covered by other speakers. By Clause 2.5.1-4 of the Conditions with Contractor's Design:

> "In so far as the design of the Works is ... the Contractor's ... the Contractor shall have in respect of any defect or insufficiency in such design the like liability to the Employer ... as would an Architect ... or other appropriate professional designer ... Any references to the design which the Contractor has prepared or shall prepare or issue for the Works *include a reference to any design which the Contractor has caused or shall cause to be prepared or issued by others*".

Suppose a contractor employed under that form leaves it to manufacturers or suppliers to design plant such as a pump, or adapt a proprietary item of theirs specially for the works. Is the liability of the contractor for their design limited to reasonable care? If so, is the chain of liability broken, so that the manufacturers or suppliers effectively benefit, and the owner suffers, from a

9 At pp. 123, 128.

reduction to the professional designer's level of duty (with all the problems of proving their negligence), below their normal sale of goods strict warranties? Has history repeated itself by reopening here the structural cracks so laboriously papered over in nominated sub-contracting ?

Nominated sub-contracting itself is as an example of the difficulty of distinguishing the distinctions listed above. Confusion within and between all of Distinctions 1 to 5 has been compounded from time to time during the development of the system to its climax in the opposite result to that intended by its supporters. In particular, the "risk" argument that because the employer chooses a nominated sub-contractor the main contractor should not be fully liable for him, led to *Bickerton* etc. But delay or insolvency of a sub-contractor is not caused by the Employer's nomination merely because it follows it. The employer's decision is an effective cause only if he adds a risk - chooses a sub-contractor who is more likely to delay or become bankrupt than the industry norm. If the relief to main contractors had been limited accordingly, the JCT and others might not have had to introduce by popular demand the substitutes by which contractors take wider responsibility for an employer's nominee.

> "...the poorer the quality of the drafting, the less willing any court should be to be driven by semantic niceties to attribute to the parties an improbable and unbusinesslike intention...Their Lordships cannot help thinking that much of the difficulty felt by both courts below.. arose from the attention they devoted to reported decisions on the construction of other contracts containing supposedly similar provisions..To fasten on ...phrases [mirrored in another contract and] comparison of one contract with another can seldom be a useful aid to construction and may be...positively misleading".[10]

In *Home & Overseas Insurance Co. Ltd.* v. *Mentor Insurance Co. (UK) Ltd. (In Liquidation)*[11], an "honourable engagement" clause in a reinsurance agreement read:

> "The arbitrators and the umpire shall interpret their reinsurance as an honourable engagement and they shall make their award with a view to effecting the general purpose of this reinsurance in such reasonable manner rather than in accordance with a literal interpretation of the language".

Held, the clause entitled "arbitrators to view matters of construction more leniently and with regard more generally to commercial considerations" than would otherwise have been permissible.

Distinctions 1 to 5 in planning

Technical and legal contract planners may take special care to keep a wide awake eye on construction, payment, liability and compensation, from several directions separately and all together. Planners will also keep in mind that programmemanship for claims bears as much relation to programming for construction, as deliberate risk distortion bears generally to risk assessment

10 *Mitsui*, above, at pp.14, 18.
11 *The Times*, 11 August 1988.

and allocation, and "forensic engineering" to engineering. The two groups deserve quite different treatment. No doubt, contractors' organisations and committees producing standard forms are urgently debating whether or not the judicial notice in *Glenlion* of a programming racket is right to any extent and, if it is, what they can do to stop it - unless they classify it as Tendermanship and Claimsmanship without the irony the name intended.

Planners will note that the difference between having experience and knowledge of construction disputes and experience and knowledge of construction has not been judicially noticed yet. On the authorities quoted above lawyer-interpreters need not be supplied with old entrails into which, naturally, to read their own magic. Contracts, codes, standards and regulations could use the language and forms nowadays best suited to construction. They could make clear in various ways that they are intended as practical guides to achieve the purposes of design and construction, and that intention is to be given paramount importance in their interpretation. With refinement those methods could help progress towards lawyers approaching contracts and codes on the construction industry's terms, not their own, and reduce construction semi-legal jargon on other minds and tongues.

6. Primary performer/checker

Under the Law Reform (Contributory Negligence) Act 1945 the compensation awarded to a claimant found to have been negligent in caring for himself, is to be "reduced to such extent as the court thinks just and equitable having regard to the claimant's share in the responsibility for the damage" which he is claiming against the defendant. The *Vesta*[12] decision that, on the one hand, the defence of contributory negligence applies to a claim made in contract, and on the other hand it applies there only "where the defendant's liability in contract is the same as his liability in the tort of negligence independently of the existence of any contract", was not made in a construction case. Does the result need special adjustment by contract or otherwise to avoid special construction problems?

Liability for negligence "based on a general public sentiment of moral wrongdoing"[13] requires a party to do for himself at least as much as he requires everyone else to do for him. When a claimant casts the first stone, on the grounds that the defendant has failed to take reasonable care, the defendant retaliates in kind. Whenever a claimant does (see below) have potential rights both in contract and tort, the courts tend to give him the best of both combined. Indeed, much law of tort has been made by judges to rectify shortcomings in the law of contract of their own making. It may seem that, contrary to that principle, a claimant in contract subjected to the defence of contributory negligence imported from tort in favour of the defendant, is receiving the worst of the two worlds. But arguably that defence is in the nature of a counterclaim, so that the defendent is in the position of claimant As such he should not lose the right to have the defendant look after himself, analagous to the tortious duty of care, merely because he has made a contract with him,

12 *Forsikringsaktienlskatet Vesta* v. *Butcher* [1966] 2 All ER 488, CA, and the article by Michael J Smith in (1988) Const. L J 75.
13 *Donoghue* v. *Stevenson* [1932] AC 562.

but only so far as he has contracted to give up the right. If more or less mutual obligations to take care have been re-allocated between parties to a contract because one has agreed to take care of the other, obviously that may make the tit-for-tat contributory negligence principle inapplicable. But there is a danger that one kind of re-allocation will be ignored, as follows.

A contracting party may directly add to losses caused him by the other party although it is not practically possible to separate the results of their combined efforts - defects by the builder and improper maintenance by the owner together cause a pipe to burst. Alternatively, one party may fail to defuse, to intercept and prevent, the effect of the other's negligence, which then by itself causes a catastrophe and all his losses. In the former case, a defendant obviously should not pay on the grounds of his carelessness for extra losses actually caused by the claimant's own carelessness. But in the latter case there are logical and policy reasons why contributory negligence should not reduce the damages recovered by a claimant from a defendant who has broken his contract to do for the claimant what he could not, or chose not to do for himself. It is not in itself negligent in law to rely on another for what he holds himself out as capable of doing, certainly not in relation to that other. If he would have been entitled to omit completely to supervise or otherwise check the efforts of a purported expert, one who does check them inadequately or incompetently is doing more, not less, than the law requires him to do to look after himself.

That conclusion is fully supported by authority where it is a consultant or other independent agent who is employed as "checker". But, by the principle of vicarious liability (largely developed to provide someone worth suing by an injured third party), every employer (in the general sense) is identified with his own full employees. It follows that normally "the contributory negligence of a servant of the claimant is a good defence"[14]. The possible distinction (without a difference in this context) between employees and consultants, obviously becomes more important the more a party involves himself directly in checking what is being done for his benefit. That affects not merely the obvious cases of local authorities and other experienced project owners with their own in-house project team checking construction or shop drawings, but a managing contractor supervising works contractors. There may be effects from the mere mechanics of having an RE or clerk of works employed by the owner, not by his consultant.

Those examples have in common that to reduce the claimant's compensation, would be to penalise him because the defendant knew he was double-checking, and therefore relied on him to check carefully. It would benefit the defendant accordingly, and reduce any deterrent effects on him of the risk of liability. Those results could be produced only by mistaking the doctrine of contributory negligence for a duty owed by the claimant to the particular defendant and ignoring the contract between them. Unfortunately, a danger of such mistake appears from results of the general rules of contribution, discussed elsewhere at length[15]. (Of course, those are the rules analagous to the rules of contributory negligence but applying not as between a

14 *Salmond and Heuston on Tort*, 19th Ed. 587.

15 Abrahamson, Contractors' Rights-over etc. in the Liability of Contractors (1966). This paper is trying to develop conclusions reached in that article.

claimant and defendant, but between defendants who together have caused "the same damage" to a claimant. The rules require the compensation for which each is fully liable to the plaintiff, to be "justly and equitably" divided between whichever of them is solvent).

Precautions may be necessary: either in the contract, or on site by forewarning, or even removing, those whose presence may add the insult of a plea of contributory negligence to injury to their employer. There are common form contract terms to the effect that the acts or omissions of a supervisor or designer on site or in the office, will not absolve the contractor from any of his construction or temporary work etc. duties. But they do not seem to remove the danger that the doctrine of contributory negligence may be applied against the checker's employer, since in theory the doctrine does not reduce duties, only compensation.

It may be appropriate to try to improve such terms (although it may not be easy to help some arbitrators resist the argument that a supervisor has duties to intervene, save the contractor from his own mistakes, reduce his responsibility for any missed, and certify payment for interfering with his business by raising any that are arguable). Liability for contributory negligence may be written out, despite the terms of the Act. According to *Vesta* it does not apply anyway to strict contract duties - such as the contractors' traditional srict duty independent of fault to provide specified work and materials. For design duties (whether for permanent or temporary works), duties to avoid noise or other pollution, and many others - the choice between imposing a duty of care and an absolute warranty of success (and the problems of finding insurance for the latter) become crucial in this context, as in others. That distinction itself is becoming confused by long lists of duties added in construction and service contracts without making clear whether they are examples only of a general duty of care or are specially strict.

A combination of contracts can go further and alter the general rules of contribution just mentioned. It is possible contractually to take away from a defendant who is the primary performer of a duty performed negligently any claim to a contribution from a checker towards the compensation payable to the injured party. The primary performer then knows that he has no one to turn to, or on, for help in paying compensation if he does not make proper arrangements and pay for his own supervision of his own operations. So, his chance of benefiting from systematic negligence (that is, of counter-insuring himself, next) is reduced. As a result, a project owner may be more likely to get the full preventative benefits of double supervision, as well as double liability.

There has been much activity in courts and contracts about the possibility of a duty to warn between separate specialists - particularly between primary performer and checker. When considering whether to clarify that duty in a contract, it is relevant that a party may give fullest rein to his sense of responsibility by issuing warnings when he does not have to implement them at his own expense. That could be one reason for the progress over the last 30 years from too little writing during construction to too much. Changes have just been mentioned that could remove cross-contributions between the primary performers and checkers themselves for any absence of warning from one to the other, without affecting any joint and several liability of each to the injured party (so useful to him if either is insolvent).

7. Insurance/counter insurance

There are proponents of both self-insurance and counter-insurance for claims. Some think a contractor should save profits made on the many jobs that go right to pay for losses on the few that go wrong; others that a contractor should make surpluses on jobs that go claimably wrong to pay for his own mistakes on those that go right. There are the similar alternatives of paying premiums from profits for insurance against accidents, and skimping systematically so as to be in credit even if the odd accident has to be paid for. But all the distinctions so far are relevant to the large risk of claims.

Distinctions 1 to 7 on claims

In some classes of claims, instead of preferring construction to legal language at the start, as described above, the actual contract legal language is rewritten as late as arbitration. Clause 12 may be interpreted to cover not only conditions that could not reasonably have been foreseen by an experienced contractor, but conditions of a foreseeable kind that could have been more fully exposed by experienced advisors of the owner, or even fully foreseeable conditions that the owner failed to wave under the contractor's nose. A less than careful and effective analysis and division of ground condition risks infringes each of the "theoretical" principles summarized at the start of this paper and, not coincidentally, is in danger of becoming as self- defeating as the development of nominated sub-contracting (see above).

Applied theory has a good deal to do about claims. As a small example, it is risky for owners to overlook that if contractors they employ to insure them against ground or other risks as well as to construct go bankrupt as insurers they will do so as constructors, and vice versa; but the common advice that owners should not delete Clause 12 because ground conditions may be so unforseeably severe as to drive the contractors into liquidation, with all the resulting costs and delay to the owner, overlooks that it is precisely such a disasterous risk that owners and their financiers will least wish to carry themselves.

The simplicity preferable in risk allocation, despite such difficulties, is not the same as coarseness. It is hardly justifiable to trade-off swings with roundabouts, as some drafting committees seem to do. A party taken for a ride on one may not have the opportunity, or live, to enjoy the other. This factor, and not only lawyers, makes simplicity hard to achieve, although no less needed.

Down to basics, where the benefits of some old customs of the industry, such as the published schedules of plant charges, make compensation pay better than prevention. That is specially possible when claims are paid not only with the usual uncertainties of calculating cost-plus, but added uncertainties about what work should be included - so that some work is paid for at cost-plus plus contract rates and prices. Of course, it is not only contractors who may get something for nothing by law (see next Section), and even counsels' brief fee for preparing sometimes is combined with a refresher for each day the hearing is prolonged by failure to prepare. Even apart from that, it is perhaps not surprising that contractors sometimes prefer claiming to estimating, given the levels of accuracy achievable (or achieved) in estimating even straightforward work.

Improvement on claims is likely to be made by relatively small practical steps, including for the record the following that are old in theory but still untried:

- Because the dimension of time gives most trouble, contract draftsmen and reporters on tenders will include in their checklists review of the economics of repetitive charges and percentage add-ons, in case there are many more or less of them than expected, and contract procedures to deal with them realistically. Should a contractor give some basic figures about the cost of any supervisor, item of plant, car, or site installation before he bring him or it on site - annual salary, percentages of time to be spent on site and elsewhere on the business of the works, purchase price and age, rental charge and to whom paid, arrangements for maintenance (as relevant)? With that information, it would be relatively easy to work out reasonable charges varying with the length of delay - of course, with computer help. It could also be easier to avoid dividing an annual cost between an average of 1,000 hrs. p.a., and then applying the hourly rate to a claim for six months standing on a double shift 18 hour day.

- Is it possible for the geologists etc. said to wait at one end of a tunnel, perhaps in partnership with the lawyers at the other, to prepare information sheets, trying to meet the practical needs of tenderers? The questions on the sheets could be completed in stages. First site information known to the owner and his advisers would be catalogued, with fact divided from comment and opinion; then each tenderer would (be bound to?) add any extra information relevant to tenders that he happened to have (for distribution to all tenderers), and to identify aspects and paramaters of particular importance to him because of his choice of plant etc; leading if necessary to a joint review between tenderers, their soils advisers, and the owner's Engineer and site investigators. Such open government of contracts no doubt horrifies those who concentrate on liability, but the main test of preventative measures is what they prevent, not what they don't.

- It is sometimes claimed to be too demanding for tenderers seriously to consider and give details before contract on the above matters and the real make up of pricing, when fears for confidentiality are raised as well. But an over-run in time or budget may be serious, even disastrous, for the owner, and confidentiality does not seem to inhibit the barrage of such information to support claims. At least, a full tender breakdown could be deposited in some safe place, in case anything turns on it after contract.

- Could standard procedure be reversed by way of cosmetics to reduce pressures to choose a "lowest" tenderer, and improve select tendering by relating the final selection as closely as possible to real planning for the actual works? First open envelopes containing only tenderers' resourced programme, method statement, information on key personnel and plant etc. Only those tenders that show a verifiable expectation of doing the job satisfactorily are classified as valid. Return unopened to the other tenderers the second envelopes with their prices and tender make-up. Politicians might be satisfied by selection of the lowest valid tender.

- During construction, the contractor must quote for a variation, with separate particulars and a separate price for delay costs, and for each factor for which bill rates may be adjusted under the contract system of valuation. For example, for work not of a similar character to that billed, or that significantly changes billed quantities, or with problems of access, or working space or hours etc., as under the JCT and, to some extent, ICE forms. If the quotation is not accepted or is waived to avoid delay, nevertheless the contractor still is bound to give as much as possible of that information before obeying the order, and complete the information from time to time as soon as practicable. Obviously, the owner's representatives may withdraw or change the order, or at least monitor its execution, knowing which aspects of the variation have most cost and claims potential.

- Accept that in cost-plus contracts the allocation of risk in relation to a target price can be robust, since the contractor's exposure is limited.

8: Floodgates, strict logic, and negligence

Consider a short history of judicial and other research :

> "... the position has now been reached that in order to establish that a duty of care arises in a particular situation, it is not necessary to bring the facts of that situation within those of previous situations in which a duty of care has been held to exist"[16].(1977)

> "The history of the development of the law in the last years shows that fear aroused by the 'floodgates' argument have been unfounded ... The argument, that extension of liability will produce a flood of claims, has been described ... as specious and the argument against allowing a cause of action such as was allowed in *Dutton*, *Anns* and *Bowen* as 'in terrorem or doctrinaire'".[17] (1982)

> "Their Lordships venture to think that the ... [Anns] test ... for determining the existence of a duty of care in negligence has been elevated to a degree of importance greater than its merits, and greater than its author intended".[18] (1987)

> "Plainly this decision contained within it the seeds of a major development of the law of negligence ... It remained to be seen whether those seeds would be encouraged or permitted to germinate. The clear trend of authority since ... has indicated that, for the time being at least, they will not ... Indeed I find it difficult to see that future citation from *Junior Books* can ever serve any useful purpose"[19]. (February 1988)

> "There is no precedent for the application of strict Nottingham logic in treading the path leading from the basic principle established in

16 *Anns* v.*London Borough of Merton* [1977] 2 All ER 492, HL.
17 *Junior Books* v. *Veitchi* [1982] 3 All ER 201 at 213, HL.
18 *Yuen Kun-Yeu* v. A-G of Hong Kong [1975] 2 All ER 705, HL.
19 *Simaan Glass Contracting Co.*v. *Pilkington Glass Ltd.* [1988] 1 All ER 791 at 796, CA.

> *Donoghue* v. *Stevenson* towards the Pandora's box of unbridled damages at the end of the path of foreseeability"[20]. (March 1988)
>
> "In Cork (motto "Statio Bene Fida Carinis" - a safe port in a storm) two families are now comfortably housed because of the good luck that their previous houses founded partly on made-up ground and partly on rock chose to fall down after *Anns* and before *Pirelli*.
>
> "Absolute freedom from danger cannot be attained, no matter how much money be spent on the structure."[21]
>
> "The simplest systems are now seen to create extraordinarily difficult problems of predictability. Yet order arises spontaneously in those systems - chaos and order together...orderly disorder ... long-range weather forecasting must be doomed"[22].

Whether the celebrations to the music of floodgates swinging shut are most swinging at site parties with relief from fear of lawyers (apparently the main cause of construction collapses, defects and disputes), or in law offices expecting business, or insurance offices because they can reduce premiums, when the noise has stopped we all do have to try to forecast and dress for the new judicial weather.

Now that the law of negligence independent of the contracts of the parties is available only to protect basic interests - safety from carelessness for our lives and limbs, our own property and information on which we and others must rely about our affairs, there is an intimidating list of new elements to allow for in forcasts. Each stage is affected, from negotiating, pricing, drafting insurance policies, guarantees and contracts (including disclaimers and limitations of liability), through site relations, to claims. There should be effects on all stages of legal proceedings also, from investigations, proofs of evidence (including expert evidence), compensation and even decision-making procedure.

So much has been written already on the new decisions, with unanimous rudeness unusual about the highest courts, that little can usefully be added here. What would seem most useful is a checklist for those who fear they may need either to avoid or use the actual practical results of the decisions as a whole, and need to plan accordingly. An attempt physically to illustrate those results with the "famous and (appropriately) baffling Chinese ring trick" has been found to need much more R & D. But the analogy is surpringly useful because the differant contract arrangements have been designed mainly by varying the links in chains of responsibility - for example the sub-contractors linked to the main contractor in the standard system compared to the trade contractors linked to the Employer in managing contracting compared to the single link in package deals. So the following is an interim and trial checklist :

- Note where the change is to one remedy against one party only instead of several, so that before taking on a risk it is most important to form the one remaining link carefully, to investigate the ability to pay of the sole surviving liablity party at the end of it , or to negotiate adequate contractual security.

20 *Nottingham Co-op* v. *Cementation, The Times,* 28 March 1988.
21 The Institution of Structural Engineers, "Aims of Structural Design", 1975.
22 James Gleick, *Chaos* (1988), pp. 8-17.

- Watch boundaries between places where added links by contract are and are not possible in place of those removed by the courts. Information is readily available about adapting the standard forms of collateral contracts to the new complications. Multi-party contracts might give more help, with each constructor party linked in liability to each of the others in a full circle. For example, it is possible to conceive of a contract by which one 'head' contractor (main or managing) and each trade- or sub-contractor agree to indemnify the others and the owner against any delay or disruption he may cause, exonerating the owner and head contractor from liability in the middle (except for their own fault). If questions about control of admission to membership of this circle and security for liability could be solved, the result would be consistent with the concept of a construction "team".
- Before joining the middle of a contract chain only as strong as its weakest link, try to secure a strong link on each side to avoid having to bear the weight of liability if a neighbour to whom there is a right to transfer it happens to become insolvent. (The courts have not noticed that particular risk recently, but in several cases have complained that the claimant should have used the main contractual chain, instead of trying to bypass a, presumably, weak link by using the safety chain of concurrent liability in tort, which the court then proceeded to remove).
- Of course, trace out each chain and sub-chain, so as to avoid missing links and dangling ends as far as possible The most important place where no contract link is possible in traditional practice, is between consultants and contractors of the same Employer. At tender stage if possible, contractors should allow and plan for the fact that cases of the following kinds will not squeeze into what is left of the tort of negligence:

> A supervisor's tender design or specification for a detail of the permanent works is short on buildability, or costs more money and time to build than tenderers could reasonably have foreseen. Contractors pursue the supervisors for their losses in completing the work as designed, or for their costs of trying and for damages paid to the employer for failing.
>
> Clause 19.3 of JCT 80 allows the employer to supply lists to tenderers from which they must choose sub-contractors. The chosen then rank as domestic and not nominated sub-contractors. A supervisor includes in a list sub-contractors who for reasons he should have known but the main contractor could not easily have found out in time, do not have the ability to perform the sub-contract. They are the choice of the main contractor, who becomes liable to the employer for their delay and defective work, and claims-over against the supervisor.
>
> There may be a similar claim if a main contractor loses because of a supervisor's careless choice of a nominated sub-contractor, or by a nominated sub-contractor appointed early who loses because of the later choice of main contractor.
>
> By a specification a supervisor has an absolute discretion to refuse consent to excavate rock by blasting. He refuses consent, because he negligently overestimates the effect of the blasts planned on nearby houses. The contractors claim from the supervisor their extra costs of excavating. Alternatively, the specification gives the discretion to the

employer's project manager, who uses it on negligent advice from the supervisor.[23]

- Separate "physical" catastrophies from the above types of "claims" to recover money losses, and try at least to be insured against the former. But judges appear to have lifted the covers that with Victorian modesty they previously kept over insurance policies in court, and to like what they see. Compare now the drafting of insurance policies and tort , and consider the practical implications of the new close relationship between the two:

  One of 1,000 foundation piles in a building near completion fails due to faulty workmanship, with progressive failure of the rest, and total collapse about to follow. The contractor's agent remembers the Dutch boy and the dam, and puts his head in the gap made by the failed pile, to allow time to place supports and save the building. The contractor should reward his courage by dismissing him from site as quickly as possible. There is a common policy exclusion of faulty design or workmanship but not usually (in most countries) damage caused by it, that causes endless trouble and can remove almost the whole cover paid for. So, if the building is saved insurers may pay only for making good the pile that has failed, and go off cover unless the others are made good at someone else's expense (including removal and rebuilding of the superstructure). If the whole building collapses, the cost of replacement other than the extra cost of improving the design or workmanship of the piles, will be repaid by insurers under most exclusions of this kind.

  "However, it may well be arguable that in the case of complex chattels, one element of the structure should be regarded for the purpose of the application of the princples under discussion as distinct from another element, so that damage to one part of the structure caused by a hidden defect in another part may qualify to be treated as damage to 'other property' [so as to allow an action in negligence although the defect is discovered before damage to some distinct building or property or personal injury is done] and whether the argument would prevail would depend on the cicumstances of the case".[24]

  This may be a good example of the risks in the common practice of transfering notions from other parts of the law, without allowing for the peculiarities of construction. And construction is not all that peculiar, at least in this respect. If it were found that some medicine taken caused no immediate injury but was negligently manufactured so as to involve a risk of future harm, would the patient have no right to compensation in tort from the drug manufacturers for the surgical opening-up necessary to remove their product from his system?

- Survey the places where the law of negligence and the market availability of secure contracts and insurance leaves the client high and dry and reliant on self-insurance (or counter-insurance). Most of the places where constructors meet public (non- privatised) authorities are now there, so

23 These examples are discussed in anticipation of the latest decisions in the Liability article already cited.

24 The quotation is from Lord Brook in *D & F Estates*. The insurance example is from the Liability article. Insurance policies were said to have "...in parts unintelligible language" by Lord Wilberforce, in *Amin Rasheed Corp.* v. *Kuwait Insurance* [1983] 1 All ER 879.

attention in time to precautions and remedies in public law becomes most important.[25]

Whatever way the legal rings and chains of liability are arranged, the actual construction chain must have all the rings of expertise in design, consruction, management in all its forms, cash flow and other resources, and the employer's brief as to his physical and economic requirements for the works (possibly conflicting), all linked more or less effectively by communications and co-operation. What a particular contract chain gains by reducing liability risks, it may lose by adding to construction risks. But unfortunately a lawyer gets little blame for trampling over such considerations with unmuddied boots, although it is so essential to remember when conjuring with the rings that each represents both aspects - the more a ring is distanced from a party for reasons of liability the more access to the particular skill and specialisation and assets of the party it represents is distanced too. A single ring which is good for liability may be bad for flexibility, and so on. It is hoped in future to develop existing foundations on this aspect of risk amongst others.

For the construction industry generally,the main outcome of the latest decisions has been to renew doubts about what the law does achieve in the area of risk and liability. It is a fallacy to believe that even primitive or basic rights need only primitive remedies. Whatever the law, it has to be applied to a complicated matrix of construction facts , bringing with them difficulties of making fine "bright lines" with dull instruments. It also has to be applied to deliberate misconduct and conduct that systematically increases the likelihood of human error. Of course, such conduct is quite different from isolated "casual" error itself, whether the conduct is continuing to sell a drug known to be risky, or neglecting to maintain a potentially dangerous structure, or deliberately skimping design or construction, or "bottom-line" pressure to produce profits at all costs, or sometimes even accepting the lowest tender.

The courts have always found systematic negligence most difficult to deal with, in respect both of deterring it and of bringing into the pool of compensation the profits earned by it (No.7 above), to an extent that should cause heads to be lowered were it not that wigs would fall off. The systematically negligent themselves are most vocal in seeking the benefit of the sympathy for those "convicted" of casual negligence by chance misfortune, although the plea that court intervention will open floodgates and lead to defensiveness against the public interest comes badly from them, and even belt and braces design was not invented by lawyers. All these issues too need further investigation, outside the scope of this paper.

It may be that law that must distribute its prizes and penalties in a lottery (at least until we find how to sue the Almighty for natural disasters, including original sin) should make way for an alternative. To return to the beginning of this paper, although pragmatism can lead there, do we have to start out with chaos?[26]

25 See *Rawlings* v. *Takaro Properties Ltd.* [1988] 1 All ER 163, HL, *Hill* v. *Chief Constable of West Yorkshire* [1988] 2 All ER 238, *Business Computers International Ltd.* v. *Registrar of Companies* [1987] 3 All ER 465, and *Jones* v. *Dept. of Employment* [1988] 1 All ER 75, CA. This is not the place to deal with "administrative" prevention and precautions.

26 Since this paper was delivered there has been a great deal of attention to systematic negligence and the concept of "Chaos" (note 24 above), unfortunately because of several calamaties.

4 Fitness of the Product

Humphrey LLoyd

Synopsis

This paper is directed to the objective of this Conference which has been described as: "To debate and identify a coherent set of ground rules for the drafting of standard forms of contract; to identify where and to what extent these matters should be governed by principle and where they are purely matters of commercial choice." The paper examines the existing law on implied warranties and then considers the nature of warranties and the problem of ascertaiing compliance. Finally, a list of questions is suggested as requiring debate and resolution.

Introduction

It is as well at the outset to set out a standpoint in relation to standard forms of contract and the more contentious issue of whether there is truly a distinction between principle and commercial choice in relation to the topic the subject of this paper.

First, do the forms of contract with which this Conference is primarily concerned fall into some of the more typical categories of standard form contracts? Do they for example, fall within Kessler's description:

> "Standard contracts are typically used by enterprises with strong bargaining power. The weaker party, in need of goods or services, is frequently not in a position to shop around for better terms, either because the author of the standard form contract and the monopoly (natural or artificial) because all competitors use the same clauses. ... With the decline of the free enterprise system due to the innate trend of competitive capitalism towards monopoly, the meaning of contract has changed radically.... Standard contracts in particular can thus become effective instruments in the hand of powerful industrial and commercial overlords enabling them to impose new feudal order of their own upon making a vast host of vassals."[1]

1 F Kessler "Contracts of adhesion - some thoughts about freedom of contract" 43, *Columbia Law Review* 629-642 quoted by Trebilcock & Dewees in *The Economic Approach to Law*, (1981) Ed. Burrows and Veljanovski.

The Joint Contracts Tribunal would presumably not wish to be placed in that category. The emergence of the ACA form of contract and the initiatives of the British Property Federation and others nevertheless suggest strongly that the JCT forms had fallen into the vice described above. The ICE form of contract is probably immune from that criticism: it is published by engineers for engineers - engineers who are clients - engineers who are contractors - engineers who are the custodians of other engineers. Probably the IMechE/ IEE forms are in the same category. Many of the sub-contract forms are now ones which appear to be negotiated with no one faction having a particularly dominant role; although the FCEC/FASS/CASEC standard form of sub-contract has perhaps some way to go before it is truly "balanced".

Further afield however we see the signs of monopoly influence in the standard forms for professional engagements of architects and engineers, one faction having a particularly dominant role; by the RIBA and the Association of Consulting Engineers. The FIDIC form of contract also seems now to be one which is more representative of a sectional interest although it purports to represent other interests. Whether contracts incorporating the FIDIC Conditions or other standard forms are truly "effective instruments in the hands of powerful industrial and commercial overlords enabling them to impose a new feudal order of their own making upon a vast host of vassals" remains to be seen: certainly some of the amendments which the overlords would wish to make will make vassals of contractors. But then some of the forms devised by main contractors for sub-contracts have also that effect.

In the main however this paper assumes that we are not concerned with contracts of adhesion but with that class of standard form of contract described by Lord Diplock in *Macaulay* v. *Schroeder Publishing Co. Ltd.*[2] as those which facilitate the conduct of trade. We must nevertheless note the existence of the dominant and potentially offensive standard form of contract for it is in relation to that form that much of the more recent consumer legislation has been passed (to which I shall be referring later in this paper). It should also not be assumed that the true consumer is properly represented in the discussions which lead to the publication of our major standard forms of contract, namely the JCT form and the ICE forms although, in the latter case, such interests were probably more influential than in any other form. That does not mean that the standard forms of contract are not worthy; it merely means that they should not be immune to the imposition of statutory and other legal controls over certain terms. These considerations are of great importance to the question of liability for fitness of product and the extent to which there are parameters beyond which any development of policy will not be allowed to pass.

So far as the subject of this paper is concerned, subject to some mandatory legal constraints, commercial policy is treated solely as a response to or barometer of what the market is prepared to accept. The role of a lawyer is not to criticize the policy of standard forms although attention may be drawn to the probable consequences in law of the language chosen and any omissions, unless perhaps the lawyer works so closely with policy makers in the industry as to be properly informed about its current needs. Nor is it a useful exercise

2 [1976] 1 WLR at 1316.

for this Conference for a lawyer (other than the type that I have described) to suggest what policy should be in the future. Policy is the province of those who run the business not those who serve it in times of crisis. Like others on the periphery a lawyer can draw attention to general considerations of social policy which may affect the implementation in law of commercial policy. I have already mentioned the "revolt" led by the ACA and the British Property Federation against the JCT form. Even before this, dominant employing bodies took steps to amend the ICE Conditions, Fifth Edition, because it was felt that they were too favourable to the contractor. In the main amendments were not made in the direction of imposing greater liabilities on contractors for the quality or suitability of the work carried out but rather controls on cost so that an employer may have reasonable certainty as to his budget and that it will not be exceeded, at least without proper notice. These objectives appear to fall well within the broad band of policy which any free market economy is bound to permit.

The question of liability for the fitness of the product - sometimes inaccurately equated to issues of liability for design - is a matter for broad commercial policy. There is no magic question of principle here - certainly there should not be. If a person wishes to engage another person to design the works in outline or in detail and then to contract with a third party, whether the main contractor, management contractor, or indeed a series of contractors, any of whom is prepared to undertake in contract that the design proposed is sound or will be implemented so that it is sound, who is to say that that is against principle or against commercial policy? One has only to look at the I Mech E /IEE Conditions of Contract and their evolution to see that it is possible for responsibility for the ultimate fitness of the product or works to be shared between the contractor and client. The Model Form A Conditions have for some time made provision for the contractor to be liable for the proper preparation of the drawings that may be required for the execution of the works (usually those set out and called for in the specification) - see Clause 4. Clause 5 of those Conditions makes the contractor responsible for "any discrepancies, errors or omissions in the drawings and information supplied by him, whether they have been approved by the engineer or not", so that responsibility for the evolution of the design and its ultimate implementation may rest on the contractor even though the engineer may have approved the contractor's proposals. The contractor is only exempted from liability if "such discrepancies, errors or omissions be not due to defective drawings or information furnished to the contractor by the purchaser or the engineer" (Clause 5(i) proviso). These provisions coupled with the standard requirement calling for the contractor to test and commission not merely the individual parts of the works but also the works as a whole on completion can place upon the contractor a liability jointly with the engineer for demonstrating to the client that the works on completion met the standards specified by the client. Such an overlap is both necessary and desired.

It is but a short step from such a standard form of contract to one in which it is for the contractor himself to ascertain the client's requirements and to produce works that meet those requirements. There are so many ways of completing projects that it is foolish to argue that there is any one "right" way or that as a general rule "design should not be the responsibility of the contractor". Design is a word that reflects only a choice or decision. It has no meaning in law, once divorced of its context. Questions of "legal liability for design" can only be discussed sensibly by reference to a specific factual situation or with limited application by reference to a standard form and typical factuals. What however does need to be defined and what this paper is concerned about is whether some of the potentially troublesome areas should be clarified in the contract, either as a matter of policy or as a matter of commercial choice.

Before examining the law let us dispose of a red herring, namely that in general contractors only have expertise in execution and not design. On some projects the professional skills of the contractor are equal to if not greater than the professional skills and advice available to the client. Even in competitive tendering a contractor will have been selected for his experience and specialist knowledge, usually viewed corporately rather than by reference to the individuals who will be employed to manage the contract (some of whom may prove to belie their employer's reputation). Even at the humbler end of the construction industry contractors will, even if they do not employ people with qualifications obtained by examination and subsequently fortified by experience, nevertheless have or should have on their staff people with sufficient knowledge of the industry's practices to have at least "a nose" for what is wrong and what is right. Is it therefore correct to approach the interpretation of a contract, whether as a matter of principle or policy, on the basis that a client, in entrusting work to a contractor, did not rely upon the contractor's experience, judgement and advice (should the contractor be required to carry out work which in his view appeared likely to cause trouble)? It is not simply a matter of self-interest, although in many cases the contractor's advice may be tempered by those considerations but it is also a question of what a person is obtaining under the head of "workmanship". For the purposes of discussion one may take the location of services in a duct: is a contractor not expected to point out difficulties of access to maintain one service if it might be blocked by other services, whether or not any thought has apparently been given to the provisions? Surely, one does not need express clauses in the contract requiring the contractor to scrutinise the "design" and advise the client as to whether or not it is likely to fulfil its purposes: it should be quite sufficient simply to rely on basic legal obligations as to competence and skill.

The Law

I now intend to turn to the existing law as I understand it and to discuss it and its implications. I take as my starting point what I believe to be the basic common law principle applicable to "fitness of the product", namely the statement approved in *Young & Marten Ltd.* v. *McManus Childs Ltd*[3].

> "A person contracting to do work and supply materials warrants that the materials which he uses will be of good quality and reasonably fit for the purpose for which he is using them, unless the circumstances of the contract are such as to exclude any such warranty."

3 [1969] 1 AC 454; 9 Build LR 77.

Lord Reid in his speech made it clear that there were really two warranties, one as to quality and one as to reasonable fitness for the job.[4]

The origin of this warranty goes further back beyond the case approved by the House of Lords, (*G H Myers & Co.* v. *Brent Cross Service Co.*)[5]. It appears to owe its origin to the same source as liability for the quality and fitness of goods. In *Christopher Hill* v. *Ashington Piggeries Ltd.*[6] Lord Guest referred to what he regarded as the "classic passage" in *Jones* v. *Last*[7] as the basis of the enactment of Section 14 of the Sale of Goods Act 1893 where Mellor J said:-

> "Fourthly, where a manufacturer or dealer contracts to supply an article which he manufactures or produces, or in which he deals, to be applied for a particular purpose, so that the buyer necessarily trusts to the judgment or skill of the manufacturer or dealer, there is in that case an implied term or warranty that it shall it shall be reasonably fit for the purpose to which it is to be applied: *Brown* v. *Edgington* (1841) 2 McN & G. 279, *Jones* v. *Bright* (1829) 15 Bing. 533. In such a case the buyer trusts the manufacturer or dealer, and relied upon his judgment and not upon his own. ..."

From this we may take it that the common law regarded such a term as socially desirable in so far as the law reflected the needs and aspirations of society, at least in the mid-19th century. As regards sales of goods such an approach of course received Parliamentary approval in the Sale of Goods Act 1893. It took nearly 100 years for Parliament to extend it to work and services but that does not mean to say that the law did not contain a comparable provision before the Supply of Goods and Services Act 1982. Nor, contrary to what Lord Bridge has supposed in *D & F Estates* v. *The Church Commissioners*[8] did the enactment of the 1982 Act imply that the law was then changed, as Lord Bridge considers the law to have been radically changed by the Defective Premises Act 1972.

Next, what type of implied term is it? How does it fit into the classification of implied term; is the term implied "in fact" or "in law"? The distinction is important for reasons which are canvassed by Treitel.[9] It is in my view clear that, having regard to the discussion in *Liverpool City Council* v. *Irwin*[10], the term is one which must be implied as a matter of law. This much is clear at least from the concluding words "unless the circumstances of the contract are such to exclude any such warranty". The warranty postulated seems to be one which will be found as a matter of law unless displaced. It is a matter of "status"[11] or "legal incident".[12] It is therefore a question of policy: it is policy that a contractor should be subject to that undertaking unless it is displaced.[13] The

4 [1969] 1 AC 468; 9 Build LR 89.
5 [1934] 1 KB 46 at 55.
6 [1972] AC 441 at 474.
7 (1868) LR 3 QB 197, 202-203.
8 [1988] 3 WLR 368; 41 Build LR 1.
9 *The Law of Contract*, 7th Ed, (1987) pp 158 *et seq*.
10 [1977] AC 239.
11 [1957] AC 555 at 576.
12 *Mears* v. *Safeguard Securities Ltd.* [1983] QB 54 at 78.
13 The displacement argument was advanced by the writer in a paper "Contractor's Liability for Design: an English Point of View" in *The Liability of Contractors* (1986) at 139.

warranty seems to fall into the category described by Lord Salmon in *Liverpool CC* v. *Irwin*.[14]

> "Unless the law, in circumstances such as these, imposes an obligation...the whole transaction becomes inefficacious, futile and absurd."

Or, to use Lord Wilberforce's term[15] a "legal incident of this kind of contract".

How will the warranty be excluded or displaced? This question is considered fully later. Nevertheless, having regard to the common law and Parliamentary legislation it is suggested that the proper approach would be to see whether the warranty is to be displaced, but as Lord Diplock said in the *Christopher Hill* case "the choice depends largely upon one's personal view as to whether the swing of the pendulum ...from *caveat emptor* to *caveat venditor* has now gone far enough and ought to be arrested, or whether it should be given a further impetus, albeit a minor one, upon its current course." It is nonetheless tolerably clear from the legislation passed in the last two decades that whatever the principles of the common law may have said and whatever commercial policy may supposedly require, social policy now militates very much against the displacement of that implied term. Four illustrations of this policy can be given:

- The re-enactment of the Sales of Goods Act 1979 retaining the implied term as to fitness for purpose of goods sold by a seller in the course of his business: Section 14(3);
- The introduction of implied terms as to fitness as regards goods supplied under a contract for the transfer of goods (Section 4 of the Supply of Goods and Services Act 1982) and as to the necessity to carry out services with reasonable care and skill (Section 13 of the same Act);
- Liability for defective products established by the Consumer Protection Act 1987 pursuant to the Product Liability Directive of the Council of European Communities of 25 July 1985 (see Sections 2 and 3) with the very limited defences given by Section 4(1) and in particular the defence in paragraph (*e*) of that section coupled with the prohibition on exclusions of liability in Section 7 of the same Act;
- The restrictions on exclusions of liability contained in Section 3 of the Unfair Contract Terms Act 1977 which appear to be now of general application to construction contracts between employers and contractors in the light of the attitude of the Court of Appeal to the words "dealing as a consumer" in *R & B Customs Brokers Co. Ltd.* v. *United Dominions Trust Ltd. (Saunders Abbott) (1980) Ltd. Third Party*.[16]

The Nature of the Warranty : I

First, is the warranty absolute or qualified? It was not thought that there could be much doubt about this but for the reference to a lower standard in *Liverpool C.C.* v. *Irwin* where Lord Wilberforce said:[17]

14 [1977] AC 239 at 262A.
15 *Ibid* p 255.
16 [1988] 1 WLR 321.
17 [1977] AC 329 at 256.

> "It remains to define the standard. My Lords, if, as I think, the test of the existence of the term is necessity the standard must surely not exceed what is necessary having regard to the circumstances. To imply an absolute obligation to repair would go beyond what is a necessary legal instant and would indeed be unreasonable. An obligation to take reasonable care and to keep in reasonable repair and usability is what fits the requirements of the case. Such a definition involves - and I think rightly - recognition that the tenants themselves have their responsibilities. What it is reasonable to expect of a landlord has a clear relation to what a reasonable set of tenants should do for themselves."

He also went on to deal with the nature of the obligation as to the provision of lighting and the maintenance of lifts both of which he also regarded as not requiring absolute standards of compliance.

On the other hand the traditional view has been, and contracts have clearly been drawn up on the basis, that the standard is an absolute one. Clause 2.5.1 of the JCT Standard Form of Building Contract with Contractors Design 1981 Edition imposes only on the contractor an obligation comparable to that of an architect or other appropriate professional designer together with some possible further restrictions on liability contained in Clause 2.5.3 and, in relation to the design prepared by others in Clause 2.5.4. These reservations may have arisen for example, from what Lord Scarman had said in the leading case of *Independent Broadcasting Authority* v. *EMI and BICC*:[18]

> "Counsel for the appellants, however, submitted that where a design, as in this case, requires the exercise of professional skill, the obligation is no more than to exercise the care and skill of the ordinarily competent member of the profession. ... I do not accept that the design obligation and the supply of an article is to be equated with the obligation of the professional man in the practice of his profession."

An earlier and possibly more helpful illustration of the application of policy to this principle may be seen from the decision of the Court of Appeal in *London Borough of Newham* v. *Taylor Woodrow-Anglian Ltd.*[19]

The contract there stated, amongst other things:-

> "1(2) The Contractor shall be responsible for the design and construction of the works... (the 'Tower Block Works')
>
> (4) The Contractor shall notwithstanding previous examination or approval by the Architect of drawings, data, evidence or documents submitted or supplied by the Contractor be held responsible for any miscalculation, error or fault in the Tower Block Works...
>
> (5) The Contractor shall be held responsible for all works designed by him...
>
> (6) The Contractor hereby guarantees the work which he has designed and when so instructed by the Architect shall make good at his own cost any defective work which is due to any fault or defect in the design."

At trial O'Connor J held that Clause 1(6) was one by which the contractor warranted that his design was free of fault or defect. He said:

18 (1980) 14 Build LR 1 at 47.
19 (1981) 19 Build LR 99.

> "Design necessarily imports the purpose for the product, in this case blocks of flats; so that the warranty is that the design will produce blocks of residential flats of the type identified in Clause 1. Insofar as the design fails to produce these results it is faulty or defective, and the work - namely, the building or parts thereof - is defective work. The warranty is absolute and if it is broken it matters not that the designer has exercised all due care and skill in making his design."

The contractor's appeal was dismissed; so too was the plaintiff's cross-appeal against the finding that there was no negligence on the part of the contractor. This illustrates that there may be liability without negligence. Whether this is of great practical importance may at times be doubted.

In *Holland Hannen & Cubitts (Northern) Ltd.* v. *Welsh Health Technical Services Organisation (Alan Marshall & Partners Third Party)*[20] the Court of Appeal was concerned with the impact of a contractual warranty and the liability of professional engineers employed by a sub-contractor in circumstances comparable to those found in *Greaves* v. *Baynham Meikle & Partners*[21] - a case on its own special facts. In that case Robert Goff LJ said this when considering the question of breach of warranty:

> "Next, I do not consider that it is open to us to interfere with the judge's conclusion that the floors were in fact unserviceable. I feel bound to say that, having regard to the strength of the evidence to the contrary, this may well have been a borderline case; but it is impossible for us to say that there was no evidence upon which the judge could make his finding on this point, and I do not think it would be right for this court to interfere with that finding. The floors were unserviceable because the effect of the deflection was that there was 'double-dishing' on either side of the spine-beam, leaving a significant and plainly visible hump over the spine-beam itself. Like the judge, I consider that this meant that the floors were unserviceable, both as to function and as to visual effect. They were unserviceable as to function, in particular because the profile of the flooring resulted in more than usual difficulty and adjustment in the erection of partitions, of which the main contractors, HHC, justifiably complained, and also, though to a much lesser extent, because of the effect, observed by the judge, upon trolleys passing over the hump. They were also unserviceable by reason of their visual effect, observed by Mr. Pickup when he came to visit the hospital in the spring of 1976.
>
> "I turn then to the judge's conclusion that CED were in breach of their warranty to WHTSO. On this point it was the submission of Mr. Gardam that the judge erred in that he did not ask himself the correct question, viz, whether CED could reasonably have thought that the design was satisfactory in the material respect. In this connection, he suggested that there was a danger in cases of professional negligence that professional men, whose duty is only to exercise due care and skill, may be treated as though they had given absolute warranties relating to the products of their work. Speaking for myself, I recognise this danger; but the present case does perhaps illustrate how, in certain circumstances, a breach of the duty of care can come close to a breach of warranty. Let me take the case of suitability of the product of a design, where the customer contends that a product is unsuitable whereas the professional designer contends that it is not. The circumstances may well be such that the requisite criteria are not precise; and the

20 (1985) 35 Build LR 1.
21 [1975] 1 WLR 1095; 4 Build LR 56.

professional man may either have produced a design which, though not perfect, falls within the acceptable bracket, or he may have produced one which falls short of the acceptable standard. Plainly, in the first example he is not negligent; but in the second, it may be difficult not to draw the conclusion that he is negligent. For, with the exercise of due skill, he should have known what the acceptable bracket was, and he should have been able to form a correct judgment whether or not his design would produce a product which did or did not fall within that bracket.

"It is this that produces the feeling that, in cases such as these, a professional man is being treated as though he gave an absolute warranty. The true answer must be to recognise that his obligation is only to exercise due care and skill, though, where he is held to have been negligent, to identify precisely the negligence of which he is held guilty. Bearing this in mind I do not think that, having studied his judgment, the judge failed to ask himself the right question. His criticism was that a defective design was prepared and persisted in; but if the relevant passage in the judgment is read as a whole, it appears that he concluded that this was due to a failure by CED to exercise due care and skill in relation to the design. Given that the floors were unserviceable, and having regard to the fact that the deflections in the floors were on the evidence a predictable consequence of the design, the judge was, in my judgment, entitled to reach that conclusion, the relevant negligence of CED being a failure to exercise due skill in assessing the serviceability of the product of their design."

The Nature of the Warranty - II

Secondly, what is meant by "reasonably fit"? This is allied to the question "how is the 'purpose' to be ascertained"? "Fitness" is not a standard to be measured except by reference to the purposes for which the works are to be required. These are questions of fact and degree. For the purpose of construction contracts some obvious steps may be taken such as by the incorporation in the contract of a list of the purposes for which the works were required. However even that list may not be sufficiently clear in relation to matters such as durability. What is the standard of the services that are required? How easy to maintain are they to be? If they are not easy to maintain then costs will obviously be incurred in the long run. How frequently will the major components of any air-handling system have to be renewed? So far little if anything has been said in the English courts on these subjects. These are of course not matters of principle but commercial choice. There is a strong case to be made, in my view, for establishing a model regime in the construction industry whereby the purposes are fully and carefully defined. On the simplest basis the regime could be in the nature of a check list.

Allied to this there is the problem of the fitness of a product when it is used in conjunction with other products or incorporated in work done by others or in materials and goods produced by others. Some guidance is given by Section 4 of the Consumer Protection Act 1987 which affords a defence on the grounds that the defect was "wholly attributable to the design of the subsequent product or to compliance by the producer of the product in question with the instructions given by the producer of the subsequent product" (Section 4(1)(*f*)). This is necessary because the definition of "product" includes "a product which is comprised in another product" and accordingly the producer of the product may be liable for the defect in the subsequent product resulting from a defect in the product which he himself originally supplied. The position at common law is tolerably clear, certainly if one uses the analogy of the sale of goods. Whether it is acceptable as a matter of commercial choice is not for me to say.

The first approach is to determine who is responsible for securing the fitness: to whom did the contract leave the relevant decision? It seems quite clear from *Cammell Laird & Co.* v. *The Manganese Bronze & Brass Co.*[22] that the defect must lie in the region within which the contractor is to exercise its skill and judgement.[23] In the same case Lord Wright, holding that the suppliers of the propeller were liable for the defects which affected the performance of the ship, dealt with the question thus[24]:

> "In some cases [what is the particular purpose] may be very simple: the purpose for which a hot water bottle is required is easily determined and equally easy is it to determine the extent of reliance on the seller: similarly in the case of a piece of mechanism, intended to fit into a complete machine, the relevant purpose as between the buyer and the maker will normally be simply that it should be of the specified plan and, when properly fitted, work in its place: there is no reliance on the maker for the general performance of the machine as a whole. Similarly in *Manchester Liners Ltd.* v. *Rea Ltd.* [1922] 2 A.C. 74 the bunkers were to be fit to burn in the furnaces but not to raise any given head of steam. The definition of the particular purpose will vary according to the contract in question. To apply these considerations to the present case: the propeller is, as I conceive it, to be fit for ship and engines No. 972, but only as a propeller; that is, it has to work efficiently when fitted properly on the vessel; for instance, the blades must not snap, there must not be corrosion, it must work without excessive noise, and must revolve reasonably smoothly with the actual engines, these being Diesel engines, but the propeller makers are not concerned with matters relating to the ship and engines as a whole, such as matters of speed; for instance, if the propeller worked efficiently as a propeller, it would not matter to the respondents if owing to something in the design of ship or engines, it could only propel the ship at two miles an hour.
>
> "I think the true position is that the respondents accept the plan and specification and agree, by using what appears on these pieces of paper, to produce by their skill and experience a material object in Parsons manganese bronze capable of being properly described as a propeller and being, in addition to being of the prescribed design and dimensions, also fit to operate as a propeller with ship and engines No. 972. The appellants stated what sizes, shapes and so forth they thought would suit their vessel and engines. No doubt they had in mind some ideas as to the speed and the power to be achieved with the help of the propeller, but what the respondents had to do was to follow the instructions given them as to design and so forth, and produce something which being of that design and size would function as a propeller. The conclusion I arrive at is that in all matters relevant as between these parties to the creation of a propeller for No. 972, there was reliance on the sellers' skill or judgment within the section. But it is said this conclusion would throw on the makers responsibility for defects in the plan and design, for instance, if a propeller of the specified plan and design could not be physically cast, or would be too weak, or otherwise could not be fitted to or worked on No. 972. I have

22 [1934] AC 402.
23 *Ibid per* Lord MacMillan at 419.
24 *Ibid* p 424.

pointed out that on my view of the facts none of these difficulties arise here.

"It has been laid down that where a manufacturer or builder undertakes to produce a finished result according to a design or plan, he may be still bound by his bargain even though he can show an unanticipated difficulty or even impossibility in achieving the result desired with the plans or specification. Such a case as *Thorn* v. *Mayor and Commonalty of London* (1876) 1 App. Cas. 120, where under a building contract the contractor sought to set up an implied warranty by the other contracting party that the bridge could be built (or built without undue expense) according to the plans and specification, but this House decided against any such warranty. Again in *Gillespie* v. *Howden* (1838) 4 M. & W. 399 the Court of Session held it was no defence to a shipbuilder who had contracted to build a ship of a certain design and of a certain carrying capacity, that it was impossible with the approved design to achieve the agreed capacity: the shipbuilder had to answer in damages. Though this is the general principle of law, its application in respect of any particular contract must vary with the terms and circumstances of that contract, but I see no reason why in regard to this contract the respondents should not be held to be subject, under the terms of S. 14(1), of the Act, to the implied condition that the propeller they made should be reasonably fit for use on Ship No. 972. Obviously it was their business to supply propellers."

He later said this[25]:

"It follows, I think, that a reliance partial but substantial and effective, will bring the implied condition into play: it would then be a matter of construction of the particular contract whether the condition that "the goods shall be reasonably fit for such purpose" is to be read without qualification or whether it is to be limited to the matters within the particular province left entirely to the seller's skill and judgment."

Thus in principle we may assume that a contractor may well be liable to ensure that every part of the work even parts specified to him will be suitable for the ultimate purpose for which it is required (subject of course to apportionment of liability under the Civil Liability (Contribution) Act 1978. Nevertheless this approach does give rise to the problem posed by Lord Diplock in the *Christopher Hill* case[26]. He said this:

"The way in which the principle of reliance which underlies subsections (1) and (2) should be applied to a more complex contract of this kind, which was not in the immediate contemplation of the draftsman of the code, poses another stark question of legal policy. In large part this decision was made by your Lordships' House in 1934 in the *Cammell Laird* case [1934] A.C. 402. It was there laid down that if the defect in the goods which rendered them unfit for their purpose was due to a characteristic which it lay within the sphere of expertise of the seller to detect and avoid, the responsibility for their unfitness lay with the seller. The ratio decidendi leads ineluctably to the corollary that if the defect was due to a characteristic which it lay within the sphere of the expertise of the buyer to detect and avoid, the seller was not contractually responsible for it. It did not attract the implied condition under subsection (1). The field of the seller's undertaking as to the fitness of the goods for the purpose corresponded with the field of the buyer's reliance upon the skill and judgment of the seller. My Lords,

25 At 428.
26 [1972] AC 441 at 508.

this seems to me to be consistent with commonsense and business honesty. It was accepted as the correct principle by both courts below and by all parties to the appeals in this House. But the *Cammell Laird* case leaves open for decision an ancillary question of legal policy which your Lordships are now called upon to decide for the first time. That question is whether, in a case of partial reliance of this kind, once the goods have been proved to be unfit for the purpose for which they were required the onus lies upon the buyer to prove that the defect was due to a characteristic which it lay within the field of expertise of the seller to detect and avoid; or does it lie upon the seller to prove that the defect was due to a characteristic which lay within the sphere of expertise of the buyer."

The Nature of the Warranty - III

Thirdly, we have therefore another major question of policy with which this Conference may be concerned. How are we to answer Lord Diplock's question? He would have answered it in favour of the seller or contractor. Is this right in today's world? Or is this a matter for which the House of Lords should not shirk their responsibility to ensure that the common law is in contact with the development of the times and not duck the issue by pretending that it is only a matter for Parliament? Legislation is at times a harsh and unnecessary way of achieving law reform, when the way surely is clear.

Ascertaining Compliance with the Warranty

Another problem that commonly occurs is that of determining at what point do the works comply with the warranty. The common law rule, drawing on analogy with sales of goods, would be to take the date of delivery, *i.e.* upon completion. However in certain contracts the completion will mean the second stage of completion rather than the first of so-called "practical" completion or "substantial" completion. Indeed few if any clients would be satisfied with the state of the works upon initial handover. The proof of the pudding is in the eating. Should part of the basic ground rules for ascertaining compliance be to allow a measure of time to see whether in fact the works work in practice, and if so, how much time?

This undoubtedly will cause difficulties in certain parts of the industry where traditionally tests prior to completion are used to demonstrate compliance, such as under the IMechE/IEE form of contract although found elsewhere. The majority of cases will be where the employer/owner's use of the works could materially affect a decision as to whether or not the warranty was complied with. In contrast it is sometimes very difficult even to establish proper tests if, for example, the owner has not provided sufficient material for the plant to work on, *e.g.* sugar cane, to demonstrate the effective use of a sugar mill.

This problem cannot be divorced from the problem now known, colloquially, as the "state of the art" problem. It will be recalled that the United Kingdom decided in the Consumer Protection Act to exercise its option to have as a defence in Section 4(1)(*e*):

> "That the state of scientific and technical knowledge at the relevant time was not such that a producer of products of the same description as the product in question might be expected to have discovered the defect if it had existed in his products while they were under his control."

Of course this is a defence which has to be established by the defendant in the case of a defective product that the state of knowledge at the time that the producer supplied the product was such that no producer of products of that type might have been expected to have discovered the defect, at least according to Lord Nathan in the debate in the House of Lords.[27] The time is, by Section 4(2), the date of supply, and not the date of conception, manufacture or transportation (assuming that the risk passes upon physical delivery to the buyer's place of business and not otherwise). The Act is of relevance to the construction industry by virtue of Section 46(3) which reads:

> "The performance of any contract by the erection of any building or structure on any land or by the carrying out of any other building work shall be treated for the purposes of this Act as a supply of goods insofar as, but only insofar as, it involves the provision of any goods to any person by means of their incorporation into the building, structure or works."

The model regime to which I refer might perhaps therefore make provision for determining the date at which compliance is to be determined.

The next question then is, by what standards is compliance to be determined at the relevant date? Here however the answer in the common law is not as clear as it should be. To look once again at the analogy with the sale of goods and what was said the House of Lords in the *Hardwick Game Farm* case (*Henry Kendal & Sons* v. *William Lillico & Sons Ltd.*[28]). In relation to the question of judging merchantable quality (the distinction between merchantable quality and fitness for purpose is irrelevant for present purposes) Lord Reid said this:[29]

> "So the question at once arises - do you judge merchantable quality in light of what was known at the time of sale or in light of later knowledge? It is quite clear that some later knowledge must be brought in for otherwise it would never be possible to hold that goods were unmerchantable by reason of a latent defect. By definition a latent defect is something that could not have been discovered at the time by any examination which in the light of then existing knowledge it was reasonable to make. There is a question as to how much later knowledge ought to be brought in. ...I think it would be very artificial to bring in some part of the later knowledge and exclude others. ..."

Lord Guest said this :[30]

> "It is clear that the quality of the goods has to be assessed at the time of trial when the latent defect has become known. But it is said that you must not, in ascertaining the condition of the goods and their merchantability, attribute the knowledge that they would not be harmful... This is, in my view, to approach the true situation with blinkers."

27 ex. p.34 noted in *Halsbury's Statutes* (4th Ed.), Vol.39 at p 194.
28 [1969] 2 AC 31.
29 *Ibid* at 75.
30 *Ibid* at 108-109.

Lord Pearce, with whom Lord Wilberforce agreed, however dissented:[31]

> "But what additional after-acquired knowledge must one assume? Logic might seem to indicate that the Court should bring to the task all the after acquired knowledge which it possesses at the date of trial. But I do not think that this is always so. For one is trying to find out what market the goods would have had if their subsequently ascertained condition had been known. As it is a hypothetical exercise, one must create a hypothetical market. Nevertheless a hypothetical market should be one that could have existed not one which could not have existed at the date of delivery. The supposed goods contained a hidden deadly poison to which there was discovered by scientists two years after delivery a simple, easy, inexpensive antidote which could render the goods harmless. They would be unmarketable at the date of delivery if the existence of the poison was brought to light, since no purchaser could then have known the antidote to the poison. Hypothesis is no reason for complete departure from possibility. One must keep the hypothesis in touch with the facts as far as possible."

These considerations are obviously also relevant to the question of damages. Take two instances:[32]

1. A building is erected which on completion contains a latent defect; on its discovery panic ensues; remedial work is carried out. However at the date of the trial of the action to recover those damages it is proved that the defect was not one which in the light of the knowledge at the date of trial (but not at the date of discovery) would render the building unfit: one could have lived with it. What is the answer: to deprive the plaintiff of the damages which he incurred on a bona fide basis simply because knowledge marched on?
2. The reverse example: the building contains a defect which when it is discovered is in the light of the knowledge at the time thought to be unimportant; it is only later that its gravity is appreciated. Should the defendant pay more because the fault was not nipped in the bud?

Circumstances of the Contract

At the outset of this paper it was suggested that social policy required the implication of a warranty for fitness for purpose and that the common law permitted such a warranty to be excluded only if "the circumstances of the contract" so required. What are "the circumstances"? This Conference might usefully consider the extent to which, as a matter of commercial policy in relation to a given standard form of contract, there should be a clear indication as to whether or not the warranty is or is not to be excluded. Occasionally this can be done by reference to the use of the word "design". That however only provides an answer in relation to the decisions embodied in certain documents to which the contractor has undertaken to work. Where the contractor or his sub-contractor is left to reach other decisions, there will still be residual designer liability. Even some of the standard forms are not as clear as they

31 *Ibid*.
32 For a further stimulating case and study counting problems both the date of ascertainment and the applicable standards: see the *Blaisbach Valley Case* discussed by Dr. Christian Wiegand in *The Liability of Contractors cit.sup*. at 137-138.

might be. For example, although Clause 8(2) of the ICE Conditions, Fifth Edition, declares:

> "The Contractor shall not be responsible for the design or specification of the Permanent Works (except as may be expressly provided in the Contract) or of any Temporary Works designed by the Engineer"

It therefore leaves open two questions. First, what is meant by "design" and secondly what is a sufficiently express provision in the contract by which the contractor would be responsible for the design of the works. For example, if the contractor had in his tender put forward an alternative design which had been accepted by the employer, even though the word "design" might not have been used in the alternative tender which formed part of the contract documents, would the contractor be responsible? Commonsense suggests an affirmative answer, notwithstanding *Yorkshire Water Authority* v. *Sir Alfred McAlpine (Northern) Ltd.*[33] On the other hand, in relation to the subject of Provisional Sums or Prime Cost Items, Clause 58(3) states that if the services to be provided include:

> "any matter of design or specification of any part of the Permanent Works or of any equipment or plant to be incorporated therein such requirement shall be expressly stated in the Contract and shall be included in any nominated sub-contract. The obligation of the Contractor in respect thereof shall be only that which has been expressly stated in accordance with this sub-clause."

On the face of it such an express statement would appear to be an express provision for the purposes of Clause 8(2) to the effect that the contractor should be liable for the design of the work the subject of the provisional sum or prime cost item. But does this also make the contractor responsible for the satisfactory incorporation of the design or specification of that work with the remaining part of the permanent works? In other words has the implied warranty been sufficiently displaced by the provisions of Clause 8(2)?

I draw attention to the ICE Conditions because they deal with the question of work which would probably be sub-contracted (although not necessrily since the main contractor might himself undertake the work the subject of the provisional sum or prime cost item). Most of the instances in which the questions of the displacement of the implied warranty will arise will be where the relevant work, materials or services are provided to the main contractor by some other person.

Do we get any assistance from the cases as to what circumstances may be regarded as excluding the warranty and what types of circumstances will not exclude the warranty? The answer is: not much. We may start with the Irish case *Norta Wallpapers Ltd.* v. *John Sisk Ltd.*[34] In that case the Irish Supreme Court held that although there would normally be implied in a building contract a term making the builder liable to the employer for any loss or damage suffered by the employer as a result of the work not being fit for its purpose, but that such a term, being based upon the presumed intention of the parties to the contract and the reasonableness of the term, could not be implied

33 (1985) 32 Build LR 114.
34 [1978] IR 114; 14 Build LR 49.

in a main contract in respect of roof lights designed by a nominated sub-contractor.

When the House of Lords came to consider this case in *IBA* v. *EMI & BICC* it was distinguished by Viscount Dilhorne on the grounds that EMI had accepted responsibility for the design of the mast prepared by BICC, even though "EMI had nothing to do with its preparation and were not consulted in relation to it and were bound to accept BICC as sub-contractors and to accept their design"[35] and by Lord Fraser[36] on the grounds that the main contractor had not been given an option either as to the identity of the sub-contractor or as to the design or price. Nevertheless the House of Lords unanimously held EMI liable in contract for the failure of the design so that, at least, it is far from clear whether the House of Lords would have arrived at the same decision as the Irish Supreme Court on similar facts, notwithstanding Viscount Dilhorne's and Lord Fraser's apparent approval of *Norta*.

The *IBA* case does not appear to be authority for the proposition that the warranty is displaced by the fact that the relevant work was provided by a nominated sub-contractor any more than it is authority for the proposition that because design work was in fact undertaken by a sub-contractor gives rise to an implication which would not otherwise be present. It has already been suggested that the implied warranty is imposed as a matter of law and needs to be displaced; the undertaking by a sub-contractor of design work merely fulfills the warranty and could not lead to it being displaced, (at least to the extent of the relevant work designed or executed by the sub-contractor).

Nevertheless there has to be set in the balance the judgment of Robert Goff LJ in *Comyn Ching & Co. Ltd.* v. *Oriental Tube Co. Ltd.*[37] Observing that in *Young & Marten Ltd.* v. *McManus Childs Ltd.*[38] there were passages to the effect that a main contractor would not be liable where materials had been selected by the employer, he said:

> "In my judgment, therefore, it must be taken as a normal rule that where the builder owner does specify particular goods there is no warranty of fitness, which indeed must generally be eminently reasonable."

However it is not clear from that observation whether Robert Goff LJ was doing more than approving a proposition earlier described by him as:

> "That where a building owner specifies particular goods which are inherently unsuitable there is no warranty of fitness"[39],

thus not discussing the question of liability where goods are specified which need not be unsuitable but prove to be unsuitable. This is a relevant factor in relation to construction work for the mere selection of a person to carry out certain work albeit by a certain method or to a particular standard does not of itself necessarily displace the warranty especially if the person providing the work was under a duty to ascertain the purpose for which the work was required.

35 14 Build LR, paraphrasing Kenny J in *Norta* at [1978] IR 130; 14 Build LR 68.
36 14 Build LR 46.
37 (1979) 17 Build LR 47.
38 *Ibid* at 81.
39 *Ibid*.

In *Viking Grain Storage Ltd.* v. *TH White Installations Ltd. & Anor.*[40] His Honour Judge John Davies QC approached the question almost *ab initio* before coming to the conclusion that there was an implied warranty as to suitability.

He was there dealing with a contract by which the contractors had undertaken to build a grain drying and storage installation. It was a contract by which the contractor had undertaken at least part of the design. The issue was whether there was an implied term of the contract as to fitness for purpose. Judge Davies had this to say under the heading of "package deals", amongst other things in a passage which is worth reproducing in full:

> "In the case of some contracts of a readily definable and uncomplicated kind, the law has for so long recognised both the need and the reasonableness of attaching certain incidents to them that it would be unrealistic to presume that the parties would have intended otherwise. Examples in the field of warranties of quality and work and materials were to be found in the sale of goods before 1983, and in contracts for work and materials. ... In the case of the sale of a house in the course of erection, the initial presumption has long been in favour of warranties for fitness of purpose, since as a general rule the very nature of the contract admits of little doubt regarding either its purpose or the purchaser's reliance on the seller's skill and judgment. In contracts of the kind I have just mentioned, the law will imply the appropriate term, unless it is shown that there is a compelling indication to the contrary. Other contracts are of a more heterogenous and complex kind. They do not fit so readily into an established mould. In such cases, it is for the proponent of the implied term to show that it ought to be implied.
>
> "It has been strongly urged upon me that "package deals", of which kind this contract is one, fall into the first category I have mentioned, and are to be deemed to carry a warranty of fitness for purpose, unless the contrary is shown. I doubt whether in most transactions of any complexity it makes much difference at the end of the day whether one approaches it on the basis of an initial premise and proceeds to enquire whether the facts of the case refute it, or whether one embarks on the enquiry with an open mind since (i) this is an issue in this case; (ii) transactions generally described as 'package deals', or 'turnkey contracts', or, somewhat more specifically, 'design and build' contracts, are becoming an increasingly common feature of the building scene; and (iii) in some cases the category into which a particular contract falls might prove decisive, I will deal with it.
>
> "Whether transactions so called are to be deemed to contain implied terms of one kind or another will depend on the contents of the package, and the nature of the term sought to be implied. There are many possible shades of the spectrum and this is particularly so where the term sought to be implied is one of fitness for purpose. The purpose is often obvious. In this case it was, as the parties well know and accept, to build a grain drying and storage installation of a specified capacity, capable of one man operation. The problematical area in this contract is to be found in the sphere of reliance on skill and judgment, especially when, as here, the fitness of the installation for its known purpose depended as much on the suitability of the ground on which it was to be built as on the suitability of its constituent parts. It may or may not be that the purchaser depended on the judgment of the supplier for the latter, but even if he did, it would not necessarily follow that the same could be said of the former. Again, whilst in the ordinary case of the sale of an article other than under its trade or patent name, if the purpose is known to the seller so as to show reliance on his skill and judgment, a

40 (1985) 33 Build LR 103.

> warranty of fitness will be implied irrespective of whether he is the manufacturer. Does the analogy hold good in the case of the supplier of a multi-partite installation like this one, where a variety of different parts of the entity are the subject of specialist sub-contracts? Or is it that his liability, if any, is to be founded only in negligence, as White contend? It is for these reasons that I feel driven to approach this case without any preconceived notion as to whether a term of fitness for purpose should be implied."

At the end of his judgment Judge Davies incorporated by reference:

> "the arguments against cutting the chain of responsibility in a case like this, with its tally of sub-contracts which would be the consequence of not implying the terms sought..."

Judge Davies referred in particular to what Lord Reid had said in *Young & Marten* v. *McManus Childs*[41]:

> "There are, in my view, good reasons for implying such a warranty if it is not excluded by the terms of the contract. If the contractor's employer suffers loss by reason of the emergence of the latent defect, he will generally have no redress if he cannot recover damages from the contractor. ... and, if that seller had in turn bought from someone else, there will again be liability, so that there will be a chain of liability from the employer who suffers the damage back to the author of the defect. Of course, the chain may be broken because the contractor (or an earlier buyer) may have agreed to enter into a contract under which his supplier excluded or limited his ordinary liability under the Sale of Goods Act. But in general that has nothing to do with the employer and should not deprive him of his remedy."

Judge Davies also relied on what Lord Upjohn had said in the same case:[42]

> "Under our principles of jurisprudence, apart from a so far scarcely chartered sea of the law of tort in this area, the practical business effect and just solution to this type of breach of contract is that each vendor or contractor of labour and materials should warrant his supply of materials against patent and latent defects so that by the well-known chain of third party procedures the ultimate culprit, the manufacturer, may be made liable for his defective manufacture."

Since *Young & Marten* v. *McManus Childs* was decided we have seen efforts to chart the sea of the law of tort; but the hydrographers have finally returned to port following the decision of the House of Lords in *D & F Estates Ltd.* v. *The Church Commissioners of England*.[43] Thus the policy considerations referred to by Judge Davies seem to be wholly apposite today.

The last and latest case to which reference may be made is *University of Warwick* v. *Sir Robert McAlpine & Others* a decision of Garland J[44]. That also was a case in which complaint was made about the fitness for purpose of work done by a sub-contractor who was not a nominated sub-contractor. The first defendants, McAlpines, were main contractors to the University under a 1963 JCT form. Cementation Chemicals Limited were specialist sub-contractors employed by McAlpine on the basis of the "green" form of sub-contract but

41 [1969] 1 AC 454 at 466-67; 9 Build LR 77 at 89.
42 *Ibid* at 475 and 494.
43 [1988] 3 WLR 368; 41 Build LR 1.
44 (1988) 42 Build LR 1.

who were not, technically, nominated. The University alleged that McAlpines were in breach of an implied warranty of fitness for purpose. However the University had not relied on the skill and judgement of McAlpines and had relied on the skill and judgement of Cementation. The architects had however instructed McAlpines to enter into sub-contracts with Cementation which, according to Garland J, constituted variations to the main contract. McAlpines were however free to enter into whatever form of sub-contract they wished with Cementation; the terms of the sub-contract were not prescribed by the University. A direct warranty was not provided by Cementation.

The submission which Garland J had to deal with was that there was no clear authority governing the question where the employer instructs a main contractor to order goods or services of a sub-contractor relying on the skill and judgment of the sub-contractor but not that of the main contractor. Garland J came to this conclusion:

> "In my view the correct approach is to ask, as between the employer and the main contractor, what warranty is prima facie to be implied into the contract, (or in the present case, the contract as varied) and then to ask whether the circumstances are such as to exclude one or both of them. On this basis there can be no implication of the warranty of fitness because there was no reliance on McAlpine.
> "Can there nevertheless be an implication that because the University relied on Cementation to McAlpine's knowledge, and McAlpine was not obliged to contract with Cementation on particular terms, or, indeed, at all? In fact they obtained an indemnity. The issue is a finely balanced one, but in my view the first approach is correct. I do not accede to the suggestion that if there is no implication the University are left remedyless. They could have taken an express warranty from McAlpine or they could have taken a direct warranty from Cementation."

He therefore found McAlpines not liable in contract to the University. It is not clear why the fact that there was actual reliance upon the sub-contractor should displace the warranty of fitness which presumably existed prior to the contract being varied by the introduction of the sub-contractor. The contractual chain of responsibility described in *Young & Marten* v. *McManus Childs* did not, on the face of that case, depend upon actual reliance on the main contractor. If it were so dependent then there would be very few cases in which there could be an implied warranty of fitness. Nevertheless it is for consideration at this Conference whether the implied warranty of fitness should be excluded or displaced simply by the lack of express reliance on the main contractor. If there were an express reliance on the main contractor, then, to follow Garland J, there would probably be an express warranty. Certainly he considered that the University "could have taken an express warranty from McAlpines". Would they have done so - or should they have done so - but the purpose of this part of the law is to impose such terms because it is not necessary to express it.

The last remarks of Garland J also call for debate. First, is it right that one of the circumstances of a contract which might exclude the warranty is the existence of a remedy against another person - even if that person is somebody who would otherwise have been liable in the chain of contracting? Is this not another means of weakening the contractual links? (In fact the University were left remedyless in contract.)

Secondly, is it right that the mere possibility of a right of action against the person who might primarily be held liable should be considered to be a relevant circumstance which would exclude or displace the warranty? This latter question is of course of potential importance to the whole of the construction industry. On the building side collateral warranties are quite commonly used and have now been institutionalised. They give a client some additional protection but probably not all the protection that the client should have. They have the pernicious effect of relieving main contractors of responsibilities which had traditionally been theirs. Their use in other parts of the industry is much limited mainly because they owe their origin to the system of nominating sub-contractors, the deficiencies in which have been perpetuated by some court decisions. Many clients have called for and obtained a reversion to the traditional system. If this Conference is to make recommendations as to policy it might usefully consider whether the present system of nomination together with its complex of warranties should continue in or should spread from the building side of the construction industry or whether some simpler form of liability for suitability should not be devised based upon the implied warranty and the lack of any circumstances to exclude it. For this purpose some model regime or guidelines might be helpful. If it is desired that the system of nomination should continue in its present form then equally ought there not to be clear statements as to the effect of that system upon the implied warranty? Obtaining tenders and letting contracts is difficult enough as it is. Perhaps there should be some simpler system whereby the fact that the client has, for example, an alternative or additional right of action against his professional advisers will be regarded universally as an irrelevant circumstance for the purposes of determining his rights of action against other parties, such as against the main contractor based upon an implied warranty. Such an approach would probably find favour with many; why should it not also be applied where the client has a possible right of action against a nominated sub-contractor, whether or not he actually obtains a warranty or agreement or avails himself of it?

In summary therefore it is suggested that the following questions deserve debate and answer:

- Should the implied warranty as to fitness be absolute or dependent only on proof of negligence?
- What is meant by "reasonably fit"? How is the "purpose" to be ascertained?
- Where is the line to be drawn when a defective product is incorporated into another product or work - in what circumstances should the original producer be liable for the unsuitability of the other product or the work and should the person receiving the defective product also be liable?
- Is it for the producer or consumer to prove unfitness where the defect is one which the other could have detected or avoided? Is legislation necessary or desirable to make this clear?
- When should compliance with the warranty be ascertained in the case of construction works: as at the date of handover or final completion or at some other date?
- What standards are to be used to determine compliance? May after-acquired knowledge be used and if so, is it to be imputed detrimentally to the plaintiff or to the defendant?

- Should any circumstances of the contract exclude or displace the warranty? If so what circumstances would be relevant? Should there be model guidelines for determining the relevance of actual or possible collateral undertakings?

Risks in the Method of Construction 5

John N Barber

Synopsis

This working party paper examines the concept of fairness in relation to the terms of and performance of construction contracts. The nature of supervision is examined in the context of responsibility and risks involved in the choice of construction methods.

Introduction - The Need for a Policy

The great American thinker and essayist, Ralph Waldo Emerson, observed[1] "Nature is tugging at every contract to make the terms of it fair". Those involved in the heavier end of construction, directing the great sources of power in Nature for the use and convenience of Man, will recognize the truth of Emerson's words. Nature is harnessed more readily by directing it than by attempting to disregard or deny it.

Fairness is not the sole aim of a form of contract. The pursuit of fairness should not be allowed to lead, either by inadvertence or slavish adherence to preconceptions, to consequences which are inconsistent with the essential objectives of a contract as regards quality, price, time and security. On the other hand, a contract which is blatantly one-sided or, in effect, a trap for the unwary is not conducive to a satisfactory outcome of a construction project for either party.

The terms of a contract can be made fair partly by appropriate drafting, but equally important is the interpretation placed on the words used. Shakespeare illustrated in fiction[2] that the terms of a contract which are repugnant to nature can be interpreted, with sufficient ingenuity, to produce a just result even to the point that the party seeking to impose and enforce oppressive terms might be deprived of all benefit. More recently, the courts have uttered guidance at the highest level that a similar approach should be adopted in the interpretation of commercial contracts, to produce results which accord with sound business sense.

1 Ralph Waldo Emerson, *Conduct of Life* (1860).
2 Merchant of Venice, Act I.

While the basic position has been re-affirmed that there is no equitable jurisdiction to rewrite an improvident contract[3], Lord Bridge delivering the judgment of the Privy Council in *Mitsui*[4] and, in the House of Lords, Lord Diplock in *The Antaios*[5] and Lord Wilberforce in *Reardon Smith* v *Yngvar Hansen-Tangen*[6] have commended that commercial contracts should be interpreted or construed, so far as possible, to give effect to what prudent businessmen and responsible government departments would be expected to have agreed. Excessive semantic and syntactical analysis is to give way to business common sense. The secondary or loose meaning of general words may be taken in preference to the primary or strict meaning to avoid contrary results. The guidance is not limited to considerations of fairness, but more generally, to the pursuit of the proper aims of commercial contracts, as perceived by the courts.

The debate on contract policy at this Conference is thus of relevance not only to the few concerned with drafting and agreeing contract terms, but also to the whole mass of professionals who have to interpret and apply contracts. Escape from excessive literalism to a healthier regime of contract interpretation lies in popular acceptance of contract policies which reflect the presumed common aims of the parties and reconcile their conflicting needs and aspirations in a manner consistent with good practice, sound construction, and timely completion. Then we might avoid the problem of quite rational provisions being interpreted - or misinterpreted - to produce the converse of what was originally intended.

The most glaring example of this problem concerns provisions included to allow the time for completion to be extended. Such provisions are intended to keep a date for completion in place for the benefit of the employer, both to promote timely completion and secure his entitlement to liquidated damages. Instead, they are commonly interpreted and applied in a manner reminiscent of the courts in Lewis Carroll's Wonderland[7], as stepping stones leading to claims against the employer for extra payment. A similar problem arises in relation to methods of construction. Contractual provisions intended to ensure a satisfactory outcome by means of specifications, supervision or the supply of information come instead to be sources of disputes, delays, denials of responsibility, and demands for extra payment.

3 *Clea Shipping* v.*Bulk Oil* [1984] 1 All ER 129 at 137.
4 *Mitsui* v. *A-G for Hong Kong* (1986) 2 Const LJ 133 at p139. *Per* Lord Bridge, the courts should uphold "an interpretation which attributes to the parties an intention to make provision for contingencies inherent in the work contracted for on a businesslike basis .... It seems to their Lordships somewhat improbable that a responsible public authority on the one hand and responsible engineering conteractors on the other, contracting for the execution of public works worth many millions of dollars should deliberately embark on a substantial gamble."
5 *Antaios Cia Naviera SA* v. *Salen Rederierna*, "*The Antaios*" [1984] 3 All ER 229, *per* Lord Diplock at 233: "If detailed semantic and syntactical analysis of words in a commercial contract is going to lead to a conclusion that flouts business common sense, it must be made to yield to business common sense."
6 *Reardon Smith Line* v. *Yngvar Hansen-Tangen* [1976] 3 All ER 570, at 574-75.
7 " 'Write that down,' the King said to the jury, and the jury eagerly wrote down all three dates on their slates, and then added them up, and reduced the answer to shillings and pence."

The Non-interventionist School

One response to the problem is to minimize the extent of intervention by, or on behalf of, the employer. In law, the contractor can be made responsible for producing a satisfactory end result and for completing the works by the stipulated date. He can be left to obtain all the information he needs. He can be required to undertake the design to meet specified functional requirements and to warrant that the end result will be fit for the specified purpose. The employer is under no obligation to supervise the works and, even if he chooses to do so, his appointed supervisor is under no implied obligation towards the contractor either to warn him of dangers[8] or to check that the works comply with the specification[9].

The non-interventionist response has its supporters and is quite appropriate to certain situations, but three conditions for its adoption are suggested. Firstly, the end result required must be adequately defined in advance. Responsibility may not survive change or inadequate definition of requirements. Secondly, there must be reasonable grounds for faith in the contractor's capability, competence and intention to perform. Disappointment at the end of a construction period of one or two years may find the prospect of monetary compensation inadequate comfort, particularly if stage payments have been made. Thirdly, the possibility of recourse in the long term should be secured either by the contractor's financial stability or by appropriate insurance. (The French system of contracting, which is very much along these lines, provides security by means of decennial insurance. Insurers then insist, however, on independent checking and supervision as a condition of insurance.)

Turnkey contracting is the obvious example of this approach. It now accounts for a substantial proportion of construction work in some sectors. The extent to which it provides satisfaction and reliability in practice can therefore be judged by experience. In a recent research project by Rowlinson[10] into different contracting methods used for design and construction of industrial framed buildings, experience of turnkey contracting was reported by employers to be most satisfactory where the contract had been negotiated rather than obtained by competition. The proportion of contracts awarded by negotiation was, nevertheless, limited. Contractors complained that employers were not prepared to be flexible in their approach, that they invited too many tenders without regard to the high cost of submitting turnkey bids, and that adjudication of proposals was inconsistent. These comments accord with expectations, but it would be dangerous to extrapolate from the results of research related to industrial framed buildings to other types of works. It is understood that the research is being extended to cover civil engineering works. — has, + ?

8 *Clayton* v. *Woodman & Son (Builders) Ltd.* [1962] 2 QB 533 at 542. See also CA, [1962] 1 WLR 585 at 591-93.

9 *East Ham* v. *Bernard Sunley & Sons* [1966] AC 406 at 449.

10 S.M. Rowlinson, (Brunel University) *Evaluation of Design and Construction Processes for Industrial Buildings* (1986).

Independent Design and Supervision

Such research may reveal whether the continued use of "conventional" systems of contracting is merely the result of history, inertia and vested interests, or whether it offers greater reliability of satisfaction. Historically, the early contractors were craftsmen, not possessed of professional skills. They did not have the capability to undertake major works independently of the great engineers or architects. In earlier days, the design of projects had necessarily to evolve during construction to take account of the ground exposed, the results of proof tests and experiments, and observation of the behaviour of completed sections of the works. This militated against conferring total responsibility or power on the contractor. The situation has changed. Today, contractors have professional skills. Knowledge of how materials, soils and structures behave has advanced and techniques for investigation have developed to allow the design largely to be settled, given sufficient time and money, prior to construction.

On the other hand, the system of design and supervision by independent professionals has proved its effectiveness over two centuries. It has two immediate advantages apart from keeping closer control of the conduct of the works. It admits more readily of competition in the letting of construction contracts - a major consideration in the bureaucratic environment of public works. Secondly, it minimizes the inevitable problem of professional judgement and advice being coloured by commercial enthusiasm, as illustrated by the legacy of industrialised building systems of the 1960's with their poor design and inadequate supervision.

Independent design and supervision also enables a greater degree of flexibility, allowing ready modification of requirements and detail during construction. That may be considered a benefit; it may also be the root of the problems which cause dissatisfaction with the system. The ability to change and supply details tempts people to procrastinate and prevaricate instead of finalizing matters before inviting tenders or entering contracts.

The crux of the argument for independent supervision, however, is the need to maintain sufficient control over the conduct of the works. The need derives from the fundamental limitations of the law and the legal system in the context of construction. A contract is merely an agreement recognized by the law. The concept of any law, such as embodied in a contract, is not that it is a statement of what will or will not be done, but merely of what ought or ought not to be done. The significance of the law is that the statements of what ought or ought not to be done are backed up by sanctions, or the availability of sanctions, through the courts[11]. The law does not purport to be capable of ensuring directly that services are correctly performed.

Construction typically consists of services performed and materials supplied and fixed on the employer's land over a long period of time. If the power to apply sanctions for non-compliance is deferred until the contract has been completed unsatisfactorily, the sanctions are of limited value. The works are fixed to the employer's land. He cannot easily reject them; any defective parts must therefore be rectified. The law gives no guarantee that rectification can or will be satisfactory, nor that the contractor will remain solvent. The earlier a defect is spotted, the lower will be the cost of rectification and the greater the

11 HLA Hart, *The Concept of Law* (1961).

likelihood that satisfactory rectification can be carried out. The earlier that slippage on progress is noticed, the more feasible and less expensive it is to catch up. Construction contracts thus need to permit supervision and provide powers to insist on immediate correction of faults or slippage when noticed. The problem is how to arrange for independent supervision so that it reinforces or supplements the contractor's responsibility, rather than detracts from it.

The primary role of a supervising officer (be he architect, engineer or surveyor) is to check by inspection and testing that work has been completed satisfactorily in accordance with the design. Such inspection must not, however, be taken by the contractor as displacing his own responsibility in this respect. As mentioned above, the House of Lords has held[12] that a contractor is not excused from his responsibility to comply with the specification by reason of failure of the supervising officer to notice the non-compliance. Contractors may, however, be misled and responsibilities may even be affected by the frequent reference in the standard forms of contract to the "satisfaction" of the supervising officer. Are contractors expected to be psychic and anticipate what standard will satisfy the supervising officer's subjective opinion on the matter? As pointed out by Professor Wallace[13], such references probably require no more than compliance with the specification applied objectively. The confusion would be avoided if the myriad references to the supervising officer's satisfaction were removed and replaced, (except where specifically intended) by a general term empowering him to reject and require removal of work not complying with the specification. This would leave intact for the benefit of the employer the super-added protection of the supervising officer's powers, without suggesting that dual standards or cumulative standards might be applicable concurrently[14]. Sweet has commented[15] on the American AIA forms, that they have evolved to serve and protect the design professionals, rather than to serve the needs or desires of owners or contractors. The excessively frequent reference to the engineer or architect in United Kingdom standard forms may be a manifestation of the same failing.

Methods of Construction

The secondary role of the supervising officer is, arguably, not to check that the work has been satisfactorily completed, but to check that the methods of working proposed by the contractor are such as to provide satisfactory completion, and that the contractor then performs the work in accordance either with the approved methods or with methods specified by the designer. The supervisory input can thus be increased and brought to bear at an earlier stage. Attitudes to this are subject to divergent fashions: on the one hand, architects decide they will limit themselves to inspection rather than

12 *East Ham* v. *Bernard Sunley & Sons* [1966] AC 406.
13 IN Duncan Wallace QC "The Architect, the Arbitrator and the Courts" (1986) 2 Const LJ 13. Cf. *Neodox* v. *Swinton & Pendlebury* (1958) 5 Build LR 34 at 47 where Diplock J (as he then was) held that there was not even an implied term that the Engineer's decisions on methods of working would be reasonable.
14 Cf. *NCB* v. *William Neill* [1984] 1 All ER 555.
15 *Sweet on Construction Contracts* (1987) see review by Stipanowich (1988) 4 Const LJ 21 at 22.

supervision while, on the other hand, Quality Assurance (or, as it might be called, supervision by ticked boxes) attracts favour.

A dilemma arises because such an approach to supervision requires that the methods of construction be first approved or specified. What happens if the approved or specified method, properly performed, will not lead to a satisfactory end result? Where the success of a method is established by experience or research relevant to the conditions pertaining, reference to the method may be the most effective means of specification. Benefit should be taken of available knowledge. What better way to specify breakfast requirements in normal conditions than to ask for a "4-minute egg" if that suits the taste? One must, however, be alert to special conditions and the need for adjustment. At the top of a mountain, water boils at a lower temperature: a longer time is required to obtain the same end result.

If a contractor specializes in a process, requiring him to produce a method-statement may be counter-productive. Would one give the recipe to a renowned chef, or demand that he submit his recipe for approval, before allowing him to prepare his speciality? As Hazlitt remarked, rules and models destroy genius and art. But the real problem arises when method statements are specified or approved without adequate knowledge. The propounding or approval of an untried method lends a spurious verisimilitude of expertise where none exists. In such circumstances, unless a method is first proved satisfactory by trials and tests, requirement of its observance is surely unsound, both legally and technically.

Requiring the contractor to submit details of his proposed methods provides the benefit of ensuring that he has thought about problems in advance, and it permits comments to be made. The drawback is that it may freeze the thinking too early and discourage critical evaluation of the method. Forms of contract and Quality Assurance systems should avoid elevating unproven methods to a status where they may conflict with the end result requirements. The value of proving tests in individual contracts should not be overlooked, and the wider benefits of an adequate programme of research and development into construction materials and methods should be recognized. The ability of the legal framework alone to ensure a satisfactory technical outcome is always limited.

Temporary works are principally the fixed hardware of construction methods although the term is commonly used to refer more widely to anything which has to be constructed in addition to the permanent works. Temporary works are generally designed by the contractor, but they may be partly designed by the permanent works designer. In either case, the design can be checked usually on established principles. Checking is important not only to ensure the safety of the temporary works themselves, but also to examine their effect on the permanent works. The example given by Goudsmit[16], of temporary works for bridge erection overloading a bridge pier, illustrates the potential complexity of responsibility in this area and the dangers of the supervising officer relying on the contractor, or the contractor relying on the supervising officer, to appreciate the effect of the temporary works on the permanent works.

16 Dr J J Goudsmit "Legal Liability in Contract Structures" in *The Liability of Contractors*.

Mode and Manner of Construction

The distinction is sometimes drawn between those aspects of a contractor's activities that are essential to satisfactory completion of the works and those elements which are non-essential. In established usage, the former category is referred to as methods of construction while the latter is classified as mode or manner of construction. Currently accepted wisdom is that methods should be strictly supervised but mode and manner ought to be left to the contractor. This wisdom is not beyond question. For the reasons set out above, supervision of method may be inappropriate in certain situations. On the other hand, matters classified as mode or manner may be significant to aims considered important by the employer. There is no intrinsic reason why such matters should not be dealt with by the contract, although attempts to incorporate provisions in the main pricing structure are not always successful. Provisions may either be unsupported by any effective sanction (the ultimate sanction of determining the contract is usually impractical as an effective sanction) or the exercise of relevant powers may be seized and exploited as a ground for claiming additional payment. Contractual provisions regarding programme and rates of progress are a particular example. Conventional forms of contract have tended to concede defeat in this area to avoid the potential for claims, but the growing popularity of management contracting demonstrates that employers, particularly commercial enterprises, value more effective control. Experience suggests that greater influence can be achieved by the inclusion of separate collateral incentives to support collateral requirements. For example, bonuses (despite Rimmer's brief advice[17] against them) are far more effective psychologically than liquidated damages in obtaining performance and timely completion. The sophisticated payment systems used for the construction of the Diego Garcia Naval Base[18] also achieved encouraging results; on that project, a set of award fees, determined on a six-monthly basis, was applied to a wide range of management, safety and other objectives; the fees awarded demonstrate the response of the contractor in satisfying the objectives.

Allocation of Responsibility and Risk

It is too much to hope that any form of contract will invariably lead to a satisfactory and harmonious conclusion: a form of contract that failed to address the possibility of an unsatisfactory outcome and discord would soon be found wanting. But construction contracts can and should provide a practical framework to maximize the probability of success, by allocating clear provinces of responsibility to those persons within the aegis of the contract; by providing adequate powers, with effective means of enforcement, to enable the discharge of powers imposed; and by providing for the timely transfer or delivery of information or decisions necessary for the fulfilment of responsibilities.

17 E J Rimmer "The Conditions of Engineering Contracts" (1939) *ICE Journal* Vol 11 p3 at 15: "That provision (viz, for payment of bonus for early completion) cannot, however, be recommended except in very exceptional circumstances."

18 Tucker & Doughty, "Naval facilities, Diego Garcia, British Indian Ocean Territory: management and administration", Proc ICE Part 1 (1988), 84, Apr. 191-215.

Clear allocation of provinces of responsibility does not eliminate the possibility of disputes in the event of the works being found unsatisfactory. Supervision entails responsibilities being overlaid for the added protection of the employer, while the contractual chains to sub-contractors and suppliers extend the potential burden to others. The problem is that the common law, with its concept of several liability on each person to whom legal responsibility can be traced, can expose a large number of persons to risks which are completely out of proportion financially to the remuneration received. Such exposure can only be dealtwith by insurance. Under the arrangements now standard in the United Kingdom, each party requires separate cover. The premiums paid, although cumulatively substantial, may individually be as little as perhaps one quarter per cent. of the potential amount involved. This surely cannot be sustained. The time must come soon when single project insurance, latent defect protection insurance, whatever it may be called, becomes standard, providing cover to employer, main contractor, sub-contractors and professionals involved. This will, however, require some assistance from the legislature in reducing the long-stop limitation period, as well as a change of attitude amongst insurers.

For risks which are insurable, the solution may only involve arranging collective insurance and regulating the payment of premiums and liability for excesses. More problematical are those risks which are not insurable. Whilst allocation of responsibility for satisfactory completion or for completion by a given date should be clear, such allocation does not necessarily entail responsibility without adjustment of the price. Conversely, the provision of powers or duties to give instructions or supply information does not necessarily entail that there must be an entitlement to adjustment of price. The contract must allocate the risk as well as the responsibility.

Sweet[19] has expounded the philosophy that control should determine risk. Wallace[20], on the other hand, has suggested that there is no reason why a contract cannot be drafted to avoid entitlement to payment. Whether either of these approaches is appropriate or workable cannot be judged on abstract legal theory alone. A contract is an artifical framework, subject to nature rather than controlling it. The framework should be compatible with the realities of construction and of nature.

Nature tugs at a contract to make the terms of it fair, but fairness does not demand that contractors be treated as innocents abroad, incapable and inexperienced. Observe the consideration with which main contractors treat their sub-contractors. The reality is that contractors worthy of the name have the experience and capability to evaluate most risks with a sufficient degree of certainty on a broad approach, rather as insurers are able to evaluate insurable risks. Like insurers, however, contractors cannot evaluate the risk if information is withheld or they are not given an opportunity to price it; nor can they break down the risk into minute detail. If contractors are expected to act as quasi-insurers, perhaps construction contracts should be treated as subject to the doctrine of uberrimae fides, at least as regards the supply of information.

19 Sweet, "Defects : A Summary and Analysis of American Law", in *Selected Problems of Construction Law: International Approach*, 79 at 118.
20 IN Duncan Wallace QC, "Prices under Common Law Systems", *ibid*, 145 at 164, para 31.

Certain risks, such as variable ground on a tunnelling project, cannot be quantified with sufficient certainty, having regard to the limited profit margins involved. In such cases fairness requires that the price be related to what is actually encountered. In other cases, fairness may only require the provision of adequate opportunity to price the risks. Committees responsible for standard methods of measurement have commendably sought to make such provision. Unfortunately the answer adopted of itemisation of the work in minute detail as to classification and location is misguided, at least in civil engineering. In building, where most of the work is sub-contracted and the risk thereby sub-divided between the sub-contractors, extensively detailed bills of quantities may be useful and appropriate. In civil engineering, risks and costs cannot be broken down in such detail; detailed itemisation does not correspond to the way in which contractors assess the risk and costs involved. If bills of quantities are to be merely bills of enormous quantity of paper and little quantity of thought, the system has lost its way. The other development of providing items for method-related charges should be useful. Unfortunately there is no compulsion on contractors to relate their prices to costs, so the itemized prices do not provide a reliable basis for adjustment. If the aim is to gain access to the details of the contractor's pricing, that can surely be better achieved more directly.

Foreseeability has become enshrined in UK construction contracts as a basis for risk allocation and entitlement to additional payment or extensions of time but, as explained by Lord Radcliffe[21], this is not part of the common law and need not be regarded as sacrosanct. Nor is it essential: the construction industry in Hong Kong has functioned since at least 1977 with non-foreseeability of conditions specifically excluded as a basis for additional payment on Government contracts. Where forms of contract depend on foreseeability, determination of what is considered foreseeable has unfortunately come to be an exercise of detailed retrospective analysis of the information supplied to the tenderers. As with detailed analyses of semantics and syntax, business common sense should surely rebel against such an approach. Contractors are expected to be experienced - they should be expected to price the work primarily on the basis of their actual or presumed experience. Information supplied should be seen as supplementing or qualifying experience, not as a substitute.

Providing fairness within a workable contract, avoiding excessive administrative effort and limiting scope for exploitation, are not simple objectives. They require not only changes to the words used in the contract, but also a change in prevailing attitudes. Contractors, employers and supervising officers all tend to complain so much that it is difficult to appreciate which are real problems and which are imagined. Perhaps the following extract from a report[22] of a behavioural modification experiment in pain response at Washington University Medical Centre serves as an appropriate fable. (It should not be assumed that the young man is necessarily a contractor).

21 *Davis Contractors* v. *Fareham UDC* [1956] AC 696 at 733.
22 *South China Morning Post*, 24 July 1988.

"A young man was in such terrible pain and screamed and moaned so much that his parents found him unmanageable at home. A team carefully analysed the man's behaviour and found that complaining brought rewards. Whenever he complained, the parents paid a lot of attention, often massaging his muscles to relieve his pain. Sometimes the attention was in the form of anger or despair but it was attention all the same ... The pain was real and the physicians needed to know when or if the pain was better or worse during treatment ... so the task was not to stop the complaining but the way it was done. The treatment began by having the physicians, nurses and the man's parents give him the same amount of sympathy whether he complained and cried or not. Soon he learned he didn't need to scream and cry to get attention. From there, the therapists moved to a program in which they gave him more than the usual amount of attention only if he rated his pain as better or worse and did so without screaming and crying. In a short time, the man was complaining only when the pain became worse - a clear signal that he needed more help and got it. The parents were able to conserve their strength and help for times when they were confident more help was needed and they were able to keep their son at home."

The Concept of Design 6

David Cornes

Synopsis

This paper offers a definition of design and analyzes what design may effect. It reviews the way in which standard forms deal with communication of and liability for design. The most important area is found to be communication both within the design team itself and between the design team and the construction team. It concludes by asking a series of questions which point to ways in which contracts may influence the quality of a project.

Introduction

Those who procure construction work have for years been searching for better contracts. This is reflected in the proliferation of contract forms, each one with a slightly different allocation of risk, method of payment or mode of obtaining the end result. These forms include the traditional standard forms, the various management contracts (both in-house and JCT), design and build contracts which cater for a range from full design element down to a minimum input by the contractor, and a plethora of purpose drafted one-off contracts.

The quest for new methods of procurement can only arise from dissatisfaction with the old. The secret of finding the correct balance in a new form of contract must lie in discovering the causes of that dissatisfaction, and combining a cure with the practical realities on site. The reasons for dissatisfaction are complex but would appear to relate to quality of design and of construction, the difficulty of forecasting at the outset of the contract a reasonably accurate cost , and the time taken from conception to completion. It is certainly true, at least in the building industry, that the architect is no longer able to design the whole of the building, because modern buildings contain complex mechanical and electrical systems, computer systems and a high level of interior decor. At the same time the tradition of contractors employing their own tradesmen has substantially gone and the employment of labour only sub-contractors has given rise to a new range of problems. These developments mean that the design and the co-ordination of that design has become more fragmented, and the communication of the design to the workmen carrying out the construction is no longer one-to-one, but is now a many-to-many relationship. Consequently the satisfactory control of the project as a whole is harder to achieve. There is a clear need for better, more detailed co-ordination and communication, which may ease the dissatisfaction.

What is Design?

For the purposes of description rather than legal definition, design may be considered as:

- all the decisions that need to be made as to the location in three dimensions of every component part of the project, the definition of the quality and quantity (including the specification of workmanship) of each component and how each fits in with another;
- all the same decisions in relation to any temporary works (not being part of the finished project) needed to achieve the construction of the project.

All the standard forms of contract assume that the temporary works should be left to the contractor on the basis that he is best placed to deal with such matters. Subject to that point the design, as defined, affects a number of areas:

Aesthetics

What will the project look like when it is finished? The employer will be very much more concerned with this question than the contractor. It is this aspect of the design function which leads the employer and his professional team into wishing to control parts of the overall project design, largely because it is of lasting effect and may influence the financial viability of a project.

Function

This relates to the use of the project after completion and whether it is fit for its intended purpose. It is linked both to quality and cash flow of the employer. In general, the cheaper the original materials the lower the quality and the higher the maintenance cost. The function and intended use must be weighed in conjunction with cost, quality and cost of maintenance.

Cost

The design affects cost in two important substantive ways and in a third indirect but equally crucial way. First, there is an obvious effect on the quality of the finished product. If the architect specifies materials of the highest quality the product is likely to be high, but at a price. The substantive cost of materials, in general, increases commensurately with quality.

Secondly, any particular design may predetermine the methods of construction, the order of work and the labour and plant required. All of these matters, and their related operations affect the cost of the project. It can be argued that the involvement of the contractor at an early stage will allow the consideration of such issues during the formulation of the design and produce substantial cost benefits to the project.

Thirdly, design can affect the cost simply by delay in its provision. How often does the phrase "fast tracking" cover up the reality of inadequate pre-contract design and pre-planning? As long ago as June 1963 the Committee on the Placing and Managing of Contracts for Building and Civil Engineering Work, under the chairmanship of Sir Harold Banwell said, of the philosophy of pre-planning:

> "The more that is known of what is involved in any project, the less will be the degree of uncertainty against which tenderers will be obliged to make provision; this applies to all construction work but is of particular importance where contractors are asked to quote firm prices. Only if the work has been settled in all its critical details is it reasonable to expect a contractor to tender for a firm price and a fixed period."

The Standard Method of Measurement of Building Works, SMM6, requires that "Bills of Quantities shall fully describe and accurately represent the quality and quantity of the works to be carried out". How many projects go out to tender with the quality and quantity of the work either properly or fully described? More often the period between conception of a project and going out to tender is cut short in an attempt to save time. The amount of time that is then spent by contractor's staff chasing lack of detail, information and necessary instruction will often more than outweigh the time saved in early tendering. The contractor's time would undoubtedly be better spent managing the construction and safeguarding the quality of the project.

Co-ordination

On a building project a number of organisations are involved in producing the design: the Architect, the Structural Engineer, the Mechanical and Electrical Engineers and the Nominated Sub-Contractors. Each one produces a different element of the design which must be integrated with the others to produce the overall project. Lack of co-ordination between the various designers often gives rise to problems of lost time and extra cost. On design and build projects, although such problems may arise, the risk, and the responsibility, can be placed on the contractor. In the traditional contracts it is desirable that one party is allocated the responsibility for co-ordination. This party will then carry the liability for increased cost and delay if co-ordination is insufficient.

Standard Form Arrangements

JCT 80 : Standard Form of Building Contract

In the traditional scheme the design is carried out by the architect, or other professional designers employed by the employer or by nominated sub-contractors. The contractor has no contractual right or duty to contribute to the design. Conversely he has no liabilities for inadequacies in, or late delivery of, the design, unless he acquires liability, for example, by inadvertently accepting a nomination containing a design element. It follows that the contractor will usually have no responsibility or liability in respect of the design of the permanent works. Consequently there is no contractual chain of liability from the employer through the contractor to a nominated sub-contractor who has undertaken an element of design. The employer must look to a direct warranty agreement (NSC2) and to his architect and other professional designer for redress for design faults. There is rarely consistency between the disputes procedures contained in the nominated sub-contract direct warranty, the conditions of engagement of the architect and the main contract. Therefore where there is a dispute as to whether a fault is caused by poor design of the architect or of a nominated sub-contractor, or whether it is caused by poor workmanship of the main contractor, no proper procedure exists for resolution of the dispute between all the parties.

JCT 80 with Contractor's designed portion Supplement

This scheme is substantially the same as JCT 80 save that certain elements of the project are to be designed by the main contractor and/or sub-contractors. Insofar as the design is part of the contractor's obligation,a contractual chain will exist between the employer, the contractor and the sub-contractor, so that disputes can be settled under the arbitration procedure set out in the main contract. Insofar as any dispute impinges on other areas and obligations, the same potential problems arise as in JCT 80.

JCT 81 Design and Build Contract

By so specifying in the Employers Requirements, the employer may design as much, or as little, of the detail of the project as he wishes. The contractor, in his proposals, is left to design the remainder. There are no direct warranty agreements with the sub-contractors or their professional designers (or at least, none drafted by JCT) but in theory a contractual chain exists between the employer and those persons who design the project for the contractor.

ACA/BPF System

In this scheme also the employer is enabled to specify how little or how much of the design he wishes to provide, with the obligation resting on the contractor to complete the design. The BPF system also provides for one professional to be nominated as the party responsible for co-ordination and for all aspects of the design. He has to ensure that the design is produced according to a predetermined timetable and if delays to the timetable occur he is prima facie responsible

ICE 5th Edition

There is no provision for design by the contractor except under Clauses 8(2) and 58(3). This latter clause allows for design by the main contractor or any sub-contractor but only in respect of provisional or prime cost items where the exact requirements of the design are expressly stated in both the main contract and any nominated sub-contract. Except by way of the exacting requirements of Clause 58(3) there is no contractual chain of liability from the employer to the sub-contractor in respect of design. Clause 8(2) similarly requires any design liability placed on the Contractor to be "expressly provided in the contract".

Achieving Quality on Building Sites

Effects on quality

In 1987 a report "Achieving Quality on Building Sites" was prepared by NEDO on behalf of the Building Economic Development Committee. The objective of the report was:

> "to suggest improved methods of quality control for building works by identifying the extent to which quality achieved falls short of expectations and by assessing the contribution of management procedures, project information, site supervision and inspection to the standards achieved."

In order to consider these matters, the BRE observed some 50 projects spanning the public and private sectors and involving a wide range of contractual procedures including the traditional method, management construction projects and design and build projects. The key findings of this report are:

- serious quality problems are too common and too often remain unresolved;
- realistic and well understood time constraints do not adversely affect the achievement of good quality;
- motivation and commitment to producing good work are essential to the achievement of good quality;
- site management has to spend too much time chasing late drawings and other project information which inevitably reduces the time available for quality management;
- traditional specifications are often unrelated to the quality requirements of a particular contract and are therefore rarely referred to;
- specifications based on or similar to the National Building Specification seem to produce better results;
- contractual arrangements, as such have little effect on the quality achieved, but management structures have considerable influence;
- site management is more likely to be successful in achieving good quality where lines of authority are clearly understood and site staff have the opportunity to contribute to and take responsibility for quality achievement;

- where deficiencies in quality are identified, responsibility and authority to effect remedial action are often unclear;
- where project quality is going wrong, clients cannot rely on being informed of this by any member of the building team;
- site managers often have to spend a lot of time dealing with technical queries to the detriment of other aspects of management;
- projects exhibiting good quality are characterised by an appropriate level of site management resources, with managers who are properly trained and who exercise more authority than usual;
- inadequacies in the quality, completeness or accessibility of information are a major handicap in the achievement of quality;
- meetings between consultants and the contractor on site are all too often concerned merely with progress and rarely consider quality;
- the clerk of works finds it difficult to act as an effective quality controller because of lack of contractual authority.

Despite the finding of the report that contractual arrangements have little effect on quality, it is worthwhile examining how far a contract can influence those matters which form the major findings of the report. The traditional object of the contract is to allocate risk and define liability, so that any attempt to deal with matters which essentially cover good practice and management is a departure into new ground.

It is suggested that the contract may affect or influence matters of practice and management, and that the following questions need to be considered in regard to the drafting of appropriate clauses or provisions:

- how carefully should the procurer of the contract define the design brief at the outset of the project?
- at what point in the preparation of the design is it appropriate to go out to tender and enter into a contract?
- who is to co-ordinate the design between the various parties preparing it so as to ensure that the elements inter-relate, work together and the project as a whole is buildable?
- who is to ensure that the construction team receive information from the design team so that the project can be planned and constructed in a proper and logical sequence without disruption?
- should contractors and their designers be required by their contracts to operate on the basis of critical path analysis?
- should standard specifications be adopted in contracts insofar as it is possible so as to bring the empirical approach in the construction industry to quality and standards nearer to that required by contracts?
- should there be a requirement that contractors and designers only work within spheres n which they are competent and that specialist sub-contractors/specialist designers be used where appropriate?
- should designers spend more time on sites directly involved in the design process, as opposed to making brief inspections in relation to quality and progress?
- should the Clerk of the Works/Resident Engineer/Site Inspectors have express contractual powers in relation to design problems that arise?
- should the construction contract require the contractor to have a specific person or category of persons to deal with resolving design problems and production of the design to suite the contractor's programme?

- should major sub-contractors be required by contract to have their own supervisory agents on the site?
- should contracts spell out in clear terms who is responsible for design, or specified parts of the design, as opposed to being virtually silent on the subject?

Finally it is appropriate to ask whether the above matters should be left to the drafting of workable codes of practice, such as the Code of Procedure for Selective Tendering for Design and Build produced by the NJCC. Experience will indicate whether contractual provisions backed by appropriate sanctions are more conducive to good quality than codes of practice.

7 Risk Theory for Contracting

Professor C.B. Chapman, S.C. Ward, B. Curtis

Synopsis

The possibility of constructing a theory of risk is considered. After discussing practical and theoretical difficulties a model is put forward and examined from the viewpoint of the employer and contractor. Possible benefits from this analysis are suggested together with further areas of work to be explored.

Introduction

It is well known that a variety of sources of risk can affect the performance of construction projects. Such sources of risk include unforeseen site conditions, inadequate co-ordination of work, work changes, and so on. Several writers have argued for the systematic identification and assessment of all sources of risk for all projects.[1],[2] Identification of risks as early as possible in a project's life is important, not only to enable project constraints and appropriate cost estimates to be determined, but also to focus project management attention on ways of controlling and allocating risk.[2]

Risk analysis incorporating the identification of both sources of uncertainty and appropriate preventative and responsive contingency plans in relation to project planning and costs have been advocated elsewhere by the present authors[3],[4] The extent to which sources of uncertainty and contingency plans ought to be considered at a detailed level will vary from project to project, as a function of the size of the project, the importance of uncertainty, and

1 Martin Barnes, (1984) "Effective project organisation", *Building Technology and Management*, Dec. pp 21-23.

2 John G Perry and Ross W. Hayes (1986) "Risk Management for project managers", *Building Technology and Management*, August/September, P 811.

2 John G Perry and Ross W. Hayes (1986) "Risk Management for project managers", *Building Technology and Management*, August/September, P 811.

3 Chris B Chapman (1979) "Large engineering project risk analysis", *IEEE Transactions on Engineering Management*, Vol. EM76, pp 78-86.

4 Dale F Cooper and Chris B Chapman, (1987) *Risk Analysis for Large Projects*, Wiley.

improvements in risk efficiency associated with such planning[5]. For example, an oil company about to release funds and contract for a major offshore development may find it worth identifying some 30 or 40 sources of uncertainty for each of 50 activities encompassing the whole project, and considering three or four responses for each source of uncertainty, in a highly structured, formal, probabilistic manner. Alternatively, a shopping development sponsor may find it worthwhile to identify only half a dozen major risks for a dozen major activities, and consider a single response for each source of uncertainty in an informal non-probabilistic manner.

This paper is particularly concerned with the allocation of risk between a client (owner, investor, promoter, or employer) and a contractor, but this needs to be seen as an integrated part of an overall risk management strategy. Perry[6] has suggested that the form and conditions of contract can contribute to the management of project risk by:

- clarifying definitions of risk and their allocation;
- including incentives linked to risk allocation;
- emphasising good management practice, particularly working to time.

Figure 1 illustrates key influences on the form of contracts.

Figure 1 Influences on the Form of Contracts

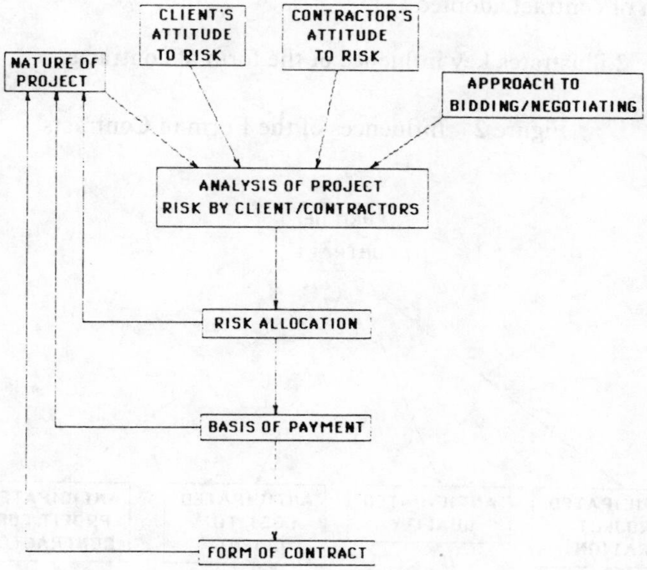

Figure 1 indicates why attention to project risk is important for good project performance. In particular, it suggests that analysis of project risks should be

5 Chris B Chapman, ED Phillips, Dale F Cooper and Lynne Lightfoot, (1985) "Selecting an approach to project time and cost planning", *International Journal of Project Management*, Vol. 3, No. 1, February.

6 John G Perry (1986) "Dealing with risk in contracts", *Building Technology and Management*, April, pp 23-26.

undertaken early in the project to determine how risks should be allocated to contractual parties. An analysis of risks should strongly influence the choice of method of payment and form of contract. The allocation of risks to contractual parties, the method of payment and the form of contract will all influence the nature of the project. The analysis of project risks needs to consider how the nature of the project is changed by the way risks are allocated, the basis of payment selected, and the form of contract adopted. Accurate anticipation or iteration is required.

The client's attitude to risk is clearly important, but the contractor's attitude is important even if not consulted and simple selection of the lowest bid used. For example, many contractors may be prepared to take a high risk of loss on a contract as agreed because this is preferable to the certain bankruptcy associated with no work, or because of an optimistic view of the scope for variations or claims related to the client changing his mind. This in turn means the approach to bidding/negotiation is very important.

Based on the nature of the project, professional, advice and other considerations, the client forms a view of project risks. This leads in Figure 1 to the client deciding on the appropriate allocation of project related risk, indicating either a cost based or price based method of payment or some combination of the two. This choice then influences the choice of a particular organizational form of project procurement and the resulting contractual form. In most competitive situations, contractors will have little influence over the form of contract adopted.

Figure 2 illustrates key influence of the form of contracts.

Figure 2 Influences of the Form of Contracts

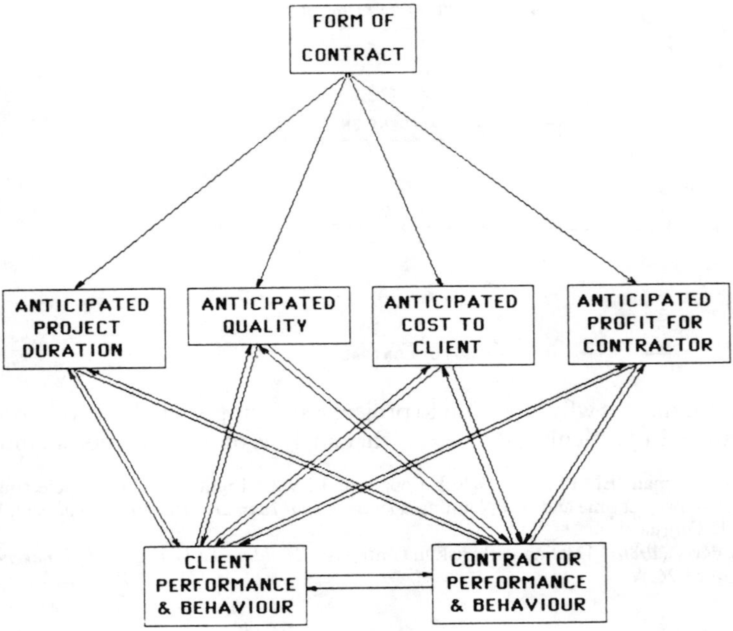

As shown in Figure 2, the form of contract adopted will influence the anticipated time to build, the cost to the client, and the quality or performance of the completed structure. It will also influence the contractor's anticipated profit. All four of these expectations will in turn influence both client and contractor behaviour and performance, which will in turn influence each other and all of these expectations. Perhaps the clearest message the authors received from other papers at this Conference, informal discussion, and subsequent correspondence, might be summarized as follows.

A fixed price contract will work well if:

- the client and the contractor have a clear mutual understanding of what is required;
- the client is prepared to avoid changes to his specification;
- the client remains comfortable with the anticipated project duration, cost and quality; and
- the contractor remains comfortable with his anticipated profit.

If any of these conditions are violated, particularly the last, co-operation will change to confrontation and the project will be in trouble. As projects become larger, more complex, and more subject to technological changes, the risk of violation of one of these conditions becomes greater.

Once the contract is let, the terms of the contract motivate the contractual parties to a greater or lesser extent to manage project risk. In general terms, a price based approach to payment places risk with the contractor and might therefore be expected to motivate the contractor to minimize and control risk. Conversely, a cost based approach places risk with the investor who will reimburse actual costs to the contractor. In this case it may be necessary to introduce appropriate controls to ensure efficient contractor performance. Behaviour will also depend on the contractor's perceptions of, and attitude to, risk. Where the contractor is suitably motivated he will adopt the role of risk manager seeking to avoid undesirable events and minimize the adverse effects of events that do occur. For example, in the early stages of a project, prior to commencing construction, risks may be avoided or reduced by amending designs or work packages, development work, or further investigations. Certain forms of procurement such as management contracting facilitate this by increasing the contractor's involvement in the design and construction phases.

To manage project risks effectively the contractor may undertake his own analysis of project risks. This analysis may be completely independent of any analysis previously carried out by the client. The purpose of this analysis is to evaluate and control costs. It plays no part in allocating project risks except in so far as it causes a contract to be partially renegotiated or it gives rise to a claim for additional payment.

As far as the client is concerned, any attempts at risk management ought to lead to enhanced project performance via reduced costs, reduced time to build, and/or improved quality of the completed project. Conceivably however, the cost and time savings of the contractor's risk management may not be passed on to the client, as in for example, a fixed price contract.

If the contractor's analysis is less complete than the analysis carried out earlier by the client, then it may be in the client's interests to provide the contractor with this information. It is certainly in the interests of the contractor that the client should do so.

If the contractor's analysis is more complete than the analysis carried out earlier by the client, an opportunity to allocate and price project risks on a more mutually beneficial basis may have been missed.

The acquisition of information about project risks plays a key role in the ability of contractual parties to allocate and manage risk. Given the potential conflict of contractual party objectives a central issue is the extent to which contractual parties can obtain mutual benefit by sharing risk information. A related issue is how this information can be used to allocate risks on a rational basis and the extent to which risks can be allocated in a mutually beneficial way.

The Problem of Risk Allocation

How should project risks be allocated?, or what amounts to the same thing, what method of payment should be adopted for a given contract? Price based contracts usually require the contractor to carry more risk than cost based contracts. However, it is by no means clear which method of payment is to be preferred by a client putting a project out to competitive tender.

In the case of high risk projects, a cost based contract may be attractive to contractors, but the final cost of the project to the client is uncertain, and contractor incentives to control costs, in particular to identify and control project risks, may be lacking.

A fixed price contract may appear more attractive to the client, particularly where project risks are high. However, contractors may require what the client regards as an excessive price to take on these risks, and more seriously, even a price based contract may not remove all uncertainty about the final price the client has to pay. For some risks, such as variation in quantity, or unforeseen ground conditions, the contractor will be entitled to additional payments via a claims procedure. The nature of risk and claims, coupled with the confidentiality of the contractor's costs, introduce an element of chance into the adequacy of the payment, from whichever side of the contract it is viewed[7]. Client insistence on placing "fixed price" contracts with the lowest bidder may only serve to aggravate this problem.

Competition and Conflict

If, in a competitive tendering situation, the client accepts the lowest bid, subject to prior or post bidding screening out of any contractors not deemed capable, reliable and sound, the successful bidder will have to be that member of the viable set of contractors who scores best overall in the following categories.

- Most optimistic in relation to cost uncertainties. This may reflect expertise, but it may reflect a willingness to depart from implicit and explicit specification of the project, or ignorance of what is required.

7 Perry (1986) *ibid.*

- Most optimistic in relation to claims for additional revenue.
- Least concerned with considerations like impact on reputation or the chance of bankruptcy.
- Least informed about the likely behaviour of other contractors.
- Most desperate for work.

This suggests that selecting the lowest fixed price bid is an approach which ought to be used with care in a limited set of circumstances. It is particularly risky if any of the following apply.

- Uncertainty is important. It may not be clear to potential contractors what is required, and what may be required.
- Performance specifications are not comprehensive, clear, and legally enforceable.
- The expertise, reputation and financial security of the contractor are not beyond question.

The situation is summed up by Barnes[8]:

> "The problem is that when conditions of contract placing large total risk upon the contractor are used and work is awarded by competitive tender, the contractor who accidentally or deliberately underestimated the risks is most likely to get the work. When the risks materialise with full force he must then either struggle to extract compensation from the client or suffer the loss. This stimulates the growth of the claims problem."

The remedy seems to be to take factors other than lowest price into account when appointing contractors. In particular, a reputation gained for finishing fast and on time without aggressive pursuit of extra payment for the unexpected should be given very great weight and should be seen to do so.

An additional remedy is to carry out an analysis of project risks prior to contract formulation, to determine an appropriate allocation of risks, and to provide all bidders with this information. Unfortunately the implied systematic approach to risk allocation and pricing is unusual in current practice.

One reason for this may be unwillingness or inability on the part of the client to identify sources and consequences of project risk. A difficulty here is that perceptions of risk are dependent on assessment of subsequent risk avoidance and risk reduction actions likely to be taken by the contractor and other parties. Such actions depend in turn on the form of contract agreed and the consequent motivations and behaviour of the contract parties, as shown in Figure 2. Rational allocation of risk depends on systematic evaluation of risks under different project scenarios characterised by different contractual arrangements. This is potentially a time consuming and demanding exercise.

An additional problem is that even with the help of advisers, the client may not be in a position to assess many of the risks associated with construction. Such risks are best assessed by the potential contractors. Unfortunately, in a competitive tendering situation it is not usually possible to tap this source in such a way as to materially influence the basic form of the contract. Yet the

8 Barnes (1984) *ibid*.

form of the contract will motivate the contractual parties to attend to a greater or lesser extent to the management of risk.

If project risks are to be allocated in a manner which improves each contractual party's position, this must involve a greater sharing of knowledge and expertise about project risks, not only during execution of the contract, but at an earlier stage where the contract is being formulated.

For many contract parties such requirements to assess risks and share information may be unacceptable. Abrahamson[9] has put it this way:

> "The strange thing is that the pricing of risk items ... is resisted by both sides. Some contractors prefer a contentious right to their extra costs to a chance to price a risk, and indeed rely on the increase in their final account from claims to make up for low tenders. On the other hand, some employers and engineers prefer to refer to risks generally or as obliquely as possible, presumably in the hope of finding a contractor who will not allow for them fully in his price. These two attitudes are equally reprehensible and short sighted. What a sorry start to a project when they encounter each other!"

Much of the current difficulty with risk allocation and associated claims and arbitration may arise because of contractual parties' preoccupation with transferring risk to other parties. As long as parties believe that risks can be transferred or offloaded onto someone else, perhaps inappropriately, then inadequate attention may be given to risk avoidance or reduction measures, and any quantitative assessment of risks will be halfhearted.

General Guidelines for risk allocation

Abrahamson[10] has suggested that it is proper for a contracting party to bear risk in any one of the following five cases.

1. The risk is of loss due to his own wilful misconduct or lack of reasonable efficiency or care;
2. If he can cover a risk by insurance and allow for the premium in settling his charges, and it is most convenient and practicable for the risk to be dealt with in this way;
3. If the preponderant economic benefit of running the risk accrues to him;
4. If it is in the interests of efficiency to place the risk on him;
5. If, when the risk eventuates, the loss happens to fall on him in the first instance and there is no reason under any of the above headings to transfer the loss to another, or it is impracticable to do so.

These guidelines are a useful first step in addressing the problem of risk allocation, but they do not provide a complete solution.

Point 1 deals with risks associated with unreasonable behaviour. Allocation of such uncertainties in the manner indicated must be uncontentious, but it is important for each party to recognize and deal with such risk related to the other party.

Point 2 deals with that set of project risks that can be externalised from the contractual parties. In so far as the client ultimately pays the insurance fee, the

9 Max Abrahamson (1973) "Contractual risks in tunnelling: how they should be shared", *Tunnels and Tunnelling*, Nov. pp 587-598.

10 Abrahamson (1973) *ibid*.

issue of allocating insurable risks is a question only of who can obtain the cheapest cover. In an efficient insurance market both parties will be able to obtain cover at the same price, but in practice inefficiencies may be important.

Point 3 recognizes that economic benefits and risks ought to be matched, but it does not provide guidelines as to how this should be done, or deal with the need for an adequate level of reward for taking on a particular risk, or with differences in such rewards depending upon willingness to take risk, which may be unrelated to ability to take risk.

Point 4 recognizes the importance of efficiency, but there is some ambiguity about the nature of this: efficiency with respect to which contractual party and what objectives? Presumably Point 4 represents the widely accepted notion that "risk should be allocated to the party best able to anticipate and control that risk"[11] but this may not be the party best able to bear it.

Taken together points 3 and 4 suggest a fixed price agreement for contractor-controllable risks, and a cost reimbursable agreement for client-controllable risks, such as changes to designs. However, this is a naive interpretation because it ignores the pricing of risks, and the differing attitudes to risk of the contractual parties. In addition, points 3 and 4 offer little help in allocating risks which are uncontrollable, or controllable to a degree by more than one contractual party. The possibility of risk sharing is ignored.

Point 5 is a useful catch-all, but does not resolve any of the difficulties noted above. As Abrahamson[12] has acknowledged:

> "one of the problems of the construction industry is that although decisions have to be made about allocating risks, in negotiating contracts and revising standard contract forms very little consideration has been given to basic principles, and what one might call a philosophy of risk is lacking."

Successful, appropriate allocation of risk along the lines proposed by Abrahamson presupposes an atmosphere of trust between contracting parties, and a clear, mutual appreciation of all relevant project risks and their effects. In the absence of one or both of these conditions, and given the limitations of these guidelines, it is perhaps not surprising that the debate about appropriate allocation of risks is often diverted to investigating and clarifying the effectiveness of allocation mechanisms such as contract clauses.[13]

Towards a Theory of project risk allocation

If a proper theory of risk allocation underlay the allocation of project risks, it would be clear how and why risks were allocated in a given contract. Further, contracts would be documents carefully designed to encourage both parties to act in their mutual interest in the face of uncertainty, with litigation an unlikely outcome. Legal input would be "up front" and preventative, providing a framework for co-operation rather than confrontation, which both parties perceive as fair and attractive.

11 John E Beard III (1982) "Risk allocation through contract clauses", *Proceedings of ASCE Symp. on "Managing Liability"*, Nevada, April.
12 Abrahamson (1982) *ibid.*
13 Beard (1982) *ibid.*

The next section seeks to develop an understanding of the principles involved in allocating project risks. To do this it first considers a simplified situation involving the allocation of a single source of risk which must be allocated in total either to the client or to the contractor. Only a fixed price or cost reimbursable method of payment is possible, where fixed price means precisely that no claims are possible. Later sections build on this basic framework, working towards more realistic situations by considering controllable risks, risk sharing and multiple risks, offering further insights into the risk allocation problem.

The Basic Framework

This section develops a basic framework to describe the risk allocation problem from general economic risk theory concepts. This implies that uncertainty about project outcomes, including time taken for completion and the quality of the completed project, can be quantified in terms of uncertainty about project costs. This makes it possible to compare alternative risk scenarios and consider in a quantitative way the risk preferences of contractor and client. An initial model addresses the effect of willingness to take risk, everything else being equal, in the context of a choice between a simple fixed price or a cost reimbursable contract. This allows assessment of who ought to take on project risk in a particular context, and the information required to achieve this.

Representing uncertain project costs

Uncertainty about project related costs can be quantified in the form of a cumulative probability distribution of possible cost values, or PC curve, as shown in Figure 3(a). P(C) is the probability of a cost equal to or less than C.

E is the expected value of C, and the best estimate of what will happen on average relative to the associated probability distribution. E usually has a chance of achievement greater than 0.5, in the region 0.55 to 0.70, because of asymmetry in the probability distribution: relative to a most likely or modal value there is more scope for cost overruns than there is for cost savings.

U is a value of C with virtual certainty of achievement: the probability of a value of C less than U is nearly unity.

Z is a value of C with virtual certainty of non-achievement: the probability of a value of C less than Z is nearly zero.

Variability in project cost could be represented by an equivalent probability density form, but the cumulative form is easier to use for most purposes. Cost distributions like that of Figure 3(a) may be based on detailed analysis of costs and uncertainties, or relatively crude subjective assessments. Distributions may be measured with some precision using unrestricted forms, or crudely approximated by simple linear forms.

The analysis that follows employs PC curves which are assumed to be either client or contractor perceptions of C, the contractor's total project related costs, incorporating an "appropriate" contribution to profit for the contractor. The appropriate contribution to contractor's profit may be either a fixed

Figure 3 Representing Project Cost Uncertainty

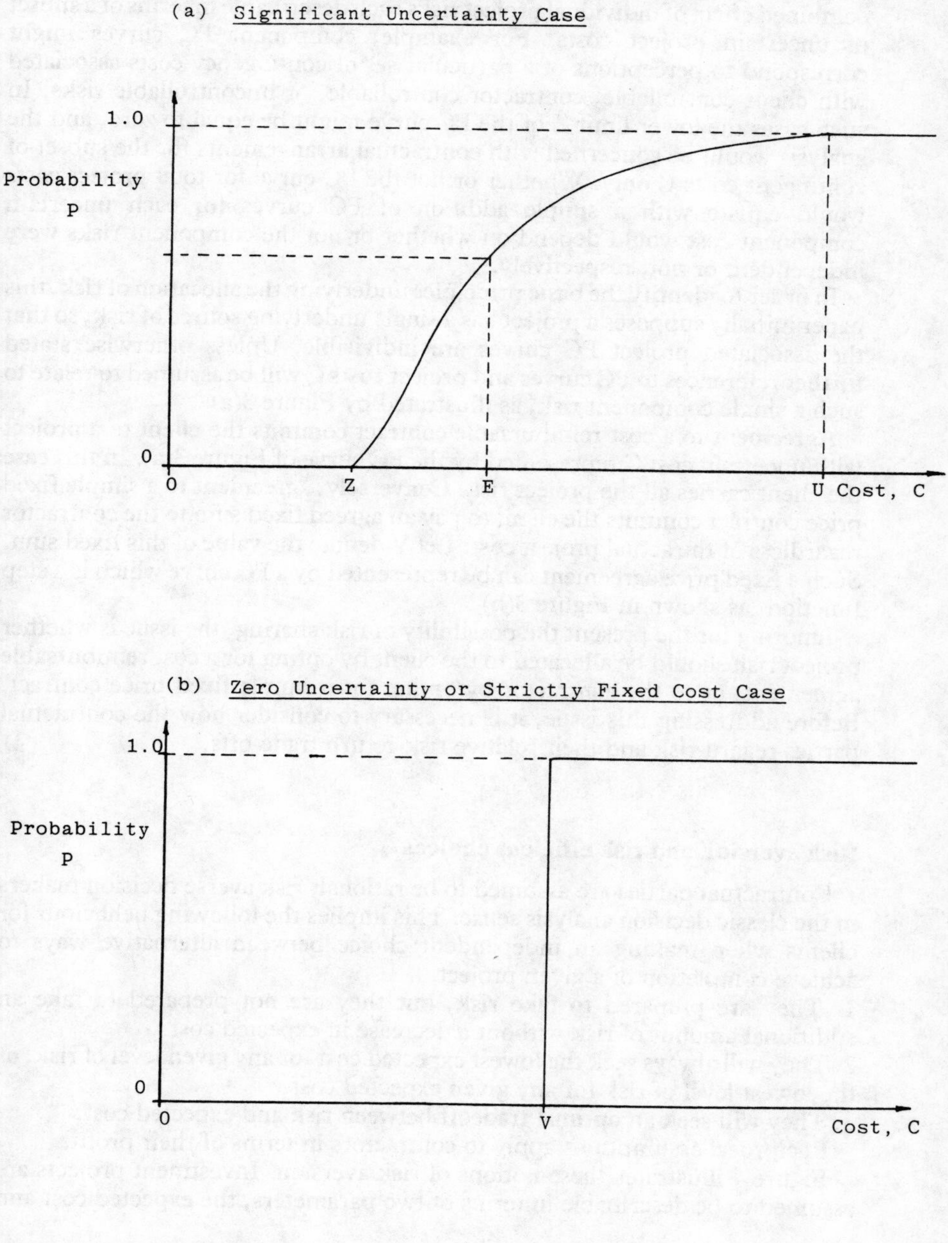

amount or a percentage of project related costs. These arrangements have potentially different effects on contractor behaviour, but the analysis does not address this issue. Clearly an appropriate contribution to profit may involve a loss if there is strong competition for work; or an "abnormal" profit if competition is limited or absent altogether. C is the uncertain amount the client pays to the contractor under a cost reimbursable contract.

The PC curve of the project cost C as defined above can be regarded as the combined effect of individual project risks each describable in terms of a subset of uncertain project costs. For example, component PC curves might correspond to perceptions of a particular set of contingency costs associated with client controllable, contractor controllable, or uncontrollable risks. In such cases the lower limit Z of the PC curve might be equal to zero, and the analysis would be concerned with contractual arrangements for the subset of contingent costs C only. Whether or not the PC curve for total project costs would equate with a simple addition of PC curves for each uncertain component cost would depend on whether or not the component risks were independent or not, respectively.

In order to identify the basic principles underlying the allocation of risk, this paper initially supposes a project has a single underlying source of risk, so that the associated project PC curves are indivisible. Unless otherwise stated further references to PC curves and project costs C will be assumed to relate to such a single component risk, as illustrated by Figure 3(a).

Agreement to a cost reimbursable contract commits the client to a project with uncertain cost C represented by the PC curve of Figure 3(a). In this case the client carries all the project risk. Conversely, agreement to a simple fixed price contract commits the client to pay an agreed fixed sum to the contractor regardless of the actual project cost. Let V denote the value of this fixed sum. Such a fixed price agreement can be represented by a PC curve which is a step function, as shown in Figure 3(b).

Ignoring for the present the possibility of risk sharing, the issue is whether project risk should be allocated to the client by opting for a cost reimbursable agreement, or to the contractor by opting for a simple fixed price contract. Before addressing this issue, it is necessary to consider how the contractual parties regard risk and their relative risk-return trade-offs.

Risk aversion and risk efficient choices

Contractual parties are assumed to be rational, risk averse decision makers in the classic decision analysis sense. This implies the following behaviour for clients when making an independent choice between alternative ways to achieve completion of a given project.

1. They are prepared to take risk, but they are not prepared to take an additional amount of risk without a decrease in expected cost.
2. They will always seek the lowest expected cost for any given level of risk, or the lowest level of risk for any given expected cost.
3. They will seek an optimal tradeoff between risk and expected cost.

Reciprocal assumptions apply to contractors in terms of their profit.

Figure 4 illustrates these notions of risk aversion. Investment projects are assumed to be describable in terms of two parameters, the expected cost and some univariate measure of cost uncertainty or risk such as the variance of the project cost C. The point H on the indifference curve A represents a project like the one shown in Figure 3(a). By definition a decision maker is indifferent between any projects lying on curve A. Behaviour 1 is evident in the shape of curve A, which, moving from T, slopes to the left (risk aversion). In addition curve A is assumed to become progressively flatter the greater the risk (increasing risk aversion). This is not a crucial assumption for most of our analysis, but reflects common preferences between alternative investment opportunities. The risk averse decision maker is indifferent between the project at point H on Figure 4 and a simple fixed price contract of value T with zero risk, where T is greater than E. The shallower curve A is, the bigger the distance between T and E, and the more risk averse the decision maker.

Figure 4 Illustrating Risk Aversion and Indifference Curves A Client Perspective

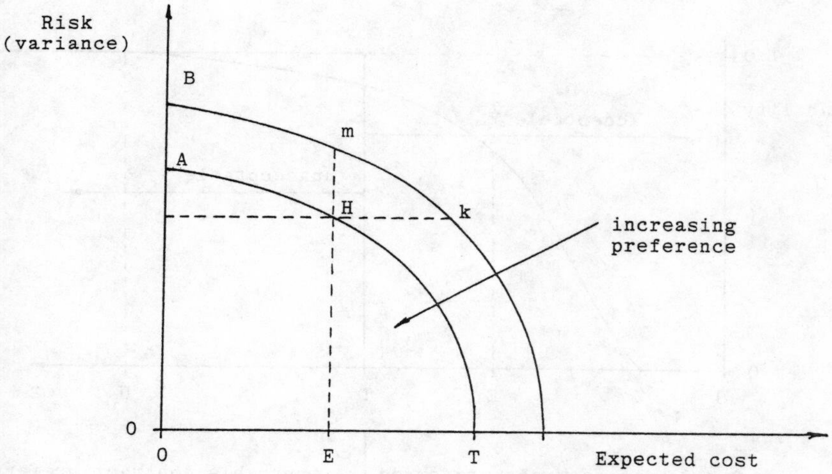

Curve B in Figure 4 represents another indifference curve, parallel to curve A, such that the decision maker would be indifferent between projects like k and m lying on this curve. Behaviour 2 implies that point H is preferred to points k and m, and consequently that any point on curve A is preferred to any point on curve B.

Where indifference curves are parallel straight lines, the decision maker exhibits constant risk aversion at all levels of risk, a limiting special case of interest later.

Behaviour 3 implies that, given the opportunity, a decision maker will prefer alternative projects which lie as far to the bottom left hand corner of the risk expected cost space of Figure 4 as possible. This choice of project will be risk efficient in the sense that no other project or contractual arrangement lies to the left and below the indifference curve passing through the point representing that project. In Figure 4 if H is such a project or contractual arrangement, then any other project alternative lying on curve A is also a risk efficient choice, such as T. Points like k and m may be feasible options, but they are not risk efficient given the availability of options like H or T on curve A.

The Client's contractual preferences

The above characterization of risk-cost preferences should underlie a client's preference for a cost reimbursable or fixed price contract in respect of a single, given project with uncertain cost C. Figure 5 illustrates this choice using the project cost representation of Figure 3(a). The cost curve in Figure 5 represents a client's perceptions of the project cost C and the uncertain cost of a cost reimbursable contract. The vertical line shown at C = T represents the assumed alternative of a fixed price contract of value V = T.

Figure 5 Basic Concepts: The Client's Viewpoint

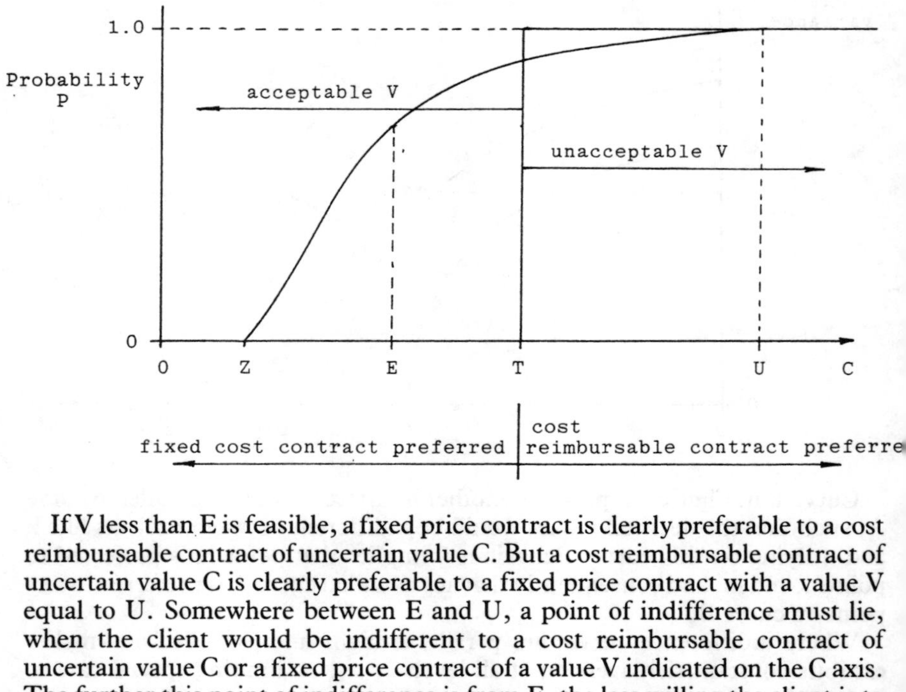

If V less than E is feasible, a fixed price contract is clearly preferable to a cost reimbursable contract of uncertain value C. But a cost reimbursable contract of uncertain value C is clearly preferable to a fixed price contract with a value V equal to U. Somewhere between E and U, a point of indifference must lie, when the client would be indifferent to a cost reimbursable contract of uncertain value C or a fixed price contract of a value V indicated on the C axis. The further this point of indifference is from E, the less willing the client is to take on the project risk, in the sense that the client is prepared to accept a higher fixed price contract to avoid accepting the uncertainty associated with a cost reimbursable contract. In Figure 5, T indicates an example point of indifference for the client. If V is less than T, then the client will accept the fixed price contract of value V in preference to a cost reimbursable contract of uncertain value C. If V is greater than T, then the client will prefer a cost reimbursable contract of uncertain value C to a fixed price contract of value V.

TE is the maximum risk premium the client should be prepared to pay to avoid the uncertainty associated with a cost reimbursable contract. The more willing the client is to take on the project risk, the smaller TE will be.

A Contractor's contractual preferences

A contractor's view of the risk-cost trade-offs between cost reimbursable and fixed price contracts can be represented in a similar manner to the client's. As for the client, assume the contractor is a rational, risk averse decision maker, implying similar (but not identical) risk-cost choice behaviour as discussed for the client. The curve of Figure 6 represents a contractor's view of the uncertainty associated with a project of interest in terms of the contractor's cost incorporating an appropriate contribution to profit for the contractor, C. The nature of this curve is similar to Figure 5, but there is no need for the curve to be the same as the client's perceptions in Figure 5.

Figure 6 Basic Concepts: The Contractor's Viewpoint

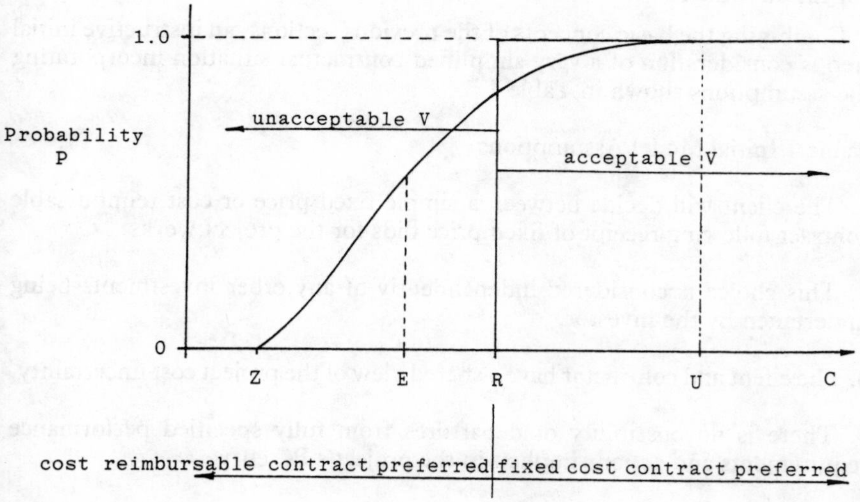

As in Figure 5: E in Figure 6 is the expected value of C; U is the value of C with P nearly unity; Z is the value of C with P nearly zero.

A contractor does not normally have a choice between a fixed price contract and a cost reimbursable contract. However, if this choice were possible, a cost reimbursable contract of uncertain value C is clearly preferable to a fixed price contract with a value V less than E. But a fixed price contract with value V equal to U is clearly preferable to a cost reimbursable contract of uncertain value C. Somewhere between E and U, a point of indifference must lie, when the contractor would be indifferent to a cost reimbursable contract of uncertain value C or a fixed price contract of a value V indicated on the C axis. In Figure 6, R indicates an example point of indifference for the contractor. The further this point of indifference is from E, the less willing the contractor is to take on the project risk, in the sense that the contractor is prepared to forgo as much as the risk premium R-E to avoid accepting the uncertainty associated with a fixed price contract. If V is less than R, then the contractor will accept a cost reimbursable contract of uncertain value C in preference to a fixed price contract of value V. If V is greater than R, then the contractor will prefer a fixed price contract of value V to a cost reimbursable contract of uncertain value C.

RE is the minimum risk premium the contractor should be prepared to accept to undertake a fixed price contract. One effect of strong competition for work, or great need to win a given contract, will be to reduce R and hence RE. This may reflect the contractor's willingness to accept the project risk, but it may not reflect the contractor's ability to take on the project risk, which may be reduced by the effects of strong competition for work. With such adjustments, R represents the lowest fixed price bid the contractor is prepared to submit for the project. Unless otherwise stated this definition of R is assumed in the analysis and discussion that follows.

An Initial model

Combining the basic concepts of the previous sections, an instructive initial step is consideration of a very simplified contractual situation incorporating the assumptions shown in Table 1.

Table 1 Initial Model Assumptions

1. The client will decide between a simple fixed price or cost reimbursable contract following receipt of fixed price bids for the project works.

2. This choice is considered independently of any other investments being undertaken by the investor.

3. The client and contractor have a shared view of the project cost uncertainty.

4. There is no possibility of departures from fully specified performance requirements and actions implicit in the project's PC curve.

5. The client has received a fixed price bid R from a given contractor to undertake the project. R might be the lowest fixed price bid received from a number of bidders.

6. An appropriate contribution to profit rate for the contractor is agreed which would apply if a cost reimbursable contract is agreed.

In order to decide on appropriate allocation of project risk, assume the client superimposes information about R on his own perspective of the project as represented in Figure 5.

Figure 7 An Initial Model of Risk Allocation

(a) Contractor More Willing to Accept Risk

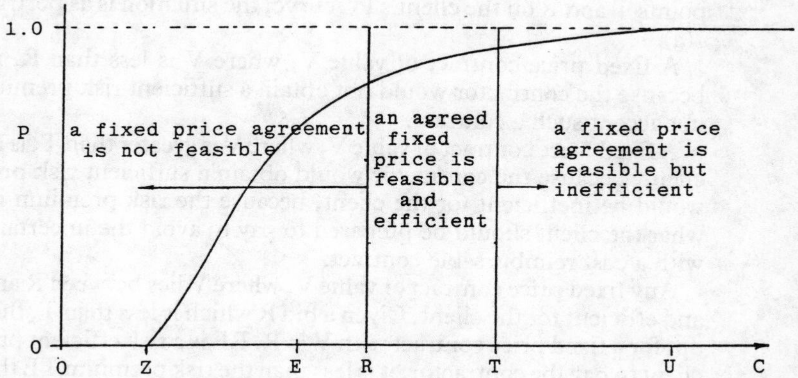

(b) Client More Willing to Accept Risk

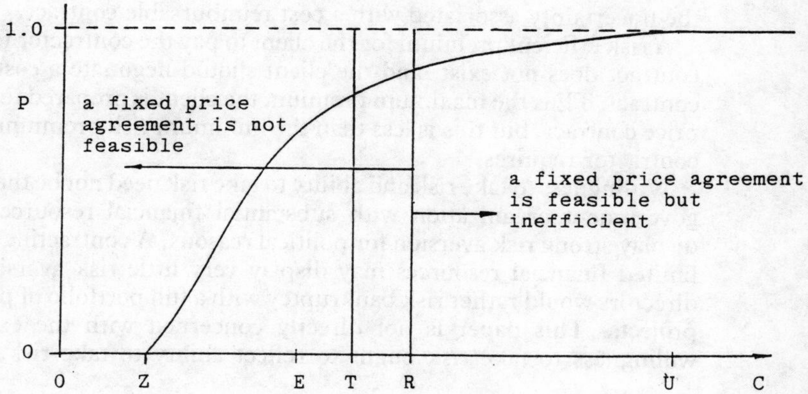

The client can view R as an indicator of the contractor's willingness to take on project risk with respect to the client's perception of the project PC curve, even if the contractor has a different perception of the project PC curve. For the moment, however, it is convenient to assume that client and contractor have a shared view of the project cost uncertainty. This is not essential for the argument that follows, but allows us to postpone discussion of the effects of optimism or pessimism about project risk on the part of either party.

There are two cases to consider, one where the contractor is more willing to take risk than the client, and the other where the client is more willing to take risk than the contractor.

If the contractor is more willing to take risk than the client, as defined by points T and R on the client's PC curve, the situation is as portrayed in Figure 7(a).

A fixed price contract of value V, where V is less than R, is not feasible because the contractor would not obtain a sufficient risk premium and would not accept such a contract.

A fixed price contract of value V, where V is greater than T, is feasible for the client, because the contractor would obtain a sufficient risk premium; but it would be inefficient for the client, because the risk premium is greater than what the client should be prepared to pay to avoid the uncertainty associated with a cost reimbursable contract.

Any fixed price contract of value V, where V lies between R and T is feasible and efficient for the client. Given a bid R which is less than T, the client should opt for a fixed price contract with V = R. RE is a risk efficient premium for the client to pay the contractor; it is less than the risk premium TE the client would be prepared to pay to avoid a cost reimbursable contract.

If the client is more willing to take risk than the contractor, as defined by points T and R on the client's PC curve, the situation is as portrayed in Figure 7(b).

As in Figure 7(a), a fixed price contract of value V, where V is less than R, is not feasible for the client, because the contractor would not obtain a sufficient risk premium and would not accept such a contract.

A fixed price contract of value V, where V is equal to or greater than R, is feasible for the client, because the contractor would obtain a sufficient risk premium; but as in Figure 5, it would be inefficient for the client, because the risk premium is greater than that the client should be prepared to pay to avoid the uncertainty associated with a cost reimbursable contract.

A risk efficient premium for the client to pay the contractor for a fixed price contract does not exist, and the client should negotiate a cost reimbursable contract. TE is the maximum premium the client is prepared to pay for a fixed price contract, but this is less than the minimum risk premium RE which the contractor requires.

Willingness to take risk and ability to take risk need not be the same thing. A government organization with substantial financial resources on call may display strong risk aversion for political reasons. A contracting firm with very limited financial resources may display very little risk aversion because its directors would rather risk bankruptcy with a full portfolio of projects than no projects. This paper is not directly concerned with the extent to which willingness to take risk ought to reflect ability to take risk, but there are

Figure 8 The Effects of Overstating Risk Aversion

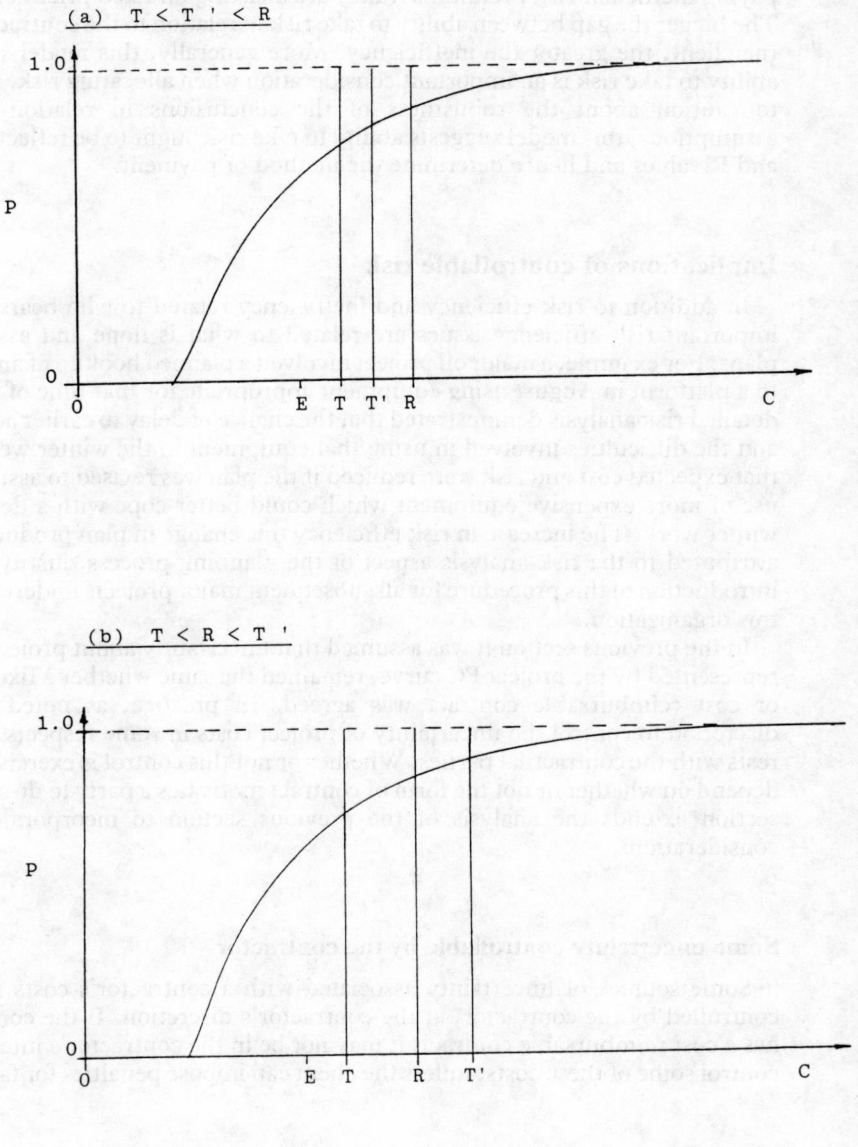

grounds to argue that it can be inefficient for clients who can afford to take risks to refuse to do so.

This attitude can be represented in the model by a tendency to make decisions about risk allocation with an implicitly inflated value for T, T' say. In the case of Figure 7(a) this is of no concern. However in the case of Figure 7(b), there are two possibilities to consider, $T < T' < R$ and $T' > R > T$. These are shown in Figure 8.

In the event that $T' < R$, a cost reimbursable contract is indicated as in Figure 7(b). Where $T' > R$, but $R > T$, instead of choosing a cost reimbursable contract, the client will opt for a fixed price contract of value $V = R$. Thus clients who are more able to take risks than their contractors may be paying inefficient risk premiums if they are insisting on fixed price contracts. The bigger the gap between ability to take risk in relation to the contractor and the client, the greater the inefficiency. More generally, this model suggests ability to take risk is an important consideration when allocating risk. Subject to caution about the robustness of the conclusions in relation to the assumptions, this model suggests ability to take risk ought to be reflected in T and R values and hence determine the method of payment.

Implications of controllable risk

In addition to risk efficiency and inefficiency related to who bears a risk, important risk efficiency issues are related to what is done and associated plans. For example, a major oil project involved a planned hookup of an oil line to a platform in August using equipment appropriate for that time of year. A detailed risk analysis demonstrated that the chance of delay to earlier activities and the difficulties involved in using that equipment in the winter were such that expected cost and risk were reduced if the plan was revised to assume the use of more expensive equipment which could better cope with a delay and winter work. The increase in risk efficiency this change in plan produced was attributed to the risk analysis aspect of the planning process, justifying the introduction of this procedure for all subsequent major projects undertaken by this organization.

In the previous section it was assumed that uncertainty about project costs, represented by the project PC curve, remained the same whether a fixed price or cost reimbursable contract was agreed. In practice, as noted above, discretion to control the uncertainty of project costs in some respects usually rests with the contractual parties. Whether or not this control is exercised may depend on whether or not the form of contract motivates a party to do so. This section extends the analysis of the previous section to incorporate these considerations.

Some uncertainty controllable by the contractor

Some sources of uncertainty associated with a contractor's costs may be controlled by the contractor, at the contractor's discretion. If the contractor has a cost reimbursable contract, it may not be in the contractor's interests to control some of these costs, unless the client can impose penalties for failure to do so, through the courts as in a negligence claim, or through dissemination of information leading to a loss of reputation. For example, a contractor might purchase more expensive equipment to perform a task than would seem to be necessary in the context of that task on its own and in normal circumstances, because the expected overall project cost is less and project risk is reduced. However, if the client does not understand this possibility, or could not successfully demonstrate that the contractor should have recognized it, the contractor's expected profit will be increased if the contractor fails to take such risk efficient action. Indeed, the contractor will have a strong incentive not even to identify such a possibility, because a "moral hazard" is involved if the contractor has done so but not responded. Some of these actions will involve different equipment, some different base plans, some carefully developed contingency plans, some insurance policies, some different arrangements with suppliers or sub-contractors or employees, and so on. There is a wide range of possibilities. Some may reduce risk with a slight increase in expected cost: for example, the contractor taking out insurance which would allow rapid replacement of damaged equipment. But the net effect if all feasible possibilities are pursued by the contractor is likely to be a substantial reduction in risk with a significant reduction in expected cost. Figure 9 portrays such an effect, maintaining all six assumptions of the initial model, and adding a further assumption to allow the affect discussed above, as follows.

7. The PC curves of Figure 7 portraying uncertainty about project costs can be moved to the left and made more vertical, if the contractor is made to control all the uncertainty which the contractor can control.

In Figure 9 curve A represents the original curve, without such complete control by the contractor. Curve B represents the shifted curve, with such control by the contractor.

Such control and curve B might be associated with a sufficiently low fixed price contract, and a lack of such control and curve A might be associated with a cost reimbursable contract. However, identification of that version of curve B which is most vertical and farthest to the left also implies careful risk management by the contractor and client. Such risk management could involve a tight cost reimbursable or risk sharing contract specification which required the contractor to use curve B, as will be discussed later.

In Figure 9, U_A, U_B, Z_A and Z_B values are identified as for earlier curves. EA and EB expected values as for earlier curves, are not shown in Figure 9, but could be. TB represents the point of indifference in relation to curve B for the client between a fixed price contract and a cost reimbursable contract. T_A is a similarly defined point for curve A. R_B represents the point of indifference in relation to curve B for the contractor between a fixed price contract and a cost reimbursable contract. R_B might be expected to correspond to the contractor's fixed price bid. RA would be unspecified, as contractors would be bidding assuming they will have to work to curve B.

If the contractor is more willing to take risk than the client, then R_B is less than T_B, as shown in Figure 9(a), and a fixed price contract of value RB is the best choice for the client.

In Figure 9(b), T_B is less than R_B, the client is more willing to take risk than the contractor, and R_B is less than T_A. If a tightly specified cost reimbursable

Figure 9 Some Uncertainty Controllable by the Contractor

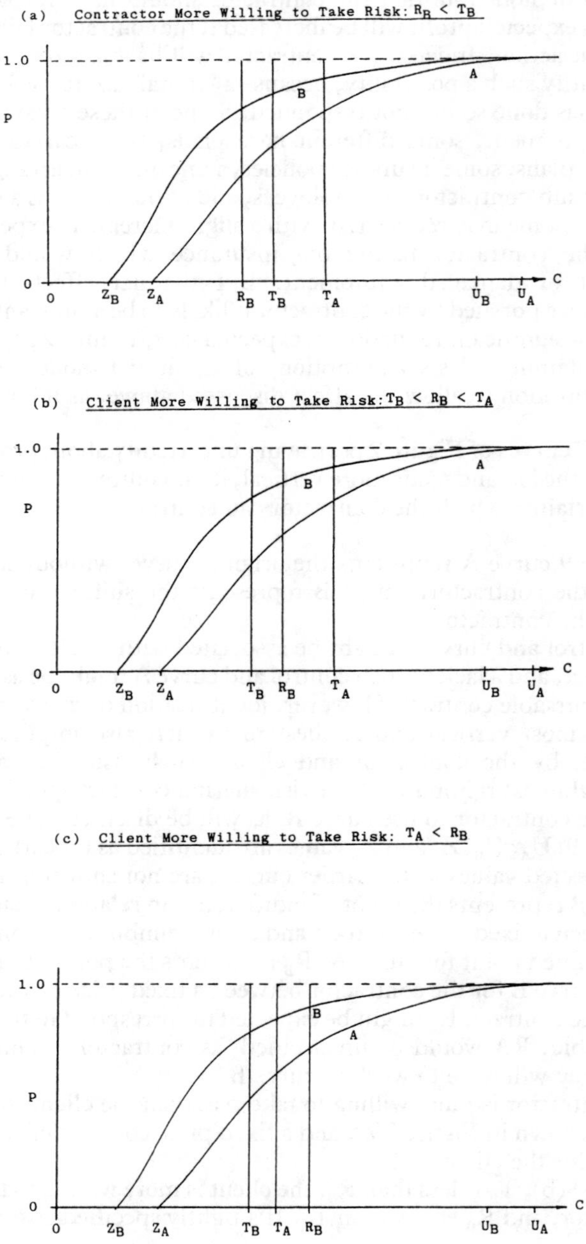

contract implying curve B is feasible, the client ought to take this form of cost reimbursable contract. If not, then the client ought to settle for a fixed price contract of value R_B, paying the premium $R_B T_B$ for the risk control provided by the fixed price contract. Even if the client was so willing to take risk that T_B coincided with E_B, and the contractor was so unwilling to take risk that R_B coincided with U_B, this would still be the case.

In Figure 9(c) the situation is as for 9(b), except that RB is greater than T_A. In this case if a tightly specified cost reimbursable contract implying curve B is feasible, the client ought to take this form of contract. If not, the client ought to settle for a cost reimbursable contract implying curve A will be the basis of its execution, with an opportunity cost $T_A T_B$ associated with the client's inability to obtain a form of reimbursable contract making curve B feasible. A fixed price contract of value R_B will be even more inefficient.

Hence, if a client is more willing to take risk than a contractor, and a cost reimbursable contract which requires the contractor to exercise tight control over risks is not feasible, a client may find it necessary to use a fixed price contract which involves a premium to obtain contractor risk control. Depending on the particular form of the curves A and B, this premium could be very large. Even if it is considered worth paying such a premium, substantial inefficiency may be involved.

Any uncertainty which may be controlled by the contractor at the contractor's discretion will in general suggest fixed price contracts, to force the contractor to exercise full control. If all uncertainty is of this nature and the contractor is more willing to take risk than the client, this is a reasonable outcome. If the client is more willing to take risk than the contractor, this may not be an appropriate outcome. In such cases, if a cost reimbursable contract implying curve B could be made feasible at a cost less than the premium $R_B T_B$ illustrated on Figure 9(b) or $T_A T_B$ illustrated in Figure 9(c), it would be worth organising such a contract.

For example, if the dominant risk for a construction project is ground conditions as measured by one or two parameters like rock content of soil removed, a price might be defined as an agreed function of these parameters. This is a cost reimbursable contract in relation to the ground conditions, but fixed in other respects, leaving the contractor with maximum incentive to manage controllable risk. Contracts for the construction of tunnels often use this approach, but it is not generally used to the extent that it might be appropriate to do so.

In many cases it is not straightforward to achieve a cost reimbursable contract on a curve B basis, but it is still feasible, if the client takes an active management role. This might be via detailed prior contingency planning and control, or it might involve a management contract. Both are feasible alternatives to direct management of the project with the contractor acting as a sub-contractor. Oil companies often maintain a strong management presence in their contractor's organization, to good effect, even for fixed price contracts. Other organizations, for whom such an approach has obvious merit, often take a "hands off" or "back seat" approach which is difficult to rationalize.

Some uncertainty controllable by the client

Some sources of uncertainty associated with a contractor's costs may be controlled by the client at the client's discretion. If, in some of these cases, a client has a fixed price contract, it may not be worthwhile for the client to control such costs, unless the contractor can impose penalties for failure to do so through a claim which may require legal proceedings. For example, a senior member of the client's staff might see the incorporation of a design change related to new technology as extremely desirable from his or her perspective, and have the political power to insist that it be incorporated. Such a change may imply a substantial shift in the contractor's cost curve, to the right and to a more horizontal shape, but the contract may not allow fully for such changes. In a more positive context, a client might decide to forgo all new technology, and copy exactly a previous project, because the expected cost effectiveness is greater, given the perceived risks associated with new technology, including problems induced by contractors. However, if those responsible for drawing up a contract on behalf of the client and the contractor do not appreciate such possibilities, the technical members of the client's team will have strong incentives not even to identify such a possibility. Actions which a client can take to control uncertainty may involve less new technology, more up-front design, prototype testing, insurance, revised base plans, carefully developed contingency plans, and so on. There is a wide range of possibilities.

Figure 10 portrays such an effect, maintaining all six assumptions of the initial model, and replacing assumption 7 with the following.

7a. The PC curve of Figure 7 portraying uncertainty about project costs can be moved to the left and made more vertical, if the client can be made to control all the uncertainty which the client can control.

In Figure 10, curve A represents the original curve, without such complete control by the client. Curve B represents the shifted curve, with such control by the client.

Such control and curve B might be associated with a cost reimbursable contract. A lack of such control and curve A might be associated with a fixed price contract. As noted in the last section, identification of that version of curve B which is most vertical and furthest to the left also implies careful risk management by the client and the contractor. In the present case there is no question of requiring the client or the contractor to use curve B on a fixed price basis. Unless the contractor feels able to rely on the client controlling costs to curve B, the contractor will only consider curve A, and a fixed price contract of value V less than RAwill not be acceptable. This means that contractors will bid assuming curve A, and R_B will not be specified. For R_B to be specified, the client would have to negotiate with the contractors on the basis of a contract which clearly compelled the client to operate with curve B. For present purposes this is assumed non-feasible.

If the contractor is more willing to take risk than the client and R_A is less than T_B, as shown in Figure 10(a), then a fixed price contract of value R_A is the best choice for the client. However, an inefficiency is involved, equivalent to R_A-R_B, because of the inability of the client to provide a contract that the contractor is convinced will keep him on curve B.

Figure 10 Some Uncertainty Controllable by the Client

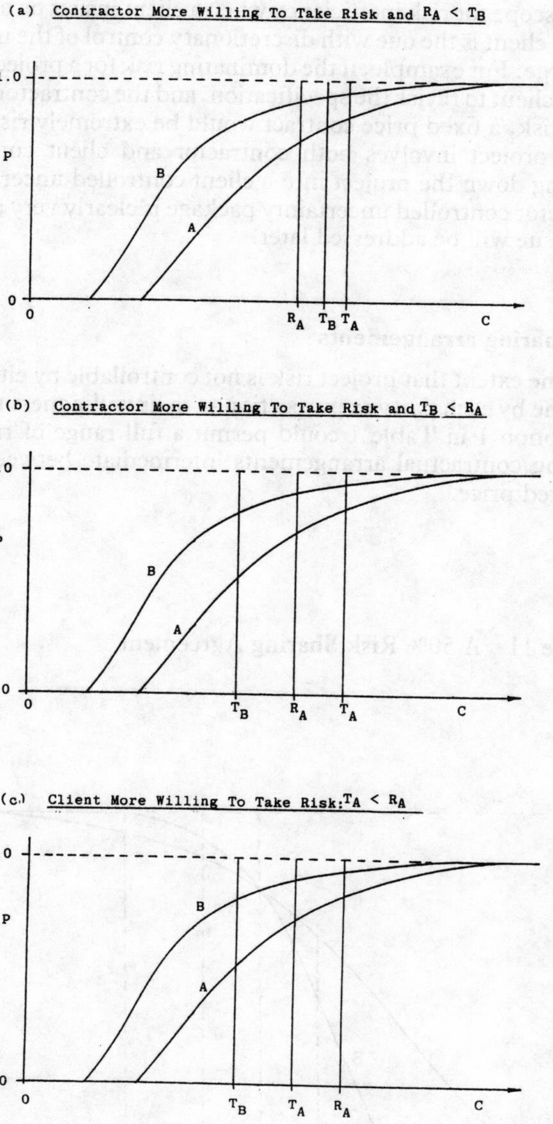

If the contractor is more willing to take risk than the client and R_A is greater than T_B, as shown in Figure 10(b), then a cost reimbursable contract is the best choice for the client, operating on curve B. A fixed price contract will involve an inefficient risk premium R_A-T_B, plus an inefficiency equivalent to T_B-R_B akin to that for 10(a).

If the client is more willing to take risk than the contractor, as shown in Figure 10(c), then a cost reimbursable contract is the best choice for the client, operating on curve B. A fixed price contract will involve an inefficient risk premium R_A-T_B which incorporates the R_A-R_B effect.

The scope for risk inefficiency when a client insists on a fixed price contract, but the client is the one with discretionary control of the uncertainty, is clearly very large. For example, if the dominating risk for a project is the possible need for the client to revise the specification, and the contractor is not willing to take much risk, a fixed price contract would be extremely risk inefficient.

If a project involves both contractor and client controlled uncertainty, breaking down the project into a client controlled uncertainty package and a contractor controlled uncertainty package is clearly very attractive, if feasible. This issue will be addressed later.

Risk sharing arrangements

To the extent that project risk is not controllable by either party, risk might be borne by each party in proportion to their willingness to bear risk. Relaxing assumption 1 in Table 1 could permit a full range of risk sharing contracts covering contractual arrangements intermediate between cost reimbursable and fixed price.

Figure 11 A 50% Risk Sharing Agreement

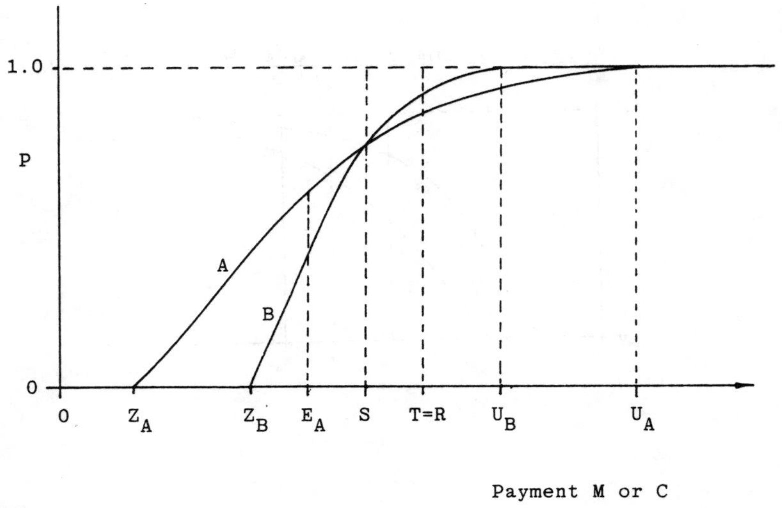

As a useful starting point for examining risk sharing arrangements, consider the initial model with the assumptions of Table 1, but with the contractor and client equally willing to take on cost uncertainty. In these circumstances T = R and both parties are indifferent between a fixed price contract of value V = T = R and a cost reimbursable contract. Insistence on a choice between these two extremes of payment method results in one party taking all or none of the project risk. A more balanced contract would involve the client and contractor each bearing half the uncertainty with an expected risk premium over E of (T-E)/2.

Figure 12 Client Payments to Contractor Under Various Risk Sharing Agreements

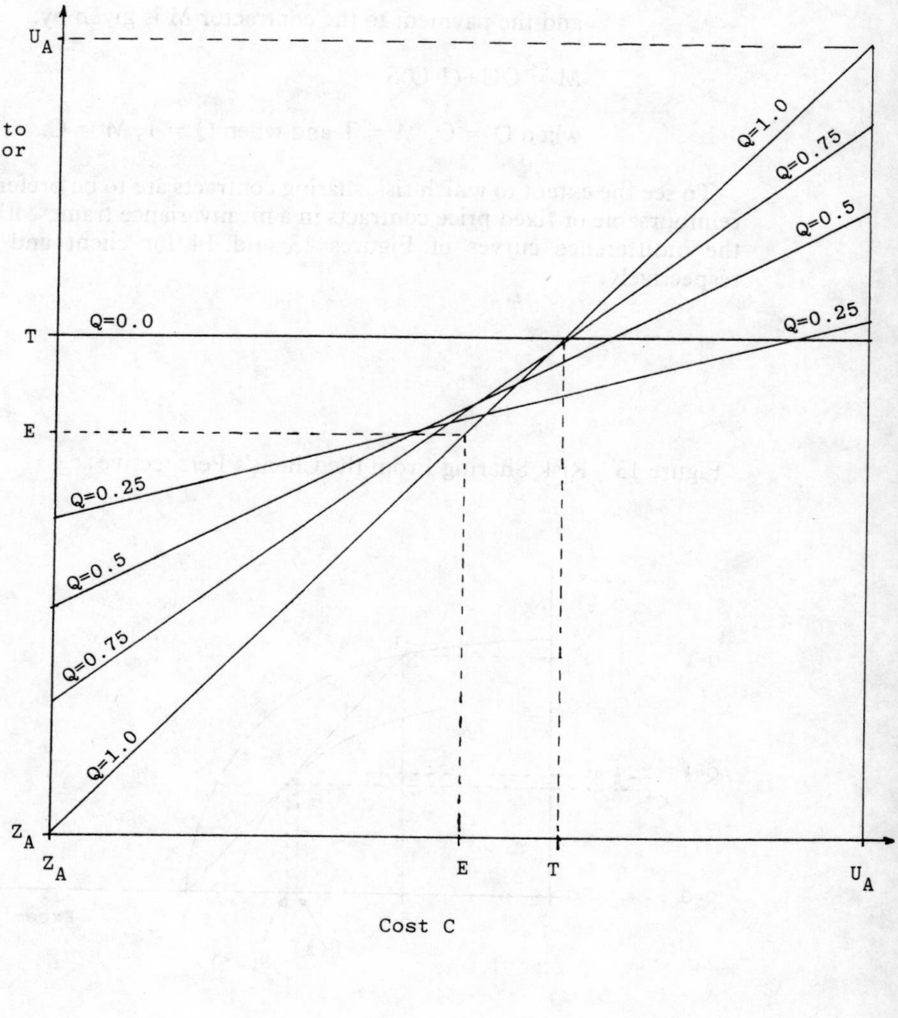

Figure 11 illustrates this arrangement: curve A represents the C distribution of Figure 7 with T = R. Curve B portrays the payment to the contractor by the client implied by a 50/50 risk sharing agreement. The expected value of curve B is S, where S = (T+E)/2, and curve B splits the difference between S and the value of C indicated by curve A. Uncertainty is split 50/50 relative to S.

In the event that C corresponds to S, the payment is S. If C corresponds to U_A, the payment is $U_B = (U_A+S)/2$, which splits the difference between U_A and S. In the event that $C = Z_A$, the payment is $Z_B = (Z_A+S)/2$. For the client, relative to a cost reimbursable contract, taking this shared risk agreement involves 50% of the increase in expected value a fixed price contract would provide, and 50% of the decrease in uncertainty.

Figure 12 illustrates a number of alternative risk sharing arrangements, where the proportion of risk born by the client, Q, varies between zero (fixed price contract) and unity (cost reimbursable contract). In Figure 12, S is a function of Q for a given PC curve and associated T = R value. Thus:

$$S(Q) = (1\text{-}Q)T+QE$$

and the payment to the contractor M is given by:

$$M = QC+(1\text{-}Q)S$$

when Q = O, M = T and when Q = 1, M = C.

To see the extent to which risk sharing contracts are to be preferred to cost reimbursable or fixed price contracts in a meanvariance framework, consider the indifference curves of Figures 13 and 14 for client and contractor respectively.

Figure 13 Risk Sharing From the Client's Perspective

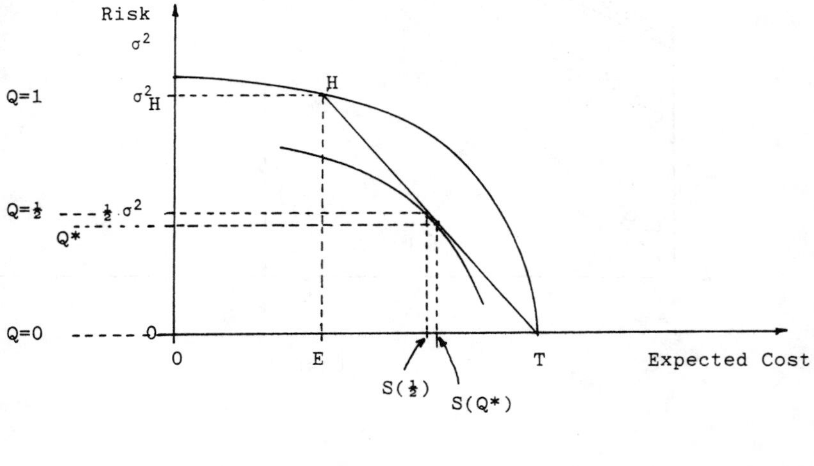

Following Figure 4, Figure 13 shows the client's indifference curve, IT, that passes through the points H and T corresponding to alternatives of a cost reimbursable contract with expected cost E and fixed price contract of value T. Risk sharing agreements involving a payment M with Q between zero and one, lie on the straight line HT. Any such option is preferred to either the fixed price contract of value T or the cost reimbursable contract of expected value E. The most preferred risk sharing agreement is at Q = Q⋆ where the straight line HT is tangential to an indifference curve, but Q⋆ is unlikely to equal 1/2 owing to asymmetry in the indifference curves.

Figure 14 Risk Sharing From the Contractor's Perspective

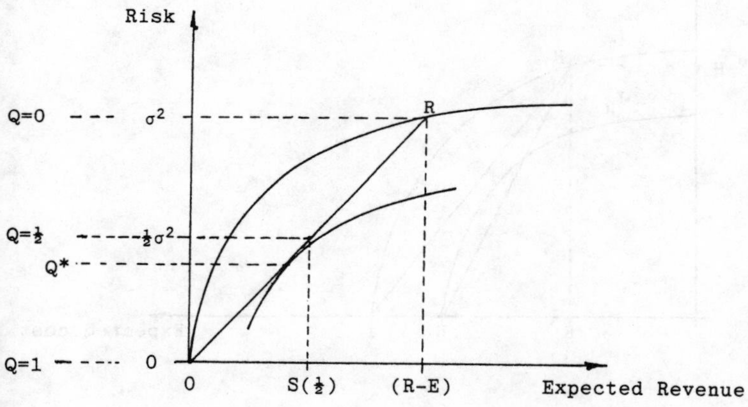

Figure 14 shows the corresponding position for the contractor who exhibits similar risk aversion. As for the client the contractor prefers any risk sharing agreement involving a payment M with Q between zero and one. Any such option is preferred to either a fixed price contract of value R = T or a cost reimbursable contract of expected value E. If the shape of the contractor's indifference curve IR is the same as the client's (in addition to R = T) the optimum risk sharing arrangement will correspond to Q⋆ for the client. In general the optimum points will be different for the two parties.

Only in the special case where both client and contractor exhibit constant risk aversion, and the indifference curves of Figures 13 and 14 correspond to straight lines, will a risk sharing contract not be preferable to a cost reimbursable or fixed price contract for both parties.

For a fixed price or cost reimbursable contract to be preferred to a risk sharing contract, the indifference curves of Figures 11 and 12 must be convex rather than concave, contrary to the basic assumptions of rational decision taking discussed earlier.

Figure 15 Risk Sharing when Contractor More Willing to Accept Risk

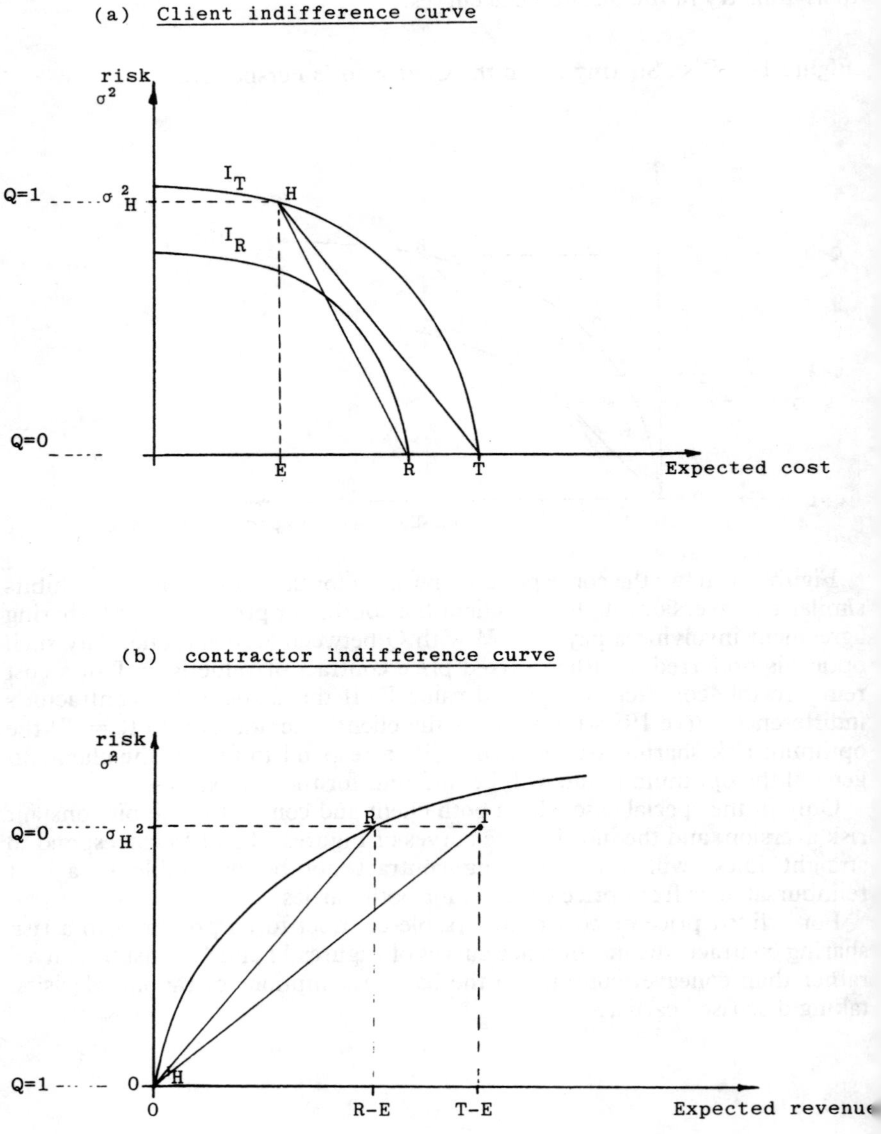

Contractor more willing to accept risk

Figure 15 illustrates the position where the contractor is more willing to accept risk than the client, so that R is less than T.

In the absence of risk sharing, both parties would agree to a fixed price contract of value R as indicated in Figure 7(a) (point R in Figure 15). However the position of both parties is improved with risk sharing. In particular, Figure 15(b) shows that the contractor would prefer any risk sharing arrangement involving a payment.

$$M = QC+(1\text{-}Q)[(1\text{-}Q)K+QE]$$

where K = R and Q lies between zero and one.

The extent to which the client also prefers a risk sharing arrangement depends on the shape of the indifference curve through point R, I_R. In particular risk sharing is not preferred for some values of Q and K = R only if the slope of I_R at point R is less than $\sigma h^2/(R\text{-}E)$. If risk sharing with K = R is preferred at all, it is confined to lower values of Q. (If I_R intersects the chord HT, risk sharing with K = T may be preferred by the client for some Q to a fixed price contract V = R. In this case the client would prefer risk sharing with K = R.) In all cases the contractor would prefer risk sharing with K = T, but the contractor would remain ignorant of the size of T unless it was revealed by the client in negotiations.

Figure 16 Risk Sharing when Client More Willing to Accept Risk

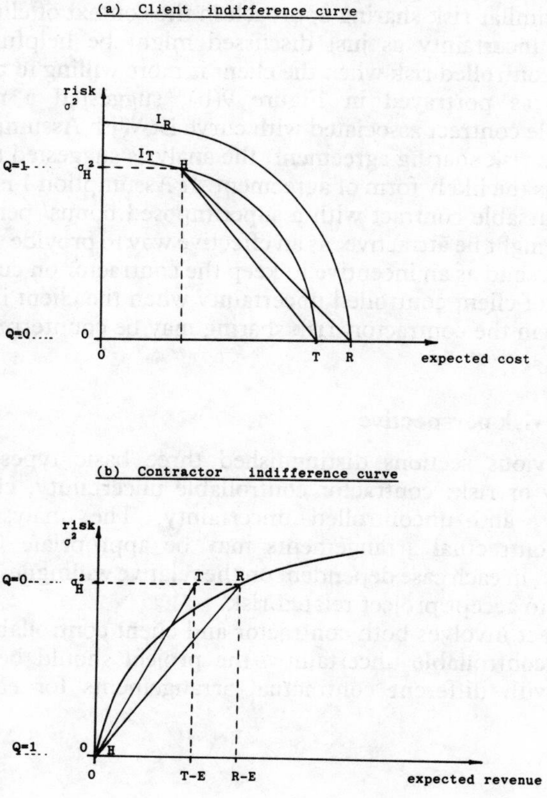

Client more willing to accept risk

Figure 16 illustrates the position where the client is more willing to accept risk than the client, so that T is less than R.

In the absence of risk sharing both parties would settle for a cost reimbursable contract as indicated in Figure 7(b) (point H in Figure 16). However, the position of both parties is improved with risk sharing. In particular Figure 16(a) shows that the client would prefer any risk sharing arrangement involving a payment M with K = T where Q lies between zero and one. The contractor will also prefer such a risk sharing arrangement to a cost reimbursable contract for higher values of Q, but the precise range of preferred risk sharing arrangements will depend on the shape of the contractor's indifference curve. Additionally, the contractor would prefer any risk sharing arrangement with K = R to risk sharing with K = T, a cost reimbursable contract, or a fixed price contract of value R. However, the client would prefer any risk sharing arrangement with K = T to risk sharing with K = R, and negotiation of a risk sharing arrangement with K = T and high Q value should be possible.

This analysis suggests that the implications of the initial model may be misleading: if uncertainty is uncontrolled, both fixed price and cost reimbursable contracts are inefficient. Sharing the uncertainty is always preferable, unless one party is so much more willing to take risk than the other as to make the other's appropriate share too small to be worth accounting for. It should also be noted that this general conclusion is not dependent on Assumption 3 in Table 1, that the client and contractor have a shared view of project cost uncertainty.

Using a similar risk sharing approach in the context of client or contractor controlled uncertainty as just discussed might be helpful. For example, contractor controlled risk when the client is more willing to take risk than the contractor, as portrayed in Figure 9(b), suggested a need for a cost reimbursable contract associated with curve B. With Assumption 1, *i.e* in the absence of a risk sharing agreement, the analysis suggested that a fixed price contract was the likely form of agreement. If Assumption 1 is dropped, then a cost reimbursable contract with a superimposed bonus/ penalty related to a target cost might be attractive, as an effective way to provide some appropriate risk sharing, and as an incentive to keep the contractor on curve B. However, in the case of client controlled uncertainty when the client is more willing to take risk than the contractor, risk sharing may be counterproductive.

A multiple risk perspective

The previous sections distinguished three basic types of project cost uncertainty or risk: contractor controllable uncertainty, client controllable uncertainty, and uncontrolled uncertainty. The analysis suggests that different contractual arrangements may be appropriate for each type of uncertainty, in each case dependent on the relative willingness of the client and contractor to accept project related risk.

If a project involves both contractor and client controllable uncertainty as well as uncontrollable uncertainty, the project should be split into three packages with different contractual arrangements for each set of risks.

Considering risk in a meanvariance framework suggests that sharing uncontrollable uncertainty will be mutually beneficial to both contractor and client, being preferable by both parties to either pure cost reimbursable or fixed price contracts.

The case for risk sharing in respect of client or contractor controllable risk is less clear, highlighting the desirability of distinguishing between these three basic types of risk in negotiating contractual arrangements.

To the extent that individual sources of cost uncertainty independently contribute to each of the three categories, it may be appropriate to subdivide categories and negotiate different payment agreements for each major independent risk source. For example in the case of the uncontrollable risk category, different levels of risk sharing could be agreed for each of a limited number of major risks and all residual uncontrollable risks. This implies explicit recognition of project risks in the tendering procedure. To a limited extent this already happens in practice when a client undertakes to pay a lower fixed price if he agrees to carry a designated risk via cost reimbursable in respect of that risk.

In the procedure envisaged here, the client first identifies appropriate constituent groupings of project risks, constructing associated PC curves and identifying T values for each. The PC curve for the project as a whole is then obtained by combining the component PC curves. The total project PC curve together with the associated T value is used later for checking consistency and completeness of submitted bids rather than to determine a single payment method for the whole project. Tenderers are asked to submit for each group of project risks designated by the client, (a) fixed price bids (R values) and (b) the contribution to profit (fee) required if a cost reimbursable contract is agreed. In addition, tenderers might be required or choose to submit their perceptions of constituent risk PC curves to demonstrate the depth of their understanding of the project risks and to justify the level of bids, should these be regarded by the client as unusually low or high. Equally, a client might provide tenderers with the client's perceptions of constituent risk PC curves to encourage and facilitate appropriate attention to project cost uncertainties. If a spirit of co-operation and willingness to negotiate mutually beneficial risk sharing arrangements prevailed, the client and individual tenderers could exchange perceptions about constituent risk PC curves with a view to developing a consensus view of project risks. Such views expressed as PC curves would facilitate the negotiation of mutually beneficial risk sharing agreements without the necessity for the PC curves themselves to have any legal status in the contract.

One effect of this approach would be to further question the practice of accepting the lowest total bid, given in this approach by the sum of a contractor's constituent risk R values.

In assessing bids, the client would be concerned about the relative sizes of R and T values for each constituent risk PC curve. The contractor bidding with the lowest total sum of R values would not necessarily be the contractor with the most preferred pattern of R values.

Building up a bid

Within this procedure, consider how rational contractors ought to proceed, in theory, in the absence of information and decision cost. Each contractor ought to construct a distribution for contractor cost reimbursable an appropriate contribution to profit, a PC curve, as illustrated in Figure 6. It can be argued that any contractor does so, implicitly if not explicitly, with a similar argument applying to the following.

In relation to each value of C on the PC curve, each contractor should have specified an associated set of probability distributions which define the extent to which the contractor is planning to depart from all implicit and explicit performance specifications. A separate distribution is required for each performance specification. Where these departures will reduce the contractor's costs, and where they will involve claims payable to the client or legal fees borne by the contractor, these costs and their associated probabilities ought to be reflected in the PC curve.

In relation to each value of C on the PC curve, each contractor should specify an associated probability distribution which defines additional revenue obtained via claims less associated legal costs. Strategic and tactical choices underlying the PC curve ought to reflect this claims distribution.

All effects of importance other than direct costs and revenues associated with all these cost and revenue distributions should also be considered, measured and related to a probability distribution, like impact on reputation which may have longterm profit implications. Strategic and tactical choices underlying the PC curve ought to reflect these distributions.

In relation to each possible bid value, each contractor should assess the probability of winning the contract, based on that contractor's perception of all other contractor's PC curves, all associated curves, and how they will use those curves. This distribution, when combined with the contractor's PC distribution and extra revenue via claims distribution, provides an extra profit/loss distribution for each possible bid value. These distributions should then be considered, in conjunction with the distributions for all affects other than direct cost, like impact on reputation, for a series of possible bid values. A choice should be made considering the trade-offs between perceived chance of winning, the perceived distribution of extra profit/loss, and all effects other than direct cost, like loss of reputation. Apart from concerns like loss of reputation, the contractor will have to consider issues like how badly the work is needed, longer term marketing implications of success or failure to obtain the contract, how large an exposure to risk of bankruptcy is appropriate, and so on[14].

Assessing bids

Still within the proposed procedure, consider how a rational client ought to proceed, in theory, in the absence of information and decision costs. When assessing the bid from each contractor, the client should define an associated total direct cost probability distribution. A number of elements are involved, which need to be identified and integrated.

14 Stephen C Ward and Chris B Chapman (1988). "Developing competitive bids: A framework for information processing", *Journal of the Operational Research Society*, 39(2), pp 123-134.

The client's perception of that contractor's PC distribution is a starting point, but it needs to be transformed to reflect the client's legal costs in relation to claims and failures to meet specifications, rather than the contractor's legal costs. The costs of these failures to meet specification should be considered next. Such costs may be substantial, and may vary considerably from contractor to contractor. The separate distributions for each performance specification which underlie the PC curve will each need separate and joint consideration. The cost of additional revenue claims against the client by the contractor also needs consideration.

These distributions can be combined and the bid incorporated to obtain a probability distribution for total direct cost to the client including lost benefits from failure to meet explicit and implicit performance specifications. All effects on the client other than the total direct costs just considered will also need identification, measurement and related probability distributions, like impact on the client if the contractor goes bankrupt part way through a badly managed job. A choice between contractors needs to consider trade-offs between total direct cost distributions and distributions for all other effects.

Conclusion

The analysis described in this paper has considered the problem of risk allocation in a relatively simple framework ignoring many of the complexities of real bidding situations. Such a simplified analysis is useful because it clarifies problem issues and the nature of the information required if risk allocation is to be carried out in a rational and efficient manner.

As previously noted, much of the current difficulty with risk allocation stems from a failure to carry out this kind of analysis at an early stage. The analysis highlights the need for clients to consider project cost uncertainties explicitly and to identify T, the "equivalent" certain cost. Some may consider this information requirement to be too onerous, if not unrealistic, even though the initial model at least merely formalises what must already be for many clients an intuitive process. However, experience with risk analysis of large engineering projects suggests that problems of information acquisition about project uncertainties are not insurmountable and can be cost effective. In practice the level of precision adopted could be varied to reflect the nature of the project, and the amount of information available. Moreover, uncertainty about the specification of PC curves or T (and R) values could easily be treated explicitly in the analysis.

An important feature of the analysis is the robustness of many of the conclusions. Depending on the relative sizes of T and R values, it may not be necessary to identify PC curves or T values with a high degree of precision in order to reach decisions about risk allocation. Most of the conclusions about the mutually beneficial nature of risk sharing only rest on the assumption of risk aversion; they do not require the specification of contractor or client indifference curves.

This paper has argued that contractors and clients need to undertake considerable detailed analysis of contract risks and contingencies. Contractors need to develop insuring skills, assessing risks, deciding which may and may not be accepted, distributing appropriate premiums over similar jobs and defining risks in precisely drafted terms[15]. It is clear that most contractors do not do anything like this. But implicitly they must do so if they are to fully appreciate the nature of their situation. It is clear that most clients are even less inclined than contractors to do anything like this explicitly. However, it is arguable that the bid price submitted by a contractor is unimportant relative to the other information considered above.

There are a number of possible benefits of using risk analysis and contingency planning as a basis for developing a contracting strategy:

- Potential contractors will have a much better idea about what work is or may be required as a consequence of uncertainty. This should reduce the chance due to ignorance, of low bids which are not subsequently enforceable, and increase contractors' willingness to take on risks;
- Contingency responses can be costed, and responsibilities and costs can be allocated, between the client and contractor, in a risk efficient manner. Hence the expected cost of the work and the necessary risk premiums can be minimised;
- Legal costs and other costs associated with disputes concerning additional revenue can be minimised. If uncertainty which can be controlled has associated risk appropriately allocated, and prior agreement is reached about critical contingency plans, there should be limited scope for disputes;
- A more effective and less confrontational approach to departures from performance can be made part of the contract, with direct and indirect benefits;
- Client or managing contractor control of contractors can be made more effective and efficient without being excessively intrusive.

These benefits will have to cover additional pre-project legal and other contracting costs, but there are good reasons to argue that they ought to do so. Indeed, the net savings may make such contingency planning worthwhile purely for contracting reasons, the other benefits being useful spin-offs. The only way to test this argument is to try it out, although the argument itself might be considerably developed if it is not already convincing.

As the best way to proceed is not intuitively obvious, there will be some additional costs associated with the learning process for the first cases. Such costs should be expected and allowed for when assessing the effectiveness of the result. They should not be so large as to discourage experimentation. As in the context of developing a method of risk analysis for oil companies, to allow them to use risk analysis models effectively and efficiently[16], a methodology for contracting which incorporates contingency planning will have to be developed. Once this has been done, further applications of the ideas and approaches should be relatively straightforward.

Further work is needed to develop the approach presented here in more complex, realistic situations. For example, the following need to be considered in more detail:

15 Abrahamson (1973) *ibid*.
16 Cooper and Chapman (1987) *ibid*.

- Methodology for identifying constituent risk cost curves including the treatment of time to build;
- The effect of percentage fees in cost reimbursable and other related payment methods;
- Situations where an appropriate contribution to profit rate for a cost plus contract has not been agreed;
- Situations where client and contractor do not have a shared view of cost uncertainties and the associated effects of optimism and pessimism about project costs;
- Consideration of risks which are controllable to some extent by one or both contractual parties;
- Situations where the performance specification is incomplete, not fully enforceable, and may be expensive to enforce partially . In these situations claims will be made for works at variance with the contractor's understanding of the project specification;
- The pricing of risk by clients and contractors, that is factors which determine T and R values. In particular, consideration of portfolio effects and the extent to which a market price of risk ought to apply (determined for example in a capital asset pricing model framework);
- Implications of the analysis for risk allocation in more complex forms of procurement, for example management contracting, and effects of subcontracting.

The authors believe the ideas presented in this paper are of sufficient interest to warrant further development, and would welcome constructive criticism on content or presentation.

Acknowledgment: This research was supported by SERC grant GR/E/48343 as part of the specially promoted programme in construction management.

8 Risk Assessment and Allocation Discussion and Debate

Plenary Session

In relation to risks in construction (Paper 3) Professor Abrahamson said that hard pressed employers were known to hold part of their construction budget in reserve for disputes and risks. Neither the industry nor its clients could afford to allow such a situation to continue. Where a constructional problem arose, the allocation of risk could result in the parties seeking to make a profit out of what had gone wrong. It was not unknown for parties to engineer a situation where such constructional problems would arise.

In regard to the resolution of disputes, Professor Abrahamson regarded litigation and arbitration as equally costly and suggested that conciliation might be adopted for resolving disputes at a much earlier stage. This would require an end to the hyper-adversarial attitude of lawyers, who tended to see problems only in the light of their own clients' possible advantage. Many conventional disputes tended to settle immediately before the start of a hearing, when massive costs had already been incurred. There was no reason in principle why settlement could not be reached at a much earlier stage. Conciliation together with an early and proper assessment of the documents would assist this process. Professor Abrahamson agreed that a much fuller breakdown of prices from a successful contractor, given soon after acceptance of his tender, would assist in the avoidance of disputes.

Mr. LLoyd's paper dealt with the subject of risks in relation to the product itself (Paper 4). Discussion focussed on whether a warranty of fitness for purpose required to be absolute or whether it should be dependent on proof of negligence. It was suggested that warranties and questions of fault should be separate. The consumer preferred absolute warranties, such as those given under NHBC contracts, where the party giving the warranty would still retain rights of contribution based on fault, against third parties. If warranties required negligence to be established, there was a case for arguing that the burden of proof should be reversed, placing it upon the warrantor to prove in his defence that some other party had been negligent.

Mr. LLoyd agreed that this suggestion would be attractive to consumers whose resources were less than those of the defendant. But many plaintiffs in the construction industry were not impoverished and liability based on fault would generally be covered by insurance. It was pointed out that changing the burden of proof could break the chain of liability and simply give the third party in breach the opportunity to align himself with the defendant in order to resist the plaintiff's claim.

A speaker from the National House Building Council pointed out that their schemes included an absolute warranty to be undertaken by builders and a conciliation service. NHBC contracts provided for arbitration, but this was regarded as too like litigation and from 1989 conciliation was to become a condition precedent to arbitration.

There was discussion on the problems of defining for the purpose for which the building or works was required. The general purpose could be inferred from the circumstances of the project; but specific purposes could evolve even during the construction stage. Too early a definition could defeat the object of the warranty.

Working Party on Risks in the Method of Construction

Introducing Paper 5, Mr. Barber said he had approached the topic as a practising civil engineer. For the satisfactory outcome of a project the contract had to achieve reliability of price, quality and time, and it ought also to provide fairness between the parties. Fairness should not be treated in the abstract, but had to be based on realities. The distinction between a commercially acceptable risk and an unacceptable "gamble" was illustrated by the facts of *Mitsui*[1]. For a rock tunnel project, the employer had caused only a few bore-holes to be drilled. The conditions actually encountered resulted in increases in quantities which had the effect of doubling the construction period. Accepted tender margins in Hong Kong at the time were only of the order of five per cent, so that the risk was out of proportion to the margin. In similar vein, in the field of design responsibility, potential liabilities tended to be imposed on individual firms which were completely out of proportion to the fees received. All such liabilities should be covered by insurance. The overall contractual arrangements for a project ought to recognize the proper cost of insurance needed to cover claims, whether due to faults of design, materials, workmanship or supervision. What was needed was single project insurance, with rights of subrogation being waived.

As regards non-insurable risks, if contractors were to be treated as quasi-insurers, insurance law and practice might provide appropriate rules by analogy, for example:

- If the contractor is to bear a risk, that risk ought to be identified and the contractor given an opportunity to price it;
- All relevant information available to the employer ought to be supplied to the contractor prior to contract and ought not to be withheld;
- The basis of pricing should be on broad categories of risk, rather than related to small details;
- A contractor should not be expected to price certain types of risk which are more properly classified as gambles.

1 *Mitsui* v. *A-G Hong Kong* (1986) 33 Build LR 1.

Discussion on paper 5 concentrated on two issues: disclosure by employers in building contracts and single project insurance. It was proposed that, in regard to disclosure by employers, building contracts ought to be on an *uberrima fides* basis, by analogy with insurance. The intention was to move towards a situation where employers would be obliged to disclose all relevant information. Similarly, it could be argued that contractors had a right to expect full design information at tender stage. It was frequently the case that full design information did not become available until long after commencement of construction.

It was pointed out that an insurer under a contract to which *uberrima fides* applied had a right to disclaim for non-disclosure, even if the non-disclosure bore no relation to the claim. If applied to construction contracts, the principle would be that the employer would have to warrant the completeness and sufficiency of the information disclosed, and the contractor would be entitled to rely on it. The point was made that contractors often say that they require more information, but when a dispute arises, claim that they have encountered conditions which could not be foreseen. In the United States and in other Commonwealth jurisdictions, the courts have said that there is no duty to disclose, and that there is only a duty not to misrepresent. In a building contract, it was difficult to define what an employer was bound to disclose. There was support, however, for the view that the employer should not be permitted to avoid liability merely on the grounds that there had been no misrepresentation, and that there ought to be some positive duty regarding disclosure of information.

Further discussion took place on the question, if a duty to disclose were to exist, whether such duty should be absolute or based on fault. There was general support for the creation of a duty in the following terms:

that there should be a general duty of disclosure of information reasonably within the employer's knowledge which was material to the project, including its design and implementation.

It was considered that the creation of such a duty was necessary even where the contract contained a provision such as Clause 12 of the ICE Conditions, since under these Conditions employers sometimes felt inhibited from disclosing information which might subsequently be used as a basis for a claim.

On the question of single project insurance (SPI) the need could be said to arise from the disparity that may exist between the risk undertaken and the financial interest of the risk-bearer, particularly in the case of consultants; and also from the unco-ordinated nature of ad hoc insurance cover. As regards consultants, the current feeling was that potential liability might lead to over-conservative designs, which was not to the benefit of the client or the public. As regards contractors, the opposite point was made, namely, that compulsory comprehensive insurance might lead to cutting of corners knowing that insurance cover was available. In fact, it was pointed out, SPI was not generally available except for design.

The proposal was made that the construction industry, the professions and insurers should co-operate to consider whether it was viable to produce a comprehensive basket of insurance cover for whole projects. In relation to any particular project, it should be possible to identify whether the risk lay primarily in design (as with a novel type of structure) or in the construction (as with a well established design). One of the difficulties with SPI was the need for further independent checks which would involve both time and additional cost. It was recognized also that SPI would be less practicable for smaller projects.

Replying to the discussion, Mr. Barber said that premiums of the order of one to three per cent. on the cost of the project had been indicated for SPI cover.[2] This should be compared to the individual cost of professional indemnity insurance, where premiums were of the order of 0.25% to 0.50% of the project value. It followed that employers who chose to rely entirely on one level of PI cover were not paying the true cost, and this was reflected in the serious likelihood that a particular loss might not fall within the cover provided. If proper and adequate cover was to be provided employers must bear the true cost. The reluctance of insurance markets to provide the necessary long-term cover must be overcome and suitable arrangements for bringing such cover into effect had to be worked out.[3]

Working party on the concept of design

Opening the discussion on Paper 6, Mr. Cornes stressed that one major cause of dissatisfaction amongst employers arose from defects or deficiencies in the design procedure. Particular problems arose from insufficient co-ordination between various parties involved in the design. This could result in a situation where it was unclear where responsibility lay, for example, between management, supervision and control of the work. A second cause of dissatisfaction was inadequately prepared pre-contract and pre-construction information which could result in further work or re-work at a late stage with consequent delay and disruption. A third problem was dispute resolution procedures, which are often inadequately covered by contract documentation. In particular, it may be difficult or impossible to ensure that all those who may potentially be involved in a dispute are joined in the same proceedings or before the same forum. This arises from the difficulty of multi-party arbitration and inconsistent arbitration clauses.

The report prepared in 1987 by NEDO on behalf of the Building Economic Committee "Achieving Quality on Building Sites" made it clear that responsibility for increased costs, lack of co-ordination and delay could not necessarily be offloaded onto contractors. The report records the results of a survey of 50 sites of differing natures and suggests, at least in the case of quality problems, that design is more likely to be the cause of dissatisfaction than faulty construction work. Conversely, in other parts of the construction industry, for example the process and oil sectors, particularly in the United States, defined procedures existed to enforce design discipline. Such procedures required a designer to certify the design as complete before going out to tender, and a contractor might be required to certify that his bid complied with particular standards.

2 Report by Atkins Planning for Latent Defect Protection Insurance Committee.
3 See now report on Building Users Insurance against Latent Defects (BUILD) HMSO.

There was discussion concerning the proper cost of design. It was felt that design difficulties would be minimized if greater consideration were given to following established design procedures at an early stage. Attempts to economize on design fees was considered to be counter-productive in that a small saving in design costs involved a greater risk of increased cost at the construction stage, for example through the need to amend or finalize design details. There was a widespread although not unanimous view among the professionals present, that fee competition adversely affected the quality of design work. It was recognized that government policy and economic conditions both encouraged competition between designers. A representative of the PSA, however, said that the experience of the PSA was most fee competition did not adversely affect the quality of design work, and it also had the advantage of maintaining realistic pricing. There was some support for the view that clients were in a better position to know how much they could spend on design. It was considered that designers, in addition to tendering a price, should specify the approach they proposed to a particular project, so that the client would then be in a position to compare different offers and to make an informed decision as to the balance he wished to achieve between cost and quality.

It was agreed that design problems often arose from the insufficiency of pre-tender information. It would be in the best interests of the construction industry to learn to avoid such problems, but it was recognized that tendering contractors could not be expected to tell the employer that more time was needed before the work could be commenced. There was substantial agreement that new procedures should be developed to ensure that, at the date of invitation to tender, all design work necessary for tendering had been carried out. This could be indicated in the tender documents, for example, by the designer certifying both to the client and to tenderers, the adequacy of the information provided. The contractor's tender, programme and method statements could then be based on the adequacy of the information provided. A similar process could be followed in relation to the actual commencement of work.

As regards responsibility for design, it was agreed that contract documentation needed to identify more clearly where liability for various aspects of design lay. Any such liability should be created by contract so that the parties had no need to seek to establish liability in tort. It was felt, however, that this would be workable only if a clear line could be drawn between design and construction. It was felt that contractual responsibility ought not to be forced upon parties in respect of design features for which they had no practical responsibility or in which they had no interest.

In regard to co-ordination of different functions within the design team, there was general agreement that major projects too frequently proceeded without adequate identification of the parties responsible for co-ordination and supervision. The construction contract documentation should specify who is to take responsibility. Co-ordination was seen as crucial for the satisfactory progress of the work. Regarding supervision, it was generally thought desirable that the current system under JCT 80 (whereby architects are assumed to provide only periodic inspection rather than full supervision) ought to be reviewed. Opinions differed as to whether inspection should be the contractors' responsibility or whether there should be a person appointed for this purpose. There was substantial support for the view that a new style "Clerk of Works" within the contractual supervisory authority could provide a satisfactory answer, but there was doubt as to how far the authority of such a person could extend. The current role of the Clerk of Works is that of an inspector, and adequate qualification would be required to fulfil a full supervisory role.

In conclusion, the working party agreed that:

- It was important that those involved in construction should recognise the central importance of the design function. Attempts to economize should be discouraged as likely to lead to even greater problems.
- There was a particular need for fuller pre-tender information. To achieve this there should be greater concentration on design at an early stage in the project. One possibility was to have a certificate, on which tenderers could rely, to the effect that the design was sufficiently complete.
- There should be clearer contractual identification of responsibility for design, co-ordination and supervision.

Working Party Risk Theory for Contracting

Professor Chapman outlined the basis of Paper 7: first, that it was possible to construct a theory of risk and, secondly, the shape which such a theory might take. The working party then considered a number of difficulties that might arise in the implementation of the theory.

The paper suggested that both contractors and employers should bear appropriate degrees of risk and that the allocation of the particular risks should be agreed before the contract was made. However, current standard forms of contract were drafted in such a way that a party was encouraged, if an adverse risk did materialize, to seek by litigation or other means to shift the resulting loss to the other party. As a possible solution Professor Chapman suggested that the contracts should be drafted in such a way that it was made clear precisely what were the risks involved in performance of a particular contract, so that the chance of an entirely unforeseen risk arising was greatly reduced. For example, a contract might contain a number of priced items, the one to be applied depending upon the precise ground conditions discovered upon excavation. Many similar examples could be given. A finite list of variables would need to be drawn up for each contract or project, but experience indicated that the risks which materialized in practice were relatively few in number so that it should be feasible to construct a sufficient list of variables.

A further major difficulty lay in persuading employers of the benefit of accepting some risks under a construction contract. Reluctance might be due to policy decisions or simply misconception as to the supposed benefits of a fixed price contract. As a means of guarding against contractual risks, a fixed price contract was particularly unsatisfactory. The reasons for this were, first, because there was no way of telling precisely how much of the contractors price was assessed, effectively, as an insurance premium; and secondly, because the contract effectively compelled the employer to purchase insurance against all risks that might materialize, without knowing the premium.

Acceptance of the lowest tender for a fixed price contract necessarily involves placing the maximum risk on the contractor. This in itself involves a further risk in that the contractor has himself assumed more risk than he is properly able to bear, involving the danger of default or bankruptcy. Paradoxically, employers would take the view that the sort of risk that might cause a contractor to default was exactly the type of risk that they did not wish themselves to bear. Logically, such risk ought to be one that the employer takes, and controls or reduces in such manner as he chooses. For example, the risk of adverse ground conditions is peculiarly within the employer's control since he must decide on the appropriate level of investigation and therefore of uncertainty.

A third perceived difficulty was that the theory assumed a large degree of co-operation between contractor and employer before signing the contract. In practice, particularly in the context of competitive tendering, that might be difficult to achieve and too much to expect. However, a representative of a major oil company described their approach to this particular difficulty. The procedure adopted was to invite contractors to submit bids for a particular contract and at the same time to submit comment on the proposed terms of contract. Contractors submitting bids were thus invited to identify particular terms which they regarded as (*a*) completely unacceptable (*b*) acceptable, but only at a price. The effect of this procedure was two-fold: first, individual contracts might be amended to reflect a risk allocation more acceptable both to employer and contractor; and secondly, the standard form of contract used by the company could be amended to reflect the preponderance of views of tenderers over a period of time.

The conclusions of the working party were, first, that it was essential for the construction industry to grapple with the problem of risk, however complex in theory that might seem. Secondly, it was necessary to identify a method of measuring risk so that parties could be in a position to identify particular risks being undertaken, and to provide for them financially in a more precise manner. Thirdly, it was essential for contracts to contain incentives to both parties to minimize risks. Professor Chapman's theory provided one means of achieving this. Fourthly, current standard forms of contract tended to refer to risk obliquely. There was no good reason for this, and the contract ought clearly to address the question of risk, its allocation, and the incentives to both parties to minimize the impact of risk.

Part III

Project Management and Quality Control

The Role of Contracts in Management 9

Martin Barnes

Synopsis

A summary of proposals for a new style of contract for engineering and multi-disciplined projects is presented. The objectives of these proposals include achieving flexibility in application and clarity and simplicity in drafting, as well as stimulating improved project management. The paper considers the relationship of contracts to project management together with the other objectives of the New Style Contract.

Introduction

Managers of projects often adopt the attitude exemplified by the policy of keeping the contract in the drawer, only to be taken out if co-operative relationships break down and the prospect of major disputes has to be confronted. The opposite view, now increasingly widely held, is that a modern construction contract could itself be a force stimulating good relationships, effective management and a reduction in the incidence of disputes. Instead of being kept in the drawer, it could be the core of the management procedures used on the project, implemented every time a significant decision influencing the management of the work has to be taken which involves more than one of the parties.

Few forms of contract yet accommodate this approach. No standard form yet does so but this may soon change. In 1986 the Institution of Civil Engineers commissioned preparation of a specification for a New Style Contract which was to have the characteristic, *inter alia*, of stimulating good management of projects. The Council of the Institution of Civil Engineers, having consulted interested parties and canvassed opinion about the specification of New Style Contract, decided in June 1988 that drafting should go ahead. Completion of the new standard form is due in 1989.

The specification for the New Style Contract for engineering and multi-disciplinary projects was designed and produced for the Institution of Civil Engineers by Martin Barnes Project Management with help from Dr. John Perry of UMIST.

The objectives of the new style contract are to achieve the following :

Stimulus to good management

The new style contract should embody responsibilities for the parties to a construction contract and procedures for them to use which collectively have a major influence towards good management of the project. The result should be greater efficiency and economy of the work carried out by engineers, contractors, sub-contractors and suppliers and more frequent achievement of the employer's objectives for the completed project in terms of its performance in use and completion on time and within budget.

Flexibility

The new style contract should be applicable to any type of engineering or construction project whether carried out in the United Kingdom or overseas. It should permit design work to be carried out by the contractor to any extent up to full design and build. It should embody the newer contract strategies such as management contracts, target cost contracts and cost-reimbursable contracts.

Clarity and Simplicity

The new style contract should be arranged and expressed simply and clearly so that :
It is easy to learn and to understand
It generates little dispute
It can be used easily by people outside the United Kingdom.
It can be administered by engineers/managers with only occasional help from lawyers.

The summary of the specification of the new style contract which follows includes information about :

- The principles of engineering contracts and project management which have been adopted in the design of the new style contract;
- The techniques and procedures which have been designed to provide the required flexibility, stimulus to good management, clarity and simplicity.

The appendices contain a full schedule of the clauses in the new style contract and examples of clause function statements. Extracts from the schedule of contract data, one of the devices introduced to give effect to the flexibility, clarity and simplicity objectives of the new system, are also reproduced.

The need for a New Style Contract

For many years model forms of contract have dominated the management practices of the British engineering and construction industries. As recently as ten years ago, the dominance of these forms of contract could have been expected to have continued in perpetuity within the United Kingdom and in areas of British influence overseas. Since that time, this situation has changed dramatically. The principal changes have been:

- Employers are using a wider range of contract strategies, including management, design and build and target cost contracts. Using these strategies, the responsibilities of the parties, the allocation of risks and the methods of payment may differ significantly from those embodied in existing model forms. Collectively developed model forms of contract for these new approaches do not yet exist.

- Proliferation of a widening variety of forms of contract for specialized sectors of construction and engineering has gathered pace steadily. The initiators of each new document are clearly well-intentioned, but the effect of their activity is to require practitioners in the construction and engineering professions and industries to familiarize themselves with a variety of contracts of different styles, comprehensiveness, precision and commercial sensibility.

- The international engineering community is now much more broadly based as to culture and legal and commercial systems. The erstwhile British system is no longer accepted as the norm and both its principles and its details are being questioned. New initiatives from within the United Kingdom must be seen to have international relevance and application.

- An unwelcome proportion of contracts are affected by contractual disputes between the parties. These make co-operative management and attention to unexpected problems difficult.

- Research into the effect of different allocation of risks in construction contracts has shown that this is a principal factor governing the influence achieved by different forms of contract. Better understanding of risk now enables conditions of contract to be designed which strengthen motivation to manage particular aspects of the work well.

- The traditional separation of design from construction has been questioned and has been discarded for certain types of project. Merging design and construction can help to meet the increased pressure from employers to complete work quickly. Also, it is said that, only if the contractor has himself influenced the design of the works are the best methods of construction likely to be used.

- The boundaries of the engineering disciplines have become less clearly marked. This has led to greater awareness of the differences between managerial practices in the various sectors and to questioning of the practices formerly used only within the boundaries of particular sectors.

- The science of project management has achieved wider acceptance and more effective application. This has raised expectations for the successful outcome of engineering projects. New conditions of contract can embody requirements which stimulate more effective teamwork, planning and foresighted decision making. They can also shift the emphasis from having carefully designed procedures for working out how much extra the contractor is to be paid if things go wrong towards arranging matters so that the likelihood of things going wrong is reduced.

- Management contracting has hugely increased its penetration in the building industry. The main advantage of the system is that it is more robust than the conventional when dealing with the unexpected. The growth of the system within the building industry suggests strongly that it has advantages which could also be obtained in engineering projects. This has been demonstrated in many process plant and offshore projects. Management contracting can have particular advantages in multi-disciplinary work and in work in developing countries.

The combination of all these factors makes now the opportune time for a new approach to conditions of contract to be defined and for a new standard form to be drafted.

The benefits to be obtained from producing an improved contract and taking it into use are considerable. Employers stand to benefit from achievement of more rigorous targets for their projects. Consulting engineers stand to gain from more efficient administration of projects and greater scope for applying their technical skills to their work. Contractors stand to gain from more economic construction and greater scope for applying their technical skills. All will benefit from the reduced incidence of disputes. The British engineering professions and industry will benefit from being masters of an up to date and effective management and contractual technology for use throughout engineering generally in the United Kingdom and world wide.

Objectives of New Style Contract

Flexibility

The new style contract should be usable for any of the following:

- Contracts involving any combination of engineering and construction disciplines;
- Contracts to be carried out either in the United Kingdom or elsewhere;
- Large and small projects;
- Contracts with design carried out by the contractor either entirely, in part or not at all;
- Management or traditional main contractor contracts;
- Cost-reimbursable or target cost contracts;
- Contracts with or without bills of quantities;
- Multiple contractor and single contractor projects;
- Contracts with the role of the engineer adapted to fit the employer's requirements for the particular project;
- Contracts with the allocation of risks adapted to suit special circumstances.

Stimulus for good management

New provisions are required which will motivate each of the participants to manage their own contribution well and in accordance with modern principles and practices of project management. The intention is that use of the new style contract will lead more frequently to achievement of the employer's objectives for each project in terms of its ultimate quality and performance, its cost and its completion time. It is also intended that it should be possible to set more rigorous targets for these objectives with greater confidence in achieving them.

Clarity and simplicity

The wording of the contract is to be clear and effective and as brief as these constraints permit in order that:

- The incidence of disputes founded upon uncertainty about the meaning of the contract is minimised;
- Translation of the contract and use of it by people accustomed to languages other than English are made easier;
- Training of engineers and others who will use the contract is made easier;
- The necessity to seek advice and help from lawyers in the administration of contracts is diminished.

At this stage, drafting has been confined to the proposed structure and functions of the new conditions. The clause function statements, examples of which are given in Appendix 2, are intended to be the starting point for drafting of the clauses themselves. However, it may be possible for the function statements to become the actual clauses.

The significant advantages of this systematic approach are :

- The document will have very much stronger logic and consistency than other, older standard forms
- Drafting the clauses will be made very much more straightforward by the existence of a clearly stated and agreed function for each clause.

Characteristics of the New Style Contract

Flexibility

The measures adopted for applying the new style contract to the range of situations listed as flexibility objectives are of three types.

- Clauses in the contract which are to be used for all situations are called core clauses. Other clauses used in only some of the situations are called optional clauses. For example, most of the clauses describing the roles of the participants are core clauses. Those which set out how the contractor is to be paid are optional clauses as are the clauses only needed when the work is carried out outside the United Kingdom.

- The situations which are not discrete but gradations between extremes are catered for by core clauses. For example, clauses are included which assume that some design work will be carried out by the contractor and that some work will be sub-contracted in the general case. Both groups of clauses are worded so that they can accommodate intermediate gradation between the extremes, *i.e.* any amount of contractor design from almost all to almost none and any amount of sub-contracting from all to none.

- A Schedule of Contract Data is used which allows parameters to be set for the particular contract which tune it to the required circumstances. For example, if target cost share formula co-efficients are set in the Schedule of Contract Data so that very little share is allocated to the contractor, the contract becomes almost a cost-reimbursable contract. If the co-efficients are set so that most of the share is allocated to the contractor, the contract requires almost a full commitment to price from the contractor.

In combination, these methods produce a very simple, robust and easily understood arrangement for achieving flexibility. A remarkably small amount of text and small number of options can achieve applicability to a full range of situations.

Users of the new style contract must decide upon the combination of blocks of clauses which will make up the version of the system they require and identify the combination they have chosen in the Schedule of Contract Data. The reference to the conditions in the schedule is simple. It might comprise, for example, a statement that the conditions of contract are the Core Clauses and the Clauses for Options 1, 4, 10 and 12 of the New Style Contract. The new style contract has been planned as a single document which allows for use of a variety of contract strategies. Publication of separate forms for each contract strategy can be considered. Whatever is decided later, the contracts used in different situations will be entirely consistent in their provisions, style and wording, whether printed separately or in a composite document.

The necessity for ad hoc special conditions should arise very seldom. As the new system is so flexible, they should be necessary only for particular contracts where either a local legal, commercial or statutory provision so dictates or where the work included has a quite distinctive requirement which cannot be covered by the Specification or by a special risk allocation clause. Special conditions should not be introduced to the published core and optional clauses merely in order to impose harsher trading conditions upon the contractor.

The new style contract is intended for contracts which include all types of engineering installation. It includes, therefore, comprehensive obligations for design, testing and commissioning of mechanical, electrical and other functioning equipment installed within the contract.

Management

In the new style contract, stimulus to good management means good management by everyone contributing to the project, not just those contributing to construction. The conditions of contract can have a strong influence upon the activities of the employer, the engineer, the designers, the sub-contractors and the suppliers. Examples of characteristics of the new style contract specifically designed to achieve good management follow.

Design changes

The conditions of contract govern the procedure for issuing variations to the work and making consequent changes to the contract price. These procedures have been modified in order to make it much more apparent when a variation becomes necessary which the designer could have avoided. He is, consequently, strongly motivated to avoid unnecessary variations. This example shows how the new style contract uses new procedures and control techniques to provide increased stimulus to good management by means of changes to motivation rather than new sanctions.

Tender information

The new style contract contains some options which assume a firm initial commitment to a price by the contractor (measure and value, lump sum) and some which do not (target cost, management contract and full cost-reimbursable). For the firm price options, it is assumed that a complete statement of what the contractor will be required to do will be made when tenders are invited. This is a fundamental factor in the pursuit of improved management of projects. Ever since mechanisms were introduced into contracts making it possible to invite tenders without making a complete statement of what the contractor was required to do, their misuse has grown. The task of the designer is not to do only enough design to get a tender, it is to make a complete (but not necessarily final) statement to the tenderers of what they are to be asked to construct.

This is a reversion to a very simple principle. When the main contractor is required to commit himself to a price which is complete, the information given to him on which to base the price must also be complete. It should be possible for the contractor to construct the works without further instruction, unless either the employer instigates changes or unforeseen events necessitate changes. Changes of these types will occur but they will be dealt with as changes to a previously complete statement of what the contractor had undertaken to do. Consequently, any instructions to contractors which are merely statements filling in previous gaps in information or clarifications of requirements previously only vaguely expressed are treated as variations. These variations may or may not justify increased payment to the contractor and extension of time.

Control by the Employer

Engineering projects are managed most successfully when the employer makes an appropriate contribution to the management decisions. Under the new style contract, the engineer is the employer's project manager and it is one of his jobs to alert the employer to impending decisions which the employer should take himself. The engineer must also ensure that forecasts are available to the employer to enable him to make a sound decision.

The new style contract stimulates this aspect of good management in a number of ways. For example, it provides for forecasts of both the cost and time effects to be to hand at points of decision by the employer such as whether to make a particular change and whether to accelerate the work.

Formerly non-standard arrangements, such as target cost and management contracts, are included in the system so that the Employer is able to select contracting arrangements which allow him to exert closer control of the work if necessary.

Co-operation

Co-operation between the organizations making up the project team is essential if the assaults of the unexpected are not to throw the project severely off course. Most projects, even those managed with no particular professionalism and which use traditional contracts, start off with an expectation of success and an intention on the part of employer, designers and contractors to co-operate. Many of the projects which become management failures do so because the early intention to co-operate is just too fragile to survive the real pressures caused by the unexpected events and the tendency of the members of the team to react to them self-interestedly.

The new style contract seeks to remedy this by strengthening the incentives upon the participants in the project to maintain co-operation right through to the end and by including procedures and "checks and balances" which make it easier for them to co-operate. The most obvious example is the early warning system. This is a very practical procedure for ensuring early joint consideration of foreseen problems. The contract includes provisions designed to motivate the contractor to participate in the early warning procedure fully and effectively.

The system also requires management meetings to take place at which the business is to organise the future, not to review the past. Reporting upon the disappointments of the past and allocating blame for them does not benefit the conduct of the remaining work. Making good decisions about the remaining work in the light of recently acquired knowledge is much more purposeful and stimulates co-operation. The new procedures are designed to ensure that the parties to the contract generate and are obliged to exchange the information needed for this style of management.

Tender programme and planning

In the new style contract, the need for a comprehensive, realistic and up-to-date plan for the remaining work and for this to be communicated around the team in the form of a programme on paper is pervasive. When a firm price contract is used, the contractor submits such a programme with his tender and later expands it and backs it up with method statements and resource plans. The contract is designed for the tender programme not to be binding upon the Contractor or for it to be prepared in great detail.

Whatever unexpected events befall or changes are made, the contractor reacts by reviewing the programme and plan for the remaining work and modifying it in the light of new decisions taken. In all this he is monitored by the engineer who is empowered by the contract to ensure that the process is carried out, although not empowered to interfere with decisions which should be made only by the contractor. The central role of the plan in management is reinforced. For example, when the option of using an activity schedule instead of a bill of quantities is used, the contractor earns payment by completing planned activities shown on the programme.

Personnel

It is fundamental to effective management that the key personnel working on projects should be appropriately equipped as to personal qualities, training and experience. Few appointments of contractors for major projects are now made without the employer checking the abilities and experience of the proposed key personnel. This practice is adopted in the new style contract. The contractor is not bound to employ the proposed key personnel. If any of them become unavailable, he may replace them with people of equivalent ability and experience.

Responsibility zones

The new style contract establishes the clearest possible perceptions of where the boundaries between the responsibilities of different members of the team are to be drawn for each project. For example, the specification issued by the engineer is used to establish a number of important boundaries. Perhaps the most important is the place where the boundary is to be drawn between design carried out before the contractor becomes involved and design to be carried out by the contractor. The system relies upon the simple but novel rule that the technical statement in the specification of what the contractor is required to produce is the boundary. All further design decisions required to convert this statement into a constructable design are by definition to be taken by the contractor, his sub-contractors or his own design specialists.

Nominated sub-contractors and suppliers

The new style contract does not provide for any sub-contractors or suppliers to be nominated. This change is made in order to eliminate the harmful effect upon the management of projects which shared responsibility for choosing sub-contractors and for controlling their activities and payments produces.

For example, contractors will have total responsibility for choosing who should do the work in their contracts (which will make control and co-ordination easier), incompatibility between nominated sub-contractor's commitments and those of main contractors will be eliminated, and the employer will not carry responsibility for delays by nominated sub-contractors, for replacing defunct nominated subcontractors and for paying them preferentially.

The quid pro quo for these improvements is that a direct contract must be used when selection by the employer of a specialist who is to do part of the work is absolutely essential. This transfers responsibility for co-ordination at the interface between the main contractor and the specialist to the engineer.

Payment mechanisms

Using new style contract, payment will normally be based upon an activity schedule, not a bill of quantities. An activity schedule is a schedule of the activities comprising the work in the contract with a price shown against each one. It is used as the basis for assembling a tender by the contractor and subsequently for assessing interim payments and valuing changes and variations. It differs from a bill of quantities in two main respects. Remeasurement of quantities is required only for variations. The breakdown of the contract sum is into separate sums each associated with a design, manufacture, supply, construction or commissioning activity. Interim payments comprise payment for completed activities. Variations are valued by altering the lump sums for varied activities and by adding or deleting activities for additional or deleted work. The activity schedule is supported by a programme which includes a method and resources statement. It may also include quantities in order to simplify valuation of variations.

Relating payment to activities provides a key stimulus to contractors to prepare the schedule in enough detail to secure a satisfactory cash flow. For example, if the contractor wishes to be paid for materials on Site, he must show delivery of the affected materials as separate activities on the schedule.

An advantage of the arrangements for improved management collectively will be that contractors will benefit from improvements they are able to make in the efficiency of their construction operations and in their own management. So long as the majority of their work is obtained in competition, this should enable the firms which are good at doing construction and are innovative and enterprising in development of new construction methods to prosper by getting contracts at reasonable prices. The pursuit of efficiency in construction should become more rewarding in relation to the pursuit of additional payment than under current arrangements.

Clarity and simplicity

The presentation and drafting of the new style contract have the following characteristics :

- Simple language and commonly occurring words are used;
- Legal jargon is avoided wherever possible;
- There are no cross references between clauses;
- Identical phrases are used for matters which can be expressed similarly;
- The procedures are logically complete;
- Only provisions which are important or frequently needed are included;
- Contract specific data is in a separate schedule so that nothing has to be added to the text of the conditions;
- Clarity is given priority over fairness in minor matters where this avoids complex text which would itself generate uncertainty and contention;
- The definition and use of prime cost items is drastically simplified;
- Blocks of optional clauses are provided which are to be used in special cases, making it almost never necessary for Employers to have to draft non-standard clauses;
- Terminology which is common to all engineering disciplines is used wherever possible;

- The contractor's obligations under local law are not set out or paraphrased in the contract;
- Matters which are more effectively covered in the Specification are not included in the conditions.

Phrases like "in the opinion of the engineer" are almost entirely avoided. Instead, the duties of the engineer are set out clearly and there is a general right for the contractor to refer any of the engineer's actions to an adjudicator. There should be few such references as the functions of the engineer are expressed very precisely. For example, the circumstances in which the engineer should extend the completion time are listed specifically, not left to his opinion of what is fair.

As a result of their long evolution, existing standard conditions of contract have little remaining structure. Logical clarity can be restored by drafting from first principles. An example of this is provided by the arrangements proposed for dealing with the risks of foreseeable events which it is not intended that the contractor should allow for in his tender.

Seventeen types of event are identified in the ICE Fifth Edition which, if they occur, entitle the contractor to additional payment and sometimes to additional time. They are referred to in differently worded clauses spread unsystematically throughout the document and the procedures which they call into action are inconsistent. In the new style contract, one clause sets out how all such events are dealt with for adjustment of the contract price and one for extension of time. The events themselves are listed as compensation events. One such list is given as a core clause and other lists are given in those sets of optional clauses where they are required.

The style adopted for the function statements for the clauses in the new style contract is intended to be adopted in the conditions themselves. Semi-legal expressions familiar only to British professional and amateur lawyers have been avoided. Minor differences of tense and mode have been avoided so that users of the contract whose first language is not English are likely to understand the text relatively easily.

It is striking how the arrangement using blocks of optional clauses simplifies the conditions. For example, a number of the clauses can be used unaltered in more than one option, such as the clause defining actual cost which is used in both the target cost and cost-reimbursable options. The arrangement is so simple that many of the options require only one special optional clause.

The Role of the Engineer

In the new style contract the traditional role of the Engineer is seen in its four constituents. These are :

- Project manager
- Designer
- Supervisor of construction
- Adjudicator of disputes

The first three of these functions are carried out on behalf of the employer, the fourth is carried out independently.

In order to give the greatest possible flexibility, all the traditional constituents of the role of the engineer are retained but they are defined separately so that they can be allocated to different individuals or organizations however the needs of the employer for a particular project dictate. The role always to be designated to the engineer is that of the employer's project manager. Management of the project on behalf of the employer is the core of the engineer's role under the new style contract which should not be allocated to anyone else. The engineer does not, of course, interfere with the construction management responsibilities of the contractor such as responsibility for the choice of construction methods.

In current practice the role of designer may not be carried by the named engineer under the contract. Similarly, the engineer's representative (called the supervisor in the new style contract) is not always an employee of the engineer. These flexibilities are retained.

A number of advantages are obtained from regarding the engineer principally as the employer's project manager, not only as the designer. For example, the engineer is appointed for his managerial abilities not just for his design abilities. This will stimulate greater professionalism amongst engineers with respect to management and substantially strengthen the role of the engineer. Recent moves by some major employers to shrink the role of the engineer under traditional forms of contract can be effectively resisted when the new style contract becomes available for use. Their misgivings about the traditional role would not apply to the new style contract.

It remains the engineer's duty to manage the design process and to be fully conversant with the emerging design. The new style contract only makes it unnecessary for the engineer to have carried out the design himself.

The principal role of the supervisor is to monitor the contractor's performance for compliance with the Specification and drawings. The engineer is not empowered to delegate any of his responsibilities to the supervisor. This ensures that the full management of the project on behalf of the employer is, in practice, carried out by the engineer. The engineer should not be the most senior engineer in the organisation who is only nominally in charge. By ensuring that management responsibility is taken at the working level, the new style contract provides for young chartered engineers to develop as managers by carrying responsibility as the engineer on smaller jobs.

At this stage, the role of an adjudicator, whose function is only to decide disputes which arise in the course of carrying out a contract, is defined separately from that of the engineer. To use a separate adjudicator can be a significant contribution to reducing the incidence and severity of disputes. In many situations outside the United Kingdom the employer will regard this detachment as an advantage.

The Contractor's design responsibility

As the new style contract is to be used for non-civil engineering contracts, which characteristically involve some off-site fabrication or manufacture in which there is a contractor design element, it is essential that provision for contractor design should be made. It must also accommodate the extremes of contractor design responsibility such as full "design and build" and "design and manage".

The text of the new style contract will provide for the contractor to make design decisions and to take responsibility for them. These provisions will apply when the contractor is to take nearly all of the design decisions (as in a design and build contract). They will apply equally to when he is to take only relatively minor design decisions such as the positioning of construction joints in concrete (as in a conventional contract).

The definition of the extent of the contractor's responsibility for design in each case will be in the contract specification and drawings. Where the contractor is to do most of the design for a component of a project, the specification will be in outline, mainly stating the performance required of the component. If the contractor is to design the whole project, the specification will comprise only a statement of the performance required of the whole project. Where full specifications and drawings are supplied, the contractor has responsibility only for the remaining minor decisions.

The new style contract requires that the specification issued to tenderers should be sufficient to ensure that, if the design carried out by the contractor after appointment is in compliance with the specification, the resulting work will be satisfactory. It is not intended that tenderers should normally submit the results of design work with their tenders. Some outline design assessment may be necessary in order to be able to prepare an estimate, but tenderers should not be put to the significant expense of preparing detailed designs which may not be used if their tender is not successful.

Using the new style contract, contractors will often take responsibility for more of the design than they do at the moment. They will be free to subcontract their design responsibilities to specialist design firms if they wish. It will be necessary for contractors to insure their design liability or to satisfy themselves that their specialists carry such insurance. The total amount of design liability to be insured is not affected by the new system and the total cost of providing it, to be borne eventually by the employer, will not be increased.

Risk Allocation

If a risk is carried by a party to the contract, he is motivated to minimize its effect. For example, old-fashioned variation of price clauses took the risk of materials costing more than was expected off the contractor. He was then not motivated to buy materials as cheaply as he could and the cost of the work to the employer tended to increase. Modern formula-based price adjustment clauses leave the contractor with any benefit from buying materials cheaply and he is, therefore, motivated to do so. The new style contract is designed on this principle. It uses risk allocation to place motives towards good management of the project with the parties who are most likely to be able to respond to them beneficially.

For example, traditionally the contractor is assumed to have inspected the Site and carried out his own site investigation. This does not leave the employer with a strong motive to do enough site investigation to establish the effect of ground conditions upon construction cost. The new style contract says that the contractor is to assume that the ground conditions will be as they are described to him in the tender documents. Consequently, if only a minimal amount of site investigation has been done, the contractor is likely to base his price upon a wrong view of the sub-surface conditions he will experience. As this will increase the employer's risk of later programme delays and extra costs, the employer is now more strongly motivated to do enough investigation. This ensures that the contractor does not carry a very large risk which he can do little to shrink.

Another example is that the effect of variations upon the completion date and the price of the work is likely to be very much more unwelcome to the employer using the new style contract. This is achieved by ensuring that the full consequential cost of variations is paid to the contractor. The traditional basis of valuing variations using bill of quantities rates is discarded in favour of valuation according to the full effect of the variation upon timing and methods of work and upon the use of resources. The likely cost of a variation is intended to be made known to the employer before the variation is ordered. This is achieved by providing an incentive for the contractor to quote for variations in advance. This motivates the employer to ask for only those variations to be made for which the benefit to him is more than the full cost. This makes a contribution to the foresightedness and the climate of planning ahead which characterise effective project management and which are intended to be stimulated by the risk allocations built into the new style contract.

Similar provisions for valuing variations in advance are included in the improved system for management of building projects introduced by the British Property Federation in 1983. There was some doubt at the time that the motives built into the system for doing this would be strong enough. However, experience of the system in use has produced clear evidence that they are. The improvement in the management of variations using the BPF system has been striking and is just one example of the effect which a collection of measures designed to improve attitudes to management and co-operation generally can have.

Where the total amount of risk which would otherwise be carried by a contractor would be excessive, a contract providing for comprehensive reduction of his risk may have to be used. The target cost contract is the appropriate option within the new style contract. When none of the cost risk is to be carried by the contractor, the full cost-reimbursable contract option will be chosen.

Three types of risk of unexpected events are covered in the new style contract :

- Risks which are to be insured;
- Risks which lead to determination of the contract;
- Risks which lead to cost and time compensation to the contractor.

In each case a list of the events in the class of risk is given and a simple clause states the procedure to be followed should any of the listed events occur.

The events which the contractor is required to insure against are listed in the Schedule of Contract Data and are specific to each project. It would be possible to put some of these events in a core clause so that they became standard insurance requirements. The events which lead to determination of the contract are also listed in a core clause.

The events which entitle the contractor to cost and time compensation are called compensation events. Due to the pervasive inter-relationship of cost and time effects, all events outside the contractor's risk entitles him to extra time and extra payment. Events which are always to be compensated are listed in a core clause. Those which are compensated only when particular options are in use are listed in the optional clauses. Those which are specific to a particular contract are listed as special risk events in the Schedule of Contract Data. Normally no such special risk allocation will be necessary. Occasionally, however, relieving the contractor of a risk associated with the particular contract may be preferable to using one of the methods available for reducing the contractor's risk generally such as the target cost or cost-reimbursable contract options. The new style contract does not provide for allocation of special risks to the contractor.

Appendix 1: Schedule of Clause Function Statements

The functions and purposes of each clause in the new style contract are set out in the specification of the New Style Contract. The proposed clauses cover everything which is needed to provide for the options. Standard forms which have been checked to ensure that the coverage of the function statements is complete include those published by ICE, FIDIC, IChemE, IMechE, IEE and the management contract form used by a contractor who has specialised in this method of working for many years.

Only some examples of the function statements are given in this summary. The full specification includes the full set of 42 core clause function statements and 39 optional clause function statements covering all of the 16 options. Clauses for which full function statements are given in Appendix 2 are marked with an asterisk.

Core clauses

Definitions
Interpretation
Supervisor
Delegation
Communications
Confidentiality
Copyright

*Personnel
Subcontracting
Other Contractors
Insurance
Supply of Issued Information
Ambiguities
Variations

*Contractor's responsibility
*Approval of the Contractor's design
Third party approvals
Programme

Extension of the Completion Time
*Acceleration
Delays ordered by the Engineer

Management meetings
Early warning
Possession of the Site
Indemnities
Property
Access to the Site
Uncovering of Work
Discoveries
Tests
Completion
Correction of Defects
Uncorrected Defects after Completion
*Compensation Events
Prime Cost

Interest on overdue payments
Final account
Determination
Payment upon determination
Frustration
*Disputes
Procedure for disputes

Optional Clauses

Option 1 : Conventional Contracts (not target cost or cost-reimbursable)

Issued Information at Acceptance Date
Assessment of profit
Cost of Defects

Options 1 and 2 : Contract which are not cost-reimbursable

Definitions
Programme Submission
*Compensation for Variations
Payment before Completion
Adjustment item
Acceleration
Compensation events
Taxes

Option 2 : Target Cost Contracts

*Definitions
Fee
*Target Share

Options 2 and 3 : Target Cost and cost-reimbursable contracts

*Actual Cost
Cost of Defects
Accounts
Programme for Issued Information

Option 3 : Cost-reimbursable contracts

Definitions
Budget and programme
Payment before Completion

Option 5: Contracts using a Bill of Quantities

Bill of quantities
Provisional sums

Option 7 : Management Contracts

*Sub-contracting
Contractor's duties
Other contractors
Method Statement and Programme

Option 9 : Contracts carried out outside the United Kingdom

Language and law
Currencies

The following options require only one clause:

Option 4: Activity Schedule
6: Price adjustment for inflation
8: Management contractor's pre-construction services
10: Retention
11: Bonus and penalty
12: Completion in sections
13: Advanced payment
14: Bonds

15: Special conditions
16: Permanent plant

Appendix 2: Examples of Clause Function Statements

Core clauses

Personnel.
The Contractor is to employ either the personnel named in the Schedule of Key Personnel to carry out the functions stated in the Schedule or other personnel approved by the Engineer. The Engineer is to approve proposed replacement key personnel if their abilities and experience are not inferior to those of the personnel listed in the Schedule.

Contractor's responsibility.
The Contractor is to complete the design in accordance with the Issued Information and to construct the Works in accordance with the Issued Information and the Contractor's design approved by the Engineer.

Approval of the Contractor's design.
The Contractor is to submit drawings and specifications showing his proposed completion of the design to the Engineer. The Engineer is to approve the Contractor's proposed completion of the design if it complies with the Issued Information. The Engineer's approval does not reduce the Contractor's responsibility for his design. The Contractor is not entitled to compensation if the Engineer correctly disapproves his proposed completion of the design.

Acceleration.
If the Engineer decides that the remaining work is unlikely to be finished within the completion time and that there are no reasons for him to make an extension of time he may instruct the Contractor to revise his programme so that the work will be be finished within the completion time and to work to the revised programme.

When the Employer wants the Contractor to finish before the end of the completion time, the Engineer obtains priced proposals for achieving the necessary acceleration from the Contractor. If the Employer accepts these proposals, the completion time is adjusted accordingly and confirmed by both the Employer and the Contractor.

Compensation Events

The following are compensation events:

[Incomplete - the complete list is given in the full specification]

The Employer does not give access to a part of the Site by the Site Possession Date stated in the Schedule of Contract Data.

The programme shows requirements for issue of information or for obtaining licences or permits and any such requirement is not met.

The Engineer does not reply to a request by the Contractor to approve part of the Contractor's design within the period stated in the Schedule of Contract Data.

The Supervisor instructs the Contractor to uncover work which is found to have no Defects.

Ground conditions more adverse than those described in the information issued to tenderers are encountered or, if no description of the ground conditions was issued, adverse conditions are encountered which would not have been apparent from a visual inspection of the Site made immediately before tenders were due to be submitted.

Adverse conditions are encountered (other than ground conditions) which an experienced contractor would not have been expected to have foreseen.

The Engineer orders a suspension of work.

The Engineer instructs the Contractor to delay the start, progress or completion of an activity within the Works.

The Engineer instructs the Contractor following an early warning given by the Contractor.

The Special Risk Events set out in the Schedule of Contract Data are also Compensation Events.

Disputes

If either the Employer or the Contractor believes that a decision taken by the Engineer or the Supervisor was either outside the authority given to them by the contract or was wrongly taken, the decision may be referred to the Adjudicator.

Optional Clauses

Options 1 and 2 Contracts which are not cost-reimbursable

Compensation for Variations

The change in the Contract Price assessed by the Engineer for a variation is to be based upon a quotation given by the Contractor before the instruction to vary the work is given by the Engineer.

Where the urgency of varying the work would prevent a quotation being given and considered without delaying the work, no quotation is given and any variation instructed is treated as a compensation event.

Option 2 Target Cost Contracts

Contract Price

The Contract Price is the Target Cost plus the Fee.
Target share. The difference between the Target Cost and the Actual Cost is shared between the Employer and the Contractor in the ratios stated in the Schedule of Contract Data. The share is calculated for each payment certificate and either added to or deducted from the payment certified.

Options 2 and 3 Target Cost and cost-reimbursable contracts

Actual Cost

The components of Actual Cost are set out in the Schedule of Components of Actual Cost. The Fee is deemed to include all the Contractor's other costs.

Option 7 Management Contracts

Sub-contracting

All completion of design, construction and commissioning is to be carried out by sub-contractors at prime cost.

Acknowledgement

This paper is reproduced with the kind consent of the Institution of Civil Engineers.

The Control of Quality in Construction 10

Donald Keating

Synopsis

The paper examines the working of Quality Control on construction projects in theory and in practice. Practical methods work with good will on both sides but otherwise tend to fall down. The theoretical method does not work because there are rarely enough skilled clerks of works and the architect visits site too infrequently. The paper then looks at Quality Assurance and suggests possible long term benefits and limitations on its use.

Introduction

"Contractual arrangements, as such, have little effect on the quality achieved, but management structures have considerable influence" (Paragraph 2.2, Proceedings of the National Quality Assurance Forum for Construction, CIRIA Special Publication 50). The writer has much sympathy with this quotation. It illustrates the wisdom of those who founded this department that it should include management with law. However, the two cannot be separated. A legal framework is essential for good management. Ultimately it provides sanctions for bad building and, as human beings are fallible and are not wholly motivated by unselfish desire for the good, sanction for the bad has been found to be necessary in most aspects of life, including construction.

What is meant by Quality in a Construction Contract?

A rigorous and wholly satisfactory definition cannot be given, but the principle is clear. It is that aspect of the construction task which can be considered as separate from the duty, by whomsoever accepted, to produce something fit for its purpose.

As regards materials, the classic exposition in *Young & Marten Limited* v. *McManus Childs Ltd*[1] is the starting point. The facts illustrate the point. The experienced agent of the main contractor chose "Somerset 13" tiles to be fixed

1 [1969] AC 454.

by the sub-contractor. After fixing and exposure to weather, defects appeared which required the replacement of the tiles. Because of the choice by the main contractor, the sub-contractor was not liable for breach of the ordinary implied warranty of fitness for purpose but he was liable for breach of the implied warranty of good quality because the tiles, due to some unestablished defect of manufacture, were not fit as tiles. The House of Lords held that there was a close correspondence in construction contracts between the relationship of quality and fitness for purpose with that set out in the Sale of Goods Act.[2]

The Supply of Goods and Services Act 1982 must be considered. A full discussion of its effect would be lengthy, but a short note is required. Part 1 of the Act and certain other clauses came into operation on 4th January 1983; Part 2 on 4 July 1983. The Act does not apply to a contract made before the provision came into operation. Part 1 deals with contracts for the transfer of property in goods and applies whether or not services are also to be provided[3]. It applies, presumably, to Construction Contracts so far as the contractor supplies goods, the property in which is to be transferred to the employer. Part 2 applies to "a Contract under which a person agrees to carry out a service"[4]. It applies "whether or not goods are also - (a) transferred or to be transferred ..."[5]. Subject to certain exceptions[6], and express or implied exclusion[7], goods are to be of merchantable quality; this means that, "they are as fit for the purpose or purposes for which goods of that kind are commonly supplied as it is reasonable to expect having regard to any description applied to them, the price (if relevant) and all other relevant circumstances"[8]. As regards services, subject to express or implied exclusion[9], "there is an implied term that the supplier will carry out the service with reasonable care and skill"[10].

The definition of Merchantable Quality in the 1982 Act follows that in the Sale of Goods Act 1979 which differed in its wording from the Sale of Goods Act 1893 to which reference was made in the *Young & Marten* case; but the Court of Appeal[11], has held that the change in wording has not brought about any substantial change in the law. As regards the duty as to workmanship implied by Section 13 of the 1982 Act it closely follows the words of Lord Reid in *Young & Marten*,[12] "...it must be done with all proper skill and care". It seems that the Act is intended to follow the common law and, as regards Construction Contracts, has brought about no change of substance, but the caveat must be entered that the writer is unaware of any authority on the subject.

It therefore appears that subject to exceptional circumstances[13] the duty as regards quality of materials is absolute, but as regards workmanship is that of skill and care. Interesting questions as to the nature of the duty in respect of

2 Sale of Goods Act 1893, S.14.
3 S.1(3).
4 S.12(1).
5 S.12(3).
6 S.4
7 S.11.
8 S.4(9)
9 S.16
10 S.13
11 *Aswan Engineering* v. *Lupdine* [1987] 1 WLR 1.
12 *ibid*, p 465.
13 Consider *Gloucester County Council* v. *Richardson* [1969] 1 AC 480.

workmanship may arise where there are express requirements as to workmanship. No general rule can usefully be stated.

A defect of quality usually makes the product unsuitable for its purpose as illustrated by the facts of *Young & Marten*. It was, perhaps, for this reason that until *Young & Marten* it was thought that the correct analysis as regards quality and fitness was to treat the contractor's implied duties as one warranty. Lord Reid, in *Young & Marten,* with characteristic clarity pointed out that the two implied duties were separate. The significance is that the goods may be of merchantable quality and the workmanship have been carried out with reasonable skill and care yet the product may be unfit for its purpose. In such a case the contractor will not be under an implied duty as to fitness unless his judgement was relied upon in choice of the goods or nature of workmanship. Some commentators have suggested that Lord Scarman in *IBA* v. *EMI*[14] does not regard reliance as essential; but the passage referred to is obiter and in the context of a contract in which the contractor undertook an express liability of design.

It is to be observed that the British Standards Quality of Assurance Documents use the term "quality" in the sense of fitness for purpose. BS 4778, Section 4.1.1 states, "the totality of features and characteristics of a product or service that bear on its ability to satisfy a given need". This does not invalidate their various suggestions as to procedures but does make it necessary to consider some of them in detail where they presume a liability for fitness for purpose which in a Construction Contract may not exist.

Employers' Remedies for Defects of Quality.

This must be considered in relation to the position whether or not the works have been performed. Where the works have been performed the ordinary remedy is damages. The measure is, "... prima facie... the Plaintiff is entitled to such damages as will put him in a position to have the building for which he contracted unless the cost of reinstatement is wholly disproportionate to the advantages of reinstatement"[15]. Thus ordinarily the cost of reinstatement is the measure of damages and not diminution in value. The usual rules as to the date of assessment of damages and mitigation apply.

The remedy in damages may not always be considered satisfactory. By the time judgment is obtained the contractor may not be able to meet it, or meet it fully with costs. In any event proceedings are a time and energy consuming process. Further, there is frequently a loss of business whilst the works are put right which is rarely fully compensated by damages even in contract if they are recovered at all. As regards a private individual, loss of amenity is now recognised as a head of damage but the awards are modest. Prevention of defects is to be preferred to damages.

Theoretically where substantial defects are discovered during the course of construction and the works are exactly defined, specific performance of a duty to build in accordance with the Contract can be obtained[16]. No case is known

14 (1980) 14 Build LR 1, 47.
15 *William Cory* v. *Wingate Investments* (1980) 17 Build LR 104.
16 *Hounslow LBC* v. *Twickenham Garden Developments Limited* [1971] 1 Ch. 233 at 251.

where such a decree has been obtained. Save in an exceptional case it may be disregarded as a practical remedy.

Where the employer discovers defects during the course of the works but has no express powers under the contract in relation to such defects his position is unsatisfactory. He may threaten a claim for damages. If this does not work he may be tempted to turn the contractor off the site. Whether or not he can obtain an injunction is a matter of some doubt but if he has possession it is thought unlikely that an injunction can be obtained by a contractor requiring him to hand back the site. The great danger for an employer who turns a contractor off the site without benefit of an express forfeiture clause is that he, the employer, may be held guilty of repudiation of the contract and have to pay the contractor damages, even though the contractor may have been in breach. This is because in general mere failure of performance is not sufficient to amount to a repudiation. There must be a breach which goes to the root of the Contract[17]. It may be held that failure to conform with requirements of the Contract before completion is not even a breach, or a breach sounding in substantial damages[18].

If the breaches of quality by the contractor are so serious as to satisfy the tests for repudiation then the employer will, at common law, be justified in ejecting the contractor from the site. This is more likely to be the case when the defects are coupled with other breaches by the contractor. Thus in *Sutcliffe* v. *Chippendale & Edmondson*[19], it was said that the contractor's

> ".... manifest inability to comply with the completion date requirements, the nature and number of complaints of Sub-Contractors and [the Architects] own admission that in May and June the quality of work was deteriorating and the number of defects was multiplying, many of which he had tried unsuccessfully to have put right, all point to the truth of the Plaintiffs' expressed view that the Contractor had neither the ability, competence or the will by this time to complete the work in the manner required by the Contract".

Hence it was held that the employer was justified in ejecting the contractor from the site.

No doubt because of the difficulties of the common law most formal contracts contain express powers of forfeiture. For example, see Clause 27, JCT 80, Clause 63, ICE, 1973 Edition. The procedures of such clauses must be exactly followed or the forfeiture may be held to be wrongful and therefore amount to a repudiation on the part of the employer.

Preventing Defects of Quality

The traditional method is to inspect the works and, if persuasion is insufficient, to exercise, or threaten to exercise, express powers under the Contract. Thus forfeiture is catastrophic to the contractor (if the clause is well drawn) and the mere threat to forfeit usually has great effect; but forfeiture causes, inevitably, a measure of delay, sometimes substantial, and extra costs

17 See authorities discussed at pp 111-118 of the author's book on *Building Contracts*, 4th Ed. and Supp.
18 See *Kaye* v. *Hosier & Dickinson* [1972] 1 WLR 146 at 165.
19 (1971) 18 Build LR 157 at 161.

which the employer may never recover from the defaulting contractor and therefore is to be considered as a last resort. Other express remedies are usually available and, provided the defect has been discovered, are usually sufficient.

JCT 80 can be taken as an example. The employer is entitled to appoint a clerk of works to act as inspector under the directions of the architect and the contractor is required to afford every reasonable facility for the performance of that duty. The clerk of works can give a "direction" which is of no effect unless given in regard to a matter in respect to which the architect is expressly empowered to issue instructions and is confirmed in writing by the architect within two days of the direction being given. If so confirmed it is deemed to be an architect's instruction. On major contracts a clerk of works is usually appointed and, in many instances there are several clerks of works, sometimes merely to cover the physical space, sometimes to deal with particular aspects of the work such as mechanical and electrical. It is contemplated that the clerk of works will inspect regularly and report to the architect. If confident of his view that work or materials are defective he will give a direction corresponding to the instructions which the architect can give under Clause 8 in relation to work or materials and the architect will then confirm it. Theoretically this ought to work quite well. Post war experience has shown that it often does not.

The reasons why it has not always worked are not really matters for lawyers, but some thoughts can be ventured. Thus, by tradition clerks of works do not have independent professional qualifications and may not have sufficient expertise in specialist matters or sufficient weight of authority to deal adequately with contractors' senior managerial staff. Frequently employers are mean and do not appoint enough clerks of works so that there is inadequate inspection of large sites; and even though the clerks of works available exercise reasonable skill and care they miss defects.

If a clerk of works misses defects through lack of reasonable skill and care and the employer brings a claim in tort against the person he alleges to be liable, the employer's damages may be reduced because of the clerk of works' contributory negligence[20]. Since the decision of the Court of Appeal in *Forsikringsaktieselskapet Vesta* v. *Butcher*[21], it appears that the employer's damages may be subject to reduction for the clerk of works' contributory negligence even though the employer's claim against the Defendant was in contract, provided the Defendant's liability in contract was the same as his liability in the tort of negligence independently of the existence of any contract. Such contributory negligence on the part of the clerk of works may in theory give rise to a claim for negligence by the employer against the clerk of works. In practice it is thought that clerks of works do not insure. It may be advisable for employers (at their expense) to require their clerks of works to insure.

A further matter to be considered in relation to the current system of inspection is the "itching palm" referred to by Lord Denning, MR in *Lewisham Borough Council* v. *Leslie*.[22] Lord Denning was at pains to state that he did not suggest that it was the position in the case before him but some

20 See *Kensington & Chelsea Health Authority* v. *Wettern Composites & Others* (1984) 31 Build LR 57.

21 [1988] 2 All ER, 43 criticized by Michael J. Smith, (1988) 4 Const LJ 75.

22 (1978) 12 Build LR, 22 at 28.

people are unkind enough to think that the occasional blind eye may, for reward be turned deliberately.

The ICE Conditions make provision for a resident engineer. JCT 80 makes no provision for a resident architect although there is no reason why the Contract should not be amended, and in any event, even if it has not been so amended it would be difficult for a contractor to object. If there is no resident architect empowered to exercise the powers of the architects under the Contract, in practice the operation of the system of inspection may be difficult. This is partly because of the English system in relation to building contracts. Despite references to "superintendence" architects do not give constant attendance upon the site and indeed visit it quite rarely. Their scale of fees reflects this in that it provides that most of the fees are payable before works commence. In the absence of a resident architect it is thought that two features sometimes occur. First, there may be delay in the clerk of works obtaining clear instructions from the architect in respect of defects which he has discovered. Secondly, a tendency sometimes develops for the clerk of works' "directions" in practice to assume the status of architect's instructions. Contractors then seek to rely on such directions both for payment of extra money and also by way of defence in respect of defective work. Ultimately they may seek to set up claims or defences arising by way of estoppel, waiver or even variation of contract. Sometimes the parties agree that the clerk of works shall issue what are termed Site Instructions. With goodwill and commonsense this can work quite well but these attributes are not always present.

The architect has ample powers of control under JCT 80. They arise under Clause 8 in respect of defective work and materials, inspection and tests. Clause 27 provides for determination by the employer. One of the grounds is the contractor's refusal or persistent neglect to comply with a written notice from the architect requiring him to remove defective work or improper materials or goods and by such refusal or neglect the works are materially effected. Further, although the architect must certify in strict accordance with Clause 30, he only certifies in respect of the valuation which he will arrive at having considered the state of the works. The powers under the Contract are ample but the control does not always work. Why should this be so?

Partly this may arise from the limitations of the clerk of works system discussed above. Partly also it arises from the limited role the architect has to play in supervision. This has been recognized by the House of Lords in *East Ham Corporation* v. *Sunley*[23] where it is said that the architect may only appear at intervals of perhaps a week or fortnight and when he arrives on the site may have to deal with many important matters other than inspection; and that he may in such circumstances, if he knows the builder sufficiently well rely upon him to carry out a good job and deal with urgent matters on the site rather than making minute inspections to see if the builder is complying with the specifications laid down. It follows that

> "... it by no means follows that, in failing to discover a defect which a reasonable examination would have disclosed, in fact the Architect was necessarily thereby in breach of his duty to the building owner so as to be liable in an action for negligence".

23 [1966] AC 406 at 443

The present position may well get worse. Fee competition now exists amongst architects. Insofar as this results in a reduction in fees, one may find architects tempted to construe their absence of duty of constant supervision even more restrictively against the employer. Further, if he is well advised and professionally secure, the architect may attempt to redefine and limit his supervising duties.

If there are defects of quality appearing after the works are complete or not dealt with during the works, the employer may seek to recover any loss he has suffered by a claim against the architect for the latter's negligence, but from the passage from the *Sunley* case cited above, it is apparent that mere proof of the existence of the defect, and even that it could have been discovered with reasonable application, may not be sufficient. The Court takes into account the architect's very limited duties of supervision. Nevertheless it must be said that the Official Referees are prepared to find and do find, architects liable in appropriate cases.

Employer's claim against the architect is of little value unless the architect is adequately insured. Because of the number of claims premiums have risen very steeply in recent years. For this and other reasons the Department of Trade and Industry has set up working parties to enquire, inter alia, into the nature, scope, extent and implications of the liability problems faced by architects, consulting engineers and construction surveyors. The reports are a little way off in time.

Self-supervision by the Contractor

This is the ideal. In construction projects, the labour is in general the same. It is the quality, quantity and method of management which distinguishes one Contractor from the other. The starting point for avoiding defects of quality is for contractors to build properly in the first place. Some Contractors seek to foster the image of good management as being good for business. How does the employer encourage self-supervision by contractors?

Where the employer is not constrained by law or practice to obtain the lowest tender by competition, he will be influenced by the advice given to him by his professional advisers. They should know of the contractors who have, or are reputed to have, good management and control. This is one of the main justifications for negotiated contracts. But one's own observations suggest that it does not always work. Even contractors of generally high repute when overloaded with work sometimes appear to spread their good management too thinly.

In any event, and despite my opening quotation, express powers in the Contract can be of assistance. Thus the ICE Conditions have more extensive powers given to the engineer to check the performance of the works than the architect has under the JCT forms. It would be interesting to know whether there is any statistical evidence showing that defects are less common in engineering contracts than in building contracts. A very personal view is that they may be and that if this is correct it may be due partly to contractual provisions and partly to the practice of having resident engineers as inspectors.

They are ordinarily qualified engineers (even if often rather early in their careers).

Can quality assurance assist?

The term is used as in the various BSI documents. Such documents vary (if the authors will forgive me) in their quality. Parts appear to be the result of careful and rigorous thinking. Other parts are somewhat diffuse and general. The doctrine is set out in a series of BSI publications supplemented by various other publications particularly those of CIRIA. The BSI documents appear in Handbook 22 of 317 pages length. Condensation and rationalization would be useful for the outsider reading them for the first time, or even it is thought for the umpteenth time. A general index would be useful. Insofar as reference to the documents is to be made in any Contract, care must be taken in inserting references. It is thought that the basic definition of quality assurance is in 5.1.1 of BS 4778, as follows:

> "all activities and functions concerned with the attainment of quality."

This is so general as to be of little assistance. The Authors of "Quality Assurance in Construction" CIRIA Special Publication 55 are aware of this in that they give different and more exact definitions in three versions of which the present author finds the following most helpful:

> "all those planned and systematic actions necessary to provide adequate confidence that a product or service given will satisfy requirements for quality".

References to quality are to the BSI definition given earlier in this paper. One of the difficulties affecting the BSI publications is that it is apparent that they were developed primarily in relation to goods where it is thought for physical and traditional reasons it is easier to set up and enforce adequate and systematic inspection than on a construction site. But considerable thought has been given in recent years to the application of quality assurance to construction, in particular by CIRIA. Technical Note 121 is of particular assistance. It gives sample documents and provides a specification clause.

The clauses require those items of work to which quality assurance is to apply to be listed in a schedule. This is practical. It may be that eventually general provisions suitable for all or most activities in construction will appear. At this stage, both because the idea is comparatively new and, it is thought, more particularly because of cost, quality assurance is intended to be limited to those items of work where it is of particular value. One pauses to observe that quality assurance in practice, if not in name, is already well recognized in certain areas, *e.g.* welding and offshore installations. Further, many insurance companies in substance require it as a condition of the grant or renewal of insurance in respect of various matters, and the certification and maintenance of aircraft schemes administered by the Civil Aviation Authority under statutory powers are classic examples of the principles of quality assurance. They require a systematic series of tests and maintenance procedures all backed up by an elaborate system of identification of the persons who actually carry them out with the ultimate threat of withdrawal of technical qualification if there is failure on the part of the individual concerned. Such systems must be expensive to operate but presumably are considered necessary where human life is in issue.

Then the model clause provides that the contractor shall not commence any item of work in the Schedule until he has submitted to the engineer a written statement of his proposed procedure for inspecting the item and recording the inspection. The statement has to identify individuals, the stages at which inspections and tests are to be made and the detailed aspects to be verified or measured. Each inspection has to be recorded with identification of the inspector and full details of the inspection would have to be available for the engineer.

Instituting Quality Assurance

A perusal of the BSI quality assurance documents makes it clear that it is essential that the employer appoints a person to advise him upon the setting up and enforcement of a quality assurance system. It is said that he will usually be a construction professional but it is immediately apparent that his duties will have to extend beyond those traditionally carried out today by an architect. Considerable time will be required both to prepare the invitation to tender and, more particularly, to enable the contractor to give details of his system. The very short tender periods customary in the United Kingdom will have to be extended. Then more time, it is thought, would be required for consideration of the systems. The project inevitably would cost more. It would be a matter for commercial judgement whether the employer decides that it is worthwhile. Thus, for an institution intending to occupy a building for many years a considerable amount of quality assurance may be thought desirable. At the other extreme a commercial developer intending to sell offices on completion and then wind-up his development company may take a different view as to the benefits of quality assurance.

If there is quality assurance, can the employer abandon his own traditional supervision? It is thought that he could not although he would have to alter it. In the first place much of the construction work would not be subject to quality assurance. Then it is apparent that quality assurance systems are likely to be of little benefit unless the systems are considered expertly and in detail and their operation continually monitored. It may be that physical inspection on the site would diminish. Inspection would consist more of the system and the reports of its operation than of the construction work itself. If inspection of the works were altogether abandoned then the scope for the operation of contributory negligence reductions in damages would be greatly diminished if not exstinguished.

It is suggested in the CIRIA documents that a side contract could be made or even that quality assurance could be dealt with by some simple clause. It is thought unlikely that one general clause would suffice. All clauses about inspection, defects and testing would have to be reconsidered. Then a fundamental decision must be made as to policy. Is it intended that compliance with a quality assurance provision is sufficient, leaving the employer with no redress in respect of bad work or materials or are the quality assurance provisions to be treated as ancillary to, but not in substitution for, the contractor's traditional duty to complete in accordance with the requirements of the Contract. If the latter is intended it will be essential to look at existing forms and probably to introduce clauses emphasising that acts or omissions on the part of the Employer or his agents, whether in reference to quality assurance procedures or otherwise, are not to release the contractor from his obligations[24]. Such clauses should encompass the possibilities of the contractor raising defences of waiver, estoppel and variation of the Contract.

The initiation of any quality assurance scheme and the extent of the activities to which it applies is a matter of cost benefit analysis. Much re-thinking of contracts would be required but it is not thought that there are any fundamental legal difficulties.

Latent Defect Insurance for Commercial Buildings.

It is understood that this is under consideration. Presumably it would be comparable to that available in respect of houses provided by the NHBC Scheme, and would be in respect of major structural defects and would be self-supporting from premiums. If introduced it may be that some of the supervisory costs at present incurred by the employer would be diminished; but presumably the insurers would institute inspection, the costs of which would be paid for out of the premiums so that it is doubtful whether there would be any saving in cost initially. The advantages, presumably, for the person entitled to enforce the policy would be reasonable certainty of his claim and protection against the insolvency of the person who would normally be a Defendant.

Who should bear the risk of latent defects and for what period?

These are matters of policy and drafting. As to policy, the first requirement is clear-headedness. In particular the errors of the Latent Damage Act 1986 should not be repeated. The parties must make up their minds as to the period and preferably define it in relation to completion and not by the use of the word "damage" with all the difficulties that that has involved. As to drafting, it would be essential to state clearly what is meant by "latent defect". Does it extend only to those defects which would not have been disclosed by reasonable inspection at a reasonable time by an architect or other inspector and if so, whom? Or does it have no such qualification so that any defect which was not known to the employer at the relevant time is a latent defect. Fraud would be excepted by the ordinary operation of law whether so expressed or not. If there were project insurance, one can see the logical advantages of having a short period for which the contractor is responsible and thereafter to grant him a full release so as to leave the claim only against the insurance company. Theoretically the pricing of the diminution of his risk ought to save sufficient to make a material contribution towards the cost of the premium.

24 This is not a draft. No responsibility is accepted. It is a suggestion.

The Employer's Agent 11

Michael Stanger

Synopsis

Three main functions of the employer's agent are considered: project management, design and adjudication. Each function requires different skills, a different degree of independence and attracts different levels of liability. The paper suggests that three separate people are required to fulfil these functions, and that the extra fees involved may be offset by more efficient running of the contract.

What is an employer's agent and why is he needed?

In the legal sense an agent is someone who directly affects the legal relations of his principal with third parties. In the construction industry the term "employer's agent" has a far wider meaning. This paper is not therefore confined to the legal principles of agency but instead addresses wider issues which are relevant to the role and responsibilities of the employer's agent in the construction industry.

The term "employer's agent" is one that is frequently used in the industry but often without much thought as to its meaning. This paper attempts to step back and analyze more critically the function of the employer's agent and his proper position in the construction process.

What then are the characteristics of an employer's agent and, in practice, who is he? To provide an answer one needs to look at the way in which the construction industry works and the features which distinguish construction contracts from other kinds of contracts where no "employer's agent" is needed.

A person who wishes to purchase a newspaper enters into a contract with the newspaper seller when he does so. In entering into this contract the purchaser must decide what it is that he wants to buy and how much he is prepared to pay. By looking at the seller's stall he can choose what he is going to buy and simultaneously identify the price which he is going to have to pay. He feels competent to make the choice himself without obtaining advice from third parties and he is confident that the price marked on the newspaper is the price which the seller is going to ask for. The transaction is completed almost instantaneously. The risk associated with it is minimal. The purchaser was not even aware that he had entered into a contract. The niceties of "invitations to treat", "offers", "acceptances", "consideration", "intention to create legal relations" and other legal principles could not have been further from the purchaser's thought as he struck the deal. The risks involved were not worth considering, irritating though it would be if a page were missing or the most interesting article were illegible.

Compare with that the man who wishes to embark upon a construction project. The simplicity and casual nature of the one transaction could not contrast more starkly with the complexity and enormity of the other. The inexperienced employer is confronted by a mine-field of technical, commercial and legal considerations which are all familiar in the industry but which an outsider would be foolhardy to wrestle with alone. The amounts of money involved, the importance of completing the project on time and the risks associated with failure are likely to be far too serious for any employer to discount.

At the outset an employer wishing to carry out a construction project will normally have an idea of what he wants constructed and some specific requirements and constraints which must be met; for example, capacity, performance, completion date and cost. The employer wants a construction company to transform his ideas into reality and in doing so to meet his specific requirements and constraints. How should he set about conveying his ideas to the contractor and ensuring that the contractor does what is required?

Suppose the employer decides to proceed without outside professional advice. The tasks which he would then find himself doing would be likely to include the following:

- conveying his ideas and requirements to the contractor;
- preparing and/or agreeing contract documentation which sets out these ideas and requirements;
- clarifying for the contractor any ambiguity or lack of detail in the contract documentation;
- during the course of the contract, making known his requirements in relation to any items which have not been fully defined at the outset;
- making changes to the original requirements and instructing the contractor to this effect;
- giving instructions to the contractor in the event of unforeseen circumstances, planning difficulties, ground conditions, antiquities, etc.;
- monitoring the work of the contractor to ensure quality and adherence to the contract;
- giving instructions for the removal or remedy of defective work;
- evaluating work carried out for the purpose of making interim payments;
- considering and evaluating the contractor's claims for extension of time and/or extra money;
- if more than one contractor is appointed, ensuring proper co-ordination/integration of their activities and work;
- confirming when the job is "practically complete";
- issuing instructions for making good defects and monitoring the making good;
- agreeing final accounts with the contractor;
- generally liaising with and instructing the contractor as necessary throughout the project.

So the employer's role is not over when he appoints the contractor. On the contrary, it is only just beginning. Any idea that he would be able to leave the contractor to it and simply be handed the keys on the date for completion could not be further from the reality. Faced with this daunting prospect, what sensible employer without experience of the construction industry could afford to go it alone? The obvious solution is for the employer to appoint someone who is experienced in the construction industry to perform all of these tasks on his behalf. It is because this person performs the tasks on behalf of the employer that he is commonly referred to as the employer's agent.

It is the agent's job to represent the employer's interests in connection with the project. He is the conduit of communications between the employer and the construction contractor. The employer will look to him to ensure that the contractor meets all of the employer's requirements and completes the project to the right quality, at the right price and at the right time. His role is a difficult one

Who is the employer's agent?

Who should the employer appoint to act as his agent? There is no general rule and, with the many varied kinds of contractual arrangements that proliferate in the construction industry today, the agent may appear in many different shapes and sizes. Furthermore, it is not uncommon for the role to be split so that different aspects are performed by different people.

The following is a list of the people who commonly perform functions as agent of the employer in the more usual contractual arrangements.

- In a traditional building project: an architect and/or a project manager.
- In a traditional engineering project: an engineer and/or a project manager.
- In a design and build project: a designer or quantity surveyor or project manager.
- In a management contracting arrangement: the management contractor itself and/or a designer.
- In a construction management arrangement: the construction manager itself and/or a designer.

As mentioned above, there are no hard and fast rules. These are simply examples. As can be seen, the nature of the contractual arrangements plays an important part in deciding who should perform the role of the employer's agent. The choice of contractual arrangements will in turn depend on the nature of the project and the constraints imposed by the employer.

On occasions, an employer will appoint one of his own employees to perform the functions of an employer's agent but for the reasons already outlined this person will need to have considerable experience in the construction industry.

The role of the employer's agent and the nature of his work

Listed above are some of the tasks which one might expect an employer to have to perform if he did not appoint an agent. It is these same tasks which an employer might reasonably require his agent to perform on his behalf. What is the nature of these tasks? They are many and varied and, as was noted above, they require a number of skills. These include:

- Technical skills - the agent has to convey the employer's ideas and requirements to the contractor. At the outset the employer's ideas and requirements are likely to be vague and incomplete. The agent has to translate these into a precise definition of what is required. This definition is conveyed through the medium of drawings and specifications. The process of translation therefore involves a large element of design.
- Legal/contract skills - the agent is required to prepare and/or agree the contract documentation which will bind the contractor to meet the defined requirements.
- Administrative skills - the agent has to ensure that the administrative procedures under the contract are complied with, that instructions are given and information is provided when required, that certificates are issued, that any notices are given and that proper records are kept.
- Quality control skills - the agent has to monitor the work of the contractor to ensure quality and adherence to the contract.
- Management skills - these will be particularly vital where more than one contractor is appointed and their activities need to be co-ordinated.
- Financial skills - needed to evaluate work carried out for the purpose of making interim payments and to agree final accounts.

It is not difficult to see why the role of employer's agent is often split between people having different fields of expertise.

Looking at the list of tasks again, one may draw a further distinction between those for which the employer's agent requires input from the employer (*e.g.* preparing the definition of the employer's requirements or giving instructions requiring variations) and those which the agent could perform in an objective way without reference to the employer (*e.g.* monitoring the work of the contractor to ensure quality and adherence to the contract or evaluating the work for the purpose of making interim payments).

For the first category of tasks, *i.e.* those where the agent can and should obtain input from the employer, the agent's position is straightforward. He must comply with the employer's wishes, although he may of course give advice to the employer where this is appropriate.

It is the second category of task, *i.e.* those which may be performed in an objective way, without reference to the employer, which present more difficulties. What procedure should be adopted for settling matters capable of objective assessment? There are three possible approaches to settling matters which are capable of objective assessment:

- leave the matter to be decided by one of the parties alone;
- allow the matter to be settled by a process of negotiation between the parties;
- arrange for the matter to be settled by an independent third party.

Each of these possibilities is considered in turn below.

Approach 1 - leaving the matter to be decided by one of the parties

It may be argued that if the matters to be considered are truly capable of objective assessment then either of the parties should come to the same answer on any particular issue. The reality is that nearly all matters of this kind are sufficiently complex or imprecise as to make a truly objective assessment extremely difficult. Both parties will have an interest in the matter to be decided and if either of them were given responsibility for this task they would be likely to be accused of bias by the other. It would thus be a recipe for disputes.

The employer's agent has been appointed to act on behalf of the employer. If he is genuinely expected to act in the employer's best interests he would be in no better position to settle these matters than would the employer. He would be equally prone to accusations of bias.

Approach 2 - allowing the matter to be settled by a process of negotiation between the parties.

This approach has more immediate merit. Each of the parties can put forward their own arguments and hopefully an accommodation would be reached. But the result might then depend upon extraneous factors. For example:

- the knowledge of the parties in relation to the matters in issue;
- the negotiating skills of the parties;
- the ability of the employer to give effect to his own wishes by withholding money;
- the ability of the contractor to apply heavy commercial pressure by threatening not to complete the job.

In these circumstances, the likelihood of achieving the right answer must be open to considerable doubt. The possibility of disputes would again be significant.

An employer's agent would in this arrangement be well placed to negotiate on behalf of the employer. He would have the necessary detailed knowledge of the project and the skills required to represent his client's interests in the best way. Unfortunately, there is no obvious reason why the involvement of the employer's agent in place of the employer would be any less likely to result in disputes. The fundamental objection to this arrangement would therefore remain.

Approach 3 - arranging for matters to be settled by an independent third party

This is the obvious solution to the difficulties associated with the first two approaches. It would mean that the person deciding the matter would be able to do so in a detached way, independent of the interests of either party. This is the approach which is said to be adopted in the more common arrangements for construction projects. A person performing this "adjudication" role could not be accused of bias. The likelihood of disputes between the parties must therefore be diminished.

The essence of this adjudicator's role is that he is independent. Is it therefore a role which the employer's agent can properly perform?

Can the employer's agent act as an independent adjudicator?

It has already been pointed out that the employer's agent is appointed to look after the employer's interests and act on his behalf in dealings with the contractor. Is it appropriate that the same person should take on the role of "adjudicator" in considering matters which are capable of an objective assessment? It seems illogical. If the employer himself is not considered the right person to take on this adjudicator's role, why should his agent, who looks after his interests, be any better qualified to do so?

In practice it is not uncommon for the same person to act as agent of the employer and to perform the function of adjudicator. One suspects that this may simply be a matter of expediency. The employer's agent is already appointed to act on behalf of the employer and it is convenient for him to perform this additional adjudication function. He will be familiar with the project and will therefore be well placed to form a view.

The usual argument in support of the view that the employer's agent can act independently in an adjudication function is that he is a member of a professional body and, as such, will apply professional standards. One can see that this argument might well be valid in circumstances where the professional is engaged purely to take on this adjudication role and where he happens to be engaged by the employer. His decisions should not in those circumstances be influenced by the fact that his remuneration comes from the employer's pocket. In other words, he could equally well be retained by the contractor and his decisions would remain the same.

Unfortunately, making the agent of the employer take on the role of independent adjudicator is not simply a question of identifying the source of his remuneration. He is in fact being asked to perform two quite distinct functions which, on the face of it, are not compatible.

In his capacity as agent of the employer, the person will be required to advise the employer, represent him and generally look after his interests. The employer will feed all instructions through him and will look to him if problems arise. He is the employer's man. So far as the contractor is concerned he is the employer.

By contrast, in acting as an independent adjudicator, the person owes no allegiances to anyone. He is to be quite detached from either party's interests. He does not have to argue the employer's case in discussions with the contractor but simply has to pronounce his decision. Would not the person who is asked to perform these two distinct roles find himself in difficulty? On occasions would he not have to perform the two roles simultaneously? He would be struggling to know which hat he should be wearing at any particular time.

Moreover, if the employer's agent is required to perform an adjudication role he may find that in doing so he has a conflict of interest. When deciding whether the quality of the work is satisfactory, would his decision be influenced by the possibility of claims for extensions of time and extra payment and the impact on the employer of delayed completion? Would he also be influenced by the fact that his decision might prompt a dispute which would be very much against the employer's best interests or which might reflect badly on his own performance as agent of the employer? How could he be expected to assess objectively those matters in respect of which he may have had some input as the employer's agent - for example, an application for an extension of time and/or additional payment arising out of late receipt of drawings or other information which it was the agent's responsibility to provide? If the consequences of a particular decision, apparently in favour of the employer, might in fact have repercussions which would be to the employer's disadvantage, should he point these matters out to the employer and seek guidance as to his wishes? That may be a highly pragmatic approach and one which the employer might properly expect his agent to fulfil, but in doing so could the agent/adjudicator be said to be acting independently?

It is not difficult to reach the conclusion that the role of employer's agent and the role of adjudicator should not be performed by the same person. But what is the alternative? Does this conclusion mean that the employer has to pay another set of fees for an experienced adjudicator who, if he is to perform his task properly, must be as familiar with the project as the true employer's agent? Alternatively, are the theoretical difficulties outlined above outweighed by the practical advantages of having one person performing this dual role?

Can the employer's agent effectively monitor performance?

The monitoring of a contractor's performance is something which ought to be capable of objective assessment by reference to the terms of the construction contract. The main aspects of performance which need to be monitored are:

- Progress;
- Compliance with technical requirements and quality control;
- Economy and efficiency (not so important in simple lump sum contracts but obviously vital in "prime cost" contractual arrangements);
- Compliance with other contractual requirements (*e.g.* security, safety, noise, dust, etc.).

How should performance be measured in each of these areas? If an objective assessment is to be made, performance must be measured against specified requirements. Looking at each of the areas in turn, the normal documentation which is used for these purposes is as follows:

- Progress: a programme;
- Technical requirements/quality: drawings,specifications and specified standards;
- Economy and efficiency: a cost plan;
- Compliance with other contractual requirements: specific standards and/or rules;

These documents should form part of the contract and thus be binding on the contractor. Normally an objective assessment of actual performance compared with the requirements of these documents will enable the assessor to establish whether or not the contractor has complied with the requirements. In some cases the assessment will require specialist skills.

There are however areas where the position is less clear cut. For example, in building contracts, it is quite usual to require certain matters to be carried out "to the reasonable satisfaction of the architect". An assessment of what is reasonable will vary from person to person and may depend on the nature of the project and other surrounding circumstances. Once again, a subjective element creeps in. Who is it that should be left with this discretion? Is it appropriate to allocate it to the employer's agent? Or should an independent person be appointed for this purpose?

Another area where there may be some uncertainty is in relation to the programme. Frequently this is not a document having contractual force. The contract merely indicates a date for completion. What then should be done if the contractor falls behind a programme of this kind? Whilst an objective comparison may be made, the real question is whether anything should be done about it. Since the contractor would not be in breach of any contractual obligation it would not be a matter on which an independent assessor could make any effective decision. The employer's agent however, acting on behalf of the employer, might wish to take steps to ensure that the completion date is not jeopardised. That again would be an area where he would have to use discretion and judgement.

That leads to another question. Should the employer's agent attempt to direct events or should he simply react to them? In other words, should he have power to direct, supervise, control and co-ordinate activities or should he simply monitor the contractor's performance against the defined standards and if a discrepancy appears, require it to be remedied?

If the employer's agent is to take a more positive role this must be clearly catered for in the contract between the employer and the contractor. The agent then moves more into the sphere of project management which may, after all, be what the employer really wants. To an extent, all employer's agents do have an element of project management as part of their function, but it is a matter of degree. In traditional building projects, where the architect commonly acts as the employer's agent, it may be argued that the degree of management is relatively slight. The contractor is to a large extent left to his own devices. Of course, the architect will monitor the contractor's performance but that is not the same as managing it. At the other end of the scale, professional project managers and "construction managers" (using the term in the context of construction management contracts) set out to provide management expertise; that is their primary function.

It is all too easy to see the disadvantages for the employer of appointing an agent merely to monitor performance and then to try to react when things go wrong. If the contractor is tempted to cut corners (and the incentives may encourage this course of action) the employer's agent will simply be left to try to correct matters after the event. At that stage there may be many factors which affect the course of action adopted by the agent. He may decide that it is better to ignore certain deficiencies so as to avoid causing further problems in other areas. Is he then acting in the employer's best interests or has he got one eye on his own position?

It would clearly be better to try to organize projects so that it is in everyone's interests to procure effective performance. If the employer's agent is to play an active part in these arrangements he cannot simply be left to monitor events. He must have the ability to manage and control. Such a role is not one which can be carried out in an objective and independent way. The closer the employer's agent comes to being a project manager, the less able he is to perform in an independent way the adjudication functions which have previously been discussed. Does this then lend further weight to the argument that these functions should be split between different people?

The impact of professional liability

Whatever functions the employer's agent performs, it is obviously important that he performs them properly. But what should his liability be for failure to do so? In traditional arrangements, even if the employer's agent does not perform particularly well, he may not have any liability for losses which flow. In some instances the remedy may lie in an arbitration between the employer and the contractor in which the decisions of the employer's agent are reviewed. In other instances there may be no such remedy and the employer may have a right of action against his agent - for example, if the agent has failed to give proper information or instructions to the contractor.

On analysis it will be seen that the areas where the right of redress will lie in a review of the agent's decision are those areas where he is required to perform the role of adjudicator. In that capacity he is determining what the rights of the parties are rather than giving advice to the employer or performing functions on his behalf. Where contracts expressly allow for the agent's decisions to be opened up and reviewed, the circumstances in which a claim could be brought against him are relatively limited.

It is in relation to the activities which are genuinely performed on behalf of the employer that the agent exposes himself to the greatest liability. The most obvious example is the agent's responsibility for conveying the employer's ideas and requirements to the contractor. In performing this task the agent has to use design and technical skills in which he must exercise reasonable skill and care. A failure to exercise such skill and care would normally be a breach of the agent's obligations to the employer rendering him liable for the consequences.

The greater the scope of the agent's responsibilities, the greater will be his potential exposure to liability. If the agent takes on increased project management responsibilities he will in principle have an increased exposure to claims.

Consideration has previously been given to whether the employer's agent can effectively monitor the performance of the contractor. Under this heading one is looking at the performance of the agent himself. How should this be measured? Is it appropriate to try to measure it in the same way that one might measure a contractor's performance? Is it really practicable to do so?

Poor performance in certain areas of activity will manifest itself more readily than in other areas. If the agent's design is defective this may result in water penetration or some other problem affecting the building. By contrast, poor performance in managing a project may be far more difficult to detect. Of course, it will be obvious if the project finishes late or outside the budget. What will not be obvious is the reason for this. The project manager is likely to argue that the reason lay outside his control. It will be an extremely difficult task for the employer to determine whether this is right or wrong.

If the employer is placing trust in his agent and is giving his agent a large measure of responsibility, is it not reasonable that the employer should expect a high degree of expertise from his agent? Quite apart from the employer's ability to recover damages for breach by the agent of his obligations, does not the risk of liability act as a spur on the agent to perform to the best of his ability?

In relation to design matters there is generally little argument about the fact that the agent should be responsible for using reasonable skill and care although there is an increasing resistance (largely driven by insurers) to any higher level of liability.

It is in the other fields of activity that views differ more widely as to the extent of the liability to which the agent should be exposed. It is sometimes argued that the agent should be treated as no more than a limb of the employer's organisation. If the employer were to appoint one of his own employees to perform the role of employer's agent (because the employee has relevant experience) he would be unlikely to bring an action against that employee for failure to perform the tasks properly. On the other hand, the employer would not be paying his own employee a fee for providing the service. Also, there may be adequate sanctions applicable to an employee (such as being sacked!) which would not apply in relation to an outside agency. The analogy therefore hardly justifies an argument that an outside consultant who acts as employer's agent should be entirely free from risk.

Perhaps the better question is not whether an employer's agent should in principle be liable for his acts but whether it is appropriate to arrange matters so that his performance can be more readily measured. Even if this were possible, would it be a worthwhile exercise or would it simply divert attention from the main objective which, after all, is to try to procure the completion of the project in a satisfactory way? Would it be possible instead to arrange matters so that there are positive incentives which encourage the employer's agent to perform well?

The future role of the professional adviser

The involvement of professionals in future construction projects is assured. They have the expertise and skills which are vital to any employer. In looking to the future, the issues to be addressed are:

- What precise roles should the professionals perform?
- Should their functions be split?
- Should an independent adjudicator be appointed?
- Should project management be given more prominence?
- What level of risk should professionals assume?

Each of these issues has been touched on in this paper. By way of conclusion, it is suggested that the various roles and functions which are required to be performed by professionals should be separated and more clearly defined than they have been in the past. In addition to the consultants who would normally be engaged in a traditional building project, it would be desirable for the employer to engage a project manager and an independent adjudicator. Such an arrangement would overcome some of the disadvantages of the more familiar arrangements. The most obvious drawback of the proposal is that it would inevitably involve greater expenditure by way of fees. Hopefully the extra expenditure would be justified by promoting a more efficient and trouble-free construction process.

New Roles in Contracting 12

J B Winter

Synopsis

The role of the management contractor is analyzed, comparison being made to the traditional approach of the standard forms. Experience in the United States is reviewed as possibly pointing the way for development in the United Kingdom, with the caveat that the concept of management contracting differs in the United States. The conclusion is that management contracting, in one form or another, is here to stay.

Introduction

Some 20 years ago (or so the story goes) some intrepid United Kingdom contractors visited the United States and came back with a creature not previously known in the United Kingdom. The creature survived the journey across the Atlantic and quickly settled in to its new surroundings in the United Kingdom. Scientists succeeded in breeding from it by taking cuttings and within a few years its offspring were to be found in major contracting companies throughout the United Kingdom, who even formed special subsidiaries to look after this creature. In 1987, following a number of years of research, scientists at the JCT laboratories succeeded in cloning a new sub-species of this creature which they intended as a super breed which would gradually force the older varieties into extinction. But wait ... reports are coming in of an autopsy recently carried out on one of these creatures, unfortunately deceased, and the results show that its genetic makeup is very similar to that of a number of species already existing in the United Kingdom and which have been around for many years. Rumours abound that this creature may be the descendant of English species shipped to the United States with the Pilgrim Fathers, if not with Christopher Columbus. The name of this creature - the MANAGEMENT CONTRACT.

The purpose of this paper is to look at the new roles which have developed in the construction industry over the last 20 years, to consider their impact on the traditional arrangements in contracting (in particular to see whether there is any future for the traditional main contractor), and to discuss whether or not there should be standardization of the forms used in these new roles. I have tried to do this primarily on the basis of first hand impressions from those in the industry, but also by drawing from experiences overseas (particularly the United States) where these techniques, which are relatively new to the United Kingdom, have been around somewhat longer. The paper will focus on Management Contracting, mainly because it seems to be the most important departure from traditional arrangements that has emerged.

The Traditional System

The new roles have developed because of general dissatisfaction throughout the industry with the traditional way of structuring a contract. By "traditional" in this paper is meant the arrangement whereby the project is fully designed by a professional architect or engineer before being let to a main contractor on what is essentially a fixed price, and the work is then carried out by the main contractor who generally sub-contracts at least part of the work to one or more sub-contractors, with the work being overseen and the contract administered by the architect or engineer. There are many reasons for this dissatisfaction, and most of them are well known. A few of the most important ones are as follows:

- To prepare a full design before going out to tender takes an unacceptably long time, particularly in times of inflation and high land costs.
- Although the design should theoretically be complete at the time of tender and contract, very frequently it is not. This leads to late information being provided to the contractor and claims arising from that.
- There is no involvement on the part of the contractor in the design and he therefore has no opportunity to provide input from his practical experience as a contractor on whether the design could be built, improved on, built more efficiently etc.
- The client has little or no control over how long the construction is likely to take and how much it is going to cost, after taking account of variations and claims and the fact that a "fixed price" contract never finishes at that price. All too often construction is completed outside the planned time and greatly in excess of the contract budget.
- The structure and the history of the traditional type of contract tends to create an adversarial relationship which leads to claims. These, whatever their merit, always involve the employer in additional time and cost.

The client's objective in construction is to obtain the highest quality product at the lowest possible price in the quickest possible time. These three elements are interrelated and the priority of the client may be different according to the type of construction. The most common constraint in building construction will be price (the client will have a fixed budget within which the project must be completed) but in some types of construction, time or quality may be the dictating force. So for example in the construction of a nuclear power station, quality is likely to be at the top of the list, given its relationship with safety. High inflation and exhorbitant land prices may make time the dominant factor; getting the project finished so that the offices may be let or the factory opened for production and give the client a return.

The traditional structure was not seen as providing clients with satisfactory results in any of the areas of price, time and quality, the particular problems being price and time.

One major element of the dissatisfaction is the quality of management in construction. In a traditional contract arrangement, the architect or engineer should take a leading part in managing the contract using the powers given to him under the contract. Unfortunately for their professions, there is a widely held view that architects and engineers do not make good managers. Professor Justin Sweet, referring to the US expresses the criticism as follows:

> "Designers were faulted because of their casual attitude toward costs, their inability to predict costs, and their ignorance of the labor and materials market, as well as costs of applying construction techniques".[1]

These views are commonly shared here in the United Kingdom. There is a view in relation to architects that the talents required to be successful in the creative art form of architecture are unlikely to be found in a person who also has good managerial skills and vice versa. Of course there are many exceptions to this rule. Although the training that an architectural student receives at university includes courses on management, contract matters and claims, it can be reasonably safely assumed that no-one embarks on a career in architecture deliberately intending to be a manager. When a student embarks on a professional career as an architect there is natural gravitation during which some will remain in design and others will go in to the administration of contracts. Given the perceived inconsistency between design skill and good management, it is likely that those who are the best designers will not prove to be the best managers. Notwithstanding this, the profession seems to have failed the construction industry in its management skills.

The new roles in contracting have been developed as a direct response to the need for better management. It may be an over simplification, but project management appears to have been developed by the professions as their response while management contracting, construction management, design and build and other variations on these themes have been the response of the contracting side of the industry. It is interesting to note that the developments have not generally come from the party in the construction process that improved management is directly intended to benefit, namely the client. Obviously one would not expect incentives to be taken by those clients who are not in the business of construction but for whom construction is merely a means to an end, that is carrying on their own, different, business. However, a very high proportion of all construction in the United Kingdom is publicly funded, and one can only guess at why incentives have not come from the public sector. The point remains that contractors and professionals alike are in business to make profits and for them to take the incentive to introduce new ways of carrying out construction must mean that they too were not benefiting financially from the disadvantages (from the client's point of view) of the traditional systems set out above. In other words everyone in the construction process was suffering in terms of price and time.

1 *Legal Aspects of Architecture, Engineers, and the Construction Process* by Justin Sweet, p 451.

In an article on project management, James McLaughlin[2] quotes from a survey carried out by the National Economic Development Organization of the United Kingdom in 1978 as follows:

> "The participants in the construction process are excessively concerned with their roles vis-a-vis other participants and insufficiently responsive to the needs of the industry".

He also refers to the commonly held belief that to build is to be robbed[3].

He goes on to say that there is a need for a shift in emphasis from a "production orientated" to a "client orientated" outlook by the construction industry. While one might initially have some doubts as to the reality of all parts of the construction industry becoming truly "client orientated", one of the objectives in developing the roles of project managers and management contractors has been to devise a system whereby there are no conflicts of interest between the client and his professional manager.

As already stated, there have been various different types of response by the industry to the perceived inadequacies of the traditional system. Before going onto examine in more detail the system known as management contracting, I will deal briefly with the other main developments.

Project Management

Any attempt at definition is fraught with difficulties so I will adopt one put forward by McLaughlin which is as follows:

> "The full definition of project management can be set down as the overall planning, control and co-ordination of a project from inception to completion, aimed at meeting the client's requirements and ensuring completion on time, within cost and to the required quality standards. Which to the client in detail means:
>
> 1.Providing a completed project which fully satisfies his original aspirations and budget.
>
> 2.Advising and guiding him from the moment of conception, in financing land acquisition, preparing the brief and appointment of consultants and selection of contractors.
>
> 3.The planning, control and direction of the project in accordance with the brief.
>
> 4.The motivation and coordination of all participants in order to achieve the completion of the project to programme and within budgeted cost."[4]

The Institute of Building, in a paper entitled Project Management in Building (1979), has stated that:

2 "What is Project Management?" Article in *Asian Architect and Contractor* by J McLaughlin, December 1982, p 17.
3 Dr Johnson "To build, sir, is to be robbed".
4 McLaughlin, p 18.

> "The objectives of project management are to apply management skills and techniques to the organisation and control of all aspects of the project and to optimise the use of resources to produce a well designed and soundly constructed facility which will meet the client's requirements of function, cost and time budget, and future maintenance. Separation of the pure management role of an entire project from the design and construction process enables project management to develop in its own right."

Given this definition and these objectives, the employment of a project manager, where the client is not in the construction industry or does not have his own in-house management team, would appear to be a necessity rather than merely an advantage. In practice however there seems to be some difficulty in establishing the professional project manager as a recognized and respected part of a management team. There is a tendency for the others involved in the process not to understand the true role of the project manager and to regard him as a barrier to communication with the client and merely an additional fee to be paid. This is particularly so when the project manager's background is in the acquisition of property and not in construction itself. It is said that the project manager has authority without responsibility. As with every task, much depends upon the quality of the individual performing it; one of the problems of the development of the new roles in contracting is that some professionals have reacted to the changes by following the trend and establishing project management arms without really changing their way of thinking and operating.

Design and Build/Design and Construct/Turnkey

Design and Build as it name suggests involves a contractor with an in-house design team (or hiring its own consultants) producing a design for a construction project and then constructing it. This avoids a number of the disadvantages of traditional contracting; that the contractor has no involvement in the design process, that there is a lack of co-ordination between designer and constructor, and that in the claims that often arise as a result of the adversarial nature of the contracts, there are very often questions of who is responsible for a particular defect and whether it is a result of defective design or poor workmanship. In design and build the client has "one backside to kick".

Despite the difficulty that at least one court has had in defining "turnkey" (see *Cable* v. *Hutcherson* which will be dealt with later in this paper), there seems to be no material difference between a turnkey contract and a design and build one. As Professor Justin Sweet has put it:

> "The core element to a turnkey contract is, at least in theory, that the owner simply tells the contractor what it wishes and does not appear on the scene again until the contractor says the project is completed and hands the owner a key and the owner 'turns it'".[5]

5 Sweet, p 453.

These types of contract have significant disadvantages which are summarized as follows:

- Where the client invites competitive tenders it will be practically impossible for him to assess properly the relative merits in terms of price, time and quality.

- The client will have difficulty in evaluating its chosen design and as McLaughlin has said it may be "at least as difficult, time consuming and costly to assess a design as it is to produce that design from scratch."

- An unsophisticated owner will not know whether the construction is being carried out properly and he may find himself the victim of paying an excessively high price, both as the construction progresses and overall.

While there will be those that disagree, it is commonly felt that design and build contracts should be restricted to those situations where fairly simple products with an established reputation and a recognised price are being built, for example warehouses. The disadvantages of design and build can largely be avoided if design and build is combined with the use of a project manager.

Management Contracts

I will turn now to deal with the principal topic of this paper, management contracting. As illustrated by the parable at the beginning of this paper, management contracting, despite being billed as a totally new concept, is in fact an amalgam of already well established forms of contract and contract practices.

In concept, the management contract is a prime cost plus fixed fee contract, a creature that has been around for many years. The ways in which it resembles traditional practices are:

- The design does not have to be completed before the initial stages of the construction are begun. This is known as "fast track". This resembles the common practice in traditional contracting that, even if it ought to have been completed, the design is often not complete as construction commences and information will be fed through to the contractor during the course of construction, often changing the design of the finished product.
- The management contractor does none of the construction work himself, but merely manages and co-ordinates a number of trade contractors in the execution of the works. This resembles the practice that has developed for major contractors to sub-let almost all of the work under traditional sub-contracting arrangements. This gradual move towards sub-contracting has meant that main contractors have had to develop management skills in priority to skills in construction.

What is it that now makes a "costs plus" contract, traditionally shunned as a blank cheque for the contractor, so popular? fifteen to twenty per cent of all new projects are now on a management basis, and the percentage is much higher in the South-east of England. Perhaps it is putting the above two features together and adding to them the imposition of responsibility for management on the contractor that makes the management contract and the "cost plus" basis the attractive package that it is now proving to be.

It is important to bear in mind that the elements do not necessarily always have to go together, for example the pure management role could clearly be applied to the traditional structure of employer/main contractor/sub-contractor, taking some of the responsibility away from the architect/engineer.

It is also as well to be aware that the term "management contracting" is not a definition written in stone; others use different definitions. For example, in the United States, the expression "construction management" is used to cover all types of contracts in which a contractor takes a management role, whereas in the United Kingdom this expression applies only to the situation where a contractor purely manages and does not have a direct contractual relationship with the trade contractors. As a reminder of this I will use the abbreviation "CM" for contract management and contract manager when referring to the United Stated. In Australia the Master Builders Association of New South Wales have a standard form "Construction Management Contract" in which the construction manager undertakes to act essentially as a consultant and enters into trade contracts, but only as agent for his principal, the employer.

The Advantages and Disadvantages

Management contracting attempts to avoid most of the criticisms of the traditional methods of construction outlined at the beginning of this paper. Unfortunately, some of the features that remove the disadvantages of the traditional system also have disadvantages of their own. The pluses and minuses will therefore be considered together.

Time

The need to complete a design before a contract is let causes unnecessary delays. Fast track construction under a management contract permits construction to begin where the design is not complete. For example, the earthworks and piling contractors can be on site commencing work before the type of cladding for a building is even chosen. Fast track therefore means that providing all goes well and the client does not excessively change the design, a project can be completed more quickly because it is started earlier in the overall process of design and construction. It should also remove the problem of variations being ordered throughout the contract because, under fast track, the work is divided into a number of small packages. Each package is let to an individual trade contractor who will execute it only when appropriate.

It might be thought that as the design does not have to be completed at the time construction commences, designers have an opportunity to delay the completion of their design even longer. In practice, it seems that delays in design are reduced for the simple reason that the management contractor is empowered (as a member of the professional team) and motivated (by his obligation to complete the works in time) to approach the design team direct and press them for information that he needs to pass on to trade contractors to enable them to do their work. In a traditional contract situation, the main contractor might be content to sit and wait for information/drawings, safe in the knowledge that late information would mean a claim and delay which he might conveniently use to disguise delays on his own part.

To a layman, one disadvantage of fast track might seem to be that, if the designer does not know the precise parameters and constituents of his final product, he cannot with accuracy design the earlier stages of construction. At its most simple, one would ask how the designer knew how many piles he required and how big they should be, if he did not know the overall weight of the structure the piles were to support. This is not thought likely to be a problem here, although it has been in the United States according to Tieder and Cox[6]. At the minimum, it seems that there might be a tendency for the designers to err on the side of caution and over-design the earlier stages. This will of course increase costs, which will (in a contract where there is a target to be worked towards) reduce the amount of money to be spent on later parts of the construction but one must weigh against that the aim of fast track construction.

Fast track's great claim to fame is speed; using it, a project should be completed quicker than it would have been under a traditional process. Taking advantage of the time saving fast track offers requires the skill management contracting is all about, that is good management. The management contractor must schedule and co-ordinate the obtaining of tenders and placing of contracts with the various trade contractors, he must then schedule and co-ordinate the execution of the work by these trade contractors, he must observe the work in progress in order to ensure that it is being carried out properly and he must revise and adapt to the changes in situation that will inevitably occur. While this is a task that the main contractor has been performing for many years, it is an extremely difficult one. Two analogies have been given in a United States context. First, in *Blake Construction Co* v. *J C Coakley Co.* it has been likened to a battle field:

> "Except in the middle of a battle field, nowhere must men co-ordinate the movement of other men and all materials in the midst of such chaos and with such limited certainty of present facts and future occurrences as in a huge construction product such as the building of this $100m hospital. Even the most painstaking planning frequently turns out to be mere conjecture and accommodation to changes must necessarily be of the rough, quick and ad hoc sort, analogous to ever changing commands on the battle field."[7]

Elsewhere it has been likened to a procession of trucks moving down the highway.[8] If one truck breaks down, all the others behind it are forced to stop;

6 Article by JB Tieder and Robert K Cox "Construction Management and the specialty trade (prime) contractors", *Law and Contemporary Problems*, Winter 1983.

7 431 A 2d 569, 575, quoted in article by RD Conner in *Contracting for Construction Management Services, Law and Contemporary Problems*, Winter 1983.

8 Sweet, p 443.

this analogy breaks down however when one considers a three lane motorway with an efficient break down recovery service. While every country is different, it would be unwise to ignore the experience of the United States where CM began. There, according to Tieder and Cox, expectations of CM have not been fulfilled and:

> "In project after project, specialty trade contractors have experienced significant delays and cost overruns due to the failure of owners, CM's and designers to fulfil the obligations imposed on them by the non-conventional techniques. The ultimate result has been a proliferation of expensive and lengthy litigation".[9]

Some of the United States case law will be referred to later, but it is also worth noting that the whole philosophy of management contracting seems to have gone astray in the United States where contract managers have attempted to place the contractual burden of scheduling and co-ordination on the trade contractors and, by "no damages for delay" clauses, have tried to absolve themselves from any liability for their own poor programming.[10]

The news in the United Kingdom certainly does not appear nearly as depressing. The popularity of management contracting seems to suggest that it does produce the results that it proclaims. It would probably be too cynical to suggest that this might be because management contracting is still in its first flush of youth and enthusiasm.

Buildability

The second major proclaimed advantage of management contracting is the involvement of the contractor in the design of the project. This avoids the complete separation of design and construction in the traditional form of contract where there is very little opportunity for the designer to obtain feed back from the contractor on the economics and practicalities of the design. The contractor's task is to advise on "buildability". This word is actually incorporated into the JCT Management Contract 1987[11] and one awaits its definition by the courts with interest (although this should be an easy task). Another way of expressing it is "value engineering" which is not simply cutting costs, but maximising the value to be obtained from expenditure. Ian MacPherson has described buildability as "the simple end of value engineering"[12]. There is little that can be considered to be a disadvantage in having involvement by the management contractor in the design. The practical difficulties that have occurred are that despite the objective of involving the management contractor as early as possible, he is sometimes only employed when the design is well advanced. No matter at what stage he is employed, the management contractor sometimes faces an understandable reluctance on the part of the design team (who may not regard the management contractor as

9 Tieder and Cox, p 46
10 Tieder and Cox, p 47
11 Third Schedule, item 4.
12 Ian MacPherson in documentation for seminar on Construction Project Management, October 1987, p.121.

being a "professional" in the same way that they are) to accept his comments on and criticisms of their design.

Experience of architects is that sometimes contractors do not make a major contribution to design meetings they take part in, apparently because their training and experience does not permit them to visualize a structure from the drawings in the same way that an architect can. There seems to be scope for litigation arising from the responsibility of the management contractor to comment on the design and this should certainly be regarded as a disadvantage. On this subject, see the later section of this paper.

Flexibility

With fast track and the division of the work into small packages comes flexibility for the management contractor, allowing him to adapt to changing circumstances. The design can be changed at a relatively late stage without effect on the overall programme or outstanding claims or variations, because the individual packages are let only at the last moment. Letting packages at a late stage means that prices obtained from trade contractors are accurate and up to date which avoids the situation that occurs in the traditional approach (particularly in times of high inflation/recession) where, when the time comes for a sub-contract task to be formed, the sub-contractor may have already gone out of business, or his prices may now be so uneconomical that he must resort to fallacious claims in order that he is not seriously out of pocket at the end of the job.

A problem that has occurred in the United States[13] and which could occur here is that with the division of the work into small packages there is increased potential for parts of the design to be omitted from work let to trade contractors, and/or arguments between trade contractors as to who in responsibile for what work.

Cost

Except to the extent that management contracts should be finished quicker than traditional projects, and reduced time means cost saving (*e.g.* by getting commercial property let or a factory producing goods), even management contractors are reluctant to hold out too many expectations of the actual cost of construction in a management contract as being likely to be less than in a traditional contract. However, there are potential savings in the following areas:

- The management contractor's fixed fee is likely to be less than the mark-up that a main contractor would add to a sub-contractor's price.
- Competition amongst management contractors is fierce and management fees have apparently remained at approximately the same level for a number of years.

13 Article by WR Squires and MJ Murphy, "The impact of fast track construction and construction management on subcontractors", *Law & Contemporary Problems*, Winter, 1983, p.55 at p 59.

- The prime cost payment procedure and the division of the work into small packages reduces the dangers arising from the vagaries of estimating.
- One of the skills of the management contractor should be in sophisticated cost estimating. This should keep costs down.
- Under a well managed contract, claims are less likely to arise and those that do arise are likely to be dealt with quickly with resulting cost savings.

On the debit side, the purest form of fast track management contract contains no maximum or even target cost and there is no real incentive to keep costs down. Management contractors argue that reputation is what gets them future work and that gives them sufficient incentive. As described above, if the project is not properly programmed and co-ordinated scope for delays and therefore additional cost is enormous. The burden of this cost will fall on the employer unless he can prove that the delays result from failures on the part of the management contractor, which may not be easy to do. The employer will pay the management contractor a fee for his involvement in the design phase which he would not do in the traditional approach. Under fast track, the architect/engineer's fees are likely to be higher. Even where a management contractor is willing to commit to a target price or gross maximum price, this target or GMP may be regarded as something to work up to.

Disputes

The consensus approach to management contracting should mean that parties do not take the adversarial attitudes that they tend to take in a traditional arrangement. The first reaction will be to sort out the problem rather than give notice under the appropriate clause of the contract. As between management contractor and employer this may well be the case, but as between the trade contractors and the management contractor there is no real reason why there should be any less claims; the position of a trade contractor is not greatly different to that of a traditional sub-contractor. It is said that the management contractor, being "poacher turned gamekeeper" will be better able to recognize some of the ploys that trade contractors might resort to, but realistically only the best management contractors will able to reduce significantly the amount of claims made by trade-contractors, and the burden of these claims (under management contracting philosophy and the present JCT form of management contract) will fall on the employer.

Management

This brings me to the final but most important perceived advantage of management contracting over the traditional approach, and that is in the management itself. Management contractors see themselves as better managers than architects or engineers. If the inherent incompatibility of creativity and managerial skill in architects is a fact, then management contractors may well be better managers than architects or engineers. However, there is really no reason why this should be so, given that the primary focus in their education is on their skills as constructors and only secondarily as managers. It does not appear yet to be generally accepted that the responsible staff of a management contractor should be managers first and technical construction experts second. Even in the project management context, where one would expect a purer form of management, this does not seem to be so. McLaughlin describes the perfect project manager as follows:

> "Such a person is likely to be a well rounded construction professional with a good grounding in one of the disciplines of building, engineering, architecture or surveying; have sufficient knowledge of building management from a client and a contractor's view point, understand fully the workings of the construction industry, have a good understanding of construction law and preferably have worked at some time as a member of a design team and for a contractor. And, perhaps most importantly of all he must have a thorough understanding of management theory, practice and techniques".[14]

In other words, construction professional first, management expert second. The problem is that not all contractors have proved to be good managers. There are complaints that the management contractor does not manage at all, and that he merely acts as a post box between the trade contractors and the client. He is therefore a barrier to communication. His involvement merely adds another layer of bureaucracy which increases cost and causes delay. There is confusion as to the management contractors role, which causes a chain of command problems for trade contractor's. Here too there is a complaint that the management contractor has authority without responsibility. Thus in the United Kingdom, as well as the United States, expectations have not always been matched by reality.

The Architect's View

So far in this paper attention has been focussed on management contracting from the perspective of the employer and the management contractor. What do the other parties to a traditional contract think about management contracting? The reaction of architects has apparently been mixed. Some have welcomed management contracting and all the other new roles in contracting with open arms, recognizing the need for improved management techniques, and the failure of their profession to provide this. Others, in the more traditional mould, object strongly to the interference of management contractors in areas which they regard as their preserve. One suspects that between this lies the majority, who rather reluctantly accept management contracting as a necessary evil. As I have said, some have reacted by setting up their own management practices, usually under the name of project management.

In one sense, architects and engineers should regard management contracting as a god-send if, as should happen, it relieves them of their obligation to supervise (as opposed to inspect) the works as they are executed. Architects have long protested that they do not have a duty to supervise but the courts have consistently declined to accept this. The new JCT Management Contract imposes on the management contractor the obligation to supervise

14 J McLaughlin, "What is Project Management? Part II," *Asian Architect and Contractor*, January 1987, p 38.

(see Schedule 3 Item 43). For the imposition of this duty on the management contractor to be of a benefit to architects (in terms of reduction in insurance premiums and sleepless nights), this must be reflected in the terms of engagement by the client of the architect. For too long, the contractual relationship between the architect and the client has been too loose, and there are not yet generally available standard forms of terms of engagement for use with management contracts. Unless the roles are clearly set out in writing, there will be an inevitable overlap which, although it will potentially give the client two parties to blame if anything goes wrong, will result in the payment of two sets of fees for the same task and the real possibility of confusion between the architect and management contractor as to who should be doing what by way of supervision.

Quantity surveyors are likely to be pleased with the development of management contracting as, in the JCT form at least they are a defined party and their invaluable contribution to the professional team is properly recognised. They may however see project management as an even better opportunity to get into the field of management in their own right.

The Trade Contractor's View

Last but not least one should consider the views of the trade contractors. Their attitude is likely to be that all the talk about management is fine, but it is they that actually carry out the work, and their position under a management contract is not that different from a traditional contract. However, given the division of the construction into small packages and the crucial importance of co-ordinating these packages properly so that no delay occurs (*i.e.* keeping the trucks moving along the highway), trade contractors will have to be made very conscious of the consequences if they delay others. Under the JCT Works Contract Conditions (Clause 4.50) they will have to pay for any loss and expense suffered as a result of any act, omission or default on their part. Even if a one-off contract fails to make such a provision, the trade contractors are likely to be liable in damages for breach of contract. This pressure is likely to increase the professionalism of the good trade contractors and force the bad ones out of business. One fact that has emerged clearly from recent United Kingdom experience is that major United Kingdom contractors acting as trade contractors do not tend to get on well with the management contracting subsidiaries of major United Kingdom contractors in a management contract context. This probably results from the inevitable rivalries between companies of approximate equal standing. In discussing management I have already referred to the experiences some trade contractors have had with management contracting. I will deal later with two further aspects concerning trade contractors - firstly their attitude to the standard form/one off contract debate and secondly some potential areas of litigation relating to trade contractors.

Standard Form v. One-off

The debate as to whether or not construction contracts should be standardized or whether they should be tailor-made to suit the circumstances is an interminable one, and it applies equally to management contracting. Most of the arguments on either side apply to all forms of contract but there are a few which relate specifically to the concept of management contracts.

The advantages of standard forms are that they are cheap, require no special drafting, little or no legal input, are easy to use, there is a short learning curve to familiarise oneself with the contract, and that familiarity will increase with regular use. The contracts are produced from consensus and therefore should be fair to all parties. There are two points specific to management contracts - the first, a simple one, is that the time it will take to prepare a one off management contract is incompatible with the basic philosophy of management contracting which is to get the work started at the earliest possible moment (the answer to this is that lawyers, quantity surveyors and whoever else is involved in contract drafting will have to learn to "fast track" their production of contracts).

The second is more complex and relates to the placing of risk. It is undeniable that the JCT Management Contract represents a low risk for the management contractor as almost all the risk falls on the employer. Employers not surprisingly are not always happy with this, and may, in the drafting of the contract, seek to transfer some of the risk back to the management contractor, for example by setting a gross maximum price or by giving the management contractor the responsibility for defaulting or insolvent trade contractors. The management contractor's answer to this is that to do so is inconsistent with the philosophy of management contracting which is that the management contractor should at all times be trying to act in the client's best interest and should not be forced to protect his own position at the same time. In practice however management contractors are commonly prepared to move away from management contracting in its purest form in order to obtain work. Some do not see the acceptance of some risk as being inconsistent with good management contracting. The client will of course have to pay an increased fee for the acceptance of risk, but he may regard it as money well spent.

A major factor that is often overlooked in the standard form/one-off debate is the attitude of trade or sub-contractors. Experience shows that where there are one-off contracts or significant amendments to a standard form, this will lead to qualified tenders by trade contractors or they will not quote at all. Trade/sub-contractors are unlikely to be armed with a battery of lawyers and other advisers to assist them in interpreting a contract that they have never seen before or complex amendments whose effect will have to be traced through the entire contract. I repeat that it is the trade contractors who actually carry out the work under a management contract, and it may be regarded as unfair to them that along with all the other difficulties that they may face, they will be working under a contract that they are not familiar with.

I will not dwell on the topic of risk but, in a management contract context, there will come a point where the imposition of too great a burden of risk on the contractor and thence down to the trade contractors will destroy the management contract ethos, and the client might as well use the traditional form of contract with all that involves.

The other side of the coin is that one should not use a standard form of contract where that standard form does not adequately protect the party proposing to use it. As is well known, the JCT forms of traditional contract have come in for considerable criticism, and some extremely strong words have been expressed about the position of professionals who recommend them to their clients, even for use as a matrix in drafting a tailor made contract. The JCT forms (including the management contract) are commonly considered to be weighted in favour of the contractor.

The JCT Management Contract has already come in for a certain amount of criticism both in general ("A low risk contract for a high risk industry?" - title of a one-day conference[15]) and in particular (Oppenheimer's *Guide to the JCT Management Contract* 1987). The overall view in relation to standard form contracts is that only if they satisfy the project requirements should they be used in unamended form. It will require skill and experience to decide whether to amend the standard form or discard it and draft documentation specifically for the project.

An argument that has been made specific to management contracts is that drafting a standard form is inherently inconsistent with the philosophy of management contracting which require that one should "keep the concepts loosely defined to permit a flexible response to the perplexing changes in the economic climate".[16]

Problem Areas

I would like now to consider some of the aspects of management contracting which cause difficulty and which may therefore lead to litigation. While lawyers are often criticized for their keenness to litigate and arbitrate, it must be borne in mind that they only act in response to instructions from their clients who are aggrieved and/or out of pocket. I am not aware of any reported case law of the English courts on what the responsibilities of a management contractor are, though it should be noted that the Court of Appeal has looked at management contracts in a slightly different context in the case of *City of London Corporation* v. *Bovis Construction Limited*.[17] This was a case in which the local authority applied to the court for an injunction to restrain breaches of a notice under the Control of Pollution Act 1974 to control noise on a construction site. In that case, the Court of Appeal had little difficulty in recognizing and understanding the role of the defendant as (in this case) construction manager:

> "Clearly, as construction managers, Bovis were in full control of the site and have been properly served with a notice; it mattered not that the actual work of construction was carried out by trade contractors, who, by the terms of their contracts, were bound to comply with Bovis' instructions".

(Admittedly without knowing the background to this case, it seems that management was lacking in that the construction manager had not prevented trade contractors from carrying out work at prohibited times and on prohibited days.)

15 Organized by Hawksmere Ltd., 11 March 1988.
16 Article by WF Pratt Jr, "Afterword: Contracts and Uncertainty" in *Law and Contemporary Problems*, Winter 1983, p 169 at p 171.
17 Times Law Report, 21 April 1988.

In looking at the situation in the United States one must recognize that the decisions which have emerged from the forms of contract commonly used over there will not be the same as the decisions emerging from those used in this country. One must keep well in mind the comment of the Privy Council in the case of *Mitsui Construction* v. *Attorney General of Hong Kong*[18] that comparison of one contract with another can seldom be a useful aid to construction and may be misleading. The principles and ideas will however be relevant to the United Kingdom context.

We have seen in this paper how important the role of the management contractor is in co-ordinating the trade contractors in the execution of their various packages of work. Failure so to co-ordinate can have disastrous consequences. In a number of United States cases where there has been no direct contractual link between the trade contractors and the CM on the one part and the CM and the employer on the other part (*i.e.* a construction management arrangement, as we know it in the United Kingdom) the employer has been held to have an implied contractual obligation to coordinate the various trade contractors to prevent unreasonable delays in the project (see for example *Broadway Maintenance Corp* v. *Rutgers*[19]). The lack of a contractual connection between the trade contractors and the CM has led to a number of tort claims by trade contractors against CM's. In *Gateway Erectors Division* v. *Lutheran General Hospital*,[20] the Court held that a trade contractor not in privity of contract with the contract manager had a cause of action in tort against him on the basis that he negligently directed the trade contractor to proceed with certain work and carelessly failed to supervise another sub-contractors work. In *J McKinney & Son* v. *Lake Placid 1980 Olympic Games Inc.*[21] a New York court held that:

> "Because there was no contractual relationship between [the CM] and the Plaintiff, an action for breach of contract does not lie. However, the negligence allegations assert legitimate causes of action... [the CM's] responsibilities under the contract appear to be such as to establish a duty of care to sub-contractors like Plaintiff. As project manager, the CM was required to 'manage, supervise and inspect the construction'. Furthermore, it was obligated to review the drawings and specifications for the contract, to continuously review the design during its development', and 'to identify defects of commission or omission in the design'. These duties can reasonably be said to inure to the benefit of sub-contractors as well as the owner, for the former are 'members of a limited class' whose reliance upon the projects manager's liability is clearly foreseeable."[22]

These cases have their roots in English law, for example *Holme* v. *Guppey*.[23] In a properly drafted contract, such as the JCT Management Contract, there is a contractual provision for payment for loss and expense in this kind of situation, but if a one-off contract is inordinantly biased in favour of the

18 (1987) 10 Con LR 1.
19 90 NJ 253, 447 A2d 906, quoted at length in Sweet, p 444.
20 102 11 App 3d 300, 430 NE 2d 20 (1981).
21 (1833) 13 M & W 387.
22 92 App Div 2d 991, 461 NYS 2d 483 (1983), quoted at p 5-102 in *Construction Law*, ed. S Stein, Matthew Bender.
23 (1838) 3 M & W 387.

management contractor and his client, it may not and these implied obligations may have to be looked for.

Questions have also arisen as to whether trade contractors may have tort claims against each other.

In the case of delay and disruption claims, such tort actions in England are likely to run foul of the courts ever growing reluctant to order damages for pure economic loss. This type of litigation may be one of the reasons why the JCT decided to opt for the management contract form rather than the construction management concept (as we know it).It is better to define mutual obligations in a contract than risk the ever-changing realms of tort law.

Then there is the question of the potential liability of the management contractor for defects in the design, given his obligation to advise on "buildability". The JCT Management Contract, Schedule 3 provides that amongst the management contractor's many duties are :

> "3. Advising on the practical implications of proposed drawings and specifications.
> "4. Formulating and agreeing construction methods with the Professional Team and advising on build-ability."

In the United States it has been said that:

> "Although the CM does not prepare the final plans and specifications, the architect/engineer and owner are relying in part on his expertise. Such reliance may result in liability if the CM's advice is negligent. It has been argued that the CM's lack of control over the design process should insulate him from liability at least third party. However, at least one court has expressed a willingness to charge a CM with liability for negligent design review".[24]

The development of a contractor's responsibility for design which emerged in the English case of *EDAC* v. *Moss*[25] but which might now be thought to be on the way out because of the drawing back of the boundaries of tort liability, may be set for a revival in the management contract context.

Then there is the question of whether the management contractor, being part of the professional team, should take on with that the higher levels of responsibility of a professional. United States commentators are not entirely at one on this. Stanley Bynum believes that "it is likely that the CM will be held to a standard of professional care analogous to the standard usually imposed by law upon architects and engineers"[26], while Professor Justin Sweet is more circumspect:

> "The professional standard has its greatest application when the design professional is performing design rather than administrative services. Inasmuch as the services performed by a CM are connected more to administration than to design, it is possible that the ordinary but not professional negligence standard will be applied, meaning that no expert testimony will be required. But if the CM is simply a

24 Matthew Bender p 5-86.
25 (1985) 2 Con LR 1.
26 Article by SD Bynum, "Construction Management and design build/fast track from the perspective of a general contractor," *Law and Contemporary Problems*, Winter 1983, p 25, at p 30.

> professional adviser performing administrative tasks for the owner, he looks less like a design professional."[27]

In concluding this section dealing with potential developments in the law on management contracts, I would like to adopt the words of Professor Justin Sweet as follows:

> "Any observations will have to be tentative, not only because of the lack of crystallized practices but because the law must deal with a series of new problems that cannot be easily solved by use of simple reference to earlier precedents or statutes. Law functions to a large degree through crude categories aided by analogies, largely for administrative convenience. Law often lags behind organisational and functional shifts in the real world. Inevitably [there will be] a period of temporary disharmony. It is hoped that predictable solutions will emerge."[28]

Unfortunately this optimism has not always been well founded. In *Cable (1956)* v. *Hutcherson Bros. Pty. Ltd.*[29] the High Court of Australia (the highest court in the country) had to interpret the expression "turnkey". Barwick CJ stated:

> "It is not a term of art and even if it could be taken to mean that the works must be handed over as a going concern, I would not have thought that in the context of these articles the word or expression meant that the builder warranted the efficacy of the works he had agreed to erect. The same reasoning would, in my opinion, deny that the acceptance of all responsibility for supply and erection and operation of the project...involved any undertaking as to the suitability of the agreed design. In my opinion, for all these reasons I conclude that the respondent promised no more than to carry out the specified work in a workmanlike manner."

It is felt that nowadays an arbitrator or court in Australia would attach special meaning to the word "turnkey" and find that it included responsibility for design, but let us hope that we do not have to wait 20 years in the United Kingdom for similar understanding of the basic concepts.

Unanswered Questions

Before summing up I would like to pose a number of questions that have occurred to me which seem to be of general interest, but to which I can only offer tentative answers.

Why is management contracting not used more in an international context?

Contracts in developing countries seem to be ideally suited to management. Given limited funds, often provided by an aid agency, and the desire of the recipient country to use as much of its local labour and materials as possible, management contracting will reduce to a minimum the amount of involvement of overseas and expensive contractors and thereby save scarce foreign

27 Sweet, p 453.
28 Sweet, p 442.
29 (1969) 43 ALJR 321.

exchange. I understand that the World Bank is presently looking at the various new roles in contracting with a view to deciding an overall policy. The PRC seems to have recognized the value of this in that commonly in construction projects there, foreign general contractors act only in a management role as part of a joint venture. In practice however the advantages of project management and management contracting have not proved themselves in the PRC for a number of reasons, amongst them being low worker efficiency, weakness of the contracting teams in co-ordination planning and control and low quality - see article by Vincent Lo Hong - Sui.[30]

Why is management contracting not commonly used in civil engineering?

I have been offered various answers to this question: that much civil engineering work is publicly funded and the public authorities are slower to react to the changes in types of contract than the private sector, that engineers by character and by training prefer to maintain a "hands on" approach to their work and would not be happy with a pure management role, and, finally (one that I hardly dare repeat!) that civil engineering is simpler than building and it therefore requires less in the way of management skills.

Is it still right that the architect should play his quasi- judicial role in granting extensions of time etc?

The answer is probably yes, as this is a vital function and gives reassurance to the trade contractors, but there will inevitably be a further blurring of roles between the architect and the management contractor.

Is the growth of management contracting and the other new roles linked to the recent growth in the economy?

The answer probably is no, because management contracting has survived a number of cycles of boom and recession in the United States and has not noticably been affected by these. In recession or boom, time is still money, and the principal perceived advantage of management contracting, namely time saving, will always be important.

Is there a connection between the growth of management contracting in the UK and the reduction of union power in the construction industry?

The answer is probably not to a significant degree, although it may have helped management contractors to reduce the numbers of their own labour force and divide construction into small packages.

Does the fact that the management arms of a number of the major UK contractors seem to be producing better financial results than their traditional contracting arms mean that they are profiting at the expense of their clients?

30 *Building Journal Hong Kong China*, January 1987, p 97.

The answer should be emphatically no, as the successful and profitable management contracting business is in no way incompatible with a satisfied client with a good quality product. The management companies are probably only taking business away from their traditional contracting arms.

Is management contracting only suited to new building?

The answer is no; management contracting has shown itself to be admirably suited to refurbishment, where occupying tenants' demands and complaints may need changes in plan or design.

Conclusion

I have put forward so many advantages and disadvantages of management contracting and considered so many factors that inevitably it is difficult to draw any firm conclusion. What can be said safely is that the mould of traditional contracting has been broken and it is extremely unlikely that there will ever be a return to the use of the traditional approach alone. Whether management contracting becomes the dominant force in the future or whether any of the other new roles (or developments from them) become dominant will depend on the success of each as they are tested in the market and everyone involved in the construction industry gets a clear idea of their advantages and disadvantages in practice.

If management contracting is not a success, the next trend may be a growth in construction management, where the manager acts as the client's agent and does not enter into contracts with the trade contractors. This is being used, seemingly with great success, on the Broadgate development in the City of London. The JCT would of course have considered construction management in deciding what form to adopt as their standard, but no doubt felt that it was too radical a departure from the current arrangements to be adopted immediately. It certainly has its disadvantages, as has been demonstrated by the United States experience and the litigation there that has arisen from CM contracts. Other variations on the general theme are already in existence and may find greater favour as other types of contract go out of fashion. The changes certainly give scope for discussion on the advantages and disadvantages of the different types of contract for many years to come.

Safeguards and Sanctions 13

Michael Pepper

Synopsis

The paper proposes that contractors should operate self regulation for Quality Assurance, that specifications should be standardized and that other Quality Assurance parameters should be defined more carefully at pre-contract stage. By such means, it is suggested that the quality problems of the 1970's can be reduced. Where loss cannot be avoided, insurance should be made available as a means of avoiding the costs of litigation or arbitration.

Introduction

The object of this paper is to stimulate debate. Contracts are, to some, boring stuff. They are sometimes seen to be, at best, an unnecessary complication of standard practice, and at worst, an incomprehensible collection of jargon produced by lawyers for lawyers. Closer acquaintance reveals a very different picture.

Contracts in the construction industry are complex documents but necessarily so because construction itself is a very complex and diverse activity which places heavy demands upon both contractor and employer, or at any rate those acting on behalf of the employer.

This paper is targetted upon the capacity of contracts to assure performance, particularly in respect of quality of product and the incidence of latent defects in completed work. The views expressed are acknowledged to be contentious.

Specification

Specification is a vital part of contract documentation in the construction industry or any industry for that matter. Traditionally, even for quite minor projects, the specification has been a bulky document which defines, trade by trade, the quality of materials to be used, establishes constraints upon working practices and matters of workmanship and imposes a regime of material testing.

Until recently specifications were standard only to the extent that they dealt with the same trades. Obviously there was at least an opportunity to standardize specifications within any one practice of organization but otherwise the documents used varied substantially. All very confusing for contractors.

Standard specifications are now available which allow individual input to suit the special demands of a specific project. Some public sector clients insist on their use. Standardization of specification must improve communication and understanding between designer and constructor. It will encourage a progressive build up of "know-how" and skill within the world of the contractor and will remove the temptation for designers to "re-invent the wheel" for every project. Standard documents serve as a sound base from which young designers may develop their experience of practice and standards expected in the industry. All this is good for the end product in qualitative terms.

Familiarity with standards demanded in construction is important both to designer and to contractor. Where specifications are "one-off" documents for each job it is unlikely, at least in building construction, that a contractor will read a specification comprehensively and assimilate its content in detail before work starts. Commonly staff and operatives on site will continue "as before" with each new job until they are pulled up short by a member of the design team waving the specification! Standardization of specification format and content means that the rules remain constant and the goal-posts stay in the place where everyone knows them to be. The learning curve on each new project is substantially reduced. Benefits include the establishment of a consistent base for project management and quality assurance.

Contract performance

Performance of contract obligations relates to both programme and quality. Traditionally contracts deal in a finite way with programme insofar as they define a date for site possession and a date for completion. Performance within those constraints is a matter of project management or, in many cases, simply site management.

Performance in relation to quality is a matter of self regulation on the part of the contractor and supervision by the designer. Contracts rarely demand a specific standard of self regulation by the contractor. Supervision by the designer may in many cases be confined to periodic inspection. In no circumstances can periodic inspection be construed as supervision. In civil engineering contracts of size it is probable that there will be a site based supervizing team. In building work a significant part of the annual building programme will be completed without any resident supervisory presence and in those circumstances at least self regulation on the part of the contractor as a function of contract is highly desirable if not essential.

Quality Assurance

"Quality Assurance" is the current "buzz word" or "in" expression in the world of construction. The interpretation of the expression is, at present, all things to all men. "Discussions", as they say, "are continuing".

In design terms, "quality assurance" may mean anything between critical perusal, with an arithmetic check of calculation and dimension, and a thorough check and appraisal in principle. On site, it can mean anything between a visit once a month by an outside agency and an established team resident on site. The principles must be established for each particular contract and before that can be done the objectives must be defined. Quality assurance parameters, in relation to the needs of any specific project, should be determined prior to contract and defined as a contract condition insofar as they relate either to self regulation on the part of the contractor or the jurisdication of either an outside agency or control by the designer. "Quality Assurance" is what everyone outside the industry, including the courts, has always assumed to exist but which has been hugely eroded by relatively recent commercial pressures on both contractor and designer and by the long term change from construction by tradesmen employed by the contractor to "construction by sub-contractor" which is the rule today.

Checking and the application of the building regulations

Fundamental design misconception and indeed direct arithmetic errors may be dealt with by current procedures. In the future even that control may disappear. Building Regulations are in any event effective only in relation to health and safety, serviceability is not a consideration. Construction on site is subject only to low level periodic inspections. External checking in pursuit of Building Regulation consent is not in any sense an effective method of assuring quality of construction nor indeed is it intended to fulfil that function.

Latent Defects

Latent defects have been a feature of construction throughout the period over which records have been kept and indeed critical examination of the better preserved historic monuments suggests that they were subject to the same basic difficulties prior to records being kept.

In the mid-1950's building projects were relatively small and most were designed in (then) conventional materials and incorporated conventional details. In the 1960's the industry "heated-up" and new methods of construction emerged. Contractors still operated largely with their own labour. With the early 1970's a heated-up construction economy combined with an increased output of potential construction professionals from the Universities (new and old); job architects got younger. New materials and magic potions to add to old materials were sold enthusiastically by an ever widening band of salesmen. It was a period of great change which embraced too much work, too little experience and/or training at the decision making level, too many bright ideas, too much confidence and too few resources. It is indeed surprising how well most of the buildings constructed at that time have done. It was a period which embraced the peak of the "lump" sub-contracting method.

No wonder perhaps that litigation relating to latent defects flowered and prospered from about that time. It shows no sign, in this age of consumer protection, of abating. Many organizations in the construction industry make provision in their annual budgetting for the cost of resisting the writs that have yet to be served.

The bulk of latent defects arise from either aberrations in detail design or aberrations in construction practice. Such design aberrations are, in design terms, quite likely to be reduced in number by a quality assurance format that includes design audit by experienced practitioners. The nature of building construction and acknowledging that it is the most labour intensive form of manufacture yet devised by man suggests that although quality assurance techniques established on site may substantially reduce the risk of major material or method problems it is unlikley to result in a noticeable reduction in random errors, often known as the Monday morning or Friday evening syndrome, until the disciplines inherent in the concept of quality assurance start to induce habit in the industry at large. That could take years.

Latent defect protection

In the previous section it is implied that, in spite of current trends towards the establishment of more formal quality assurance techniques, latent defects will continue to be a feature of building construction although perhaps the frequency of occurrence may be reduced. It follows that protection for a building owner or tenant with a full repairing lease can only be achieved by insurance. The French have such a system and there are some, limited, policies available here. There are recommendations about to be published which refer to the wider provision of such facilities in the United Kingdom.

Insurance provides a direct route to repair without the need for the insured to fund that repair. For building owners and tenants it removes the risk of litigation and hence the need to fund litigation. It removes responsibility for diagnosing the problem and defining the remedial action from the building owner and tenant.

Given the establishment of a readily available insurance facility contracts should provide for appropriate latent defects protection on a project basis paid for by the employer.

Propositions

Arising from this paper the following propositions may be advanced.

- Standardization of specification as part of contract documentation in the construction industry will improve communication between designer and contractor and thus improve contract performance.
- Incorporation of contract conditions defining standards and procedures for quality assurance and/or self regulation during the construction period, to be implemented by the contractor, is essential to achieve better performance.
- Submission of drawings and calculations for consent under Building Regulations is only a very "low key" control on quality of detail design. It is no substitute for adequate quality assurance procedures in the design office. Site visiting by a Building Inspectorate is not intended to, and does not, offer any assurance of contract performance. It can only, at best eradicate gross error or default where such error or default is on view at the time of the visit.

- Latent defects in construction may reduce with the introduction of effective quality assurance procedures on site but will not be eliminated. Insurance, on a project basis, offers the best protection to building owners and tenants.

14 Project Management and Quality Control Discussion and Debate

Plenary Session

Introducing Paper 9, Dr. Barnes said that project management was not concerned merely with critical path analysis or cost control. They should be regarded as the tools of the project manager rather than the core of his enterprise. Project management involved the following objectives:

1. Motivation of people to work together;
2. Establishment of clear objectives in construction projects;
3. Establishment of effective communication pathways within the project team;
4. Strong decision-making at all stages, with the project manager having a clear view of the direction of the project;
5. Stimulation of those involved to think ahead, with solutions being found before problems begin to affect progress;
6. In particular, integration of the processes of construction and design, so as to facilitate solution of problems rather than apportioning blame;
7. Appreciation of the effect of risk, both in the sense of allocation and also in minimizing its impact on the project.

The aim of Paper 9 was to suggest a new form of contract which would stimulate good management by the application of these techniques to the construction process. Although the particular form proposed was intended for use in civil engineering projects, the flexibility of the contract was such that there was no obstacle to its adoption in building and other forms of construction. The proposals could also serve as a basis for a form of contract for use within the European Community, should the present proposals of the European Commission be proceeded with. It was noted that the emphasis placed on motivation of the parties was a particularly desirable feature of the proposed form of contract.

It was pointed out that one inevitable consequence of creating new forms of contract was that a period of uncertainty would exist while the courts were asked to construe clauses which were unclear. This was to be contrasted with the alternative approach of gradual evolution by amendment. Dr. Barnes said that the purpose of the new style contract was to bring to an end the proliferation of standard forms by providing one generally accepted and universally available contract form. It was intended that the terms of the new form would be more clear and less susceptible to differences of interpretation than earlier forms.

Mr. Keating, introducing Paper 10 on the Control of Quality, emphasized the absence of adequate remedies against quality defects under conventional forms of contract. Consideration should be given to amendments to standard construction forms to introduce a degree of quality control as explained in various BSI documents.[1] It would cost more. It would be no more effective than the extent to which it was enforced. Quality control could not extend to the whole of the building process; but in certain areas, well prepared, detailed schemes, vigorously applied, ought theoretically to reduce latent defects.

Working party on the Employer's Agent

Mr. Stanger said that there were two main issues for discussion arising out of Paper 11:

- was it satisfactory for the employer's agent to act simultaneously as an adjudicator, bearing in mind the importance of his decisions, even where subsequent arbitration was available?
- should there be an independent adjudicator appointed at the outset, ready to intervene at short notice, who would give a decision which was binding but subject to later arbitration?

Mr. Stanger's view was that, to act in the best interests of the employer, the agent should direct rather than react to events, and should therefore assume a greater role in relation to management of the project. If the agent was to become more closely involved in project management, this would be inconsistent with acting independently, and it followed that the adjudication process ought to be performed by a different person. This applied particularly in engineering contracts. It was pointed out that the opposite approach was currently being taken by the Department of Transport. The ICE form of contract provides for the engineer and the engineer's representative to act as adjudicator as well as agent. The Department are proposing that this be modified with the engineer being an employee of the Department of Transport and the engineer's representative being an independent engineer but given very limited powers. The proposal is that decisions, hitherto given by an independent engineer under Clauses 12 (unforeseen physical conditions) and 44 (extensions of time) would be given by the engineer employed by the Department. The same engineer would render the Clause 66 decision following which the contractor could go to arbitration.

In the debate that followed it was pointed out that one of the particular difficulties under engineering contracts was the provision for the engineer to review or adjudicate upon his own decisions. If an outside adjudicator was to undertake the review, there was no reason why the engineer should not make the decision in the first instance. It was also pointed out that a distinction had to be drawn between traditional contracts where the designer need not be involved in management, and "fast-track" contracts, where the designer had to be so involved. In regard to the latter, each party would be represented by an agent and there should be a single project administrator who would give

1 See BS 4778 and Quality Assurance in Construction : CIRIA Special Publication 55.

decisions on disputes, reviewable by later arbitration. The administrator would not be involved in the design process and would therefore not be giving decisions in which he had an interest.

The system under which engineers acted independently as well as fulfilling the design role was defended. This system had been in existence for over 200 years. Combining the roles of designer and adjudicator allowed the engineer to find the cheapest solution. The key question was the provision of adequate sanctions and incentives. Arbitration as presently provided under engineering contracts was not always a sufficient sanction and it was desirable to have the option of bringing in an independent adjudicator. The question was whether an independent adjudicator should be appointed at the outset. It was also important to maintain trust between the parties and confidence in the independence of the adjudicator.

As regards the appointment of an adjudicator, it was pointed out that different disputes or issues might require different adjudicators, and any proposal for calling in an outside adjudicator should operate only in respect of major disputes. The decisions of such an adjudicator would be more acceptable to the contractor if the adjudicator was not paid directly by the employer. In relation to adjudication under engineering contracts, it was particularly important that the role and responsibilities of the engineeer be clearly set out, in relation both to the contractor and the employer.

Summarizing the conclusions of the meeting, Mr. Stanger said that the concept of an adjudicator had some appeal, but the role needed to be defined, particularly if this were to form part of the European Community proposals for 1992. The proposal to appoint an adjudicator from the outset was difficult to justify; there was a need to look at each project on its merits and more input from contractors was desirable. The Department of Transport proposals were not new and could be combined with the introduction of an independent adjudicator.

The meeting generally agreed with the proposition that it was desirable that further consideration be given to the introduction of an adjudicator who, where a decision of the agent acting in his independent capacity was challenged, could make a temporary decision which would be binding until arbitration or completion of the project. There was agreement that engineers in particular when appointed as the client's agent, could be put into a position of great difficulty where they sought to act against the employer's interest. Adjudication was a possible solution to this difficulty.

Working Party on New Roles in Contracting

In presenting Paper 12, Mr. Winter emphasized that the objective in identifying new roles in contracting was not to deal better with disputes but to facilitate the efficient execution of the work. The objective of management contracting was to avoid the conflicts of interest which could arise between contractor and client.

In response, a representative of a major company involved in building procurement said that management contracting still involved an essentially adversarial relationship between client and contractor, and that preference was for project management whereby the client entered into a series of direct trade contracts. It was pointed out that under either system - management contracting or project management - there should not be a distinction between building or civil engineering work. Both should be covered by the same principles and forms which ought to be referred to simply as construction contracts. This should embody all forms of technology that might be involved in the construction process, and the form of contract should be available to clients from a large range of industries who required construction work. There were variations in approach and terminology, but with a sufficiently flexible approach, these could be overcome.

The working party considered the effect of new contract systems on the traditional role of the architect or engineer. It was said that in Australia, while the role of the architect as an adjudicator was relatively less important, in civil engineering the role was much used and highly regarded. Mr. Winter said that the adjudication role of the architect or engineer, granting extensions of time and giving decisions on disputes continued to exist under management contracts, but stressed that it was necessary for the roles of professionals to be clearly defined, to avoid confusion with the role of the management contractor. The meeting accepted the importance of separating the independent adjudication role from other functions of the architect or engineer.

There was no clear indication as to where the impetus for the development of management had come from. It could be regarded as the response of the construction industry to the apparent desire of clients for more and more effective management of construction projects. It was important that contract forms should be available which reflected the expectation of clients. This expectation included closer involvement of the clients in construction and the lessening of the adversarial approach in the performance of construction work.

Working Party on Safeguards and Sanctions

Mr. Pepper (Paper 13) introduced the subject of quality assurance. In general terms such requirements had always been assumed to exist, but specific techniques were now being developed and implemented and, indeed, demanded by some clients. One matter which would facilitate quality assurance was standardization of specification documents. This would allow site management to achieve greater familiarity with the requirements of the contract. Few contractors in fact imposed methods of quality assurance; and where enforcement was placed in the hands of a third party, enforcement was likely to be periodic and therefore inadequate. Self-regulation by contractors was the most effective means.

It was observed that a distinction had to be drawn between quality assurance applied to management functions and its application to the quality of the end product. Quality assurance ought to be inherent in management. On site, however, where the product itself was under review, quality assurance might require staff specifically charged with inspection, reporting and recording. To the extent that quality could not be assured, the risk should be covered by insurance.

Dissemination of technical knowledge concerning defects or failures was still a problem, which could lead to the same problem recurring. Greater access to information was needed.

The meeting agreed that periodic or intermittent inspection was insufficient to achieve adequate quality control. The most efficient way of achieving adequate quality was thought to be through the provision of incentives and sanctions. The degree of control or supervision would vary according to the particular work element.However, it was necessary to ensure that decisions as to the appropriate degree of control did not displace the contractor's overall obligation as to quality.

Various means of achieving adequate quality were discussed. The provision of a range of consultants, able to deal with specialist areas of work was one possibility, but this would involve cost constraints. Certification of personnel within the management team would assist in quality assurance, but it was doubted that this procedure could be applied to specialist site operatives. Insurance should not be seen as an alternative to quality assurance. Better training would assist, in some areas. For example, architects, would acquire more knowledge of the physics of materials. It was generally agreed that standard forms of contract ought to provide a more precise identification of the functions and responsibilities of all parties involved in the work. Further, diversification of standards should be avoided and co-ordination of different standards should be achived where possible.

As regards sanctions, these were seen as a necessary corollary to the achievement of quality. There was support for the avoidance of final certificates which might prevent claims being brought against the contractor. It was suggested that for the maintenance of effective sanctions in regard to defective design, supervision or construction, an employer had to be in a position to bring effective proceedings against any blameworthy party. The major difficulty which employers encountered was that of bringing potential alternative defendants before the same tribunal. This was often impossible in practice where different contracts and sub-contracts contained inconsistent arbitration clauses, or where some contained arbitration clauses and others not. It was considered that co-ordination of contractual disputes clauses was feasible and desirable. If concurrent dispute resolution could not be achieved through arbitration, then it would have to be ensured that disputes could be taken before the courts. For this purpose it is necessary to ensure both that court proceedings would not be stayed[2] and that the court would accept jurisdiction over the dispute.[3]

2 Arbitration Act 1950 s.4(1). See *Taunton-Collins* v. *Cromie* [1964] 1 WLR 633.
3 See *NHRA* v. *Derek Crouch* [1984] QB 644, *Finnegan* v. *Sheffield CC* 43 Build LR 124.

Part IV

Control of Programme and Payment

Contract Policy for Time 15

Sir Patrick Garland

Synopsis

The origins of time provisions in construction contracts are examined. The dependence of liquidated damages on extension machinery is explained and views expressed on the effect of time becoming at large. Possible alternatives to existing contractual sanctions are discussed.

Introduction

When I was asked to take part in a conference the object of which was to take an entirely fresh look at the principles and philosophy of construction contracts, I was struck very forcibly by the thought that as a practitioner one tends to see the world from inside the standard forms and to concern oneself with what can be done within their constraints. Any radical re-appraisal, or even a more limited enquiry as to whether they justify themselves tend to be dismissed as impractical pipe dreams; and we apply ourselves once again to the niceties of a loss and expense claim or work out an argument for defeating the obvious intention of the parties who have in their innocence thought that they could produce a simple provision for liquidated damages and phased completion by saying that liquidated damages shall be levied at the rate of £100 per week for each uncompleted dwelling[1]. We all tend to be creatures of habit and to prefer the devil we know so we cling to the familiar however inconvenient it may be, hoping sometimes to mitigate the inconvenience by writing "nil" in the Appendix to JCT 80[2] or binding in a few letters as part of an ICE Fifth Edition - one of those in fact being the Contractors' Method Statement[3], both of which turn out to be the contractual equivalent of lighting the blue touch paper. And how we cling to the familiar. The reluctance to use JCT 80 was really quite astonishing. How eagerly were other new forms considered. Conversely, how well have specially drafted contracts fared? It would be interesting to know how many special forms have succeeded because we tend to know only about those which did not, my own experience including

Bramall & Ogden Ltd. v. *Sheffield City Council* (1983) 29 Build LR 73.
Temloc v. *Errill Properties Ltd.* 39 Build LR 30.
McAlpine v. *Yorkshire Water Authority*.

the Thames Barrier and its subsequent variations, also at least two contracts for oil rigs (if these can properly be called construction contracts).

Origin of time obligations

Before looking forward, it might be instructive to look back. In so doing it has to be borne in mind that the Common Law regarded time as of the essence of the contract in the absence of a contrary intention, so that failure to complete by the due date could be treated as a repudiation. Thus complete performance by one party was a condition precedent to performance by the other, so that even if time was not of the essence the party in default would not be entitled to payment until performance was complete. In practice the time obligation was often phased so that a basic programme rather than an obligation to proceed regularly and diligently was a term of the contract. There are early examples of contracts without fixed completion dates. As early as 1322 a mason agreed to build a round tower in Chester for a lump sum with provision for extras. The work was to be carried out continuously and he was to reside in Chester until it was finished. The sting was that he was not entitled to the price until he had finished. A little later a plumber contracted to do some lead roofing at Westminster Palace and to complete '*absque aliqua intermissione et dilatione*' - without any interruption or delay. Progress payments or payments by instalments were quite common. The giving of a bond in a fixed sum for the due performance of the contractor's obligations both as to workmanship and time was quite usual; an alternative was to find sureties. Payment based on quantities appears very early - in 1348 a mason was to be paid five marks for every perch in length and foot in height of a seven-foot thick wall, with the fringe benefits of hay for his horse and fuel for his lodgings.

It may surprise us to find the basic structure of building contracts in place 600 years ago; but they are, after all, undertakings to do defined work for an agreed price within a stated time or at a defined rate of progress. Breach of the time obligation was obviously a matter of concern even in an age when life is supposed to have moved at a more leisurely pace. But I suspect that then, as now, building owners, having decided to have work carried out, were quite unable to wait to see it finished and wanted it done as quickly as possible. What were the remedies? Where time was of the essence, failure to complete was a repudiation but there does not seem to be any reason to suspect that building owners rushed in to allege repudiation and call in another contractor to complete. Obviously where payment was in a single lump sum or a small number of progress payments the contractor had a healthy incentive to complete, and the building owner was well protected against the contractor walking off site by the fixed sum bond (known as a "condition bond" and virtually indistinguishable from the ICE Form of Bond) or by the giving of sureties. Conversely the bondsman or sureties had an active interest in seeing the work properly completed on time. But what if there was no bond and no surety? In 1335 a carpenter undertook to build a row of houses for 62 marks and a blue robe, completion by the feast of St. Michael '*sine ulteriore prolongacione sub pena excommunicationis*'. This would not, of course, be an effective sanction against a limited company. By 1412 the target bonus appears in the contract for Catterick Church which also provided for phased completion. For early completion of the entire works the contractor was to receive 10 marks and a gown - this represented about $6^1/_2$ per cent of the contract sum. In 1434 a more practical approach was tried, "And if it so be that the said Will Horwood make not full end of the said work within term reasonable ... then he shall yield his body to prison at my Lord's will and all his moveable goods and heritages at my said Lord's disposition and ordinance". Straightforward liquidated damages appear in 1459 in a contract for building a bakehouse for Corpus Christi College Cambridge: "This work shall be begun by St. Gregory's Day in March next coming and sufficiently be ended by the feast of Lammas next coming after the date of this present writing in pain of 40/- to be paid by the said John Loose".

On the other side of the coin, Wycombe Church was built with the parishioners providing all materials but if the mason and his men should be delayed by their default, the parishioners are to pay their wages during such period. The existence of defects was to be determined by the judgement of skilled masons. So we have extension of time, loss and expense and the reference of alleged defects to experts. So what is new apart from size, complexity and economic pressures? The incentives of non-payment until completion and the hot breath of the bondsmen and sureties on the contractor's necks seem to have provided satisfactory contractual machinery for encouraging compliance with time provisions.

The Industrial Revolution, particularly the building of the railways inevitably introduced economic pressures into construction contracts. A number of factors tended to come together:

- A strict approach to the sanctity of a bargain which enabled the courts to construe contractors as "absolute" so that even if extra work was ordered, the contractor was still bound by the original completion date[4].
- The doctrine of "prevention" whereby a party loses the right to insist on the performance of an obligation if it is his own fault that the obligation cannot be performed[5].
- The very great dependence on the expertise of the relatively small number of capable engineers leading to the philosophy of "all these matters must be left to the engineer who alone is capable of deciding them" - a view warmly endorsed and often expressed by IK Brunel.
- The need to keep construction contracts going even though physical catastrophes and unforeseen difficulties were encountered, as well as to avoid delay or disruption due to contractual disputes.

It was realized at quite an early stage that if the doctrine of prevention[6] was not to undermine the contractor's time obligation, some provision had to be made for extension for the employer's own default.

For a time "engineer worship" (which included architects) produced very widely drawn extension of time clauses coupled with draconian provisions for the settlement of disputes which effectively left all questions of time in the hands of the engineer or architect. The descendants of the time clauses are with

4 *MacIntosh* v. *Midland Counties Rly* (1845) 14 M & W 548.
5 *Holme* v. *Guppy* (1838) 3 M & W 387.
6 *Holme* v. *Guppy* (*supra*).

us still in such wording as, "Should the amount of extra or additional work of any kind or other special circumstances of any kind whatsoever which may occur be such as fairly to entitle the contractor to an extension of time ...". When these clauses were coupled with a provision for the settlement of disputes such as, "the Contractor and the Directors will be bound to leave all matters of dispute which may arise during the progress of the works or in the settlement of the account to the Architect whose decisions shall be final and binding on the parties"[7] then the engineer or architect ruled and there was no effective challenge. The grounds for extension of time had to be sufficiently widely drawn to include the employer's own default: if they were not and delay was caused by the employer, he lost his right to liquidated damages. A good example is *Wells* v. *Army & Navy Co-operative Society*[8]. This case also contains the well known aphorism to the effect that if a Contractor has to complete work within a given amount of time, then equally he is entitled to that amount of time in which to complete it. The causes of delay entitling the employer to grant an extension included any alteration or addition, combination of workmen, strikes, default of sub-contractors "or other causes beyond the Contractor's control". It was held that this last phrase was not sufficiently wide to include the employer's own default in giving possession of the site because it had to be construed "*ejusdem generis*" with the specific grounds. Even so, well worded settlement of dispute clauses (and their descendants also live on, but emasculated, in ICE Clause 66 for example) stifled a great deal of contention. It is a trite observation that the floodgates were opened by arbitration clauses. Once the absolute nature of the engineer's or architect's decision was taken away by making it open to challenge and subject to being opened up, reviewed and revised, the scene was set for the disputes with which we are now so familiar. At what stage the emphasis shifted from a battle of liquidated damages to the potentially more fruitful fields of loss and expense is hard to determine in retrospect, but I think we all have a fair idea of how matters stand today.

Liquidated damages and extensions

Before considering where we could possibly go as opposed to whence we have come, it might be useful to summarize the basic principles and to comment on a few related matters.

- A contractor is bound to complete the contract works if the contract so provides by a defined or unambiguously ascertainable date. If he fails to do so he will be liable in damages. The usual practice in the Standard Forms is to provide for the payment of liquidated and ascertained damages expressed as a multiplier of time.
- Where the contractor is delayed by the employer's own default the employer will lose the benefit of a contractual date for completion and with it any right of liquidated damages. This rule applied if the total delay is

7 *Stevenson* v. *Watson* (1879) 4 CPD 148.
8 *Wells* v. *Army & Navy Co-operative Society* (1902) HBC 4(ii) 353.

partly due to the contractor provided that some of it is caused by the employer's default.[9]

- The above rights will not be lost if the contract provides for an extension of time on grounds which include the employer's default but the wording must be apt to include the particular default and will be construed *contra proferentem*.
- Any power to grant an extension must be exercised strictly in accordance with the terms of the contract, and an extended date fixed for the calculation of liquidated damages.

I do not propose to deal with the question of retrospective extensions which at one time caused a great deal of debate but which turn largely on the wording of particular contracts[10]. Three matters can conveniently be mentioned:

First, if the date for completion disappears because the employer was in default, is time at large in the sense that the contractor's obligation is to complete within a reasonable time? Clearly, a reasonable time would not begin to run until such time as the works could have been completed but for the employer's delay. Without analyzing the cases exhaustively my own view is, and has long been, that time must be at large if only because it is difficult to provide any other satisfactory answer and it seems sensible to imply a term to that effect to give the contract commercial efficacy. It has always seemed implicit in *Wells* v. *Army & Navy* and *Peak* v. *McKinney* that this was so, and the proposition appeared to be accepted without demur in *Percy Bilton Ltd*. v. *GLC* by the Court of Appeal and also by the House of Lords[11]. It is true that this view is not supported by the House of Lords in *Trollop & Colls Ltd*. v. *NW Metropolitan Hospital Board*[12] but I would now be very surprised if something other than "time at large" was held to be the law.

Secondly, if liquidated damages have gone, the employer can still sue for unliquidated damages for such delay as is due to the contractor's default: *Peak* v. *McKinney*. But can the quantum of such damages exceed what the employer would have recovered as liquidated damages but for his own default? In my view it cannot: the principle that a party to a contract must not profit from his own wrong means that the employer cannot be put in a better position than he would have enjoyed but for that wrong.

Thirdly, where the employer is in default and causes delay the contractor can claim damages for breach of contract. Under the Standard Forms he can in many instances make a contractual claim for loss and expense or for a sum ascertained by the engineer or architect. This is part of the lifeblood of the claims industry, if we leave aside variations and the correction of errors. Is there any scope for reversing the idea of liquidated and ascertained damages and liquidating potential claims arising from delay to the regular progress of the works, for example, under Clause 26 of JCT 80? We have a precedent in the Parishioners of Wycombe. It would, of course, save an enormous amount of

9 *Peak* v. *McKinney* (1970) 69 LGR 1.
10 *Amalgamated Building Contractors Ltd*. v. *Waltham Holy Cross UDC* [1952] 2 All ER 452; *Miller* v. *LCC* (1934) 50 TLR 479; *Sattin* v. *Poole* (1901) HBC 4(ii) 306
11 [1982] 1 WLR 794 at 800 *per* Lord Fraser.
12 [1973] 1 WLR 601 at 607.

time, effort and ingenuity which goes into the calculation of loss and expense with or without an argument about the *Hudson* Formula. Apart from commercial considerations from the contractor's side, the principal difficulty would in my view lie in arriving at a genuine pre-estimate of the damage likely to be suffered. A very simplistic approach to liquidated damages for non-completion of the works is that they either represent the commercial rental value of the completed structure, or in the case of a non-commercial building, the lost interest on money invested which must be taken to represent the value of the completed works to the building owner expressed at a weekly or daily rate. In practice, liquidated damages seldom seem even to approach these figures, but at least they are fairly readily identifiable and ascertainable. There is an essential difficulty in loss and expense claims considering only prolongation and not disruption, *e.g.*, in JCT 80 Clause 26.2.1, .4, .5 and .6. It is rare nowadays to hear argument that a liquidated damages provision falls outside the rules laid down in *Dunlop Ltd.* v. *New Garage Co. Ltd.*[13], remembering always that it is no obstacle to the sum stipulated being a genuine pre-estimate that the consequence of a breach are such as to make genuine pre-estimation almost impossible. Two important principles are:

- It will be held to be a penalty if the sum stipulated for is extravagant and unconscionable in amount in comparison with the greatest loss that could conceivably be proved to have followed from the breach;
- There is a presumption (but no more) that it is a penalty when a single lump sum is made payable on the occurrence of one or more or all of several events, some of which may occasion serious, and others but trifling, damage.

It has always seemed to me that the second of these principles is the stumbling block and that in any event it would be unrealistic to attempt to separate the prolongation element, *i.e.*, the simple overall delay to completion, from the element of disruption which may be contained within the contract period but nevertheless be far more costly than just keeping the site open, particularly in the very early or very late stages of the contract.

Alternative approaches to time

Is there any way in which we can open up review or revise our approach to time obligations? Is it an over-simplification to suggest that a construction contract, like Danny Kaye's symphony, must have a beginning part, a middle part and an ending part?

It would, I think, be unrealistic to suggest that time is not of fundamental importance: budgets, interest rates, cash flow requirements and market pressures combine to make it so. The employer wants his completed building whether it be commercial or non-commercial, the accountants want to plan the finance so as to keep the cost of borrowing as low as possible, and the contractor wants to plan his operations within the constraints of price, time and risks. It seems to me inevitable that there must be a date for possession or

13 [1915] AC 79

commencement, a date (or phased dates) for completion and some obligation to proceed regularly and diligently or with due diligence in between. Exceptionally we find a programme or a method statement incorporated as part of the contractor's obligation but let us not forget that it may turn out greatly to his advantage to be able to say "you required me to do the work in this order or in this particular way and if you prevent me from so doing it or want to change your mind, claims will follow".

It has been suggested that we could revert to my 14th century examples and have only a beginning part and a middle part - an obligation (and corresponding right) to commence, and then an obligation to proceed regularly and diligently or simply to complete within a reasonable time. Anyone who has been involved in a dispute under Clause 25(1)(b) of JCT 63 or Clause 63(d) of the ICE 5th Edition will probably recoil in horror at the idea. The underlying problem is how to define "reasonable" in a vacuum - it always tends to mean "reasonable to me" rather than "reasonable for you". Ultimately the question has to be defined or decided by some referee, expert or arbitrator, usually at second hand - that is after an Engineer's or Supervising Officer's original decision has been challenged.

Could we try to revert to a simpler but stricter approach and make time of the essence again? For the moment, I leave out purely commercial considerations which are, of course, usually the determining features of a commercial relationship. Suppose we say to contractors, "You must complete by a fixed date and assume the risk of all possible causes of delay. If you do not complete by that date, we can treat your failure to do so as a repudiation of obligations and bring the contract to an end (or determine your employment) on terms roughly similar to Clause 27.4 of JCT 80".

A contractor will price the risks as best he can, so far as they are risks which can properly be laid at his door contractually. But again we come back to the old difficulty of the employer's breach or fault - let us call it "prevention" for convenience: if he delays completion in any way he cannot, in the absence of a provision for extension of time "insist on a condition if it is his own fault that the condition has not been fulfilled"[14]. Prevention is not limited to breaches of express obligations in the contract. Provided that there is no inconsistency within the express terms of the contract, there will in the ordinary course of events be an implication that neither party will prevent the other from performing it. More specifically the employer must do all that is necessary on his part to enable the contractor to perform his obligations under the contract. Prevention is both negative and positive. Of course many obligations which would be implied in the absence of express terms are made express in the Standard Forms - possession of the site, provision of plans, instructions and details for the carrying out of work or the supply of materials by the employer and the provision of access to and egress from the site. Nevertheless, breach of any of these obligations whether arising expressly or by implication, which causes delay, will defeat the time obligation and if there is no provision for extension which covers the cause of the delay and which is duly exercised, time will be at large. So there must be a provision for extension which is apt to cover a least the more usual and obvious employer's breaches. Perhaps it is wiser to cast the net wide like the ICE Fifth Edition and FIDIC. If one wishes to be a

14 *Amalgamated Contractors* v. *Waltham Holy Cross UDC* (*ibid*).

little more specific, GC/Works/1 did it very neatly with the phrase, "any act or default of the Authority". Whether such wide wording would have avoided the dispute in *Bilton* v. *GLC*[15] may be a nice point, but the case serves to illustrate the difficulty of drafting for every eventuality. Under JCT 63 the decision in *Bickerton* v. *NW Regional Hospital Board*[16] placed on the employer the duty of making a fresh nomination if a nominated sub-contractor dropped out due to insolvency, or otherwise repudiated his subcontract. Bilton's mechanical services sub-contractor went into liquidation and their employment was determined. Thereafter two distinct periods of delay occurred. The first was due to the dropping out of the original nominated sub-contractor, the second was due to the failure of the GLC to make a new nomination within a reasonable time. The second clearly fell within Clauses 23(f) and 24(1)(a) of JCT 63. The first depended upon whether a failure to keep a nominated sub-contractor on site was a "prevention" by the employer. The Court of Appeal and House of Lords held it was not. The further point, whether the re-nomination of a sub-contractor who could not complete the sub-contract works consistently with the main contractor's extended date for completion would also be a prevention putting time at large, was found not to arise on the facts although Lord Fraser suggested that the contractor could have refused the nomination under Clause 27(a). Of course, it follows that a complete failure to re-nominate would be a prevention.

Apart from the difficulties of guarding against prevention, if time is of the essence, is it realistic to have the threat of determination as a stick with which to beat the contractor even though the work is being satisfactorily carried out in other respects? Of course to be able to say "You are late, therefore you are in breach" is much easier than considering what falls short of regularity and diligence under Clause 27.1.2, but in how many cases would this be a useful remedy with all he upheaval of removing one contractor and installing another?

Let us come back to commercial considerations. What would it mean in terms of pricing, or would the need to provide for extensions for what would otherwise be preventions in effect bring us back very near to where we started? I do not suppose that anyone would suggest a provision to the effect that "upon the Contractor being granted an extension of time in respect of any act omission or other default of the Employer, the Contractor shall not be entitled to make any claim or to institute any proceedings of whatsoever nature arising out of or in connection with any such act omission or default" or to rub salt into the wound by adding that the Supervising Officer's decision is to be final and binding on the parties with no provision for arbitration. I suspect that unless contractors were in general willing to contract with commercial employers in terms similar to GC/Works/1 a search for greater simplicity would not be very fruitful or commercially acceptable. But it is, perhaps, instructive to see where the search for rigid simplicity could lead us if we pursue it to the point of logical absurdity.

That contracts properly drafted can afford some degree of control over time cannot be doubted. But once the loss of a date for completion in the event of the employer's default is duly guarded against by provisions for extending time,

15 [1982] 1 WLR 794.
16 [1970] 1 WLR 607.

one is left with the allocation of some risks which are technically the contractor's responsibility in law: Clause 25.4.7 (delay on the part of Nominated Subcontractors), Clause 25.4.10 (inability to provide labour and materials) possibly Clause 25.4.3 (insured perils) and those which are in a general sense nobody's fault. Delay means loss to both employer and contractor so that an extension without a claim leaves the loss where it falls. It is in fact in the contractor's interest to use his best endeavours to avoid delay, but once it has occurred, whether or not it is in his financial interest to reduce it (which may be expensive) as opposed to merely suffering it, may be a nice question. How many grounds for extension (apart from employer's default) one should include depends in the final analysis on whether it is more convenient to say "in this and that event time will be extended and the loss shared" rather than "you must allow in your programme for various causes of delay and let there be no wringing of hands if you miscalculate". My own inclination is to be specific rather than general, if only because by being specific one can identify the more obvious and frequently encountered causes of delay; and by defining them leave the undefined residue as contractor's risks for which due allowance must be made in price and programme. However, if a draft is to be specific, surely it is preferable to gather all grounds together in one place as in the JCT and GC/Works contracts rather than leave them scattered, indeed cunningly concealed in nooks and corners, as in the ICE and FIDIC forms.

Having decided on the allocation of risk, one asks two further questions:

- Can there be any additional financial incentive to the loss inherent in delay apart from levying liquidated damages on contractor's risks?
- Can there be more specific contractual control by way of programme, phasing or provisions analogous to Clause 46 of the ICE form?

I have not had any recent opportunity of discussing the practicalities of Target Bonus provisions with interested parties. But it seemed to me when considering such provisions in the past that, properly drawn, they could provide a better incentive than just a penalty and could be tailored, rather like shoppers' car parking rates, to be lenient for comparatively short delays and harsh for long ones with corresponding benefits the other way. There can, in my view, be no objection in law to a rising scale of liquidated damages provided that the top figure is a genuine pre-estimate of the actual damage likely to be suffered. Anything less would not be a penalty. Great care would, of course, have to be taken in arriving at the date for completion so as to strike a practical balance between carrot and stick. It is in this context that consideration can then be given to more detailed control as such, as opposed to incentive and disincentive. Programmes are not normally contractual documents in building contracts - they may be valuable guides to regularity and diligence and what is due time for the giving of instructions or furnishing of details. It was my experience that it was not unusual to find a programme bound in as a contract document in engineering contracts. Suppose a programme is made contractual: what incentives or sanctions can be attached to make it worthwhile for the contractor to adhere to it? It would be virtually impossible to levy liquidated damages because there would not be any damage to pre-estimate. There is no difficulty in paying a Target Bonus or even having a "programme retention fund" which could be released thus carrying us back to the old days of stage payments. A stick rather than a carrot is a procedure similar to that under Clause 46 of the ICE Fifth Edition, but that has to have some follow-up sanction if the contractor fails to take such steps as are necessary to expedite progress. Such sanctions can, effectively, only be determination or the threat of it which, as we all know, can often be a remedy worse than the disease itself.

If I may return for a moment to a topic I referred to earlier - loss and expense claims. It appears to me that these are inevitable where the extension is on a ground which would amount to a prevention on the part of the employer, because if there is a breach of an express or implied term the contractor is prima facie entitled to damages for the breach. It is tidier and more convenient to allow what would otherwise be damages at common law to be recovered within the machinery of the contract itself. Beyond this I see no merit in encouraging time related claims.

Can drafting be improved?

I have made one or two suggestions already and pointed out how the decision in *Bickerton* revealed a situation which could have been clarified by drafting and which could have made the litigation in *Bilton* unnecessary. Very early in this paper I mentioned the perils of well intentioned but unfortunate attempts to make a Standard Form do what it as not really intended to do. You will recall that in *Gleesons* v. *London Borough of Hillingdon*[17] a provision for phased completion was written into the Bills of a JCT 1963 contract. It was held that because this provision did not relate to the quality and quantity of the work included in the Contract Sum, the Conditions of Contract were not overridden modified or affected, by virtue of Clause 12(1) of JCT 1963. A not dissimilar situation arose in *Bramall & Ogden Ltd.* v. *Sheffield City Council*[18] when the Appendix to the same form was completed by the statement "at the rate of £20 per week for each uncompleted dwelling". Since the contract did not provide for sectional completion, (which it could have done as the JCT amendment had been introduced long before) Clause 16 applied, as possession of the completed houses was taken by the Council with the consent of the contractor. Since Clause 16 applied, Clause 22 could not. The Judge (the present Senior Official Referee) observed, "It would of course be open to the parties to have made appropriate provision in the contract itself so as to deal with the situation. My finding does not in any event prevent the Respondents [the Council] from claiming damages for breaches of the contract". I have earlier suggested that where an employer has deprived himself of the advantage of being able to rely on a liquidated damages clause because of his own breach of contract, he cannot take advantage of his own wrong to recover more by way of damages at common law. In the *Bramall & Ogden* situation the liquidated damages provisions was lost by unfortunate drafting and I see no reason why in that situation the Employer should not recover whatever damage he could prove, based either on lost rent or lost interest.

17 [1970] unreported.
18 (1983) 29 Build LR 73.

In *Temloc* v. *Errill Properties Ltd.*[19] the parties wrote "Nil" in the Appendix to a JCT 80 Form. The issue that arose was whether this meant that the liquidated damages were simply nil pounds or, as the employer contended, that the effect of writing "nil" was to exclude the whole of Clause 24. The employer's argument was rejected by the Court of Appeal. Lord Justice Nourse said,

> "I think it clear ...... that if (1) Clause 24 is incorporated as art of the contract, and (2) the parties complete the relevant part of the Appendix, either by stating a rate at which the sum is to be calculated or, as here, by stating the sum is to be nil, then that constitutes an exhaustive agreement as to the damages which are or are not to be payable by the Contractor in the event of his failure to complete the works on time".

Finally a word about binding in letters and other documents such as programmes or method statements. This is an engineering habit. I referred briefly to *McAlpine* v. *Yorkshire Water Authority* where the method statement for driving a tunnel was made part of the contract. It proved impossible to do it that way, but perfectly possible to do it the other way round. The contractor was put into the position of being able to say, "You required me to do it from south to north and I find myself in a Clause 12, or better still, in a Clause 13, situation". I think we all recognize that in the run up to a major contract all sorts of things may seem far more important than some nicety of drafting, but I hope that these examples will provide a cautionary tale - it is sometimes better to throw the lawyer a crust rather than to kick him.

19 39 Build LR 30.

16 Contract Policy for Money

Ian Duncan Wallace

Synopsis

A comprehensive criticism of current standard construction forms, particularly of those provisions dealing with payment, is presented. Comparisons are drawn with the new Singapore Institute of Architects Form and proposals are given for reconsideration both of the policy and drafting of current forms of contract.

Introduction

With regard to the title of this Paper which has been chosen for me, "money" has immediate connotations of price and the mechanisms of payment. It also, however, brings rapidly to mind the concept of "value for money". Since all risk assumption by either party in a construction contract, and all express provisions, however bizarre or anomalous, must in the long run be balanced by adjustment of price, and since the overall objective of this seminar, as I understand it, is to consider the extent to which the standard forms of contract in this country are in need of alteration or improvement, I propose to treat this expression as an invitation to examine the principal aspects of the current family of United Kingdom standard forms from this point of view. Do they give society as a whole, or the consumer (*i.e.* the private owner and the ratepayer or taxpayer as the public owner) "value for money" (*i.e.* are they price efficient)? In my view the general answer must be no. Are they good for the efficiency of the industry, or do they give the industry generally contractors and sub-contractors, suppliers, architects and engineers, undue protection and financial subventions? In my view the answer to the latter question can only be yes. If this view is correct it carries serious implications since, under systems of competitive tendering, such contracts can drive out of business the class of contractor with genuine cost and construction skills in favour of the contractor with greater claiming skills and ruthlessness in exploiting the contract opportunities.

Indeed, the steady current of change in the standard forms over the past three decades has given rise to a whole new industry - the claims industry - with a new self-appointed profession of "claims consultants" and advisers advertising their services and professing expertise in the exploitation of the standard forms, and not infrequently stipulating for a semi-champertous remuneration expressed as a percentage of the sums recovered. In the United Kingdom the huge proliferation of construction litigation, virtually all based on the standard forms, has driven both the judiciary and the legislators to seek to stem the flood by driving it away from the courts,[1] with the unfortunate result of a higher judiciary increasingly inexperienced in the interpretation or understanding of construction contracts or projects. A further result is a large increase in the numbers of would-be arbitrators seeing this as a way of making a living, often doubling-up as expert witnesses in one part of the field or another.

A danger for any academic institution such as London University becoming involved in construction law is that it can rapidly deteriorate into an up-market provider of courses in claims presentation and expertise, as does virtually every seminar on construction law, whether domestic or international. How many seminars, whether domestically or internationally, concern themselves with the public and consumerist aspect of construction contracts, or with investigating the wise drafting of those contracts in that interest so that, in appropriate cases, a higher firm price is substituted for the blank cheque of unwisely permitted indeterminate claims, or that justified claims are made administratively simpler and less controversial? Yet drafting is perfectly possible which can enormously simplify the assessment and calculation of justified claims and which can avoid the anomalous and ingenious contentions and interpretations which are such a constant feature of the cases reaching the courts today from the JCT/RIBA stable. These latter are almost invariably the result of inconsistent or obscure if not deliberately devious draftsmanship, compounded by lack of judicial knowledge in some higher courts of the subject-matter of construction projects and of their practical necessities and background. Nor is it simply a matter of the Conditions of Contract themselves. The professional institutions responsible for the ever-increasing complication of the Standard Methods, together with the more and more artificial and opaque language of their incorporating provisions in the standard forms themselves, have deliberately created whole areas of potential claims and refinements of measurement which no longer seem to have any place in real life at all, and which appear to have no practical consequence other than to create a private world of mystery where only the professionally qualified may tread and where the contractor, for some reason, can frequently snatch a plus (but never in practice lose a minus) in the final adjustment of the contract sum. In this special area of over-refined measurement the United Kingdom is unique, there being little similar Standard Method complication in the Commonwealth jurisdictions, where the influence of the United Kingdom standard forms and of the United Kingdom-style quantity surveyor and United Kingdom standard methods is much less (though in Singapore and Hong Kong their influence is naturally stronger). Nor can the ICE Conditions escape responsibility for the most open and flagrant encouragement of similar claims. Disregarding the

1 Through *The Nema* decision in the House of Lords ([1982] AC 724) restricting appeals from arbitrators, and the Court of Appeal *Crouch* dictum ([1984] QB 644) apparently limiting the powers of the Courts (as opposed to arbitrators) to depart from certifiers' decisions when seized of a dispute under a contract with a traditional "open up revise and review" arbitration clause. See on this my *Construction Contracts - Principles and Policies in Tort and Contract* (1986) Sweet & Maxwell ("CCPP" here-after) paras 17-47(e) - (g), and for the *Crouch* dictum doubted see CCPP Chap. 17 generally.

important area of "changed conditions" clauses discussed separately in this paper,[2] I am unable to understand how any informed adviser could possibly support the inclusion of the open invitations to claim contained in Clauses 55(2) and 56(2), and above all the apparent blank cheque in Clause 13(3) of the Conditions if asked for his opinion by any owner, public or private, when preparing the contract documentation. Again, the provisions of sub-clauses 14(3) - 14(6) are an ingenious and dangerous trap for consultants and their clients - an Engineer should be able to ask for information about the contractor's temporary works without finding that he is forced either positively to approve and accept responsibility for them or else to take charge of their design, with the inevitable express claim permitted on reasonable foreseeability grounds.

It is small wonder that I can report that in Singapore in very recent months one of the largest public entities responsible for commissioning construction work has approached the professional institutions with a view to seeking their support in expressly banning the use of claims consultants by contractors when advancing claims on their projects. In my own experience, I may add, United Kingdom contractors overseas with otherwise attractive tender prices have lost contracts to foreign competition because of the reputation for aggressive claimsmanship of United Kingdom contractors generally, and not necessarily of the individual contractor concerned.

The purpose of the present paper

In the present paper I propose to identify those areas in the standard forms which I believe merit fundamental criticism or reconsideration of policy in the light of the reasonable interest of the public and private owner. I make no apology for this one-sided approach, since it is now the only one possible in view of the contents of the current United Kingdom standard forms (with the exception of GC/Wks/1). In a more objective drafting landscape, and in countries where the balance of power between owner and contractor may be quite different, owners may need to be cautioned against harsh or undesirable anti-contractor provisions (see the entries "Contractor - protection recommended for" and "Contractor, counter-productive provisions against interest of" and "SIA Contract, contractor, clauses protecting" in the index to CCPP). No such advice would be appropriate in the United Kingdom It is imperative to understand just how far and how deliberately the erosion of the owner's interest has proceeded in the principal standard forms in the United Kingdom in the last two decades. In this those responsible for them appear to be largely impervious to judicial criticism or to any public explanation of defects in their forms.

Thus in 1970 the well-known Clause 23(g) of the JCT/RIBA Contracts, after a close analysis in the House of Lords, was described as "highly anomalous" and as "included...without any regard to the manifest in- justice and indeed absurdity implicit in it", and as "illogical" and "inserted and drafted without any clear appreciation of its purpose or scope". Lord Wilberforce added "I cannot believe that the professional body, realising how defective the clause is,

2 See *infra* under "changed conditions clauses".

will allow it to remain in its present form"[3]. After a decent interval of ten years to allow memories to lapse, it comes as no surprise to the informed observer that the re-drafted JCT/RIBA 1980 Contract has continued with the clause unaltered[4]. An even more astonishing perversion of the earlier wording of its own contracts was perpetrated by the JCT/RIBA in their later pre-1963 contracts, charitably noted by me in my *Building and Civil Engineering Standard Forms* commentary in 1969 as being possibly accidental, but finally confirmed in the utmost detail in the secretive interstices of the 1980 Contract. This latter Contract gives the clearest indication yet of the attitudes and motivation of this particular body (see the detailed analysis which I have recently made of this draftsmanship in CCPP)[5]. As a further instance, it has been a cause of comment for many years that the RIBA/JCT Contracts contained no provision for extension of time for failure to give possession of some or all of the site - a quite common and not necessarily always very serious incident of many construction contracts. Paradoxically, because of the wholesale invalidation of a liquidated damage clause which can occur in such a case under the well- known *Peak* v. *McKinney* doctrine, even if the delay is relatively small and trivial, this omission was potentially very dangerous for employers, the more so because many incidents of construction contracts (such as failure to give information to enable a start on part of the work, or an order postponing a part of the work, could also be said to constitute a failure to give possession of that part). Indeed, it has become a commonplace for the advisers of a contractor seriously in delay and under threat of deduction of liquidated damages to comb through the contract history in order to find some failure to give possession, however trivial, to support an invalidation of the liquidated damages clause on the ground of there being no applicable extension of time. Here again, new wording has been used in the 1980 JCT Contract which can only be described as deviousness concealed within complication in order to perpetuate the danger to the owner while appearing to meet the criticism. Thus the tortured "ingress and egress" wording of Clause 15.4.12, on close examination, excludes a failure to give possession of the site itself or of any part of it from the new ground of extension of time, and only applies to failure to give possession of other property of the owner off the site but giving access to the site - an occasional but certainly rare incident of construction contracts. That this is no accident is shown by the quite different words "or use of any specific parts of the site" in the variation Clause 13.1.2.2 when additional payment is in question. This elaborate struggle to avoid giving the contractor an extension of time covering interference with possession would bewilder even a reasonably competent lawyer from another field unaware of the special advantages to the contractor of the *Peak* v. *McKinney* doctrine, let alone the average house or property owner encouraged to use the RIBA/JCT forms, if it was explained to him that the failure to cover the commoner kinds of interference with possession in an extension of time clause represented contractor influence in the drafting of the forms. A further example of what seems deliberate obscurity is to be found in Clauses 2.1 and 30.9.1.1 of the 1980 Contract. This wording again represents a subtle concealed trap for

3 See CCPP, para 21-07.
4 See Clause 25.4.7.
5 See CCPP paras 30-06 to 30-09.

employers who may have thought final certificate immunity for defective work had been removed, if their advisers have incautiously made references to the reasonable satisfaction of the Architect when defining the quality of materials or workmanship in the Specification or Bills[6].

Obscurity or an unintended result of draftsmanship is one thing, deliberate and devious draftsmanship to attain an indefensible end is another. An institution which purports to make available a form of contract for public use must expect to forfeit respect if it seeks to achieve such unattractive ends using the new and remarkably obscurantist draftsmanship, with its convoluted cross-referencing, which is the hall-mark of the JCT/RIBA 1980 Contract (and which looks like leading to its disuse and ultimate withdrawal, though, it must be said, primarily due to difficulties of comprehension rather than of objection to policy).

Pricing Philosophy

Before looking at specific areas of construction contracts which require reconsideration, it is essential to try and define a correct philosophy of risk allocation and pricing, which I have endeavoured to do at a large number of points in CCPP[7]. Broadly speaking, all risk assumption has to be balanced by price. Thus, in describing what I had attempted to do when drafting the Singapore Private Sector standard form of contract, I stated in CCPP:

> "The principle is adopted that, wherever a transfer of risk is to occur from the contractor to the owner, there must be a counter-balancing advantage of price to balance the risk assumed by the owner, and the contract is so fashioned to bring that about. However, where owners are commercially prepared for or likely to prefer an increased contingent element in the price to balance a risk to be assumed by the contractor, there is no such transfer."
>
> "It is this basic philosophy which, in my view, must underly any apportionment of risk as between one contracting party and another in a commercial contract. It is extremely rare to find any person associated with construction law and the construction industry, whether the obviously interested parties, such as the owner on the one hand and the contractor on the other, or the owner's professionals, or academics or writers in the field, or, above all, technical arbitrators, who fully understand this basic commercial principle, which is vitally important for the correct interpretation, as well as the drafting, of construction contracts. Too often the drafting of a contract, or an interpretation or criticism of a contract, is dismissed as "pro-employer" or "pro-contractor" or "fair" or "unfair". This adversarial attitude to construction contracts and the emotion which it generates, is a serious obstacle to a proper understanding and analysis of the questions of underlying policy and interpretation which are in fact involved. It is also a great obstacle to much-needed reform. It is an understanding of this philosophy which will enable the criticisms later expressed in this paper in regard to "changed conditions" clauses, or of the use of unit-price or measured contracts, to be properly appreciated, for example. Prospective owners of all kinds, and government and consumer interest may, it is hoped, find this discussion of the

6 See CCPP para 30-25
7 See the entry "Philosophy, risk allocation and pricing, of, "in the Index to CCPP.

underlying fundamentals of value, as also arbitrators and academics and others concerned with the interpretation of construction contracts.[8]"

Again, I stated later in CCPP in regard to allocation of risk in this context:

> "While an event may be foreseen as a possibility which is in no sense the fault of the contractor, but which will increase his costs, employers may see advantages in a contract which requires the contractor to assume that risk, and to include for the cost of dealing with that situation in his tendered contract price. Where the risk is uncertain, this logically requires that a contingent element will have to be included in the original price which, in the event, may possibly not be required. If so, the employer will have agreed to an unnecessarily high price, but may regard that as preferable (since his budgeting arrangements for the project will be attended by greater certainty) than a lower price subject to post-contract upward adjustment of uncertain extent at a late stage should the risk materialise (which is the alternative if the contract requires the risk to be borne by the employer). Since an assumption of an additional risk by the contractor, however 'unreasonable' this may be said to be in 'moral' terms, must inevitably be reflected in his price, any discussion as to whether or not a particular risk should be so included in the price is in essence a question of policy, and not of 'fairness', 'morality' or 'justice'. Furthermore, the desirability of the policy may well vary with different classes of employer and different types of project. The State in its various forms, with a relatively long purse and projects which are not strictly commercial in character, may possibly prefer to be its own insurer and to have the finer quoted price (but only if absolutely satisfied that that will indeed be obtained) resulting from the risk being transferred to itself. Private individuals or commercial companies, on the other hand, may have compelling reasons for remaining within their original budgeting arrangements, whether in the case of buildings for domestic occupation or commercial developments, (particularly since, as will be seen, there is a basic and fundamental lack of precision in assessing quantum under the standard methods of measurement in the U.K.) and, in many cases, if informed that the budget was likely to be exceeded, would not continue with a project at all, or without demanding substantial savings. Only if the assumption of a risk by a contractor is likely to be self-defeating, in the sense of causing increases in tendered prices out of all proportion to any corresponding advantage conferred on the employer, is an impartial adviser entitled to counsel that employers should bear that risk."[9]

Anyone familiar with the standard forms in the United Kingdom will realize that these considerations have been entirely swept aside over recent years, and the alleged attraction of the lowest possible tender (contract) price accompanied by the maximum number of expressly permitted post-contract increases of price (claims) has become regarded as axiomatic in those circles concerned to advance the use of the standard forms generally, and this appears to have been accepted with little or no critical examination by public and private owners alike. The basic premiss of this paper is that in the present situation in the United Kingdom the over-whelming Consumer/Owner/Government interest today must lie:

- In securing more realistic firm tender (contract) prices;

8 See CCPP, General Introduction, pp 11-12.
9 See CCPP para 27-06.

- In reducing to a minimum unbudgeted and speculative post-contract increases of price;
- In promoting competition in the industry in construction skills and not in claiming skills; and
- Where claims are permitted, to secure their assessment in as uncontroversial and certain a manner as possible with, if necessary, fine-tuning and undue precision yielding to ease of administration and absence of controversy.

Subjects to be covered

It is proposed to refer to the standard forms in the context of the following specific problems:-

A. Measured or Lump Sum (fixed price or unit price) choice of contract
B. What degree of re-measurement is acceptable in measured contracts?
C. Variation and their Valuation
D. Contract Make-Up of Prices
E. Changed Conditions Clauses
F. VOP (Fluctuations) Clauses
G. Interim Payment and Retention
H. Defective Work
I. Nominated Sub-Contracts
J. Insurance
K. Design and Turnkey Contracts
L. Certification,Arbitration and Remedies (Termination Clauses)
M. Priority of Documents Clauses.

I am of course aware that these subjects traverse the territory of many other papers at this seminar. My aim in so doing is not in any way to pre-empt discussion, but rather to stimulate and provoke it.

A. Measured or Lump Sum Contracts

While the JCT/RIBA body does of course produce a lump sum (fixed price) contract, owners in the case of more substantial projects will be subjected to over-whelming professional advice and industry pressures to employ measured (Bills of Quantities) contracts permitting re-measurement (*i.e.* re-calculation of the price regardless of the existence of variations called for by the employer) in accordance with the ultimate as-built quantities. So far as I am aware there has been little or no critical discussion in recent years of this peculiarly United Kingdom-style practice of using such contracts for all but the smallest building projects, though an agreement amongst contractors not to tender for projects above a certain value without Bills was long ago declared to be against the public interest[10]. The ICE, of course, does not produce a lump sum contract at all.

10 re *Birmingham Association: of BTE's Agreement* [1963] 1 WLR 484.

It should be appreciated that in the case of superstructures which have been fully pre-planned all quantities are capable of being accurately taken off the drawings and none are inherently unpredictable, unlike foundations and sub-structures, where the quantities of excavation and of fill and unsuitable items and associated temporary works may not be capable of precise estimation. It is prima facie, therefore unclear why the administrative and professional expense of a re-measured contract should be thought to be desirable for normal building projects. It is not usual, for example, in the United States.

Undoubtedly the prime source of pressure for the use of measured contracts comes from the quantity surveying profession and their institutions, who apparently take the view that there is little or no scope for the employment of professional quantity surveyors if lump sum contracts are to be used more widely. This shows little understanding of the historical origin of quantity surveyors in providing a service to tendering lump-sum contractors, and in fact the services of the owner's professional quantity surveyor will be indispensable in any major contract, whether lump sum or measured, where the design is that of the owner's consultant, so as to reduce the cost of tendering.[11] The vital question is whether the resulting Bills should be an ex-contractual guide to the tendering contractors, with their contractual role limited to providing the basis for valuing variations under the contract, or whether on the other hand they should be contractually required to govern simple re-measurement of the work as a whole, independently of variation valuation. The principal arguments advanced to convince owners in favour of Bill of Quantities contracts are (*a*) that they are said to lead to keener contract prices, since they reduce or negative the inclusion of any contingent element in the price to cover the possibility of greater quantities being required; (*b*) that they reduce the overall professional cost of tendering in competition (undoubtedly the original function of the bills of quantities); and (*c*) that they provide a more refined and exact tool for variation or interim payment valuations.

I have myself examined these arguments in some depth on a number of occasions,[12] and have concluded that none are in fact convincing. As to the first, contractors will presumably both over-estimate and under-estimate quantities from time to time, but if they were to do either consistently they would rapidly go out of business, either because they were given no contracts on the one hand, or because their contracts were consistently under-priced on the other. On the necessary assumption that contractors will estimate their prices reasonably correctly on average, there can be no case in logic for tendering prices increased for lump sum contracts increased to take account of possible under-estimation of the quantities. As to the second argument, the proliferation of quantity surveyors on both sides of the table in the industry, having regard to the many claim opportunities afforded by the present United Kingdom measurement and contractual systems, now has the effect, far from reducing the cost of tendering, of greatly increasing the professional manpower involved in tendering on measured contracts, which a return to the use of lump-sum contracts would do much to avoid. As to the third argument (greater precision of valuation) the studied vagueness of the standard forms (as

11 For the history and current role and status of Quantity Surveyors, see CCPP para 24-15
12 See CCPP paras. 23-20 to 23-23, 24-20 to 24-21, 25-14 to 25-15 and 30-13 to 30-20.

opposed to their almost fanatical zeal in pricing the minutiae of construction processes) when considering the contents and role of Preliminary Bills, together with the failure of any standard form to require a pre-start-of-work make-up of prices, has turned measurement and variation valuation into a recondite exercise with a premium on ingenuity (and, many would consider, little regard to merit) and with the owner's advisers handicapped during negotiation of claims by the absence of contemporary evidence of the real cost-allocations genuinely made by the contractor at the time of pricing (when the ultimate outcome of the as-built quantities would be still unknown, and when tailoring of arguments to suit the ultimate outcome would not be possible).

In fact, it is submitted that there is rarely any real price advantage to an employer in the use of a unit-price contract, let alone one which could outweigh its serious disadvantages, in the shape of the potential claim liabilities to which the owner will be exposed under the United Kingdom systems of measurement and standard form incorporation. Nor is this view limited to building projects with substantial superstructure elements. The only situation in which a measured contract would seem commercially attractive to an owner would be where a real possibility was thought to exist of a reduction in a final as-built quantity (where of course the owner would stand to gain with a measured contract). It is true that in the civil engineering field a case might be argued for the use of provisional quantities in certain types of project where an item (such as removal of unsuitable material and supply of imported material) will be under the ultimate day-to-day control and decision of the engineer, and where the existence of previously agreed prices will effectively remove areas of dispute and controversy which might otherwise exist if the contract was lump sum. But even in civil engineering contracts these types of item, where it is desired to give the engineer day-to-day control over what may be unusually variable items of work, are likely to be limited in number.

Against this lack of price or other advantage to owners, measured contracts are highly attractive to the industry. So far as architects and engineers are concerned, they facilitate committing the client financially to the project by an early contract while the drawings and even the specification may still be unfinalised. So far as quantity surveyors are concerned, these contracts expressly require quantity surveyor participation in the project, in both the design and construction stage in preparing bills and sometimes the specification, and in substantial valuation services performed during the contract. All this is greatly attractive to architects in assisting them with or reducing the amount of their own work. So far as contractors are concerned, they maximize, at least as the United Kingdom contracts and Standard Methods have come to be drafted or incorporated,[13] the opportunities both for subsequent claim presentation when the as-built quantities are known, or for price manipulation at the tender stage if a differing view is taken of the likely quantities outcome, or if errors or omissions in the preparation of the quantities can be detected, or any failure to follow Standard Method recommendations, all of which will present an opportunity for price adjustments producing an ultimate increase in the contract sum for the alert

13 See on this particularly CCPP paras 30-13 to 30-20.

contractor who has been able to detect such errors in advance at the tender stage.

On this view, re-measurement of the whole of the work in a building or civil engineering contract has few advantages and very serious disadvantages for employers, while greatly increasing the administrative and professional costs of such contracts, as well as fostering a burgeoning claims industry which serves no useful social or economic purpose, with claims-pro- ficient contractors and the various practitioners in the industry as its beneficiaries, and public and private owners, together with cost-efficient but not claims-efficient contractors, its victims. Any careful public or private cost-benefit analysis would, it is submitted, come down in favour of lump sum or fixed price contracts in the great majority of cases.

Even where a decision is taken to use a measured contract, there is much to be said for a case-by-case, or rather item-by-item, approach to measurement, and for the use of contracts (see *e.g.* the Malaysian PWD Contracts) which identify (as it happens by the use of the word "Provisional") particular items in the Bills where re-measurement of the work will be permitted, with the remainder treated as lump sum or fixed.[14]

B. What degree of re-measurement?

Even where an employer sees a real advantage to himself in using a measured contract, the question arises as to the extent of re-measurement which an owner should sensibly accept. Re-measurement has been carried far beyond any normal sense of that word by the express terms of the United Kingdom standard forms, which in this respect bear no relation to re-measurement arrangements elsewhere in the world. So far have the United Kingdom forms proceeded down this road, and for so long, that the rules appear to be treated by both private and public owners, and indeed by the judiciary, as representing a normal and acceptable method of re-measuring construction work,[15] and not seen as the result of decades of remorseless erosion of simple rules of measurement and arguments of increasing artificiality reaching a point where the Bill rates and prices cease to have any serious significance except as a base upon which to erect still further allowances or increased rates or prices. The evolution of this state of affairs, which can hardly be thought to reflect any reasonable or presumed intention of owners, can be traced as follows:

- The earliest re-measurement contracts were "schedule of rates" or "schedule" contracts, consisting of a series of rates or prices for work processes, and often of a composite and simplified character (as *e.g.* of a single price per linear unit of road works constructed, notwithstanding a possibly quite complicated specification for formation, sub-base, base and surface finishes respectively). Other such schedules might simply refer to quantities of well-known traditional work, such as brickwork, concrete,

14 See also for an Australian public works example *Commissioner for Main Road* v. *Reed & Stuart* (1974) 18 ALUR 641, 12 Build LR 56, *Hudson*, 1979 Supp., p 514.

15 See, for a recent example, the Privy Council's judgment in *Mitsui Construction* v. *A-G of Hong Kong* (1987) 33 Build LR 1, criticized particularly on this aspect by the present writer in (1987) 3 Const LJ p 3

excavation, roofing and timber, with many ancillary processes and with all overheads and mobilization expenses, for example, included in these prices.

- It soon became clear that it was preferable and sensible to have, in addition to the purely construction items, a "preliminaries" bill, usually containing fixed once-for-all items such as mobilization and de-mobilization of plant, site huts and so forth (thus explaining the "preliminaries" description). This would make the application of the construction rates and prices to the as-built quantities rather more accurate, since duplication of such fixed elements of cost would be avoided.
- Later still, time-related (*e.g.* supervision) or even quantities-related items of cost (such as provision of power and services) were separately included in the Preliminaries Bills, *i.e.* the running site overheads of the project in addition to purely fixed items. Again, this led to greater precision of re-measurement, since greater or less quantities of a particular construction process might or might not be on the critical path for time, for example, or might or might not affect other quantities-related items of cost in the Preliminaries Bills.[16]

Owners should understand, therefore, that vitally important and differing degrees of re-measurement can be involved in a unit-price contract, depending on its draftsmanship. In ascending order, the draftsmanship may expressly permit re-measurement:

- Of the construction items only at the construction item prices only;
- Of the general or preliminary items as well as the construction items, in the latter case at prices deduced or derived from those in the Preliminary Bills;
- At quite different (higher) prices than those in the construction or preliminaries bills, if the contractor is allowed to advance arguments based on the changes in the ultimate quantities, whether up or down (these inevitably would have to depend on on his alleged expectations and internal allocations of cost at the time when he originally priced the contract); and finally
- Adding new prices or items where some error or omission can be alleged in the Bills, for example in failing to comply with the recommendations of an incorporated Standard Method of Measurement for separate pricing of such items (however obvious the departure from the Standard Method may in fact be). This last claim can be made, it should be noted, where no change at all in the as-built quantities has taken place, and can in principle be advanced the moment that the ink is dry on the signature of the contract.[17]

It should always be remembered that re-measurement provisions apply whether or not there have been variations called for by the employer. No employer, it is submitted, could reasonably intend, by agreeing to a contract permitting re-measurement in the light of the as-built quantities, that where no variation is in-volved the adjustment should be anything other than a simple

16 For Preliminary or General Items, see CCPP paras 8-05, 8-12, 23-21, 24-20, 24-21(c), 25-05, 26-08 and 27-21.

17 See for the dubious contractual language called to support these claims my commentary on the ICE Fifth Edition, pp 191-13, and also CCPP 26-11 to 26-13, 29-14, and 30-12 to 30-21.

adjustment, at the contractor's quoted rates and prices in the Bills, of the quantities of the con struction items and, additionally, if appropriate, of any preliminary items which can be seen to be affected by the construction item changes (*i.e.* the two re-measurements envisaged in 20(*a*) and (*b*) above). Variations, of course, are quite a different matter. If a contractor's own estimates of the likely out-turn of quantities differ from those in the Bills he is free to take a view and price accordingly; he cannot possibly, however, save in exceptional circumstances, take a view of the future variation requirements of the owner. Moreover, variations, by reason of their timing and location, may be completely outside the original pricing parameters of the contractor, so that "open-ended" valuation provisions for variations, allowing for substantial departures from the quoted contract prices in appropriate circumstances, are obviously a wholly justifiable quid pro quo for the owner's power to vary the work as of right at any time, which the variation clauses in the United Kingdom forms of course confer.[18]

It should not, of course, be thought that even the more conservative and consensually based view of re- measurement referred to above will not produce quite substantial valuation problems and controversy. In the first place, the standard methods of measurement in both industries, for all their almost fanatical concern for detail in the construction items themselves, become unaccountably vague and lacking in precision in defining the work or costs which could or should be priced in the Preliminary Bills, as distinguished from the construction items. Secondly, for some reason it seems to be accepted by quantity surveyors that the Contractor should be left free to allocate items of cost and to weight his prices wherever he sees fit, and in particular in the distribution of his costs as between the construction items and the preliminary items. Thirdly, under the standard forms in the United Kingdom the contractor has never been required to produce a detailed make-up or breakdown of his prices, whether of the construction or preliminary items, so that no genuine contemporary documentation is available to confirm or refute his alleged internal pricing arguments in support of a claim made after the as-built outcome of the quantities has become known. It is for this reason that claims for higher prices and additional payment upon re-measurement can be and are constantly advanced in whichever direction, up or down, the as-built quantities may have finally moved, (though this will naturally require precisely opposite factual arguments about the internal pricing to be advanced in the two cases). This weakness and consequential exposure of the owner to exaggerated or unjustified claims is further compounded by the practice, not in my experience ever objected to by quantity surveyors or others, of inserting very large single lump sum Preliminary or General items under very generalised descriptions in the Preliminary Bills,[19] which in the absence of detailed description can be used to increase the amount of claims, particularly where overall delay is alleged as a result of variations or other breaches of contract.

18 For no very good reason, most US contracts do not envisage variation valuation except at contrct prices or at previously agreed prices. This is not a practical formulation for a variation clause.

19 For some unexplained reason this seems to be positively encouraged by the Civil Engineering Standard Methods - see the "General Contingencies Allowance" and global "Adjustment Item" recommendations in "CESSM", referred to at pp 193-94 of my commentary on the Fifth Edition.

It seems to me self-evident that no owner should agree to re-measurement, even on the relatively conservative construction/preliminaries adjustment basis, without requiring the successful tenderer to supply a detailed breakdown of his prices, as between labour, plant, materials and possibly sub-contractors, before the commencement of work at latest, and preferably before final execution of the contract.[20]

Until the Fifth Edition of the ICE Conditions in 1973 the extremely brief and uninformative remeasurement provisions in Clauses 55 and 56 of the ICE Contracts were always thought to provide for normal construction/preliminaries adjustment, notwithstanding the difficulties created by lack of any contemporary make-up of prices.[21] On the other hand, the JCT/RIBA Contracts had for many decades expressly applied the contract variation valuation rules to re-measurement under those contracts (and hence the "open-ended" valuation concept permitting departure from the contract prices) - see the traditional "deemed to be a variation" wording re-stated in Clause 12 of the 1963 Contract and the corresponding Clause 2.2.2.2 of the 1980 Contract. Eventually in 1973 the ICE, in their Fifth Edition, for the first time not only decided to adopt the 1963 RIBA wording, but in addition expressly authorized departure from the Bill prices "if the actual quantities are greater or less than those stated in the Bills"[22]. In the Singapore Private Sector Contract, by contrast, the rules for valuing variations are kept entirely separate from those applying to re-measurement, and construction/preliminary item adjustment is all that is permitted on re-measurement, using where necessary the detailed make-up of prices which successful tenderers are required to provide under that contract before work commences.[23]

Finally, this leaves the "omitted item" or "standard method" claim which has become such a favourite in the claims industry, and which, as stated, can be made even where the quantities have not changed. The legal and logical basis for these claims is not only extremely dubious, but they in fact savour strongly of sharp practice, since they enable the alert contractor to claim additional payment literally the moment the contract has been signed, though he is rarely tactless enough to do so. There is every indication that the institutions responsible for incorporating these documents into their Contract Conditions have in fact no very precise idea of what kind of claim their wording is intended to permit, nor are any satisfactory rules laid down (as also in the case of claims based on major departures in the quantities) for their ascertainment, since it appears to be assumed by the wording that there is some objective contract intention against which the alleged "variation" due to the "omitted item" can be measured.

20 For the imperative need for such a make-up see CCPP paras 8-05, 23-18, 23-23, 24-20 to 21-21(a), 26-15, 27-22 and 30-20.

21 See the discussion on the Fourth Edition in my *Building and Civil Engineering Standard Forms* pp 382-83 and 400, and in the case of the FIDIC contracts see *Grinaker Construction* v. *Transvaal Authority* [1982] 1 SALR 78 and see CCPP paras 26-09 to 26-14 for comparison of the wording in the two contracts. See also the decision of the Privy Council in *Mitsui Construction* v. *A.-G. of Hong Kong*, analyzed and criticized by the present writer in (1987) 3 Const. LJ p 3.

22 See Clause 56(2), CCPP para 30-21.

23 See Clauses 5 (make-up of prices) and 13 (measurement).

The legal difficulties and anomalies and uncertainty of this type of claim have been pointed out by me on many occasions.[24] Here again, the ICE Contract decided upon a slavish adoption of the RIBA wording, presumably in order to encourage such claims, in the Fifth 1973 Edition.[25] In fact very careful draftsmanship is required to avoid claims of this kind, since those parts of the Standard Methods which concern themselves with describing the exact method of taking measurements of physical work are clearly very desirable for incorporation into measured contracts in order to avoid confusion, there being in theory many different methods of actually measuring physical work. The anomaly is caused by the fact that the United Kingdom Standard Methods, paying lip service to an apparent need to create standardization of tendering procedures, lay down with varying degrees of urgency recommendations as to the degree of sub-division of building work to be used for pricing purposes - effectively in some cases recommending or prescribing that certain work processes should be inclusive of other related or ancillary work processes on the one hand, but on the other hand prescribing or recommending that other ancillary or related processes should be separately priced and not included in a more composite price for the item concerned. Later still, recommendations have been made in the standard methods for the separate pricing of a large number of temporary works processes, so that an "omitted item" claim (*e.g.* if there is no "separate item" for special pumping) can frequently call for additional payment where the physical conditions in question have been fully foreseen and notified to the contractor in the specification or drawings, for example. The language of incorporation of a standard method into a contract should, therefore, seek to distinguish between those provisions in the Standard Methods which are acceptable in order to introduce certainty into the measuring process, and those which are not acceptable and must yield to the "inclusive price principle" which in the owner's interest, and whether expressly or by implication of law, should underlie all priced contracts for work and materials, whether simple or sophisticated.[26] In the Singapore SIA Contract I have tried to produce a form of wording designed to achieve this limited incorporation of those parts of the Standard Methods which it is clearly in the interest of both parties to adopt.[27]

Drafting requirements for Measured Contracts

A full discussion of the relative advantages of lump sum and measurement contracts is contained in paragraphs 23-21 to 23-23, and 24-20 to 24-21 of CCPP. The minimum drafting requirements to give owners reasonable protection, should they decide to use a measured contract, are set out in paragraphs 23-23(*b*) (*i*) - (*v*) inclusive, and in paragraph 24-21(*c*) and (*d*) (*i*) - (*iii*) inclusive of CCPP. The drafting requirements for lump sum contracts are discussed in paragraphs 23-23(*c*) and 24-21(*e*). Briefly, the requirements for measured contracts should in my view include:

24 See, for example, CCPP paras 26-11 to 26-13, 29-14 and 30-13 to 30-21.
25 See Clause 55(2) and CCPP para 30-21.
26 See *e.g.* CCPP para 24-21(d)(ii).
27 See Art. 5 and Clause 13(1)(b) and (c), set out in CCPP p 570.

- A pre-contract or pre-start-of-work make-up of prices into their various constituent parts, primarily of labour, plant, materials and sub-contracts, together with any special items of expenditure (compare SIA Contract Clause 5)[28].
- An express distinction made between the re- measurement and variation valuation provisions of the contract, limiting re-measurement to adjustment at the contract prices only, but including an appropriate adjustment of preliminary items in the light of the contractor's make-up of prices (compare Clauses 13(1) and 13(1)(d) of the SIA Contract)[29] and only permitting more flexible valuation in the case of variations.
- An express statement of the inclusive price principle, including the removal of any attempted special priority of the Bills over the other contract documents (see Articles 5 and 6 and Clause 13(1)(a) of the SIA Contract)[30].
- Incorporation of any standard method only to the extent of the actual measurement techniques laid down by that method and excluding from incorporation any separate pricing or inclusive pricing recommendations (see Clauses 13(1)(b) and (c) of the SIA Contract).[31]
- Better still, to over-ride or disregard the current over-complication of Standard Method sub-divisions of work by using larger "composite" items in the Bills (while still, of course, requiring the same detailed make-up by the successful tenderer as in (A) above). This will greatly reduce the professional time required for re-measurement, or the computation of interim payment in those contracts where interim payment is made dependent upon valuation.

C. Variations and their valuation

Reverting to first principles, a well-drafted variation clause should lay down a satisfactory code for the authorization of variations, notably one which avoids the impasse which can so easily arise under those old-fashioned clauses (still widely used in the United States) making an order in writing confirming acceptance of liability a condition precedent for payment, if bona fide disagreement on liability later arises between the A/E and the contractor when the work is ordered.[32] This the United Kingdom modern forms achieve satisfactorily, partly by according no special binding force to the A/E's instructions whether purporting to allow or disallow a variation; partly by their provisions permitting confirmation in writing of verbal instructions (which oddly, though this is a minor point, do not operate retrospectively to cover any previous compliance by the contractor with a verbal instruction, which would seem to be a reasonable protection for contractors); and partly by conferring wide reviewing powers on the arbitrator (*pace* the highly anomalous *Crouch* dictum in the Court of Appeal, which would deny such powers to the courts should they, rather than an arbitrator, happen to be seised of a construction

28 See CCPP pp 559-60.
29 See CCPP p 570.
30 See CCPP pp 550 and 570.
31 See CCPP p 570.
32 Compare *Brodie* v. *Cardiff Corporation* [1919] AC 337.

dispute in contracts using the traditional "open up, review and revise" wording in the arbitration clause).[33]

So far as variation valuation is concerned, it is quite clear, as already stated, that it must in the last resort be "open-ended", having regard to the many different circumstances of a variation order which a contractor could not possibly foresee when pricing. While correctly accepting this principle, however, the standard forms in my view lack sufficient precision in giving guidance to the valuer as to the principles he should apply when valuing variations. Moreover, the draftsmanship is diffuse and traditional. Thus Clause 52 of the ICE and FIDIC Conditions appears to be a particularly convoluted patchwork of various means by which the contract prices may be modified, which however appear largely to overlap. If a distinction is intended between Clauses 52(1) and 52(2), for example, it is not clear what it is, and it is difficult to see what further is added by Clause 52(3) of FIDIC, with its apparent 15 per cent limitation on variations, together with its own obvious attendant difficulties of interpretation.[34]

Much more seriously, however, the standard forms are open to criticism for failing to deal with the real everyday possibility that it may become desirable or necessary to vary the permanent work because of some contractor breach or because of difficulties (such as site or construction difficulties) for which the Contractor is otherwise contractually responsible to the owner. It is clear that this omission in the JCT/RIBA forms is not accidental, and the appellate courts of recent years have seen many cases where unmeritorious contractors have been enabled by the wording to make financial claims based on instructions given following their own defaults, or have even been enabled to terminate their contracts as a result of far too widely drafted JCT/RIBA provisions conferring both loss and expense claims and determination rights on the contractor based on postponement or suspension of work, or lack of instructions, in such situations. This is one of the many serious charges against the JCT/RIBA forms today, and is closely connected with another really serious charge, namely the wholly inadequate remedies which, (quite obviously deliberately in the case of the JCT/ RIBA forms)[35] the United Kingdom standard forms confer on owners in respect of defective work.

The following appear to be essential improvements required in the variation clauses of the current standard forms:

Exclusion of Liability

Liability for extra payment should be expressly excluded where a variation is ordered as a result of contractor breach or other default (including, of course, sub-contractors' whether domestic or nominated). GC/Wks/1 contains just such a clause - see Clause 9(4)(c) and, for nominated sub-contractors, Clause 31(3). The absence of such a provision in the JCT/RIBA and ICE Contracts is

33 See CCPP, Chap. 17, which analyzes and criticizes the case (*Northern Regional Health Authority* v. *Crouch Construction* [1984] QB 644).

34 See the author's book *The International Civil Engineering Contract*, p 105.

35 See *infra*, para 63 *et seq.*, and see also paras 30-06 to 30-10 of CCPP set out in the Appendix hereto with regard to the owner's right to accept defective work subject to a diminution of price, as finally perverted and frustrated by the 1980 edition of this form of contract.

perhaps to be expected in view of their consistent disregard of the owner's interest, particularly in the case of the former, but the failure of the central and local government bureaucracy, and of those of the hospital boards and public corporations for example, to require the insertion of such an obviously sensible provision into local and public authority contracts throughout the United Kingdom is inexcusable, and a serious reflection on the quality both of the public representation on those bodies, and of the central government bureaucracy concerned with the subject-matter and content of public construction contracts. A similar saving requires to be made in regard to the special postponement power in the JCT/RIBA Contracts (now Clause 23.2 of the 1980 forms) and of the financial claims permitted by those forms on postponement and other grounds. In the Singapore SIA Contract the saving is for any variation "which is the reasonable consequence of defective work or other breach of contract by the Contractor", together with, if appropriate, a deduction representing any loss of value to the owner of the varied work or any saving in cost to the Contractor in carrying out the varied work, whichever is the greater (see Clauses 12(5)(d) and (e)).[36]

Temporary Works and methods of working

Traditional United Kingdom standard forms, while frequently conferring generalized but otherwise undefined powers of approval, satisfaction and control on the A/E over all the work done, are almost always silent as to whether this extends to the Contractor's own temporary works or methods of working, as opposed to the permanent work. This is reflected in their variation clauses, which neither define the A/E's powers to give variation instructions in such situations, nor seek to provide for when or how compliance with such instructions might give rise to a claim for additional payment. (As already stated, Clause 14 of the ICE Conditions also creates a clever and dangerous trap in which an unwary engineer may find that he has ensnared his client simply by asking for information in such a situation,[37] and is a copybook example of how in the standard forms a provision originally no doubt suggested to give some needed protection to the owner, quickly becomes re-fashioned to the contractor's tactical or financial advantage.)

There are obviously important policy considerations involved in deciding whether or not to confer on the A/E powers to give instructions in this particular area of temporary works and methods of working. Given modern developments in the law of tort, and the modern tendency to saddle supervising professionals, and no doubt indirectly the owner, with considerable liabilities to third parties in the event of any failure of construction, the argument for expressly conferring and defining such powers and clarifying their financial consequences as between owner and contractor have become increasingly strong.

Certainly in 1980 in the Singapore context, with the additional factor of the primary statutory responsibilities of the licensed professional engineer under Singapore legislation, the decision was taken to deal with this very important source of everyday controversy expressly. At the same time, it is clearly

36 See CCPP p 569.
37 See Clause 14(6) and my commentary on the Fifth Edition ICE Conditions, p 57.

essential in the owner's interest to emphasize the contractor's primary responsibility for the safety and sufficiency of temporary works and working methods, and to keep powers of intervention to a minimum and avoid any implication of any duty of the A/E to intervene, however serious the difficulties may prove to be. In a Singapore context this was attempted by defining carefully certain situations in which, in spite of the contractor's primary responsibilities, an architect might decide in the interest of the owner and as a matter of discretion to give an instruction with regard to temporary works or methods of working (see Clauses 2(1) and 2(2)),[38] and to distinguish clearly between those situations where additional payment would be due (Clause 1(4)) and those situations where it would not (Clause 1(3)).[39]

In my view this is a vitally important subject with which any well-drafted contract, particularly in the civil engineering industry, should in the owner's interest deal explicitly, and not leave to the courts to endeavour to interpret from a combination of generalised "under the direction and to the satisfaction of the A/E" types of wording, a complicated 19th century case law, and from the wording of the variation clause, itself clearly not drafted with the problem in mind at all, and compounded in addition by the procedural anomalies and difficulties created by the *Crouch* case in those cases where the courts are seized of the dispute and the A/E has at some time given a decision or expressed an opinion about the matter in dispute.

The basic principle of variation valuation

The underlying intention of all the modern standard forms is, I believe, though rarely clearly expressed, what I have called elsewhere the "shopping list principle" - in other words the Bills or Schedules of Rates contain a list of prices which (subject to adjustments made to take account of possible differences in cost between the varied and original contract work) are intended to govern such varied work as the owner may choose to order.[40] This has two important closely related consequences, namely:

- That if the contractor's prices are profitable, so to that extent will be any adjusted price under the variation clause (*i.e.* adjusted to take account of different location or access, or disturbance due to late ordering, for example). If on the other hand the prices are unprofitable, so to the same extent will be the price as adjusted by the variation clause; and
- Neither party will be permitted to attack or depart from the Bill or Schedule prices when disputing a variation valuation simply on the grounds of their alleged high or low profitability.

In my view this principle needs to be more clearly stated than it is in the current standard forms and a valuer should be directed more specifically in appropriate cases to the necessary adjustments (based on comparisons of cost) which should be applied to the applicable rate or price in the Bill or Schedule, since it is becoming increasingly common, particularly in the international

38 See CCPP pp 556-57.
39 See CCPP pp 554-55.
40 See CCPP paras 8-04 and 8-09.

field, to find one or other of the parties seeking to avoid the original contract prices when putting forward a variation claim and to submit alleged "reasonable cost" prices in their place without regard to the Bills or Schedule prices originally quoted.

Make-up of Prices

It is self-evident that arriving at the correct balance between construction items and preliminary items is as important in the field of variation valuation as it is in the field of re-measurement. Accordingly, the imperative need for a contractual make-up of prices is just as great as in re-measurement, as are the correct principles to apply when adjusting Preliminaries Items in those contracts where either the Bills or the Schedule of Rates contain a Preliminaries Section. The adjustment of preliminaries in the context of variations is also discussed in CCPP.[41]

Profit as a part of variation valuation

Variation valuations, being price-based, will notionally to that extent include for off-site (fixed) overheads and profit, though this will not, of course, apply to any cost adjustments made to the prices in appropriate cases.[42] In a really meticulous variation clause this, too, should be the subject of an express provision, though I have not myself attempted it in the Singapore Contract. For example, contract rates or prices will normally carry their own overheads and profit, but additional work of the same kind might be ordered which was not on the contract's critical path, so that no additional time-related overheads expenditure would be incurred. Theoretically, this would justify a reduction in the price of a variation ordered in these circumstances. Those drafting variation clauses should remember, however, that the clauses do not only apply to additional work, but must also regulate reduced quantities of work. The framing of detailed provisions with regard to such matters as profit and overheads, therefore, will need extreme care.

D. Contractual Make-up of Prices

It will be seen from the two preceding sections on Measurement and Variations that I consider this particular requirement of a make-up of prices to be perhaps the most important practical improvement to modern construction contracts, which will not only facilitate the presentation and successful establishment of justified claims but will equally deter exaggerated or fabricated claims. This will apply not only in the particular fields of measurement and variation valuation, but also (and in particular through the improved insight into the content of the preliminary bills) in the assessment of the quantum of compensation or damages claims where overall delay or disturbance is a feature of the particular claim, whatever its precise contractual

41 See CCPP para 8-05.
42 See CCPP paras 8-03, 8-09, 8-14(a) and 8-34.

or legal origin may be. Language more appropriate to the confessional is frequently used by way of objection to this simple requirement, but it should be remembered that in France, for example, the most detailed examination of a contractor's price make-up is insisted upon and accepted without demur in all government construction contracts prior to signature, and it is not difficult to frame any contractual requirement in such a way as to protect the confidentiality of the contractor's distribution and margins of profit and fixed overheads, to the secrecy of which contractors appear to attach great importance.

The make-up of prices required by Clause 5 of the Singapore SIA Contract was the subject of considerable discussion with the local quantity surveyors before its draftsmanship was finalized. It was ultimately decided to require a break-down of the construction items in the Bills from the successful tenderer only, whereas in the case of preliminaries items, which are so often much less informatively described in bills of quantities, all tendering contractors are required to indicate whether individual items are time-related, quantities-related, or fixed, as well as giving any categories of special expenditure not included in the prices of the construction items (see Clause 5(2)). The clause is also so worded as to avoid disclosure of the profit element in the prices, and in addition permits a breakdown to be given for representative groups of prices or items rather than for every single rate or price in the Bills.

The Singapore format for the required make-up of prices is not put forward by me as a definitive description of an ideal price make-up clause, but represents what is very much a first effort at tackling this problem by drafting. It is quite possible that there may be ways of improving and possibly simplifying the Singapore formula.[43] However, the formula has now been in use since 1980 and I have been informed that in practice no difficulty has been experienced as between the owners' quantity surveyors and contractors in giving practical effect to it. The SIA Contract has, for a number of years, been the subject of the training of architects and quantity surveyors in the relevant faculties of Singapore University, and again I have had no adverse reports on difficulties in the application of this clause.

It seems to me impossible for the quantity surveying profession (given for example the extraordinary complication of the measurement of formwork and other building processes in the current building Standard Methods) to object to the provision of such a make-up, and it would certainly be strange to find quantity surveyors in private practice as the professional advisers of owners doing anything else but welcome enthusiastically such a requirement, which can only be of assistance in the correct assessment and establishment of measurement and variation claims.

E. Changed Conditions Clauses

In the United Kingdom civil engineering industry these take the well-known form of Clauses 12 of the ICE and FIDIC forms of contract respectively. Unlike their United States counterparts (which permit of reductions in the contract prices where the physical conditions turn out to be

43 See Clause 5, CCPP pp 559-60.

more favourable than expected) these are one-way upside price provisions to take account of unexpected unfavourable physical conditions (disregarding for the moment the "artificial obstructions" element in the United Kingdom forms). While such clauses are not usually present in United Kingdom building contracts, exploitation of the Standard Method "omitted item" type of claim can, as previously stated, frequently provide a plausible claim for contractors even where the physical condition is fully foreseeable - see, for example, the rather complicated series of items prescribed by the building Standard Method for dealing with ground water, where a failure to provide a specific item can lead to a claim even though a high water-table is accurately indicated on the available borehole information and detailed pumping requirements are to be found in the Specification.

Reverting to the traditional form of clause, it is submitted that on close analysis this fails the fundamental "value for money" test, in the sense that it is very unlikely that an owner agreeing to such a clause will derive any pricing advantage by so doing. The reason is a fundamental lack of logic, arising from the generalized wording used in such clauses to define the situation in which a claim can be made. The expression "not reasonably foreseeable by an experienced contractor" can arguably cover almost any degree of unforeseeability. Does it mean "totally unexpected"? Does it mean "possible but unlikely"? Or does it simply mean "unlikely in view of the available information"? On such ambivalent wording no two arbitrators can be expected to apply the same test, and many engineering arbitrators seem prepared to give way to impulses of sympathy without appreciating that in most cases the true victim requiring their protection is the unsuccessful but more experienced tenderer who made the mistake of allowing contingently in his price for a risk he regarded as foreseeable, thereby losing the contract to his more rash, inexperienced or, worst of all, his deliberately under-pricing but extremely claims-proficient competitor.

The fundamental criticism of such clauses is that if a particular condition is genuinely "unforeseeable", the prospect of encountering it is unlikely to affect the price of contractors tendering in keen competition, even if there were no such clause present in the contract. Only if a risk was indeed foreseen as likely or at least a realistic possibility would a prudent tendering contractor allow a contingent element in his price for dealing with it. Given the frequently sympathetic attitudes of engineers or arbitrators, contract prices under such a contract rapidly become of a "best possible scenario" character, and any departure from that scenario will result in at least a claim and more often than not an award of additional payment. Self-evidently such clauses, without knowledge of the contractor's pricing motivations or allowances, also make effective comparison of tenders impossible.

Such clauses therefore tend to drive more reputable and experienced contractors out of business, since experienced contractors, or those disinclined to make claims as a matter of policy, foreseeing the possibility of an adverse condition (perhaps because of a more careful investigation of the site conditions than their rivals or because of greater experience) will assume that it will not qualify for a claim and price accordingly, so failing to obtain the contract; whereas inexperienced, rash or optimistic contractors, or those with highly developed claiming skills and techniques, will either accidentally or deliberately ignore the risk when pricing, and later use such a clause to extricate themselves from any unprofitability of the contract so obtained. Indeed, it could even be said that, given the presence of such clauses, tendering contractors anxious to obtain the contract should abstain from too careful or expensive a site investigation for fear of discovering facts which, if subsequently this emerged in evidence, would destroy the success of their claim.

Thus in a well-known leading case in the United States,[44] tendering contractors were required to dredge fill material from an adjoining lake or estuary in order to provide the base-course material for an aircraft runway. One contractor rowed out to the designated part of the lake and noted that the boulder material at the lake bottom was too substantial for suction dredging and would require more expensive mechanical dredging. He then requested the Engineer to designate some other part of the lake where finer material was obtainable, but after enquiries the Engineer was unable to permit this. The successful tenderer, who alleged that he had priced on the basis of suction dredging, then made a claim for changed conditions. When the engineer retorted that a rival tenderer had inspected and made a correct appreciation of the nature of the material, the contractor altered course to a claim for non-disclosure, alleging a duty to inform other tenderers of this. The case is an extremely interesting authority on an owner's duty of disclosure with regard to the condition of the site, and the contractor ultimately failed in his claim in the Supreme Court of Alaska, but owners should note the moral of the "forgotten man" in the case - namely the unsuccessful but prudent tenderer in his rowing boat, and should draw the obvious conclusion as to the effect on the health and tendering procedures of an industry where clauses worded in this generalized way are allowed to become a commonplace.

In fact, the more common unfavourable physical conditions in civil engineering projects are relatively few in number - high water tables or pore-water pressures, unstable ground such as mud, silt or running sand, hard materials such as rock, stones or boulders, possible cavities in various types of strata, rock- slip, and so on. So, too, are the probable techniques for dealing with these conditions should they arise. Bearing in mind that most employers in civil engineering projects are likely to be governments in one form or another with comparatively long purses, there may, as in the case of some unit-price contracts, be a case for the owner being his own insurer, thus deriving a pricing advantage should a possible risk not eventuate. But this is far more effectively achieved by identifying the possible adverse conditions in the contract documents, and by providing for additional remuneration either on the basis of price (*i.e.* by requiring tendering contractors to tender unit prices or rates for provisional or estimated quantities of the special work involved) or on the basis of cost (for example, by using Provisional or Contingency Sums against specified work processes or methods of working or temporary works required to deal with identified potentially adverse conditions).

The advantages of this latter more specific approach (whether cost or price-based) over the traditional generalized changed conditions clauses are, firstly, that tenders will be much more accurately comparable (with a Clause 12-type clause there is no means of knowing what, if anything, the contractor may have allowed in his price for a particular possible contingency or

44 *Morrison-Knudsen* v. *State of Alaska* (1974) 519 P2d 834.

condition), so benefiting experienced and efficient contractors and assisting them in obtaining contracts; secondly, the employer will beyond any doubt receive the advantage of a lower tendered price, together with the real possibility of reduced final cost should conditions be more favourable than the expectation. Thirdly, the owner's advisers will be induced to give more thought to possible site difficulties during the pre-planning stages of a project and to the possible design, pricing and programming consequences. By contrast the clauses in their present form offer an easy escape from a serious pre-contract consideration of these matters.[45]

F. VOP (Fluctuations) clauses

In principle it is a purely commercial decision for an owner, depending on the state of the owner/contractor market, whether to leave the risk of domestic inflation with the contractor for him to price contingently - perhaps excessively, perhaps not - or whether to carry that risk himself. If so, a clause of this type will unquestionably give a lower contract price to the owner - no contractor could, in the absence of such a clause, fail to allow for domestic inflation and remain in business - so that if inflation is less than expected the owner will derive a pricing advantage.

The traditional type of fluctuations clause, with materials price changes based upon a basic price list, and with labour based upon notional rates of wages payable by national or other wage-fixing bodies, could and did give rise to considerable and real abuse in the case of materials, and to considerable difficulties of interpretation in the case of overtime, bonus payments, holidays with pay and other special emoluments in the case of labour. The recently introduced index-based clauses are greatly preferable, being much more certain in operation and easy of administration, though here, too, a certain degree of caution is required by the owners' advisers to avoid abuse. It will be noted that such clauses may not always operate so accurately in an individual case, but this is unimportant since any such inaccuracies can be priced for by the contractor. This is a classical example of precise accuracy yielding to administrative convenience, which should be an important pricing and drafting principle. The various considerations relating to index-based clauses are discussed in CCPP.[46] One matter requiring a drafting decision is to provide expressly as to the precise desired application of such clauses during any period of culpable delay by the contractor (*i.e.* during the period when liquidated damages will be payable). The precise extent to which such a clause will operate during this period is, again, purely a policy matter for employers since it can always be balanced by price - for the particular solution adopted by the SIA contract, see Clause 38(4)[47]. Another matter is to ensure that the percentage of the contract sum to which the clause will not apply (*i.e.* the overheads and profit element) is not under-stated - other wise the clause will become a source of profit rather than of compensation. Again, precision should yield to convenience to make certain that this cannot happen.

45 For changed conditions clauses generally see paras 23-24 and 27-67 to 27-72.
46 See CCPP paras 23-24 and 27-67 to 27-72.
47 See CCPP p 616.

G. Interim Payment and Retention

Perhaps the greatest commercial risk against which any prudent owner in a construction contract requires to safeguard himself is the widespread practice or tendency of construction contractors, whether at the highest or lowest levels of sophistication and price, to take on and "bank" additional projects - that is to say, by taking on more contracts, if possible, than their resources will strictly permit, so as to ensure a continuous uninterrupted flow of future work ahead of their current output. This can only be achieved, of course, at the expense of progress on current contracts already underway, since at least token starts, and probably more, will be required to satisfy the expectations of the new later owners in the pipeline.

This tendency is reinforced if contractors can succeed, as they will invariably attempt to do, in obtaining a financing contribution to their projects through "front-loading" their pricing, achieved by various devices such as overloading the Preliminary Bills (in respect of which a substantial element can often be obtained from quantity surveyors on early interim payment) as well as by inflating the prices of the earlier construction processes (which are often relatively simple, such as bulk excavation and mass and structural concrete) and by correspondingly lightening the prices for the often labour-intensive and difficult-to-co-ordinate finishing trades. These practices are also, of course, the easier to conceal if no detailed make-up of prices is required.

Contractors following these policies will tend to transfer sufficient resources to pacify only those owners who are best-informed and who are applying the greatest financial or other pressures at any one time. Everyone who has commissioned building work himself will be familiar with the sometimes extraordinary lull which can suddenly descend on a project for no apparent reason after what seems to have been a realistic and energetic entry onto the site and commencement of work, and also the inexplicable and frustrating delays and inactivity which frequently occur towards the end of the project when completion seems very close (and when the contractor's prices will be at their least economic and the contractor himself most active in seeking new work elsewhere). Few owners, whether public or private, seek to understand or anticipate this tendency or to consider appropriate contractual remedies to avoid this state of affairs taking place.

Traditionally, the remedy employed to ensure due diligence is the liquidated damages clause, and in extreme cases the owner's termination clause. It should be more widely appreciated that neither of these are really satisfactory remedies for an owner. The difficulties of the architect in analyzing a contractor's internal programming so as to refute unjustifiable claims for extension of time are formidable, even in an apparently strong case, with the odds heavily loaded against the owner's advisers and in favour of the contractor due to the latter's own far more detailed internal knowledge of his co-ordination and programming arrangements, and so of what might or might not arguably obstruct or facilitate progress. As for termination, this is a remedy no employer can afford to use lightly since, quite apart from the heavy potential liabilities should the determination be held to be unjustified, the termination itself, even if justified, can be expected itself to cause substantial further delay - better the devil you know can often be the despairing conclusion of many owners in this situation.

Stage payments

Far more effective remedies are ready to hand if owners and their advisers would only choose to adopt them. The obvious remedy lies in securing the precise opposite of "front-loading" (perhaps "rear- or end-loading" would be suitable expressions). This can be easily and simply achieved, firstly, by making interim payment dependent on stage completion rather than on valuation, and in weighting the pricing of the stage instalments so as to produce effective inducements to progress and completion, and, secondly, by refusing to accept the progressive reductions in the amount of retention which contractor pressures have succeeded in introducing into the United Kingdom standard forms over the past few decades.

It should be appreciated that interim payment based on valuation, which is the invariable rule in the United Kingdom standard forms even in the case of lump sum contracts, is an ideal arrangement from the point of view of the "banking" contractor. Should he decide to starve project A of resources in order to take on projects B and C, he will at least continue to be paid for whatever resources he does choose to allocate to project A, where quite often, particularly towards the end of the job, retention will have reached a contractual limit, so that there may not even be any further retention withheld should he choose to do at least some work. Moreover, if he has succeeded in front-loading his prices on projects A, B and C, he will actually improve his overall cash flow by starving the relatively well-advanced and now less profitable project A. The relatively uneconomical finishing work on that project can be postponed to times when less overall work becomes available.

The standard industry objection to "end-loading", through the vehicle of suitably end-loaded stage payments or larger retentions is that they will lead inevitably to higher prices to balance the additional financing element imposed on the contractor. That is true, but it is also fallacious, since the higher price will be balanced by the additional interest in the owner's hands resulting from his own reduced or postponed payments or usage of his overdraft or other financing facilities. Unlike the imposition of liquidated damages, which even from a contractor's point of view can be unpredictable, the extent of any "end-loading" in the contract prices will be immediately apparent to the contractor, with his own private knowledge of his pricing, at the tender stage. Being predictable, such additional financing can be accurately taken account of by all tendering contractors when pricing. Again, this has the same philosophical justification as the previously recommended use of index-linked fluctuations clauses or the substitution of provisional quantities or rates for the unpredictability of the traditional changed conditions clause - any lack of precision in assessing the stage payments may be balanced by price but will be accompanied by other overriding advantages.

It will also be suggested that stage payments are only appropriate to lump sum contracts, and this will certainly have the support of quantity surveyor vested interests. There is in fact no logical reason why valuation should be the basis of interim payment, even in measured contracts. No doubt in larger more sophisticated measurement contracts where stage payments are used, it may be thought desirable to provide for any net adjustments arising on re-measurement, together with variations and nominated sub-contractors' accounts, to be assessed and allowed in interim certificates either at the same time as the overall stage payments are certified, or possibly at more frequent periodical intervals. In most projects practical and administrative convenience will point to the former.

In the case of the 1987 Third Edition of the Singapore SIA Contracts, stage payment has been provided as an alternative in the case of the measured contract forms by Article 2 and Clause 31(3). In this case, the contractual provisions for retention and payment for unfixed materials have been dropped altogether if stage payment is adopted, but on the other hand as-built remeasurement, variation valuation and PC and Provisional Sum adjustments for nominated sub-contractors will all be made in the stage payment certificates.

Increased retentions

Whether or not stage payments are adopted (and, as stated, retention provisions can effectively be avoided altogether by appropriately fixing the amount of the stage payments) it follows that really substantial retention percentages (preferably without any limit on retention) will also act as a far more effective inducement to progress (particularly because they will, like stage payments, be automatic and uncontroversial in operation) than any liquidated damages or termination provisions of the contract. As already explained, increased retentions will be largely self-financing due to the balance between any higher contract price and the reduced or postponed financing commitments of the owner.

Assessment of Stage Payments

The assessment of the precise amounts or percentages of the various stages should of course be decided upon by the owner's advisers. It is suggested that while with a small contractor with limited resources in whom confidence is placed an early financing element may be permissible as an assistance or inducement in the earlier stages, the middle stages of construction at least should be under-financed so that the remaining finishing stages, including any payments on practical completion, or at the end of any defects liability period analogous to retention, can be correspondingly weighted so as to provide a strong inducement to complete. Just as in the case of index-based fluctuations clauses, owners' advisers should not concern themselves unduly with the accuracies of their stipulated percentages of the contract price, since the additional financing costs (if any) of such in accuracies can be left to the tendering contractors to price. Leaving tendering contractors to stipulate for differing stage percentages either at the tender stage or subsequently should be avoided, and will have the added disadvantage for owners of prejudicing accurate comparison of tenders.

H. Defective work

During Construction.

The standard forms generally limit the A/E's powers to ordering the removal of defective work, or the opening up of work for inspection with additional payment for doing so made dependent upon defective work being discovered. These remedies are not only seriously inadequate but frequently quite impractical, and can create serious problems for employers where major or disputed defects are discovered (compounded, in the case of the JCT/RIBA forms, by the ease with which the contractor is empowered under those forms to terminate the contract in wholly inappropriate situations where a suspension of work - a frequent concomitant of the discovery of serious defects - has taken place). The obviously essential additional remedies for employers are set out in CCPP,[48] namely:

- The power, once defective work by the Contractor has been established, to order further opening up and to conduct investigations and if necessary to suspend work, all at the cost of the contractor in any event, in order to determine the full extent of the defects and the best method of dealing with them.
- The power to vary the permanent work or to order different remedial work without additional payment, if that is considered preferable to or more practical than wholescale removal or demolition.
- The power to accept defective work as it stands, or only partially remedied, subject to a reduction in the contract price reflecting the reduced value of the work to the owner or the reduced cost to the contractor, whichever is the greater.[49]

It is, of course, self-evident that a suspension of work in such a situation should never confer benefits or compensation on the contractor - again, (and certainly through no accident) a real possibility under the JCT/RIBA Contracts' contractor's determination clause, as many decisions of the appellate courts have shown, particularly in the context of sub-contractors and suppliers.[50]

After completion.

Clearly the liability for undetected defects should remain for the full period of limitation in any contract drafted in the owner's reasonable interest, due to the covering up inherent in a large proportion of construction work and the difficulties and expense of day-to-day supervision. As stated, Clause 30(7)(a) of the post-l976 and Clause 30.l.l.l of the post-l980 JCT/RIBA Contracts have endeavoured to continue what appears to be a deliberately imprecise exclusion of liability,[51] albeit to an apparently reduced extent by comparison with the pre-l976 versions.

Particularly offensive examples of exclusions of post-completion liability, which no properly-advised employer could possibly be asked to accept, are to

48 See para 23-29.

49 See *supra* para 6 and CCPP para 30-06 to 30-11 showing how the JCT/RIBA Contracts have succeeded in providing to the precise contrary.

50 See *e.g. Gloucester Corporation* v. *Richardson* [1969] 1 AC 480, *Jarvis* v. *Rockdale Housing Association* (1986) 36 Build LR 48 (analyzed and criticized in (1987) 3 Const LJ 274) and see also *Fairclough* v. *Rhuddlan BC* (1985) 30 Build LR 34, *City of Adelaide* v. *Jennings Industries* (1985) 57 ALR 455, and CCPP paras 29-08 to 29-10.

51 See CCPP paras 30-04 and 30-05.

be found in the mechanical standard forms, including the FIDIC/E&ME Contract (these are usually turnkey contracts, it should be noted, where one might have expected a more strict liability than usual). There, liability after "takeover", including that for satisfactory performance of the works, appears to be excluded altogether save for a very limited period, and then only where there has been what is described as "gross misconduct" on the part of the contractor.[52] It is difficult to conceive of any adviser recommending such a form to a purchaser or owner, particularly in a "design-and-build" project.

The foregoing recommendations for defects during construction have been implemented in the Singapore SIA contract in Clause 11.[53] So far as the continuing liability of the contractor for defects for the full period of limitation after completion is concerned, this is made explicitly clear in Clause 27(5) (Maintenance following Completion),and Clause 31(1)1 (Certificates).[54]

I. Nominated sub-contracts

The owner's miseries under the JCT Contracts are nowhere, perhaps, more highlighted than in the area of nominated sub-contracting - perhaps the most profitable and risk-free area of main contractor activity when examined from the financial point of view, and in times of recession frequently subsidizing the main contractor's own work, though this underlying commercial background is never mentioned in the industry and only rarely in articles in discussion of the subject. With the exception of a few of the national main contractors, the capitalization of the average nominee sub-contractor is likely to be equal to or greater than that of the average main contractor.

The traditional system of remuneration which has grown up in relation to nominated work has had the special result of giving the main contractor, over what is an increasing proportion of the whole project (and frequently well over half of it by value) highly profitable as well as (apart from the insolvency risk) wholly risk-free remuneration, since there is no other pricing risk for the main contractor on nominated work.The traditional percentages for profit to be found in almost every Bill of Quantities prepared in accordance with the Standard Methods are l0 per cent, to which fall to be added the further profit (tactfully but entirely misleadingly described in the standard forms as "cash discounts") of 2 per cent for sub-contractors and 5 per cent for suppliers. On top of these two percentages of pure profit, attendance items are priced in the Bills, very often in the region of l5 per cent. Disregarding the attendance items, which clearly represent at least some elements of cost, the other percentages (on turnover) represent prodigiously high risk-free percentages on capital employed.

The owner's misery under the traditional pre-l980 JCT Contracts (which are, of course, very frequently used even today) arose because the appellate courts, when interpreting ambiguous and obscure provisions in those forms, gave way to immediate "hard case" and insufficiently analyzed instincts of sympathy in response to the arguments of main contractors in cases where

52 See FIDIC E & ME Contract, Second Ed.1980, Clauses 12.6, 16.4, 33.11, 33.21 and 33.13.
53 See CCPP pp 564-65.
54 See CCPP pp 584-86, and see particularly Clause 27(5) for the precise effect of the Maintenance Certificate.

nominated sub-contractors had defaulted on their obligations (a sympathy often particularly influenced by the analytically irrelevant consideration that NSC insolvency may often follow shortly after[55], or sometimes accompany[56] the original default). The other basic cause was the "calculated and devious" draftsmanship of the JCT/RIBA Contracts themselves, no doubt because of a desire to avoid drawing attention to such serious anomalies by too clear or express language. These dictated a "no change" drafting policy after the surprising decision in *Bickerton,* rather than re-drafting to give clarity to the intention, it may be surmized. The practical anomaly in the case of NSCs arises because any interpretation or draftsmanship which excuses (or worse still expressly compensates) a main contractor for nominated sub-contractor default is, at second remove, a real-life commercial encouragement to solvent NSC default or repudiation, (for instance where the NSC finds he has under-priced or obtained more profitable work elsewhere) or to disclaimer by trustees and liquidators of NSC's of sub-contracts which they might otherwise have decided to complete.[57] This is compounded in the JCT Contracts by the absence of draftsmanship in those contracts designed to prevent architect's instructions issued as a result of contractor default (including of course sub-contractors) from giving rise to compensation[58], let alone express provisions making clear the full financial responsibility of the main contractor for all NSC defaults.[59]

In the Fifth Edition ICE Conditions, and now in the post-1980 JCT/RIBA forms, the owner's misery takes the form of an extremely complicated ultimate owner's guarantee to the main contractor against all the consequences of a sub-contractor default. This is further compounded by the effective inability of the owner to intervene or control the termination of nominated sub-contracts (in spite of a misleading appearance of shared control, with the contractor in real unilateral control, conferred by Clause 59B(2) of the ICE Conditions).[60] In summary, the ICE Conditions provide a code of extraordinary complication under which the employer has a cosmetic though in reality ineffective consultative role in cases where a nominated sub-contractor is in breach of contract, but where at the end of the day all the financial responsibilities for the resultant disturbance of the main contract, or for litigation between MC and NSC, are required to be borne by the employer if the NSC is unable to meet his liabilities. This is also the objective of an even more complicated scheme provided for by the post-1980 JCT Contracts (of which it can be said that, quite apart from any substantive defects, the administrative complication of the notices and instructions required to pass between the architect and the main contractor in regard to NSC nomination or default are such as to discourage any person who actually understands them from nominating sub-contractors altogether).

55 See *e.g. City of Adelaide* v. *Jennings Industries* (1985) 57 ALR 455.
56 See *e.g. Bickerton* v. *NWMHB* [1970] 1 WLR 607 HLE.
57 See CCPP para 21-06, which develops and explains this.
58 See *contra* GC/Wks/1 Cl.9(4)(c) (and indeed any other contract properly drafted in the owner's interest).
59 As *e.g.* GC/Wks/1 Clauses 31(3) and 38(b), quoted *infra*, para 74.
60 See the detailed analysis of these new NSC provisions in my Commentary on the Fifth Edition at pp 196-222.

Viewed from the point of view of owners, the case law in this field has been a catalogue of disaster. In *Gloucester Corporation* v. *Richardson*[61] defective pre-cast concrete columns provided by a nominated supplier, and producing an immediate and necessary short cessation of work to investigate the cause, resulted in a successful termination of the contract by the main contractor against the owner. *Bickerton* v. *North West Hospital Board*[62], a "test case" on the JCT/RIBA wording, required an owner, in a case of the earlier insolvency of a heating sub-contractor, to pay the higher account of the successor sub-contractor (a much more limited decision in its effect, but, as will be seen, a subsequent albatross for the judiciary, since it is clear beyond doubt that the interpretation placed by the House of Lords on the wording of the contract had not been anticipated by the draftsman of the contract itself, with the result that none of the provisions relating to extension of time, or for compensation for loss and additional expense, have subsequently been found to be applicable to or compatible with the duty to re-nominate which the *Bickerton* case apparently laid down).

Thus the House of Lords in 1982 was compelled to hold that the JCT/RIBA provisions, due to this fundamental drafting inconsistency, brought about a legal "impasse", in a case where the employer did re-nominate, but it was impossible to find at that late date a successor sub-contractor whose completion dates would be compatible with those in the original main contract. In this situation, the House of Lords held, neither party was in breach; but in an insufficiently considered dictum, it was suggested that the main contractor could have objected to such a re-nomination, leaving the employer with the alternatives of omitting the NSC work altogether or negotiating some compromise - an astonishing interpretation to place upon a standard form of contract.[63]

Subsequently, in a confusing case in the Court of Appeal in 1985, it was suggested that such an instruction (*i.e.* one unavoidably involving a later completion date) would amount to a postponement instruction under the provisions of the JCT/RIBA Contracts (if so, of course, entitling the contractor to full monetary compensation)[64] and this appears to have been conceded, or at least the contrary not argued, in the Court of Appeal in 1986.[65] (This was a case of defective piling left behind by a nominated sub-contractor without proper testing, again resulting in a rapid and successful termination of the main contract against the owner, and was an almost carbon copy of the *Gloucester* case in 1969, and even had the same main contractor.) The *Bickerton* confusion has spread to Australia under the RAIA forms of contract (where a similar result was narrowly avoided in the High Court of Australia in a case where a heating sub-contractor did not return at the end of the defects liability period to remedy defects, and much later became insolvent after the owner had himself carried out the remedial works and debited the main contractor).[66]

61 [1969] AC 480.
62 [1970] 1 WLR 607.
63 *Percy Bilton* v. *GLC* [1982] 1 WLR 784, discussed in CCPP paras 21-19 to 21-22.
64 *Fairclough Builders* v. *Rhuddlan DC* (1985) 30 Build LR 34.
65 See *John Jarvis* v. *Rockdale Housing Assocation* (1986) 36 Build LR 52, analyzed and criticized in "The *Bickerton* Albatross Once More" by the present author in (1987) 3 Const LJ 275.
66 See the *City of Adelaide* case, *supra*.

The confusion following the original *Gloucester Corporation* and *Bickerton* cases is the more remarkable in that throughout the whole period since 1969 the Government's own GC/Wks/1 contract was freely available. Thus in CCPP I have said "Nearly all the *Bickerton* cases in the UK (and many other unreported instances) have involved Hospital Board and other United Kingdom authorities incurring enormous and unwarranted public expenditure over a period of more than 15 years, which could not have occurred had the Government's own contract been used. This must be one of the most striking examples of bureaucratic and government apathy and indifference to the contents of construction contracts which seems to be so common in Western countries."[67] The draftsmanship of GC/Wks/1 is positively lapidary in its simplicity, and is well worth quoting in this context:

> "15(2) The Contractor shall be responsible for any sub-contractor or supplier employed by him in connection with the Works whether he shall be nominated or approved by the Authority or the SO or shall be appointed by the Contractor... or otherwise.
> (3) The Contractor shall make good any loss suffered or expense incurred by the Authority by reason of any default or failure, *whether total or partial*, on the part of any sub-contractor or supplier". (My emphasis.)

This is followed by a provision obviously inserted following the result in *Bickerton*:

> "38(5) In the event of the termination of a sub-contract to which this Condition applies the Contractor shall, subject to the consent in writing of the Authority, either select another sub-contractor or supplier to undertake or complete the execution of work or the supply of things in question, or himself undertake or complete the execution of that work or the supply of those things *and the Authority shall pay the Contractor the sum which would have been payable to him.... if termination of the said sub-contract had not occurred....*" (My emphasis.)

I have pointed out the various drafting options for nominated sub-contracts in CCPP.[68] In the case of the SIA Contract, it was decided to adopt the same policy as GC/Wks/1 (*i.e.* to restore the pre-*Bickerton* position by express language), but it was also thought right to afford some further protection to main contractors in the context of the unsatisfactory impasse likely to arise in a case of a disputed objection to a (first) nomination under the then existing United Kingdom standard form wording. That arose because there was no really effective rapid arbitration or other machinery to deal with a disputed objection, so that the main contractor was compelled to risk a termination by the owner should he maintain his refusal to comply with the nomination instruction. Accordingly in the SIA Contract it was decided to provide what I have called an "owner over-ride" clause. The effect of this is that, on receipt of an objection, the owner is given the right to over-ride the objection and require the contractor to place the sub-contract in question, but in the event that the specific reason given by the contractor for objection subsequently materializes,

67 See CCPP para 21-38.
68 See para 21-32

thus showing the objection to have been valid, the owner effectively indemnifies the main contractor against loss.[69]

In my view owners should realize that main contractor's organizations' criticisms of the nomination system are a public relations exercise, and there would be a storm of protest if the bluff was called and the system was abolished, due to its great profitability without risk for main contractors. Owners should quite simply adopt the GC/Wks/1 policy and revert to the original pre-*Bickerton* position.

J. Insurance

In this field, again, there has been little or no proper analysis or understanding of the owner's exact interest in obtaining compulsory insurance through the contractor in a construction contract, and in the progressive degree of over-insurance of the works themselves being called for in successive editions of the standard forms. This increase in the extent of the contractual insurance (which on analysis must be paid for, whether directly or indirectly, by the employer in the form of higher contract prices) appears only to reflect the commercial interest of contractors generally (in particular of those contractors seeking to maximise profit by minimising protective measures and site expenditures) and of the insurance industry itself.

Owners can do much to lower the cost of their contracts and benefit contractors with good records for safety and site management by avoiding unnecessary areas of insured risk likely to give rise to minor claims only (leaving inefficient contractors free to take out supplementary insurance if so inclined), and also by a sensible use of insurance excesses, based upon the contractor's ability to pay at least a substantial first part of any claim. In addition, owners, by confining insurance of the works only to those risks which can cause catastrophic damage and excluding risks which produce only minor claims having a disproportionate effect on the size of premiums, can reinforce the pressures for improved safety and site management. These views are fully explained in CCPP[70] and have been implemented in the Singapore SIA Contract.[71]

Third party insurance also requires re-examination applying the same principles[72] and in the light of a complicated case law the associated indemnity clause in the contract requires careful drafting.[73]

K. Design and Turnkey Contracts

It is a feature of the standard forms almost everywhere in the world that they make no effort to spell out expressly the contractor's responsibilities in regard to his two most fundamental obligations. These are, firstly, the inclusive nature of the completion obligation itself (with its pricing implications for

69 See the SIA Contract, Clause 28(3)(a) and (b), set out in CCPP pp 591-2 and p 643.
70 See para 23-32.
71 See the SIA Contract, Clauses 19, 20 and 39, set out in CCPP at pp 575-58 and 616-17.
72 See CCPP para 22-33.
73 See *e.g.* SIA Contract Clause 18(3), CCPP pp 574-75 and 639.

temporary works and for the overcoming of site difficulties and also for undescribed but inherently necessary ancillary permanent work) and, secondly, the proper extent of his design obligation.

Although an attempt to define these obligations comprehensively has been made in the Singapore SIA Contract[74], and while with modern judiciaries and arbitrators this would in my view be highly desirable at the present day in other jurisdictions, notwithstanding a largely satisfactory (if properly understood) 19th century case-law in traditional owner-designed projects, the one area where correct analysis and draftsmanship is currently imperative is in the case of turnkey (or preferably "design and build") contracts.

Any adviser to an owner or government who accepts or recommends the "professional duty of care" liability currently being offered by would-be turnkey contractors, or in newly emergent standard forms purportedly designed for such contracts, will have failed to make a correct analysis of the nature of the contract and of the threat to the owner's fundamental interest if he yields to argument and agrees to substitute for an absolute warranty of suitability, independent of fault, (which is what the law would otherwise imply in commercial situations where there is reliance by an owner on a contractor for design) this much lower degree of design responsibility, at least without warning his client as to the possible consequences. The public relations plea in favour of such a reduced liability proceeds on the footing that it is unfair to ask a contractor to accept a higher liability than would be asked of the client's own architect. However, it is precisely because the commercial relationship between buyer and seller is so totally different from the relationship between a buyer and his own professional adviser, with fundamentally different and perfectly respectable pressures for under-design in the buyer/seller case as against, if anything, pressures for over-design in the professional advice case, that a different and more strict design liability is necessary as a matter of business efficacy in a case of design and build, just as in the case of sale of goods. Owners who have unwisely conceded the point will find that serious defects subsequently discovered in a building will almost invariably produce a "state of the art" defence by the contractor, or his insurers or bondsman, involving lengthy and expensive proceedings with conflicting expert evidence before it may be possible to establish liability.[75]

In fact, there is hardly an important substantive provision in a turnkey contract which does not require radical revision of its corresponding provision in a traditional owner-designed contract. The drafting requirements for such contracts are considered in considerable detail in CCPP.[76]

L. Certification Arbitration and Remedies

In no area of construction contracts is there more room for radical re-thinking and analysis of what precisely are the desired policies, and no more fertile ground for bewildering and contrary decisions of the higher courts, than in those disputes which relate to the relationship between certifiers' and

74 For temporary works see Clause 2, and for his design and completion responsibilities see Clause 3, both set out in CCPP pp 556-57.

75 See CCPP paras 23-08(f) and 24-07(viii).

76 See CCPP paras 23-05 to 23-11, 24-07 to 24-09 and see generally Chap. 25.

arbitrators' decisions and the jurisdiction of the courts themselves to deal with a dispute.[77]

It seems increasingly doubtful if either party to a construction contract at the present day desires or intends that an A/E's certifications opinions or decisions should have binding force or be a condition precedent to a contractor's right of recovery, or that there should be any limitation on the powers of the courts to deal with a disputed matter on the merits in those situations where the courts, rather than an arbitrator, are seised of a dispute.[78] The only respect in which a deliberate or coherent policy would appear to be discernible in the modern draftsmanship is in the frequent endeavour to obtain immunity for the contractor in respect of post-completion discovered defects, usually based on an expressed conclusiveness of the final certificate.

Thus in the last half-century it has been owners rather than contractors who have suffered injustice as a result of the draftsmanship relating to the finality of certificates.[79] This finality of certificates may have been rather too easily accepted by the 19th century courts,[80] and many more modern judicial decisions have in fact not supported it.[81] The ICE Contract has now stepped back squarely from this position with regard to its previously ambiguous clause governing the effect of the maintenance certificate.[82] The JCT/RIBA standard forms, on the other hand, produced a new and puzzling formula in 1976 which appears to seek to retain at least some degree of contractor immunity.[83] It is to be hoped that such provisions will now attract the attentions of the Unfair Contract Terms Act. (Perhaps it was no coincidence that the new wording emerged as the Act came into force.)

As already stated the difficulties and injustices of certification provisions have been compounded by the procedural and practical anomalies and injustices likely to arise as a consequence of the dicta which the Court of Appeal, apparently ignoring both principle and contrary authority, expounded in the *Crouch* case in 1984.[84]

The impression is overwhelming that the finality decisions of the judiciary over past decades have followed from basically accidental and unconsidered draftsmanship in the standard forms and reflect no considered policy on their part (save only, as stated, the obvious desire of the contracting side to secure immunity for post-completion defects which must certainly today be within the potential scope of the Unfair Contract Terms legislation).

On the other hand, the policy of the Singapore SIA Contract, which has adopted a rather unusual approach, has been to secure over the widest possible traditional areas of dispute between owners and contractors an early, but purely temporary, finality for the architect's certificates and related decisions, together with a contractor's right of objection to any change of architect by the

77 See particularly CCPP Chap. 15 and 17 and the recent Court of Appeal decision in *Lubenham* v. *South Pembrokeshire D.C.* (1986) 33 Build LR 39.
78 See the historical analysis of these provisions in CCPP paras 17-06 to 17-100.
79 See *e.g. Kaye Ltd.* v. *Hosier & Dickinson* [1972] 1 WLR 146.
80 See for the history CCPP paras 17-06 to 17-10.
81 See the cases cited in CCPP para 17-10.
82 See Clause 62 of the Fifth Edition Conditions.
83 See the concealed dangers of Clause 30(7)(a) of the post-1976 JCT/RIBA Contracts, and of Clauses 2.1 and 30.1.1.1. of the 1980 Contract, discussed in CCPP paras 30-04 and 30-25.
84 *NRHA* v. *Crouch* [1984] QB 644, analyzed and criticized in depth in CCPP Chap. 17.

owner, and with immediate early arbitration permitted for all but a very narrowly defined and exceptional class of disputes. This policy was decided upon since there was evidence that in Singapore a minority of building owners with considerable economic power frequently dishonoured architects' certificates, or even changed architects to obtain compliant certification, and ordinary Order 14 procedures, with leave to defend so frequently given, were not a really effective remedy for contractors in such situations. A very powerful and real remedy for contractors was therefore deliberately made available through the interim certification machinery.[85]

At the present day in the United Kingdom it is suggested that, from the point of view of all owners, both private and public,

- the courts should have full jurisdiction to deal with all claims on the merits if for any reason they, rather than an arbitrator, become seised of a dispute under a construction contract;
- no certificates or opinions of the A/E should be given binding force, whether temporary or permanent, and the draftsmanship should make clear that they are of an administrative character only;
- arbitration should preferably be left for subsequent agreement and not be the subject of an arbitration clause - in other words, either party should be entitled to require a dispute to be dealt with by the Courts unless an acceptable arbitrator is put forward by the other party. This depends very much, of course, on the view taken of the attractiveness of arbitration.

Few well informed advisers would, I believe, today advise an owner to agree to a "blank cheque" provision (which in effect is what a traditional arbitration clause is) subjecting his contractual rights in an as yet totally unformulated dispute to the decision of an unknown arbitrator whose technical qualifications might in any case not be appropriate to such a dispute. Arbitrators as a class should appreciate that, unless powerful reasons are present, most owners at the receiving end of the typical present day contractor's claim will prefer an experienced Official Referee, or other judge or lawyer with experience of construction contracts, to an unknown arbitrator selected, failing agreement, by the President of some professional institution. It will be a party who is advised that his legal case is not strong who will usually tend to prefer arbitration. These may be unpalatable facts, but I do not believe that many experienced legal practitioners would dispute them, and in my view they should be squarely faced. An absence of binding arbitration clauses will also facilitate bringing multipartite disputes under one roof before one tribunal - an important factor in many construction disputes.

Adopting the general philosophy of this paper, owners and their advisers should ask themselves "Do we get value for money if we include an arbitration clause in our contract which will govern any future dispute which may arise with the opposing party?" A full discussion of the merits and de-merits of arbitration and arbitrators is to be found in CCPP.[86] If a decision is taken to have an arbitration clause there are a number of special powers peculiar to construction contracts which it is desirable to confer on the arbitrator, and also other considerations, in particular arising from the role of the architect and the presence of sub-contractors, which call for special drafting, but which are

85 See Clauses 31(1) and 37(1)(g), CCPP pp.599 and 612-13.
86 See paras 17-47 to 17-48.

rarely in practice to be found in any arbitration clause. The SIA arbitration clause is an example of the sort of matters which require special drafting.[87] It will be seen that the clause contains no less than 12 sub-clauses, dealing with the following points:

- Clause to apply to disputes in tort as well as contract (sub-clause (1));
- Power to rectify the contract (sub-clause (2));
- A specific list of all matters which under the terms of the contract are intended to be final and binding on the arbitrator (sub-clause (3));
- The powers of the Courts to be identical if they and not the arbitrator are seised of a dispute (sub-clause (4));
- Restrictions, if any, on time for commencing arbitration (sub-clause (5));
- Power to order interest to either party in the event of over- as well as under-certification (sub-clause (6));
- Power to order repayment of sums over-paid whether or not under mistake of fact or of law (sub-clause (7));
- Single tribunal powers for main and sub-contract arbitrations (sub-sections 8, 9 and 12);
- Limitation Act lacunae dealt with (where actions are stayed or arbitrations are halted in favour of litigation) (sub-clause (10);
- Single tribunal applications where third parties involved (sub-clause (11)).

Remedies (Termination Clauses)

The termination clauses in construction contracts are generally not very satisfactorily drafted. In the particular case of the JCT/RIBA Contracts, the substantive grounds for contractor termination, other than non-payment, are, quite simply, unacceptable to any fair-minded person, let alone any properly advised owner.[88] In addition, the owner's termination clause in the ICE contracts is, from the owner's point of view, over-complicated by archaic legal jargon, and in places ineptly drafted without a sufficient under standing of all his possible practical requirements in a termination situation.[89]

M. Priority of Documents Clauses.

Many standard forms of contract contain clauses designed to give one class of document priority over another. The law, left to itself, will in any civilized country have rules which endeavour to ascertain the true consensual intention of the parties to the contract before deciding upon their resulting rights and obligations. Thus in the United Kingdom, for obvious reasons not requiring explanation, as an evidentiary matter priority will, in the event of conflict between differing documents in a contract, be given to statements or agreements prepared or made by the parties themselves with the particular project in mind, such as letters, drawings or particular conditions or specifications, rather than printed or standard documents which they may

87 See Clause 37.
88 See CCPP paras 29-20 to 29-23 and 30-24, and the comments of Prof. Werner Lorenz in the *Encyclopaedia of Comparative Law* there referred to.
89 See *e.g.* my commentary on the Fifth Edition, pp .245-49.

have chosen to employ which were not prepared by the parties themselves and did not have the particular project in mind. Most notoriously in the case of the standard forms, Clause 12(1) of the 1963 version and Clause 2.2.1 of the 1980 version of the JCT/RIBA Contracts:

- both give priority to the printed standard conditions over the Bills of Quantities (the latter being, of course, a "one-off" document prepared for the particular project); and
- in the 1963 version, give priority to the Bills and to the Standard Methods of Measurement (unless specifically excluded in particular items) over the drawings and specification in regard to the price or description of the work undertaken.

Such artificial priority between documents can only produce injustice, and will be the last resort of a party (whether owner or contractor) seeking to put forward an interpretation of the contract which departs from the parties' true intentions, as disclosed by their own, as opposed to standard, wording and documentation. Lord Denning MR found such provisions so offensive that he was even prepared to disregard them as a matter of public policy[90] but there seems no doubt that the English courts will in fact still enforce such terms. The SIA Contract has endeavoured to deal with such problems of interpretation as specifically as possible and in a way calculated to avoid injustice to either party.[91] It has also a very differently drafted "discrepancy and divergence" clause with the same objective - see Clause 14, which avoids the "upside only" implications and lack of logic of the United Kingdom Standard Forms.

90 See *English Industrial Estates* v *George Wimpey* [1973] 1 Lloyd's Rep 511 and 7 Build LR 122.
91 See Arts. 6 and 7.

Management of Finance 17

John Bishop

Synopsis

This paper analyzes the methods of cost management and payment envisaged by the current standard forms of contract. It suggests various alternative methods for both concepts and concludes that money claims can often be avoided by an early and honest appreciation and allocation of risk.

Introduction

Whilst preparing this paper, I have been provided with two indications of the areas to be considered. These are the list of "Working Group Topics" and a draft of Professor Duncan Wallace's paper "Contract Policy for Money". The list of working group topics suggests for consideration the item "lump sum v crime cost". My initial amusement at this apparent mistype gave way to a consideration as to the aptness of the reference to "crime" in the light of Professor Duncan Wallace's attack on the position of contractors under the standard forms.

In Professor Duncan Wallace's paper he portrays contractors as an avaricious group whose sole interest is the unprincipled manipulation of construction contracts to the employer's disadvantage. I, respectfully, differ from this portrayal. In today's market, contractors are ever increasingly concerned with establishing a reputation for producing contracts on time and within budget so as to cultivate a "repeat order" habit with the major building employers.

As a member of the board of a holding company with contracting subsidiaries, I can speak from personal experience when I say that "claims" are only advanced within that organization when they are seen by the contracting subsidiaries as not only contractually but also ethically justifiable.

Professor Duncan Wallace stresses that all risk assumption has to be balanced by price. He refers to his book[1], where he bemoans the failure of most of us who are associated with construction law and the construction industry fully to appreciate that contracts are neither "fair" or "unfair", nor "pro-employer" or "pro-contractor". This is particularly appropriate to bear in

1 *Construction Contracts : Principles and Policies.*

mind when examining construction contract policy. What is in my opinion equally as important in avoiding disputes as to time or money is that the parties, both employer and contractor, should at the outset of a contract "come clean" as to the risks they are accepting and the risks they are passing on.

Should payments be used as a management tool?

A building employer will want to know not only how much he is likely to pay but also when he is to make payment. It is the common practice of contractors at tendering stage to prepare a cost graph showing when payments are likely to be received and thus to establish the cash-flow consequences of the contract. The projected cash position will then be a factor in "pricing" the contract.

The criticisms of the periodic "valuation and certification" process are that it allows main contractors to front end load their pricing to obtain an advantageous cash-flow and that the process often leads to dispute. Front-end loading is probably undesirable from an employer's point of view because he remains at risk in the event of a contractor's insolvency, because it does not necessarily result in true competition between tenderers and because the advantage "taken" by the contractors is not demonstrably passed on by keener pricing.

The insistence on price break-downs showing costs profit and overhead may discourage front-end loading and may also allow quantity surveyors an opportunity to spot the loading at tender stage.

It may well be possible to limit the problems I have referred to. The first opportunity on a "valuation and certification" contract will be at tender stage. It is possible for an employer to indicate the maximum percentage of the contract sum which he is prepared to pay at any particular time or stage of the works. This can be done by breaking the contract into its elements and calculating a percentage for each element so that the maximum sum payable at any one time can be calculated by reference to completed elements. This maximum sum should then be applied as a ceiling for each interim payment.

I have been involved in drafting contracts where a graph has been prepared showing money against time, from which the maximum sum which an employer will be prepared to pay at any time is calculated. The architect or engineer or quantity surveyor may then be given the task of updating the graph to take account of approximate extra cost or saving for variations and also to extend the graph to take account of delays to the contract.

It is usually thought desirable to provide that the decision of the architect/engineer/quantity surveyor in such circumstances is final and binding during the course of the contract although it is open to review on completion. A sophistication of the system is to adjust only for delays for which this contractor is not entitled to an extension thus adding a further cost to contractors who are in culpable delay.

Other methods for using payment as a management tool also exist. A simpler system than a ceiling on interim payments is the introduction of stage payments.

This is a fair system in that the contractor has the opportunity to take into account at pricing stage the consequence of the stage payment structure and the employer has the opportunity to impose his design for stage payments. The principle is that the employer states in advance the sum or the percentage of the tender sum, or of an estimate of prime cost that he is prepared to pay at each particular stage of his project. Following receipt of the successful bid and the contractor's programme a fixed stage payment amount may be calculated. There is often an adjustment procedure to take account of variations and expenditure on provisional sums etc.

It must be remembered that it has become the practice in the United Kingdom on many contracts which are not let on the JCT type standard terms for "pay when paid" provisions to be incorporated so that, in principle, the contractor is not obliged to pay the subcontractor until he is himself paid. I do not intend in this paper to consider the enforceability of such clauses, but it must be recognized that contractors rely on such clauses as a mechanism for managing their cash-flow. Except on the largest projects, it will be unlikely that the consequence of a Stage Payment or Ceiling Payment procedure in the main contract will be incorporated into the sub-contract. Accordingly, the advantage to an employer of such mechanisms may be off-set by the main contractor tendering at a higher price because he is deprived of a "pay when paid" system.

There are an increasing number of contracts in the UK where the contractor is to provide the finance for the project and thus where the employer is only obliged to pay on Practical Completion of the whole of the works. A variation of this procedure allows an employer to pay any or all interim certificates if he so elects within a period from the certificate. By this method he can take advantage of interest payments which are lower than those charged by the contractor as the price of providing finance.

There is, of course, no reason why a contractor should not be asked to finance part of a project (*e.g.* 25 per cent of all interim payments). This balance (less retention) would be paid on practical or sectional completion. It provides an incentive for prompt completion, but employers must expect to pay a financing cost included in the contract price and to receive a claim for compensation when variations, late instructions or other acts of prevention delay completion, and thus payment of the balance.

In prime cost contracting (*i.e.* when the contractor is paid the cost of the works together with a fee) there are many ways of using payment as a management tool. The following paragraphs give examples.

The Fee assessed against an Estimate of Prime Cost

This is a very familiar system whereby the contractor assesses the prime cost at the outset and this is checked by the employer. The contractor is then paid the actual cost of the work together with a fee calculated as a percentage based on that estimate. The estimate is adjusted to take account of specified matters; usually those which would entitle an increase in the contract price on a lump sum contract (*e.g.* variations, postponement instructions, expenditure of provisional sums etc.). The fact that the contractor is paid by reference to his estimate means the contractor has no interest in maximising the actual cost and, indeed, has an interest in minimizing it thereby increasing his recovery in percentage terms.

The Target Cost Contract

The contractor agrees a target cost for the contract. The target is usually adjusted to take account of any matters which would increase or reduce the contract price on a lump sum contract. The contract then makes provision for the consequences of the cost exceeding or being less than the target; for example the contractor may have to bear a percentage of any cost in excess of the target and be entitled to a bonus for every pound that the cost is less than the Target.

The Ceiling Cost Contract

This is a derivative of the Target Cost Contract save that the "Target" is a "Ceiling" so that the contractor meets in full the cost over the specified sum.

Set Off

A further tool for controlling the management of a construction project is the right to set-off monies for breach. Save in respect of defects found after completion and liquidated damages, set-off more commonly occurs between main contractors and sub-contractors than under main contracts. *Gilbert-Ash (Northern) Ltd.* v. *Modern Engineering (Bristol) Ltd.*[2] is authority for the proposition that whether monies can be set-off is a matter of construction of the contract in question; there is no special principle applicable to certified sums in the construction industry. Thus in the absence of an exclusion, the usual rights of set-off will apply. The standard forms of main contract have, in effect, powers of set-off within their terms since the contracts only call for monies to be included in certificates for works which have been "properly executed". Such expressions sometimes result in dispute. The main disputes are issues as to how much can be disallowed for work which has not been properly executed. Is it the value of the whole of the item of work or merely the value of the imperfect part or an allowance for the cost of overcoming the imperfection.

In addition the standard contracts allow the architect to require an opening up for inspection of work covered up. The contractor meets the cost if the inspection shows materials or work not in accordance with the contract. This is sometimes thought to be unfair to contractors. Construction is not precise and it may be that a minor and possibly unrelated disconformity will put the contractor to the cost of opening up even when the condition expected by the architect when he gave the instruction is not in fact found.

The standard form seems to allow architects to reject materials or work which do not accord exactly with the specification even when the problem could be overcome by an agreed variation, with no cost implication to the employer. I have been involved in a case where an architect condemned an entire structure although the problem could have been much more cheaply overcome. The employer offered, in return for a cash payment of £100,000, to instruct the architect to accept the cheaper solution.

2 [1974] AC 689.

Reverting to the position under the sub-contract: the draftsmen of the standard forms of building contract introduced into some forms of sub-contract an adjudication provision. In the event of a set-off the sub-contractor is able to invoke a procedure whereby an adjudicator decides whether the monies set-off should be held by the main contractor, paid to the sub-contractor or paid into a trustee shareholder account pending resolution of the dispute between the contractor and the sub-contractor.

In order to present the other picture to that of the innocent employer being duped by the unprincipled main contract, it still happens that from time to time employers either put pressure on the professional team to undercertify or merely refuse or fail to pay main contractors. This can happen as an attempt to persuade contractors to waive claims.

Although the contractors may have termination rights in such circumstances they are rarely used because the consequences of termination are often more serious than the employers' breach. Very often the grounds relied upon for an undercertification are not clearly matters which fall within the exceptions allowing arbitration before practical completion. Employers rarely waive the right to resist arbitration before practical completion in such circumstances.

It would be inappropriate for me to divert in this paper into a discussion on arbitration, reconciliation and alternative dispute resolution, but I do consider that provisions should be prepared allowing for an interim decision where late payment or under-certification occurs before practical completion. Even if the contractor can fall within the exceptions which allow early arbitration, the delays in appointing an arbitrator and pursuing the claim will often discourage him for pursuing his remedy.

The unfortunate state of English law which in effect prevents, in most cases, the recovery of interest for late payment except pursuant to Section 35A of the Supreme Court Act 1987, in my opinion, means that the Standard Form Contract should include express provisions for the payment of interest. (The ICE has gone some way to actioning this in Clause 60(6) of the Fifth Edition.) I am in favour of clear provisions going beyond mere interest for late payment but also providing for interest on sums "under-certified" and providing for a commercial rate of interest. I would also like to see a contractual power to suspend work for non-payment.

From an employer's viewpoint he needs to know as soon as possible if his cost is going to be increased through claims. Many disputes owe their origins to the employer being surprised either by the very existence or by the quantum of a claim. The GC Works form of contract is sometimes held out as a model in that it contains notice provisions which at least on their face amount to conditions precedent to any entitlement. In my opinion the balance struck by the ICE in clause 52(4) is the correct one in that a contractor is penalized from bringing a claim in respect of which he has failed to give notice only to the extent that the employer is thereby prejudiced.

A recent example of abuse of the GC Works Contract which I have encountered involved a supervising officer who was issuing several instructions per day at the late stage of a major contract. He was insisting upon an immediate notice for each variation alleged to cause delay with an estimate of the amount of delay. It was of course the contractor's case that the number of variations at a late stage had a delaying result even though each one in isolation may only have had a minimal result.

How far should payments be recalculated?

A large proportion of construction disputes revolve around the recalculation of payments. The simple answer to the question "How far should payments be recalculated? would therefore seem to be "as little as possible". However this is oversimplistic. The degree to which a fixed price contract needs to have elements of that price recalculated generally depends on:

- The degree to which the design has been finalized and accurately measured.
- The degree to which the employer retains and uses his right to interfere, *e.g.* by variations, nomination etc.
- The degree to which the employer passes certain risks to the contractor and pays the cost of so doing.

In addition, but in my experience comparatively rarely, a recalculation is necessary because of an error in the original contract documents. (*e.g.* a failure to comply with the relevant Standard Method of Measurement).

In recent times, many employers are more concerned by the completion date than by the risk of price increases. They therefore go out to tender on documents which are not prepared to the degree which is desirable for fixed price tendering. Often this is done with full knowledge of the risk of claims caused by recalculation following variations or the expenditure of provisional sums.

It is often the case that the professional team advising the employer do not or cannot advise him of the alternative forms of contract because the project has proceeded too far on the basis of one form of contracting or because they cannot disclose the stage of their design or because they have some other vested interest in preserving the status quo. Very often it would be cheaper for a client to move to a design and build or design development contract with a fixed price than carry on with a standard form which is inevitably going to be the subject of massive variation.

Another reason for recalculation is the unforeseen ground condition. It is often the case that a contractor would have taken the risk of unforeseen conditions had he either been given a site survey or the opportunity to carry out his own. It is not uncommon in major contracts in the Far East for the contractor to accept the "unforeseen conditions" risk. This no doubt results in an increase in price. An employer can, of course, invite alternative quotations with or without the contractor assuming the risk.

Nomination is another reason for recalculating the payment because the prime cost allowance for the work in question has been expended. Provided that the nomination is made in favour of a sub-contractor who is acceptable to the main contractor the employer should know at an early stage the cost of this element of recalculation. Clearly this element could be avoided completely by avoiding nomination. The reservation of the right to nominate usually arises for two reasons:

- The employer or his design team are relying upon the sub-contractor to carry out an essential design element; or
- The employer wants to choose the identity of the sub-contractor because of his reputation and the corresponding after sales service.

Both these factors can of course be overcome by suitable contract provisions.

Professor Duncan Wallace criticizes the Bill of Quantities method of contracting. In my opinion his proposals of an alternative are not quite as far-reaching as they may at first sight appear. It is not uncommon for contractors to price contracts where an adjustment from approximate quantities does not amount to a variation but merely to an adjustment based on the actual quantities.

In the field of design and build contracting, contractors will give fixed prices without any quantities being drawn up whatsoever. In so doing they price the risk.

When, however, bills of quantities are provided it is more difficult in practice to avoid the consequences of inaccuracies in them. This is because of the way contractors price large elements of construction projects given the time and cost constraints of competitive tendering. In practice the contractor copies substantial sections of the tender documents and sends them to sub-contractors to obtain a price. Sub-contractors may have only a few days in which to submit their price. It would be rare either for them to have the time, or for it to be justified economically, properly to investigate and price the risk that non-contractual quantities may be inaccurate.

In the current market, I have no doubt from the informal enquiries I have made, contractors would be willing to take the risk in inaccurate quantities. This would be reflected in their price The problem is that a change to this method of contracting involves employers being prepared to meet some element of the abortive tendering cost of other contractors or a major change in the industry to this method of contracting so that contractors have the opportunity to recover abortive tendering costs on other contracts. In addition tendering periods must inevitably be extended.

In the field of Design and Build Contracts it has become increasingly common for employers to engage a professional team to undertake the initial design and then require the chosen contractor to engage that team to develop the design further. It may be that in the future an employer who offers his quantity surveyor to the chosen contractor will obtain prices which remain fixed notwithstanding a change in quantities.

The Virtue of Claims

Claims are in most cases the result of:

- Changes of mind by the employer; or
- Inaccuracies in tender documentation; or
- Late production of information to the contractor; or
- Matters where the employer reserved his right to interfere: *e.g.* nomination, expenditure of provisional sums; or
- Matters in respect of which the Employer retained the risk. (*e.g.* unforeseen conditions).

At the time of preparing this paper I can see no virtue in claims from an employer's point of view; they are simply the necessary evil arising from forms of contracting which take account of some or all of the matters listed above.

Contrary to the views sometimes expressed contractors, in my experience, only bring claims where they have suffered losses from one or more of the events I have referred to. The desire to get onto tender lists and to make profits from contracting rather than to prepare claims means that contractors tend only to bring claims when they have suffered substantial losses. It tends to be the case that a reduction in contracting activity results in an increase in claims activity. However most contractors only see a virtue in claims as an alternative when profits through contracting are not available.

Lump Sum v. Prime Cost

Lump sum contracting in most cases offers an employer a greater certainty as to the cost to him of a project. Where the project is fully designed and substantial variations are unlikely most employers will be advised to look for a lump sum price through competitive tendering.

However, in my opinion the prime cost style of contracting can provide many advantages to an employer. Some of these are:

- He can start work earlier and in the knowledge that the design is incomplete.
- He can adjust the quality of the later elements of the works to reflect the then estimated final cost.
- Claims are far fewer.
- The employer can more easily adopt alternative methods of contracting (*e.g.* Design and Build Contract and Management Contracting).
- The employer can often manipulate the speed of the work as acceleration or slowing down will be reflected in costs but not in an inflated claim.

The disadvantage of prime cost contracting from an employer's point of view is usually stated to be the loss of competitive edge of tendering and the lack of certainty and control of the cost. These disadvantages can be substantially overcome by:

- Target Cost/Ceiling Cost Clauses.
- By ensuring that sub-contractors are chosen competitively.
- By ensuring that the contractor has an interest in economy *e.g.* by making his fee dependant on an estimate of cost rather than actual cost.
- By selecting a contractor with a reputation in prime cost contracting.
- By ensuring that the prime cost is accurately defined, regularly monitored by the employer's quantity surveyor and that the likely final cost is reported regularly by contractor and quantity surveyor independently.

Is the Claims Industry Necessary?

The claims industry will be present whilst the circumstances discussed above which give rise to claims continue to exist, Many contractors do not maintain the staff to present claims and thus involve outside claims consultants to investigate and prepare claims for them. Many small contractors simply do not have the expertise to present their legitimate claims to the professionals engaged by the employer.

Unfortunately the standard of claims consultants varies very substantially, from those who evaluate and advise on claims on a very professional basis to those with little expertise who will find and pursue a claim on the thinnest of grounds. In my opinion whilst claims exist, claims consultants will continue to exist. However, it is to be hoped that with a reduction in claims through the new forms of contracting, the weaker claims consultants who often pursue poor claims into arbitration rather than abandoning or settling them will be squeezed out of business.

Conclusion

The problems of management of the money under a building contract often arise from a failure of the employer to decide at the outset which risks he can afford to take himself which he wants to pass on, for a price, to the contractor. This failure arises because of a lack of awareness of other available methods of contracting or of the safeguards that can be taken. If the problems are appreciated soon and the contractor is given a fair opportunity to consider and price the risks many of the costs overruns through claims and otherwise could be overcome.

18 Management of Time

Philip Naughton

Synopsis

An analysis of contract provisions which bear on time leads to a discussion of the more novel ways of controlling progress on site. With a warning of the potential difficulties of bonus clauses, it is suggested that detailed programme control could usefully be undertaken throughout the contract. Consideration of various categories of employer leads to the conclusion that price and the risk of delay are linked.

Introduction

The provisions which relate to time in standard contracts or in special or one-off contracts are fundamental to the distribution of risk between all the parties to the contract and in some cases to the sharing of that risk by those named as professionals in the contract. Most contracts used by the different branches of the construction industry include clauses which limit or define time related risk in terms which are, generally, very familiar: "programme", "extension of time", "liquidated damages". There are other optional or possible provisions which are more rarely seen, in particular provisions relating to bonus. In this short paper I will endeavour to identify some aspects of the standard clauses which may deserve reconsideration and discuss some of the problems relating to more novel provisions.

In this review I make no attempt to be comprehensive. As a practising barrister it is inevitable that I tend to experience those aspects of construction and engineering contracts which give rise to disputes which have not been resolved by the parties. In the result, my perception of the industry may not coincide with that of the engineer or architect. There is also a substantial lag between the introduction of changes in the standard contract terms and reports of cases in which those terms have been examined. There is still very little reported law examining the terms of JCT 80, for example, and yet it is in wide use and its terms are being broken now. In the result I have concentrated on four points of interaction between the passing of time and contractual obligations:

- Programme;
- Bonus for early completion;

- Disruption claims;
- The costing of delay claims by employers and contractors;

General Matters - the contractual environment

Standard contracts make presumptions about the spread of the risks associated with the time for completion of works. There is an almost universal assumption that the contract will not finish early. It is assumed that contractors and sub contractors will be able to pay liquidated damages for late completion for which they are responsible and that those damages will compensate an employer for any loss he may suffer. On the other hand, if delay is caused by employer, architect or engineer the contractor has no automatic right to recover anything, although he may be granted an extension of time. If he has suffered a related loss he must prove it by demonstrating that he has actually incurred some additional loss or expense. If delay is caused by a sub-contractor, even a nominated sub-contractor, it is generally the case that the contractor accepts that risk in so far as it affects his own finances.

So the nature of the claim arising out of delay differs according to which party claims. The extent of that claim and its closeness to the loss actually suffered may well be determined by price and depend upon which party to the contract has the stronger position, the whip hand. Thus, when construction work is plentiful and all reputable contractors are busy, it will be difficult for the employer to insist upon onerous provisions; although at the same time it is less likely that the contractor will finish late because he and his employees will have other work to go to. When the industry is slack the employer recovers the whip hand. Put another way, the question of whether the employer can actually cover the cost of delay by a provision for liquidated damages will depend upon the state of the industry, the size of the project and the price he is willing to pay for the project. Experienced contractors will price the cost of delay and include it directly or indirectly in their build up of costs. If the project is unusual, an effective liquidated damages provision may lead to prohibitive pricing. On the other hand even experienced and large contractors may be unable to negotiate contracts which modify their obligations or provide for adequate recovery of their true losses when the industry, or their part of the industry, is in recession. So what is "appropriate" may not be coincide with what is "acceptable".

Time and the Sub-contractor

Construction of anything, be it bridge, hospital or housing estate, involves two elements; the acquisition of materials in processed or unprocessed form and the mixing, fitting and erecting of those materials to provide a finished structure. Suppliers of materials, whether or not nominated, whether or not required to supply in accordance with programme (JCT 80 36.4) will often supply only on the basis that they will not be liable for late delivery. Quite often the value of the materials supplied will be small and it would be unreasonable to require the supplier to accept more onerous responsibility. Yet the delay in provision of, let us say glass for windows or brackets for the support of cladding or the correct grade of grout for injection behind tunnel walls, may lead to delay in an entire project with real difficulty in recovery of the cost of consequent losses. Under the JCT 80 Form of Contract, if the delay is the result of the conduct of a nominated sub-contractor, the main contractor will be able to obtain an extension of time (although note that the extension applies only to delay "on the part of" the sub-contractor - see *Westminster City Corporation* v *Jarvis*,[1]) as he will if the delay was not "foreseeable" and was beyond his control, but he may be unable to recover his own loss. Under the ICE Contract the contractor's liability to the employer may be limited to that which he can recover from a nominated sub-contractor (Clause 59A). However, a sub-contractor who is employed to undertake even a small part of project work will be required to agree to the terms of one or other standard contract form which in turn will expose him to liability for all the loss suffered by the contractor as a result of late completion (*e.g.* DOM1 Clause 12.1). As projects increase in complexity and particularly as they become more dependent upon the supply of unusual or exotic materials it may be thought necessary to improve the match between suppliers and contractors.

Programme

The obligation of the contractor to provide and work to a programme varies in the different standard forms of contract. Parris[2] suggests it is optional in the JCT Contract, although it is clearly asssumed; a programme is required under the under the ICE Contract but the level of detail is not specified. In the result its significance may be slight, yet the programme may represent the most efficient way of controlling many aspects of the temporal dimension of a contract. Effort devoted to the writing and updating of a programme may save some of the truly massive expenditure incurred on preparing and fighting a contractor's claim generated out of weak control of progress during the course of works.

It may be contended that the programme presently employed and the detail presently provided is all that is possible. However, in engineering and construction contracts I see programmes prepared at the beginning of a contract which look impressive and which appear to cover every aspect of the relevant works, then I see site minutes which record that this or that part of the works is so many weeks behind programme. There may even be prepared one or two revised prgrammes during the course of the works. Then, depending upon the type of contract, requests will be made for extension, variations will be made and arguments will be rehearsed in correspondence as to the effect of events upon the progress of the works. Gradually the clearly defined progress of the works becomes submerged under the effect of variations, delays, weather, and all the other incidents of construction. Then in come the quantity surveyors and the matter is resolved or the first Claim appears which catalogues the progress of the works as seen through the eyes of the contractor. The architect or engineer replies - and so it goes on. The JCT 80 Form of Contract endeavours to deal with these problems rather more specifically than

1 [1970] 1 WLR 637.
2 *The Standard Form of Building Contract JCT 80*, Collins.

the ICE Contract (with which I admit greater familiarity).It provides for more and clearer notices to be given "forthwith" of the fact of delay and "as soon as possible" of its expected effect. Under the JCT Contract, the architect reacts to notices seeking extensions of time by granting a period for extension of the whole works. The engineer reacts in a similar way under Clause 44 of the ICE Contract.

Having seen the lengths to which the parties drive themselves (or are driven by their claims consultants) to justify disputed positions in arbitration after completion, I am led to ask whether a greater emphasis on programme and actual progress achieved might pay dividends. I have in mind a requirement that in submitting any notice of delay or other circumstance entitling contractor to an extension of time, he is required to update his programme showing the precise level of progress in respect of each element of the works and how the relevant incident affects the critical path of the works. Would such greater precision assist the supervising professional and provide a greater discipline? It is noteworthy that in the process engineering field sophisticated progress control techniques do tend to be employed. With the appearance of a computer on every desk and fast running software, the development of a programme model for even relatively straighforward works might be attractive if it avoids the "Claims Clash" arising out of disputes as to the true effect of delay. I would be interested to learn if employers or their professional advisers are seeking to enhance their control of the works and the management of claims before they attract a capital "C". How does an architect or engineer undertake the calculation of the appropriate period for an extension of time in respect of a collection of incidents save by analysis of their effect upon a programme? If that programme is not maintained it might be wildly out of date when he undertakes his calculation.

In *Glenlion Construction Limited* v *Guiness Trust*,[3] the Official Referee, His Honour Judge Fox-Andrews QC pointed out that a contractor's programme does tend to be optimistic. It provides them with a margin which can be absorbed during the course of the contract works and provides room for exageration, or at least the highlighting, of the effects of delay. Whilst it is sensible to provide early target dates to allow for the unexpected, the adoption of unrealistic programmes, if unqualified, does appear to frustrate their true purpose of providing a reliable yardstick against which to measure each element of progress along identified critical paths. Accordingly bonus payments become difficult or impossible to provide for.

Bonus

In *Glenlion* the contractor sought to recover loss alleged to have been suffered as a result of the architect failing to provide information in time for him to complete the works in accordance with his ambitious programme. His Honour Judge Fox-Andrews held that there was no duty upon an architect to provide information earlier than required for completion by the date in the contract documents. Although this result may be irritating for the contractor it may be more important for the employer to have a certain completion date than

3 (1987) 11 Con LR 126.

to have work completed early. I should qualify this general observation by noting that in the ICE and FIDIC Contracts there is a specific obligation upon the employer to give possession to the contractor on the dates required by his programme (Clause 42 in both) even if it is unrealistic.

In some cases the early completion of development property, a road or perhaps a factory may be of great advantage to the employer. A contractor who has other work to go to or has a flexible overhead may have internal reasons for wishing to finish early, but if his off-site overhead is fixed and his on-site overhead is not high he will be content to complete to programme. Imposition of a shorter contract period at the time of commencement may deter the contractor from bidding or may result in dispute, but the offer of a bonus for early completion may enable the contractor to offer inducements to his employees and sub-contractors so as to aim for if not achieve an early completion. At first sight it appears to require only a simple provision in a construction contract, but it must be linked with consideration of the obligations of architect or engineer to provide information to match the acceleration of the work and of the employer to provide possession of and access to the site. In practical terms this would require the architect or engineer to agree to and be obliged to provide information as and when required by even an ambitious programme and might entitle the contractor to claim against the employer for loss of bonus as result of late instruction. For this reason it is easiest for the employer to permit a bonus clause either when the works are straightforward and within the control of the contractor or when the architect or engineer is required to provide all information at the commencement of the works or when the contractor is responsible for the design of the works (whether under the JCT Form with contractor's design or under a specialist design and build contract). If such a clause is permitted in other circumstances it would be necessary to provide for the architect or engineer to veto the contractor's initial programme. It would not please an employer to discover that the effect of offering a bonus was to create a new class of claims relating to matters alleged to have interrupted an unrealistically optimistic programme. Additionally the existence of a bonus clause is, or may be, of crucial significance to a sub-contractor responsible for a small element of the works. He may find that he is liable to a claim by the main contractor for loss of bonus because of a failure by him to deliver on time even though the sub-contract works were completed in time for the contract completion date.

It may be preferable for the employer who wishes to offer a bonus to link it with a clear statement that it does not impose any obligation upon architect, engineer, employer or nominated supplier to comply with any requirement before the time when the contract provides or it is otherwise necessary to enable the contractor to complete the works by the date fixed for completion[4]. It would be of interest to learn if these problems are being worked out in practice. At least the personal responsibility of the professionals may be less acute following the decision of the House of Lords in *D & F Estates Ltd* v *Church Commissioners*[5].

4 See the observations of Max Abrahamson on p 158 of his book *Engineering Law and the ICE Contracts*.

5 [1988] 3 WLR 368.

It is noteworthy that neither the JCT nor ICE Contracts make provision for payment of bonus. The FIDIC Contract permits it (Clause 47(3) and Part II) but only in respect of "achievement of target date". Whilst such an achievement may be easier to control, the problems associated with a bonus linked to time of completion must remain the same.

Words of Contract - extension of time and claims for associated costs

Commentators emphasize that the provisions of the JCT and ICE Contracts for the granting of extensions of time may protect the contractor from claims for liquidated damages but do not entitle him to a penny of extra compensation. So it may follow that as the result of delay by one sub-contractor a main contractor is entitled to an extension of time, but if the delay causes a recoverable loss to another sub-contractor, because for example, the main contractor was in breach of contract in not being able to give possession that second sub-contractor, the main contractor may be obliged to pay money but be unable to recover it. And even if he is not under any obligation to a third party, his costs may be dramatically increased by an event which causes him delay but which does not entitle him to recover his additional expense. These are problems of risk allocation which do not always operate fairly under the standard forms of contract. A contractor with "the whip hand" may be well advised to write in a link between additional overhead and extension of time, but the powerful employer will endeavour to impose much of the risk associated with delay upon the contractor.

Not only may the contractor be unable to recover the cost of delay, he may also be unable to obtain an extension of time if the delay is the result of the default of his sub-contractor. If the sub-contractor is nominated or a supplier of materials under the JCT Contract the matter may be covered, but under the ICE and FIDIC Contracts the availability of an extension is dealt with by loose wording which invites dispute. In the ICE Contract an extension can be allowed for:

> "...other special circumstances of any kind whatsoever which may occur ... such as fairly entitle the contractor to an extension of time ..."

In the FIDIC Contract the terms are:

> "...other special circumstances of any kind whatsoever which may occur, other than through the default of the Contractor, ... such as fairly to entitle the contractor to an extension of time..."

Because both contracts provide that the contractor shall be liable for the acts of sub-contractors as if they were the acts of the contractors (Clause 4) the general wording of the FIDIC Contract cannot assist the contractor when his domestic sub-contractor causes delay. The words "other than through the default of the Contractor" were added to the FIDIC Contract after forthright criticism of the terms of the second edition of that Contract. The same terms are still found in the ICE Contract and they certainly leave plenty of scope for interpretation.

But what is better: a precise contract which leaves the supervising professional with no discretion if circumstances leading to delay are not within the precise terms of Clause 25 or the ICE provisions which leave the engineer with the opportunity to preside over the contract from beneath a judicial palm tree?

Disruption

Calculation of uncertain claims for delay is undertaken by the quantity surveyor. The quantity surveyor, (I have finally concluded), practises a science which is almost, but not quite, truly scientific. As in every other field of their work, the approach of two quantity surveyors to the cost incurred by a contractor as a result of delay will not always coincide and as the number of variables in most delay claims tend to make weather forecasting look simple, the result is often a contested claim. Claims related to disruption and acceleration attract particularly impressive calculation.

In *Crosby* v *Portland UDC*[6] and recently in *London Borough of Merton* v. *Leach*[7], Donaldson J and Vinelott J respectively have upheld what has become one of the most troublesome areas of delay claims. The words used by the arbitrator in *Crosby* and which are recited every day in Points of Claim must be known almost off by heart by the dedicated claimant:

> "The result, in terms of delay and disorganisation of each of the matters referred to above was a continuing one. As each matter occurred its consequences were added to the cumulative consequences of the matters which had preceded it. The delay and disruption which ultimately resulted was cumulative and attributable to the combined effect of all these matters. It is therefore impracticable, if not impossible, to assess the additional expense caused by delay and disorganisation due to any one of these matters in isolation from the other matters."

Almost exactly the same problems arise in respect of acceleration claims. Of course, disruption and acceleration claims often concern every aspect of variation of contract and not only time related claims alone but the interdependence of such claims and the passing of time justifies some consideration here.

Disruption and acceleration claims are a delight for the contractor. They permit him to rely upon impressive generalisations to bring his claim. He will contend that to have more than one trade working in one area slows everyone down, that packing the site with extra labour dimishes the efficiency of each individual and that working out of sequence causes delay and disrupts progress. All this is of course true - but to what extent is it real (or really true)? What it does is permit him to calculate his "loss" by adding up the total sum which he has in fact expended, subtracting the net cost element of his tender and any agreed variations, topping it up with overheads and profit and underlining the resulting figure.

Employers argue that such a rolled up claim takes no account of the inaccurate tendering of the contractor or of his inefficiency. Arbitrators despair and pluck a vaguely reasonable figure out of the gap between the positions of the opposing parties. Such claims can only be made if the contract

6 (1967) 5 Build LR 121.
7 (1985) 32 Build LR 51.

permits them: is it time to look again at the contract, to outlaw unquantified claims and insist the contractor proves the real effect of delay, variation or whatever? Some suggestions:

- Introduce the percentage limit on variations as in the I Mech E conditions - no variation that will, together with those already directed to be made, involve a net addition of more than 15 per cent without the contractor's consent;
- Require the contractor to provide an estimate of the total cost of any delay at the time he gives notice of its occurrence. Compare the rather kinder provisions of the ICE Contract (Clause 52) which requires "reasonable" information to be given when "reasonably possible", and the JCT Contract (Clause 26) which depends upon the architect requesting information. One finds much tougher requirements in some process engineering contracts.
- Require that each cause of alleged delay is related to an updated programme: see my previous discussion in of this paper. The more detailed the programme, the more practical it is to compare anticipated cost with likely additional cost.
- Prohibit rolled up claims unless the contractor has agreed with the architect or engineer the basis upon which any such claim is to made in advance of the work being undertaken.

I observed earlier that there is a difference in approach which may well be inevitable, between the way in which the employer and the contractor quantify the effects of delay. I return to the point when discussing claims for overheads, below, but at this stage I cannot resist putting a general question: should we be looking for a formula or formulae which fixes the scale of any claim by the contractor at the time he tenders so that whether or not his claim is rolled up, each party knows what the employer must pay the contractor if the contractor is delayed by the employer or his agent? It could be called the "Contractors Liquidated Loss."

The cost of delay - liquidated damages

The imposition of liquidated damages will, as observed above, have the effect of increasing the price tendered by the experienced contractor. If the nature of the works is unusual, a building employing novel techniques, a process plant built as a prototype or a tunnel through a mountain, the imposition of liquidated damages may have the effect of lifting the cost dramatically, as the contractor effectively "insures" the risk. However, major projects, particularly those with a high labour content, must incorporate some sanction to ensure that the contractor does "diligently proceed" with the work (JCT 23.1), use his "best endeavours to prevent delay" (JCT 25.3.4.1) and proceeds with "due expedition and without delay" (ICE 41). Although the standard forms of contract deal with difficult works by providing for unforeseen circumstances, the more unusual the contract, the more difficult it is to control and consequently the contractor will find it harder to show that delay was not the result of his, or his sub-contractors', default. In part this may be a matter of negotiating with tenderers or making specific provision in respect of the more difficult aspects of the works, but I cannot suggest any improvement on market place negotiation to bridge the gap between the likely real loss of an employer resulting from late completion and the limits of a contractor's willingness to pay liquidated damages.

Clauses providing for the payment of liquidated damages create quite different problems for employers under some of the standard contracts. Of these problems, the most common arises from the employer being responsible for some part of the delay. Liquidated damages are not then recoverable unless the contract specifically provides[8]. It is intended that the extension of time provisions in Clause 25 of JCT should permit the employer to extend time as a result of his own default and still claim liquidated damages provided that the architect grants the relevant extension. But is it wide enough to cover the default of another main contractor? The provisions of the ICE and FIDIC Contracts do appear to be wide enough but it is clearly of critical importance that the engineer gives the appropriate extension.

In his 1979 Supplement to *Hudson* Mr Duncan Wallace questioned the effect of the employer causing delay after the date fixed for completion during a period when the contractor was liable for liquidated damages and pointed out that none of the standard forms of contract provided either for delay by the employer or subsequent variation before the delayed completion. The result was that if the employer did cause delay during this period he could lose the right to claim all liquidated damages. The JCT 80 endeavours to deal with the point by providing that the architect can refix the completion date within 12 weeks of practical completion (Clause 25.3.3), although Parris retains some doubts (see pp 201, 202). There is no equivalent provision in the ICE or FIDIC Contracts although there would appear to be no technical reason for not including a clear provision entitling the engineer to review the completion date and to grant further extension to allow for either variation or delay during the period when liquidated damages would otherwise be payable.

I should also mention the recent case of *Temloc* v. *Errill Properties*[9]. In that case the employer completed the Appendix to the JCT 80 Contract specifying the weekly figure for liquidated damages as "£ nil". The Court of Appeal interpreted this provision as meaning that the parties had agreed that the employer would have no claim for damages for late completion in any circumstances. The case reinforces how important it is for the parties to any contract to complete its clauses with care. It is not possible to draft contract terms that are proof against careless completion.

The cost of delay - overheads

This is not the place to undertake an analysis of the approaches of established writers and judges towards claims for site overheads and head office overheads[10] but if calculation is put to one side and common sense is permitted to hold the stage, the observer is struck by the difference between the framework of a claim for site and office overheads and reality. Take first the site. Very often a delayed completion which is the responsiblity of the

8 See *The Cape Hattera* [1982] 1 Lloyds Rep 518 and *Peak Construction* v. *McKinney* (1971) 1 Build LR 111 and *Percy Bilton* v. *Greater London Council* (1981) 20 Build LR 1.

9 (1987) 39 Build LR 30.

10 For a useful review see the article by Roger Knowles in the *Chartered Quantity Surveyor* (1985) Vol. 8 p 207.

employer relates to some relatively small component of the works. However, the contractor claims and the employer's quantity surveyor often agrees that all the site overhead elements of the contractors' tender build up other than preliminaries should be permitted; so two men, a site hut containing a desk and a foreman can attract a weekly rate measured in five figures. Similarly head office overhead incurred or related to a specific contract may be illusory, save for the purpose of maintaining or calculating a claim. The employer has a choice. He can either specify in the contract documents the exact sums which can be claimed by way of overheads or insist upon the contractor producing actual evidence of overheads incurred or investigate and demand proof of actual overhead incurred or risk paying a handsome profit to the lucky contractor.

The employer or his engineer might be heartened by the decision of Forbes J in *Tate & Lyle Food and Distribution* v. *Greater London Council*[11] where a claim for lost mamagement time was refused after the Plaintiff had failed to adduce real evidence of the quantum of a recognized head of loss (the case subsequently went to the House of Lords but not on this point). Nevertheless enthusiasm should be tempered by consideration of the earlier decision of the Privy Council in *Tai Hing Cotton Mill* v. *Kamsing Knitting Factory*[12] in which, after full argument that damage must be certain and must be proved, their Lordships held that although evidence of loss was "minimal" and material to enable it to be quantified was lacking, as there had been substantial loss the court could settle upon a figure as best it could on the available evidence.

The professionals

In the recent past, the construction industry has undertaken both very large projects, of which the Channel Tunnel is the obvious local example, and very complex projects in which the traditional relationships between employers, professionals and contractors has been modified to permit "professional teams", "consortiums" and, ever more frequently, "design and build" or "turnkey" projects. Such projects often involve both contruction and engineering skills. Different sorts of contracts are required for these projects and different parties may be found to be responsible for the cost of delay. One of the most evident recent changes in contract practice results from the appearance of two relatively new types of developer: the pension fund, seeking to invest in commercial development for subsequent leasing and the "tax scheme" developer, looking for a scheme which can be funded, and sometimes completed, within a timescale closely connected with 5 April in any particular year. In schemes prompted by these developers one often finds more stringent provisions related to delay and an almost equal exposure of the professional team which may be employed as a group for a fixed price. It is not necessarily surprising that against this background the cost of insurance premiums paid by architcts, engineers and even surveyors have risen sharply.

If a firm of architects takes on too much work or if a local authority's engineer's office is overwhelmed by a large project, the professional may

11 [1982] 1 WLR 149.
12 [1979] AC 91.

become the cause of sustantial delay which will then be exploited by even the most diligent contractor. In the case of the employed engineer, his employer is powerless to recover the expense incurred in additional contractor's costs and overheads: the matter must be left to sensible planning of resources. Claims against independent architects or engineers will depend upon whether there has been a breach of the obligations under their contracts. These may be either the rather generalized obligations pursuant to the RIBA conditions of engagement, or, ever more frequently, the more extensive obligations under the "professional team" contract between the developer and the team consisting of architect, engineer and surveyor. If the team can insure against causing delay they may be fortunate, if not they expose themselves to liabilities geared to the cost of the works rather than their own fees. Such difficulties reflect a thread of observations running through this paper to the effect that risk and price go together. The professional team can expect very substantial fees for their efforts and must be willing to exchange this for the risk of liability for delay. So the determination of the extent of liability can be said to be "market driven". This might be said to highlight the difference between contracts involving investors or entrepreneurs and those involving the more traditional employers such as local authorities. The former group are undertaking work in respect of which substantial profits are expected to be recovered either by sale or leasing and so they are willing to pay relatively high prices but, they fix their contractors and professionals with commensurate risk pursuant to custom-drafted contracts. The local authority will expect to employ contractors pursuant to standard forms of contract; their engineer or architect is rarely at personal risk. In the result, the initial price may be lower but subsequent claims arising out of weaker control and a standard form of contract may inflate the final price. Perhaps the difference is as much a matter of politics as anything.

Other Matters

I began this paper with a caution. I could not hope to deal with every aspect of the effect of time on construction contracts. I have to admit that there are other problems which must be faced by the parties. They include the interaction of sub-contractors and the problems of controlling the workforce if it has no new contract to go on to. Each of these issues deserves consideration.

Apparently, the expression "time is money" was coined by Benjamin Franklin in advice to a young tradesman in 1748. It remains good for tradesmen of all ages. But whilst the generalization, like all good generalizations is both concise and generally true, it is not easy to translate its meaning into the framework of construction contract law so as to discover how much money pays for how much time or from whose pocket that money should come.

UK Construction Abroad 19

John MH Bellhouse

Synopsis

This paper reviews the performance of the United Kingdom construction industry abroad, including the influence of United Kingdom forms of contract and practice. Factors which currently influence the award of major projects are considered and suggestions made for successful operation in foreign markets, including the European Community.

The Construction Industry as an Exporter

The United Kingdom construction industry has traditionally been a strong exporter, involved in major projects of Building and Civil engineering Construction in countries around the world. This has been due, in part, to historical connections arising out of ties between the United Kingdom Commonwealth countries and, in part, to the United Kingdom's reputation as a leading engineering nation.

Figures for the period 1982-86 show that overseas construction activity by United Kingdom firms tended to decrease over that period in terms of the value of contracts obtained, value of work done and value of work outstanding although provisional figures for 1987 suggest that the trend may be reversing. The following figures obtained from the Department of Employment illustrate the position.

The provisional value of new contracts obtained in 1987 was over 40 per cent greater than that achieved in 1986 although it is still less than 1982-83. The period 1982-87 has seen a continued significant decline in the Middle East with the value of new contracts there down approximately 85 per cent from 1982-83 when that region was the largest market for United Kingdom construction firms.

This decline has, however, been off-set by the welcome increase in contracts obtained in the United States, Canada and Australia, illustrating a recovery of the construction market in those regions and increased opportunities for British firms.

Overseas Construction activity by United Kingdom firms

£m (current prices)

	1982-83	1983-84	1984-85	1985-86	1986	1987 (prov.)
Value of contracts obtained						
European Community	50	37	85	108	113	213
Rest of Europe	7	19	11	28	21	96
Middle East in Asia	765	709	543	222	209	113
Middle East in Africa	24	109	255	249	149	12
Hong Kong	183	82	106	56	51	120
Rest of Asia	184	122	148	141	148	84
Rest of Africa	841	447	341	203	209	185
Americas	463	557	746	301	653	990
Oceania	263	192	221	183	190	637
All Countries	2780	2274	2456	1491	1743	2450
Value of work done						
European Community	94	65	88	79	91	83
Rest of Europe	10	14	14	23	21	32
Middle East in Asia	669	675	700	585	422	222
Middle East in Africa	62	66	48	81	92	55
Hong Kong	141	157	148	125	71	62
Rest of Asia	123	149	158	136	205	117
Rest of Africa	524	557	482	381	330	205
Americas	436	440	611	594	480	672
Oceania	255	217	237	199	237	248
All Countries	2314	2340	2486	2203	1949	1696

Overseas Construction activity by United Kingdom firms

£m (current prices)

	1982-83	1983-84	1984-85	1985-86	1986	1987 (prov.)
Value of work outstanding						
European Community	87	61	55	84	122	153
Rest of Europe	4	13	9	15	10	73
Middle East in Asia	828	854	749	380	256	131
Middle East in Africa	80	118	259	413	437	133
Hong Kong	213	136	119	53	72	121
Rest of Asia	242	214	213	245	299	162
Rest of Africa	859	723	521	345	304	239
Americas	799	944	1102	808	770	1137
Oceania	205	177	160	144	147	492
All Countries	3317	3240	3187	2487	2299	2641

The figures set out in the tables above represent the contract value for contractors alone. Overseas construction projects often also involve British professional consultants and overseas earnings of British Consulting Engineers reached £500 million in 1986 compared with a decade high of £560-75 million in 1982-83.

The decline in professional consultants' fees overseas between 1983-86 can be explained by the decline in overseas contracts as a whole. It is, however, to be hoped that in a similar way the recent improvement in the number and value of overseas contracts won by British contractors will have a knock-on effect on overseas earnings of professional consultants.

In addition, major overseas contracts will benefit United Kingdom banks and other financial institutions who may be involved in providing part or all of the finance required on competitive yet still commercially advantageous terms; benefits will accrue to the insurance markets since many of these major projects will be insured on the Lloyds market, thus bringing considerable benefits to the United Kingdom by way of "invisible earnings". In particular, overseas projects bring benefits to a wide range of sub-contractors. Figures indicate that approximately 75 per cent of the United Kingdom content of a major turnkey contract will go to sub-contractors, many of them small or medium sized firms. This work is often vital to maintaining manufacturing capability which the United Kingdom market alone cannot sustain.

Influence of United Kingdom practices and forms

Just as contractors, architects and engineers from the United Kingdom going to work abroad took with them the technical skills and practices learnt in the United Kingdom, so too they exported the forms of contract with which they were familiar.

The standard forms of contract used in United Kingdom building and civil engineering projects today have developed from contracts first drafted by lawyers in the late 19th century. As these forms developed, they were widely exported to Commonwealth countries and adopted there in the context of both public and private contracts. In consequence, it is fair to say that until the 1940's the standard forms commonly used in Australia, Canada, New Zealand and South and East Africa closely followed their United Kingdom counterparts. In more recent years, the standard forms in some Commonwealth countries have begun to diverge markedly from their United Kingdom origins but even today the standard private forms of contract in use in places such as Hong Kong, Malaysia and Kenya follow extremely closely the 1963 RIBA Forms. In Hong Kong in the late 1970's and early 1980's the government standard form for civil engineering projects, although based upon the ICE Standard Form, incorporated certain clauses (*e.g.* for loss and expense) from the 1963 RIBA Form. There has been a very substantial amount of litigation in Hong Kong in relation to the ambiguities of this particular form of contract.

Even in those countries where the standard forms have started to develop on their own in recent years, much of the structure and many of the concepts first developed in the United Kingdom standard forms, such as the role and position of the Architect/Engineer, the use of Bills of Quantities and the system of nominating sub-contractors, remain.

In addition, the ICE Standard Form of Civil Engineering Contract has had a profound influence on the form of contract for works of civil engineering construction published by the Fédération Internationale des Ingénieurs Conseils (the Red Book). The first edition of the Red Book was modelled particularly closely on the Fourth Edition of the ICE Conditions and even the recent Fourth Edition of the Red Book quickly betrays its ICE origins.

The standard forms in use in Commonwealth countries which have been modelled on their United Kingdom predecessors tend inevitably to be used in common law countries whose jurisprudence has also been inherited from the United Kingdom. The incorporation of provisions and concepts such as the role of the engineer and use of Bills of Quantities, taken from the United Kingdom standard forms in general and the ICE Form in particular into the Red Book, which tends also to be widely used in countries which have a civil law system, have helped to extend those concepts of United Kingdom engineering practice and even concepts of English law (such as the doctrine of frustration) beyond the boundaries of common law jurisdiction.

These practices and concepts which were originally designed to be used in the United Kingdom market, have not always been readily understood in some parts of the world. For example, many Middle Eastern employers have great difficulty in understanding how their faithful Engineer, who has given advice since the conceptual stages of a project, can also fulfil a separate role as an independent certifier and assessor of claims such as those for additional payment and extensions of time, sometimes against the employer's interest. Similarly, the use of and application of priced Bills of Quantities is not always understood by engineers unfamiliar with professional quantity surveying, which is a peculiarly English activity.

The domestic influence of United Kingdom practices and forms of contract is declining and will continue to decline, but at the same time the opportunities for United Kingdom contractors, particularly in the developed countries in Europe, have never been greater.

Traditional ties between the United Kingdom and countries abroad where even a few years ago United Kingdom firms could confidently expect to head lists of potential tenders have rapidly been eroded, and British firms are now having to bid for projects in a shrinking market against better and more intense competition. Many developing countries face problems from recession and mounting debt, with the result that where a project does proceed aid packages on a government to government basis and/or imaginative and attractive financing proposals from the Contractor are often the keys to ensuring competitiveness and ultimately securing the contract. Competition is particularly strong from contractors in countries such as Japan, which has a substantial aid budget anticipated to double in the period 1985-90, and contractors from countries such as South Korea and Brazil which are able to offer extremely competitive bids because of lower costs of their labour and manufacturing processes.

In its workings abroad, the United Kingdom construction industry not only has the opportunity to export its skills and services, but also comes across new situations, new practices, new ideas, new forms of Contract and new solutions to problems both technical and contractual. In recent years, the industry at home and abroad has seen the growth of management contracting, construction management, the use of turnkey contracts and a trend towards a "build-own-operate-transfer" approach to project financing. In the immediate future, the industry will be faced with prospect of the opening up, through the removal of the final barriers to free trade, of the European Community construction market worth some £225 billion, or one quarter of the entire world construction market, and seven times bigger than the UK market itself.

To meet these challenges, the industry abroad will inevitably have to adapt. United Kingdom construction firms may find it desirable subject to any constraints to EC competition law, to collaborate much more in securing major projects as many of their competitors from EC countries such as Italy, France and Germany already do. For example, I represent an Italian contractor which is a permanent joint venture of three Italian contractors, the objective of which is to build dams around the world. Marketing efforts may need to be reviewed and increased. Government support, particularly in the area of concessionary finance to enable United Kingdom construction firms to compete successfully in the international arena is essential, and may require to be increased, as finance is often the key factor in determining whether or not a project is to be secured.

In addition, the contractual approach to projects abroad may require to be reviewed and, where necessary, the industry must be prepared to depart from traditional forms and approaches. In particular, European developers are much more familiar with he "design and build" and "turnkey" approach than with the traditional British arrangement of an independent architect or engineer.

The influence of the construction industry abroad on the domestic market

Experience gained abroad where these factors will be of particular relevance will almost inevitably flow into the United Kingdom and it would be naive to expect that the United Kingdom market will remain immune from their influence or to take the view that United Kingdom practices and forms of contract are necessarily sacrosanct. If the United Kingdom industry is to remain competitive abroad, and in view of the impact of 1992 competition even at home, the industry must be prepared to take note of events abroad and to adapt to take account of them when necessary.

The two most obvious effects of the construction industry overseas on the United Kingdom domestic market are the emergence of Japanese contractors and the effect of the EC and in particular 1992 when, in theory, the EC will become one market.

Until relatively recently, Japanese contractors had a very attractive booming home market which was effectively closed to overseas contractors. Since the War there have been only one or two examples of foreign contractors working in Japan. In the last few years, the Japanese contractors have pursued overseas projects with great energy, not only in the Third World but also in developed countries like the United States and the United Kingdom.

The reasons for this were the downturn in the Japanese market; the Japanese trading houses setting up factories overseas and the fear of trade barriers being put up by the West.

In the Third World, Japanese contractors have pursued infrastructure projects but in the United Kingdom (and the United States) they have energetically pursued property development, usually as developers and often in joint venture with domestic developers. They have rarely acted as contractors and then only in name, with the work being fully sub-let. Assuming that Japanese contractors do not withdraw from the United Kingdom for better opportunities at home or elsewhere it is only a matter of time before they enter the contracting field proper, whether in joint venture with English contractors or by taking over English contractors. Japanese contractors are far bigger than English contractors and have the financial assets to take over even the biggest English contractors. We may then see the Japanese approach to contracting have an influence on the domestic market.

Their approach is to take a longer term view to contractors, emphasizing turnover (rather than short term profit); a position in the market place and long term relationships with, in particular, sub-contractors. It is not true that Japanese contractors do not make claims, although they are more likely to negotiate a settlement of them than their English counterparts.

As to the effect of the EC market, European contractors, in particular the Germans, are already positioning themselves and are considering attempting to take over English contractors, as a means of access into the United Kingdom market. However, the most immediate effect, which United Kingdom contractors should be acting on now, is that the domestic market will become (if it is not already) Europe, and not just the United Kingdom. Spain and Greece of the EC countries offer greatest opportunities.

In addition, the United Kingdom contractors will need to become more flexible and more willing to take on turnkey projects as the German, Italian and French contractors do. United Kingdom contractors will need to become more used to accepting contracts on this basis and in particular not using English type contracts with an independent Engineer.

I have represented Italian, French and German contractors in contract negotiations and in disputes. They are inherently more willing to take on the technical roles in difficult projects including the design than United Kingdom contractors. This is partly because they are often larger but also because of a different approach to contracting where they expect to be responsible for those risks.

I think, therefore, that European contracting practices will increasingly affect the domestic market which will, of course, be Europe. One possible consequence is that the English form of contract will be modified (and the role of the independent architect/engineer will be reduced) and United Kingdom contractors will be obliged to accept a greater degree of responsibility, at least in engineering projects, rather than less, as they are now doing under management contracting and construction management forms of contract in the building field.

Finally, United Kingdom contracts will have a real opportunity to expand the home market in Europe, which is likely to require United Kingdom contractors to work in joint ventures with European contractors and may result in pan-European takeovers or mergers.

20 Control of Programme and Payment Discussion and Debate

Plenary Session

Introducing Paper 15, Sir Patrick Garland said that the effect of English law was that if fixed time provisions are to be accepted, there must be suitable contractual machinery for the extension of time to cover conduct of the employer which delays or prevents the contractor carrying out his obligations in accordance with those time provisions. The extension of time clause must cover acts, omissions or defaults of the employer which impede the contractor in his work. If an extension of time could not be granted, time must become at large, that is, the work must be done within a reasonable time. A reasonable time would be the stipulated time plus a reasonable extension on account of the delay imposed.

If it were desired to exercise more control over time, it was possible in theory to limit extension of time clauses to prevention by the employer, leaving all other risks on the contractor. However, the recovery of damages for delay would still be dependent on the proper operation of the extension of time clause. There were a number of alternative approaches that might be considered. First, the contract could provide simply that the contractor was to make due and diligent progresss. Secondly, by providing bonuses instead of damages, an effective incentive could be created using a sliding scale. As a sanction against delay, periodic payments could be tied to stages of the work, rather than to valuation. Consideration might also be given to whether programmes should be made contractually binding. It had to be remembered that a programme embodied mutual obligations so that the employer himself would have to conform to the programme.

Professor Duncan Wallace, introducing Paper 16, said that in his view standard forms of construction contract were out of control in that they provided no reasonable protection to building owners. There appeared little pressure for reform even from massive users in the building and civil engineering industry, including government and public authorities. As an example, no standard form, with the exception GC/Wks/1 contains the simple provision that no additional payment would be due to the contractor for variations rendered necessary by default on his part.

The argument that contractors would refrain from abusing their position in the interests of goodwill was unconvincing and certainly not borne out by cases in the courts. Such considerations would not affect a trustee or liquidator of a contractor. Goodwill might be an incentive with large property development companies, but this is not the case with public authorities, who apparently do not consider themselves entitled to remove contractors from tendering lists on the grounds of pursuing unmeritorious claims. Moreover, many clients, including substantial public and commercial owners, are concerned with one project only, so that long term goodwill is not a relevant factor.

The current level of bias in favour of contractors does not arise from the original drafting of the forms, which in most cases was undertaken many years ago by lawyers with insufficient experience in the building industry, but rather from a consistent and steady process of alteration and amendment in subsequent editions. Unsatisfactory provisions are frequently excused on the grounds of difficulty in securing agreement to change; it is notable that forms can and do undergo change with remarkable speed to the benefit of contractors in the face of unexpected court decisions or other external developments.

When invited to draft the form of building contract for private sector work in Singapore, Professor Duncan Wallace had adopted the policy of seeking to prevent owners from cheating contractors and contractors from cheating owners. The conference paper contains practical suggestions for achieving these ends. The appropriate test to be applied to any form of contract should be: "Could I recommend this form to my client?" In the case of the ICE Conditions of Contract there were four provisions which could not be recommended to owners which amounted to open invitations to make a claim, namely, Clauses 55(2), 56(2), 13(3) and 14(3)-6. In particular, Clause 13(3) appeared to provide the contractor with an open-ended entitlement to claim where more specifically defined claims elsewhere in the contract could not be established. Its precise purpose was quite unclear. Clause 12 of the ICE Conditions was also to be criticized as the wrong way of seeking to achieve its objective.

As regards other areas of contract policy reform, owners should be made aware of the danger of heavy over-insurance. The object of such insurance is to prevent a contractor becoming insolvent in the event of a heavy claim being made by the owner or a third party. Heavy over-insurance could lead to cutting of corners by contractors and sub-contractors with the insurer footing the bill if things go wrong.

Consideration should also be given to arbitration clauses. It is difficult to justify the inclusion of a clause referring all disputes to arbitration at a time when it is impossible to know the nature of the dispute that will arise, and therefore the best means of resolving it. Disputes might be factual, technical or purely legal. The omission of an arbitration clause will not prevent the parties subsequently agreeing upon arbitration if that seems in the particular circumstances a satisfactory way of resolving the dispute.

In the discussion that followed, one speaker expressed the view that Clauses 55(2) and 56(2) of the ICE Conditions were extensions of measurement provisions which it was reasonable for owners to accept. Another speaker considered that it was also reasonable for owners to accept responsibility for the default of nominated sub-contractors, since they had been selected by the owners. Professor Duncan Wallace disagreed with these views and referred to his paper for the detailed arguments in reply.

Working party on Management of Finance

Introducing Paper 17, Mr. Bishop suggested a number of areas which might be considered as means of utilising finance as a management tool.

- Bills of Quantities: should they be contractual or only an extra-contractual guide?
- Stage payments: can they be used to regulate performance?
- Disclosure of information: how far is this desirable?
- Errors in Bills of Quantities: should the contractor warrant that none had been found?
- Reports on cost out-turn: what value are these?
- Pricing of variations: can better procedures be found?
- Loss and expense: should this be claimable on top of the variations?
- Permitted variations: should the architect be allowed to sanction departures from the contract?
- Express set-off provisions: are they desirable as a means of control?
- Payment of interest: should the employer be liable automatically?
- Notice of a claim: should it be a condition precedent?

The working party came to a number of conclusions on these questions. As regards Bills of Quantities, if they were not to be given full contractual effect (so that the contractor would be entitled to re-measurement) the question arose who should take the risk of errors in the Bills. Where a mistake occurred in drawing up the document, it was arguable that the employer should take responsibility, effectively by warranting that the Bills had been prepared with due care. Disclosure of the contractor's rates breakdown was also considered desirable.But confidentiality had to be assured, in order to prevent possible commercial damage to the contractor. As regards the pricing of Bills, it was considered that the contractor ought to be allowed to quote prices as he chose and that, for example, front loading to compensate for difficult ground conditions, should be acceptable. As regards the detection of errors in the Bill, the value of any warranty given by the contractor was questionable.

As regards stage payments, being linked to stages of the work rather than valuation, these offered the oppotunity of artificial loading in order to provide an incentive to the contractor to progress the work. It was considered, however, that this would have only a limited effect in controlling performance, and difficulties might arise through the need to reschedule the works for legitimate reasons. The contractor might also seek to reschedule the work purely to qualify for particular stage payments, and this was obviously undesirable. It was therefore considered that stage payments posed a number of difficulties in their implementation.

Periodic reports by the contractor and the quantity surveyor on the likely cost of the project were desirable, but raised questions as to their contractual status. Further, if an unacceptable cost overrun was projected, consideration would have to be given to the steps which the employer would be entitled to take. As regards the pricing of variations, the traditional contract machinery could be supplemented in a variety of ways. The contract could provide for the contractor to offer in advance fixed prices for standard variations. Where changes were to be valued during the course of the contract, there should be an option for the contractor to quote a fixed price as an alternative. Whatever method of valuation was used, the contract should make clear whether this was to be all-inclusive, or whether the contractor was to be permitted to claim additional loss or expense, for example, arising out of the number or timing of variations. It was considered desirable for the architect to have a permissive power to sanction, either prospectively or retrospectively, a departure from the contract at no additional cost to the employer.

It was considered that contracts ought to provide expressly what could be set off against certificates. Where the certifier omitted any work from a valuation, the contract should expressly require a statement as to what had been omitted. In regard to late payment or certification, the contract should provide expressly for the payment of interest at a commercial rate, to be payable whether the delay was deliberate or resulted from a bona fide dispute.

It was considered that notice provisions should be drafted so as to keep the employer informed about claims and to require the contractor to provide timeous information rather than to shut out genuine claims.

Working Party on Management of Time

Mr. Naughton, introducing Paper 18, said that there was now greater use made of programmes as a management tool, particularly in larger projects. The question arose whether the more sophisticated methods of programme analysis could be utilized to identify more precisely levels of progress in different parts of the works and to establish how individual delays actually affected the critical path of the works overall. Mr. Naughton observed that in the absence of mutual obligations to perform the contract by reference to programmes, the parties may tend to move apart, each making their separate case. This applied both during the period of the contract and subsequently if claims were pursued. In the result, the parties would only begin to investigate each other's positions shortly before the hearing of an arbitration, and therefore the potential benefit of preparing and updating programmes might be lost. Information about progresss and its effect on the programme needed to be agreed, recorded and utilized during the course of the works.

The question was raised to what extent should a programme be formally incorporated into the contract. It was pointed out that while adherence to a contractual programme might benefit the employer in terms of its requirements as to progress, it could also operate to his detriment where the employer became unable to fulfil his obligations, for example, as regards the provision of detailed drawings. The better view was to regard the programme as a key element in planning the work which was of equal value to the contractor and to the employer. Simple bar charts were no longer enough for planning purposes. For medium and large contracts, a critical path analysis was required. It was generally agreed that contractors should be required to submit regular reports on progress in relation to the programme. This could be done in conjunction with the submission of monthly valuations.

A further important aspect of planning was the pre-contract stage, where the work of the professional teams and of the potential contractors and suppliers needed to be integrated and co-ordinated. It was questionable whether a programme providing for such integration should be given contractual effect. This might be appropriate in project management contracts. It was said that this approach had been adopted in a number of contracts in the City of

London, but it required input from the employer himself and from those negotiating with proposed trade contractors. In "fast track" contracts generally, much greater emphasis had to be placed on the role of the management contractor or project manager. It was frequently the case that those undertaking such operations limited their duty to using "best endeavours" rather than accepting fixed or defined obligations. The meeting noted that "fast track" contracts tended to be negotiated rather than put out to tender in the traditional way. It was thought this was likely to become the norm for large and complex projects.

There was a discussion on the possibility of alternatives to liquidated damages. It was felt that the use of higher retention percentages should not be encouraged because this would expose the contractor to adverse cashflow problems. There was support for the use of bonuses based on the benefit that the employer would get from having the contract completed early. Bonus provisions needed to be carefully drafted having regard to other contract provisions covering delay and extensions of time. It was pointed out that contracts rarely provided for the employer to be entitled to "buy back" time by requiring acceleration, where an extension of time has been granted. It was agreed that such a provision could be of benefit to both parties and could usefully be developed further.

A number of proposals have been made for incorporating "reverse liquidated damages" into contracts, the effect of which would be to fix the payment allowable to the contractor in the event of delay caused by the employer. The view was expressed that it was impracticable to pre-estimate a sum of money relating to the additional expense which a contractor might incur. Delay at the start of a contract could have a minimal effect on cost, whereas at a later stage the effect could be much greater. The introduction of such a provision would, therefore, tend to increase prices substantially. It was possible that head office overheads could be pre-estimated on a uniform time-basis, but site overheads could not be dealt with in this way. The chairman commented that there was a further difficulty in that an arbitrary pre-estimate of reverse damages might be construed as a penalty.

The conclusions of the meeting were that:

- With regard to programming, there was a strong feeling that contractors and employers should make particular efforts to co-operate so that programming could be used as an effective instrument for monitoring progress and for establishing the best evidence of the effect of delaying events.
- There was some support for programmed pre-contract planning by the employer and his professional team leading up to the tender stage.
- While there was no easy alternative to liquidated damages, there was support for the view that standard forms should make provision for the ordering of acceleration to allow the employer to buy back lost time if he wished. Such a provision could be simply incorporated and the cost calculated from information supplied.
- There was little support for the introduction of reverse liquidated damages to cover delay by the employer. It should be possible, however, to pre-estimate certain losses including head office overheads and some preliminary items.

Working Party on UK construction abroad

Mr. Bellhouse, introducing Paper 19, said that, with the possible exception of work in the United States, the value of overseas construction work undertaken by United Kingdom contractors was decreasing. The principle cause of this, apart from the world economic recession, was an increasing lack of competitiveness displayed by United Kingdom contractors together with more attractive profit margins within the United Kingdom itself.

There were two factors which led to the lack of competitiveness. First, United Kingdom contracting companies were much smaller than their overseas competitors, especially those from Japan. This meant that United Kingdom companies either could not take on large or complex projects because of lack of resources or, if such projects were taken on, reliance had to be placed on employment of local personnel. Secondly, some United Kingdom contractors had acquired an international reputation for relying on claims to generate profit in contrast to contractors from other countries who were prepared to accept more straightforward forms of contract and to rely on technical solutions to difficulties which arose.

The first factor was generally accepted by the meeting but there was some dissent as to the second, the view being expressed that United Kingdom contractors relied on claims when operating under the terms of United Kingdom-style forms of contract, but found no difficulty in adapting themselves overseas to stricter contracts where claims were not permitted. Insofar as the principal problem was one of size, it was accepted that United Kingdom contractors had to consider joint venture agreements in order to obtain access to foreign markets.

The question arose how United Kingdom contractors wishing to enter the international field should respond to foreign standard forms of contract. Should they merely tender on the terms offered; should they seek modification of the terms of particular contracts presented; or should they make representations in advance to bodies responsible for the preparation of foreign standard forms in order to influence conditions under which future work will be carried out. It was considered that in most of the world it was appropriate to seek modification of the terms of a particular contract; but for work within the EC, it was particularly appropriate to seek to influence conditions to be used in the future. United Kingdom contractors would soon be under pressure to compete in EC markets (and this would include work in the United Kingdom itself). It was a matter for individual companies to what extent they wished to compete in the rest of the world.

In conclusion, the meeting was of the opinion that, as regards work within the EC, United Kingdom contractors were unlikely to succeed in obtaining unification of construction contracts based on United Kingdom-style forms. These forms were unlikely to prove acceptable to other EC countries, and practices were so deeply entrenched and varying throughout the EC that it was thought unlikely that any single solution would prove acceptable to all member states. There would, however, be merit in United Kingdom representatives being involved in any developments pursued on behalf of the European Commission.

The meeting considered that United Kingdom contractors were quite capable of working under foreign forms of contract, which were not regarded as a barrier to United Kingdom contractors entering foreign markets. It was considered that United Kingdom contractors ought in general to accept terms offered unless they were grossly unsatisfactory. There was no case for seeking to change terms merely because they were unfamiliar. The drop in United Kingdom contracting work abroad was principally the result of economic considerations. United Kingdom contractors were likely to prefer work within the United Kingdom, where the standard forms utilised offered the possibility of greater profit margins and lower risks. The forms of contract offered could not be regarded as a primary reason for a lower level of activity by United Kingdom contractors in foreign markets.

Part V

Developments outside the Terms of Contract

Management of Liability 21

Professor Phillip Capper

Synopsis

This paper as delivered at the Conference seeks to give a detailed and broad ranging insight into the additional liabilities that may attach beyond the expressed terms of the construction contract and into the policies that underlie the imposition of such liabilities, with a particular emphasis on how they may be managed.

A radically new approach has now to be taken to the issue of negligence liability as it affects the construction industry. The House of Lords has introduced a new, and complex, legal framework as a result of the appeal in the case of *D & F Estates* v. *Church Commissioners* in July 1988. Defects liability claims have to be re-thought. Contractors may have gained substantial relief from potential liabilities, but professional advisers, architects and engineers seem now to be even more in the firing line.

There is now explicit recognition that *Anns* v. *Merton LBC* introduced in relation to the construction of buildings an entirely new type of product liability, if not, indeed, an entirely novel concept of the tort of negligence. The English courts seem to have gone even further than the American courts. But, what is not clear is the extent of the liability under this new principle. And the Lords in *D & F* have added new criteria for defeating defects claims, but without giving a definitive ruling on what remains from *Anns*.

The policy questions

It will be seen that at root the courts have, over two decades, created a problem of social policy still requiring resolution. What are the proper limits for imposing obligations in the law of tort? How should these relate to the parties' autonomy in agreeing their own contractual responsibilities? Much of this century has seen a drift in the law away from *caveat emptor* (let the buyer beware) to a desire to lay responsibility on those regarded as *at fault*. But in relation to goods that was mainly achieved by legislative policy. Yet the abandoning of *caveat emptor* in relation to buildings and land has been by judicial intervention. Legislation should be the appropriate, and proper, vehicle for policy change: it is informed by consultation, it can distinguish policies for consumers from those for business. The present law on professional liability in the construction industry is the product of haphazard, accidental occurrences of litigation. Indeed many of these changes in the law were retrospective in effect: an intolerable constitutional anomaly. Parties proceeded, *e.g.* in repairing buildings, on what the law of negligence appeared to be, only to find years later when in an appellate court that the judges had decided to change the policy again.

What are the proper boundaries between contract and tort? What is the law of tort for? In *London Congregational Union* v. *Harriss*[1] Ralph Gibson LJ said that the ordinary relationship of client and architect, as in this case, or of client and consulting engineer, as in *Pirelli*, was not in his view such that liability for pure economic loss would arise in tort on proof of negligent design or supervision but without proof of damage to property. The concept of negligence was not intended to afford owners of buildings rights equivalent to contract rights. Justice did not require a defendant to pay damages in tort for a defect in design which, in Lord Fraser's words "may never lead to any damage at all to the building" (*Pirelli*[2]). But this paper has to ask: What policy determines what are "contract rights", rather than tort rights?

The retrenchment in negligence liability

The mood of retrenchment in respect of tort liability is manifest in a series of decisions in the House of Lords, Privy Council and Court of Appeal. The decline of influence of both *Junior Books* and *Anns* v. *Merton*[3], even before *D& F* was clearly to be seen in *Curran* v. *Northern Ireland Co-Ownership Housing Association*[4] and *Yuen Kun Yeu* v. *Attorney General of Hong Kong*[5]. The swinging of the judicial pendulum is well illustrated by *DoE* v. *Thomas Bates & Sons Ltd*[6]. Doubts arising from wide interpretation of dicta in *Anns* v. *Merton* and in *Junior Books* were treated as resolved by the Privy Council in *Candlewood Corporation* v. *Mitsui (The Mineral Transporter)*[7] and the House of Lords in *Leigh & Sillavan* v. *Aliakmon Shipping*[8]. In *DoE* v. *Bates* it was pleaded that the contractor owed an obligation in tort so to construct a building that it would be reasonably fit for its intended purpose. Policy considerations showed that was too wide. Rather, the duty in tort to use reasonable care and skill in the construction of the building so that it would not, within a reasonable time, give rise to imminent danger to the health or safety of those on the premises, nor cause physical damage to those premises. The duty was mutatis mutandis owed by an architect. But there still remain difficulties about the precise scope of the criterion requiring damage to property: see *Aswan Engineering Establishment Co* v. *Lupdine Ltd*[9], below. There had also been a proliferation of potential defendants by finding one liable in negligence for others' fault: eg by failing to warn the client. Some reversal of this trend is

1 [1988] 1 All ER 15.
2 [1983] 1 All ER 65 at 70E.
3 [1978] AC 728.
4 (1987) CILL 338.
5 (1987) CILL 350.
6 (1987) CILL 308.
7 [1986] AC 1 (CILL 204).
8 [1986] AC 785 (CILL 265).
9 [1986] 2 Lloyd's Rep 347.

shown by three judgments of the Court of Appeal in early 1987. It allowed appeals by the main contractors in *D& F Estates* v. *Church Commissioners*[10] and by the professional advisers in *Mathew* v. *Maughold Life Assurance Co*[11] and has taken a restrictive view of a valuer's duty of care (*Sutcliffe* v. *Sayer*[12]). However, by contrast, perhaps because of the personal injuries element, a rather strong view was adopted towards duties to warn by the judge at first instance in the *Abbeystead* case (*Eckersley* v. *Binnie & Partners, and others*[13]) and the Court of Appeal did not entirely remove the spectre of duties of warn even after project completion; nor was the engineers' appeal allowed by the majority there (1988 CILL 388). A renewed emphasis is being placed upon the closeness and directness of the relationship ("proximity") between the defendant and the claimant, and upon the alternative opportunities for the claimant to have avoided the loss. Although the *Peabody* v. *Sir Lindsay Parkinson*[14] case left open some latitude by declaring that the existence of a duty in any particular case depended on what was just and reasonable, its result must now be viewed restrictively not only because of the narrower terms of the subsequent appellate decisions, but also it establishes firmly the restrictive view that the extent of a duty can be limited by the narrow nature of the purpose for which the defendant was involved in the particular project (the public role of protecting occupiers' health and safety). Furthermore, following *Smith* v. *Littlewoods Organisation*[15] and *Hill* v. *Chief Constable of West Yorkshire*[16], the courts are much less likely to regard any person or organization as owing a duty to be responsible for the acts of others where those others are not under the organization's control.

Issues unresolved after D & F

However, the *D& F* decision in the House of Lords arguably raises as many questions as it solves. What is the scope of the vital new limiting criterion based on the notion of "complex structure"? Why do claims for repairs and making good now have to be assessed in a new way? Their Lordships' speeches are not free of inconsistencies. Important potential loopholes can be identified. Lawyers are already coining the phrase "the garden wall" principle. Some are speculating that the Building Regulations and breach of statutory duty could be an avenue to avoid the strictures of *D& F*.

The crucial distinction to be drawn is between "dangerous defects" and "defects of quality". Indeed it may be misleading to think in terms of "defects" at all. The "essential ingredient" is taken from the new orthodoxy of Lord Brandon's dissent in *Junior Books* v. *Veitchi*[17]: there must be danger of physical damage to persons or their property, but excluding damage to the very piece of property the defective condition of which gives rise to the danger. The major policy questions thus posed are:

10 *Cf.* (1986) CILL 230.
11 *Cf.* (1985) CILL 152.
12 [1987] 1 EGLR 155.
13 (1987) CILL 332.
14 [1985] AC 210.
15 [1987] 2 WLR 480.
16 [1988] 2 All 238.
17 [1983] AC 520.

(i)Why is there normally no tort action in English law for defective manufacture of an article which causes no injury other than injury to the defective article itself?
(ii) What developments should flow from the Lords' suggestion of a special rule for buildings?

But there are many unresolved issues which in the absence of legislation will generate more litigation: Why are different rules said to apply in the Lords' new category of "complex structures"? What is a complex structure? Why did the Lords treat walls as independent of foundations, but decorative wallpaper as not a different item of property from the plaster to which it was applied? What technical criteria can be formulated to apply this new determinant of defects liability? What is a "simple product"? Can movable products also be "complex structures"? What if the damage has yet to occur? Is the cost of averting danger recoverable? Does discovery of a defect before it causes injury to person or other property prevent recovery of the costs of making good the defect? Why is the cost of replacing, or making good, defective work now normally irrecoverable?

There also remain questions as to the interaction of the *D & F* decision with previous case-law: what are the remaining effects of *Anns* v. *Merton LBC*[18]? Will *Junior Books* v. *Veitchi*[19] and *Batty* v. *Metropolitan Realisations*[20] flourish as cases of 'reliance' on special expertise? Are architects, engineers and other consultants liable in tort for mere defects despite *London Congregational* v. *Harriss*[21]?

Then there is the relationship with statutory provisions: does the *D & F* approach to product liability (with notions of "complex structure" and "averting danger") require even the product liability provisions of the Consumer Protection Act 1987 to be re-thought? What is the impact on limitation periods: why will the *D & F* approach will start time running from new points for statute-barring claims.

The special context of the industry

There are a number of causative factors behind the newly litigious nature of the United Kingdom Construction Industry. Traditional building procurement involves a disparate team, with employer design and supervision, nominated sub-contracting, and third party monitoring of building control and quality. This is a fertile seed-bed for legal claims, both during construction and after, because multiple lines of involvement obscure the location of responsibility, and provide a wider choice of solvent 'suable' defendants. During construction there will be claims for loss and expense arising from delay to the progress of the contract works or disruption of productivity. Contractor margins are tight. Profitability may depend on successful pursuit of claims for loss and expense during construction. The rate of contractor failure by insolvency is high. Therefore, when after construction defects appear, the party primarily responsible for them may frequently be unavailable or not

18 [1978] AC 728.
19 [1983] AC 520.
20 [1978] QB 554.
21 [1988] 1 All ER 15.

worth proceeding against. Buildings are high-value, long-life, multi-owner products. Design expectations often now involve leading edge technology, which can be unrealistic in relation to traditional construction methods. Contractors' quality management systems become crucial. Defects are expensive to repair. Encouraged by courts more willing to award compensation, building owners are more likely to try to recover those repair costs and associated consequential losses of rent and profit, by seeking to shift the responsibility on to those involved in the design and construction process. The fact that there is both multi-party involvement in design and construction and successive multiple ownership of buildings has meant that few of these parties are in a contractual relationship with each other. Thus in the recent judicial climate of indulging extension of negligence liabilities, the construction industry has seen a remarkable growth in tort-based liabilities to third parties. This has added buoyancy to negligence claims even in the traditional two-party professional engagement, and raised the level of claims consciousness. Against this background, any insured or financially secure professional organisation becomes an attractive target for claims, and a very suable defendant.

The expansive period

The main explanation for this development was that the context in which the courts abandoned *caveat emptor* in relation to buildings itself involved an eminently suitable target for proceeding to litigation: local building control authorities did not disappear or become insolvent. In the mid-80s the courts began to adopt a new policy of caution, tending to restrict negligence liability and overrule some of the extensions of the previous decade. Hence, local authorities' liability in respect of building control functions has now been limited to present or imminent threats to health or safety of the occupier (and even then not an owner-builder). Indeed there are special public policy reasons for limiting the liability exposure of a control authority. Building control compliance is statutory and mandatory (and was until recently exclusively a public sector function). Professional liability has a different nature. The consulting professional volunteers to sell his own service, inducing reliance thereon, and so more likely attracts liability. The resulting problem is that as other categories of defendant (not just public authorities, but also contractors) have benefitted from the judicial reversal of its expansive trend and from its new caution, there is little evidence of any such reversal in the judicial development of professional negligence liability.

Should construction be governed by 'product liability'?

When a building is taken over by a first or subsequent occupier, what is being taken over?

- a piece of land with some fixtures on it?

or

- a product, that happens to have been put in a particular place?

If a sale of land, then should the legal principle be *caveat emptor* (let the buyer beware)? If so, consumer law would have little relevance: building occupiers should look after their own interests, with appropriate professional advice (from lawyers, surveyors, valuers etc).

If, however, the building is to be viewed as a product then the principles of law are rather different. Consumer law comes to the fore. It becomes important to determine whether the product is suitable for the particular location. There arise issues about product liability and negligence liability to third parties. Indeed negligence law is very much concerned with the deciding whether something is the appropriate, or reasonable, thing to do in particular circumstances. But consumers of products also typically expect that the product will be reasonably fit for its purpose and they will have expectations as to its quality. These raise a very different spectre of liability when compared with the relatively liability-free transactions based on caveat emptor.

Liabilities: an overview, by reference to the duties owed

The liabilities likely to arise from construction contract performance can best be approached by identifying the duties which the law requires to be observed. As an overview, those duties may be summarised as follows:

- Duties to achieve results.
- Duties to avoid particular harm.
- Duties to refrain from proscribed conduct.

This classification of duties is a functional one. It recognises the purposes for which different parts of the law impose obligations on people. This functional analysis also helps to elucidate the reason why the particular forms of liability arise from different legal conceptual classifications; principally contractual liability, and tortious liability for negligence. The analysis also helps to indicate that the remedy available to a claimant will depend very much upon the nature of the duty which is alleged to have been broken and also upon the conceptual source of that duty.

How do lawyers classify the sources of those duties?

Lawyers familiar with the details of these areas of liability will recognise that the duties set out above in functional terms are perhaps better regarded as points upon a spectrum than discrete, exclusive categorisations. Lawyers would categorise the sources of those duties in the following terms:

- Contractual obligations.
- Product liability.
- Tortious liability for negligently caused harm.
- Misrepresentations inducing contracts.
- Fraud.
- Infringement of the criminal law.

- Infringement of intellectual property rights.

Broadly, the spectrum of our functional duties set out above overlays upon this sequence of sources of those duties. We shall see that duties to achieve results arise normally only in the law of contract, though some may explain product liability as also giving rise to such duties. Duties to avoid particular harm could be said to characterize all these legal categories from contractual obligations through to infringement of intellectual property rights. Nevertheless, tortious negligence liability is more readily explicable when realised to be a duty to avoid particular harm. The difference between it and contractual liability then becomes clearer. In this respect, product liability in the English jurisdiction is a conceptual form of tortious liability and so may best be viewed as a duty to avoid particular harm rather than a duty to achieve results. The third of our forms of duty on the spectrum, duties to refrain from proscribed conduct, again could be viewed very widely: in one sense, *e.g.* there is a duty to refrain from breaking a contract. However, this end of the spectrum correlates more with infringements of intellectual property rights, and with criminal misdescriptions and other forms of legally unacceptable behaviour such as fraud and misrepresentation. These obviously shade over into duties to avoid harm, though the harm is likely to be identified in social terms as a general harm which these rules of law will thus deter (rather than a particular harm being an actionable source of loss).

Duties to achieve results: fitness for purpose.

The phrase "duties to achieve results" is intended to connote the legal obligation to achieve a certain level of performance. The person responsible has to meet a performance objective: that the product will perform as required. In the ordinary context of contractors supplying goods or services this performance objective will be in essence a quality or fitness obligation. So the performance will be measured by the extent to which the goods or services supplied achieve the characteristics required. However it should be noted that the duty of a professional person giving advice is rather different. A professional still has certain duties to achieve results. The law assumes that, in the absence of contrary indications, the result intended is that the professional should take reasonable care and skill in the giving of the advice. Hence the professional person is not normally taken by English law to warrant that the advice will lead to a successful result. The professional's performance obligation is normally limited to the requirement that reasonable care and skill be exercised in rendering the service.

The notion of a "results-orientated" duty, at least in the context of quality or fitness for purpose obligations, has traditionally in English law been the province of the law of contract. Consistently with that tradition, European product liability (which was implemented in England by the Consumer Protection Act 1987) is an extension of tort, not contract, and it arises only where an unsafe product causes personal injury or damage to other property: the liability does not arise merely because the product itself is defective in terms of quality or fitness for purpose. Indeed, quality and fitness for purpose obligations would unarguably be the exclusive province of contract law were it not for a remarkable of expansion in tortious liability for negligence in the decade or so from the mid-1970's to the mid-1980's. For a while, it appeared that the mere failure of a product to perform as well as the user reasonably expected could be redressed by a claim framed in tort. Appellate court decisions in the late 1980's however suggest a return to the traditional view that users who want rights to a certain level of quality, fitness for purpose, or freedom from defects in goods and services (which are not otherwise dangerous or damaging) must make their contract to that effect with whomsoever they wish to make responsible. The only significant qualification to this is the contractual context of professional advice: perhaps the reason is precisely that that context bears a marked similarity to the tortious context of negligence. If the professional person's contractual obligation is only to take reasonable care and skill in providing a service, and not to warrant the result, then the obligation in performance terms is hardly distinguishable from tortious liability for negligence.

Contractual obligations

Contractual obligations can of course be express or implied. Terms may be implied in contracts as a matter of usual implication at common law, or because a judge regards particular terms as necessarily implied in a particular contract. However, unlike statutory implied terms, common law or "judge-made" terms will not be implied if they would be inconsistent with the express terms of the contract. The extent of this non-statutory power to supply terms which are not expressed is set out by Lord Wilberforce in the House of Lords in *Liverpool City Council* v. *Irwin*[22]. Where there is an apparently complete contract the courts are sometimes willing to add to terms: this is very common in mercantile contracts where there is an established usage - the courts are spelling out what both parties know and would, if asked, unhesitatingly agree to be part of the bargain. In other cases, where there is an apparently complete bargain, the courts are willing to add a term on the ground that without it the contract will not work. A further category is where the court is simply concerned to establish what the contract is, the parties not having themselves fully stated the terms.

The courts do not have the power to imply terms into a contract simply because such terms would be reasonable. However, judges have shown themselves able and willing to adapt statutory implied terms (for example as to quality in sales of goods) to new factual contexts by implying analogous terms at common law. An important example of this was the decision of the House of Lords in *Young and Marten Ltd* v. *McManus Childs Ltd*[23]. But, the courts cannot also adapt by analogy the specific statutory controls on disclaimers or clauses excluding or restricting liability.

We shall see that contractual obligations in respect of quality and fitness for purpose (the duties to achieve results) are therefore relatively controllable. First, there has to be a contract between the person liable and the claimant. Second, the terms of that contract can (unless private consumers are involved)

22 [1977] AC 239.
23 [1968] 2 All ER 1169.

be whatever the parties bargaining positions reasonably permit. Awareness of the law's power to imply contractual obligations leads to appropriate drafting counter measures. However, it should be recognized that, on appropriate facts, the law may even go so far as to imply the whole contract, eg directly between a manufacturer and a third party end user, particularly with regard to collateral warranties of performance or durability of a product.

The doctrine of privity

A central pillar of English contract law is the doctrine of "privity": namely, that only the parties to a contract are entitled to the rights it creates, and only the parties to it can be burdened with the obligations it imposes. Third parties who are not privy to the contract, as contracting parties, cannot take advantage of the contractual duties. This doctrine puts a natural limit on the range of possible claimants in respect of quality and fitness for purpose obligations. Only contracting parties can claim. Therefore in contract law there is no particular policy need to restrict the kinds of losses that are recoverable as damages if a duty is broken. We shall see in the next section that tortious liability to third parties does need to be restricted in some way to prevent the courts being flooded with claims: the normal mechanism is to allow losses to be recoverable only where these relate to physical harm to person or property. We shall see that pure economic losses are not normally recoverable in tort. Contract law does not make this distinction. It allows all losses (whether physical or wholly financial) to be recoverable as damages so long as they may fairly and reasonably be considered either: (*a*) as arising naturally, according to the usual course of things, from the breach of contract; or (*b*) such as may reasonably be supposed to be in the contemplation of both parties at the time they made the contract, as the probable result of breach of it. Hence, even unusually remote, purely economic, losses can be recovered in contract if within the contemplation of the parties when they made the contract. (See *Hadley* v. *Baxendale*[24], *The Heron II*[25] and *Parsons (Livestock) Ltd* v. *Uttley Ingham & Co Ltd*[26].)

Duties to avoid particular harm: negligence liability.

The modern English law on the tort of negligence has been developed almost entirely by the judges in case law rather than by legislation. The impetus to the development was the decision of the House of Lords in *Donoghue* v. *Stevenson*[27]. Its major significance was, broadly speaking, that it allowed a short cut for the end user to claim directly against an original manufacturer (if the manufacturer was negligent). This cut out the need to channel claims through the chain of supply contracts from the end user back to the manufacturer. The third quarter of the 20th century saw the limits of this new principle being explored by litigation. Claimants found the courts increasingly

24 (1854) 9 Ex 34.
25 [1967] 3 WLR 1491.
26 [1978] QB 791.
27 [1932] AC 562.

indulgent. People in the business of design, manufacture or supply were held responsible for a wider range of risks, so long as it could be established that they had not taken reasonable care.

The dramatic expansion in negligence liability was most marked over a decade or so from the mid-1970's through the mid-1980's. This expansion had two principal characteristics. The first was to extend the range of claimants to whom a tortious duty could be said to be owed. The second was to allow claimants to recover, in a tort action, losses which were wholly financial.

These two emphases in the expansion of negligence liability are interrelated. To the extent that the courts have come to regard purely economic losses as a form of harm which ought to be remedied and deterred by imposition of duties in tort, then the range of claimants to whom such a duty is owed will also be increased. The reason for this is that physical damage is naturally limited in extent and in a sense self extinguishing (except where, *e.g.* there is a catastrophe with the release of harmful replicating organisms, or of nuclear radiation). By contrast, financial losses are conceptual only, with no necessary relationship to the physical world. Thus there are no natural limits to the extent of the financial losses that could flow from a causative negligent event, so far as tortious negligence liability to third parties is concerned. Contractual liabilities are, by contrast, naturally limited in any event to the parties to the contract (the "privity" principle). Therefore, contract law does not need to distinguish between physical and financial losses.

As the modern law of negligence has developed the principal activity has inevitably been at its boundaries. A concern of the courts has been to set acceptable limits. On the one hand, judges are concerned that carelessly caused harm ought not to go uncompensated. On the other, if all the losses to all the affected parties were actionable simply because they were the result of someone's admitted carelessness, it would open the "floodgates" to a multiplicity of legal proceedings. Even if some of these legal actions were justified, it would prove practically impossible for the courts to handle them.

The "floodgates" principle has therefore frequently been invoked by the courts in order to impose limits on potential tort liabilities. However, it appeared from the mid-1970's to the mid-1980's that the courts' desire to protect claimants from losses resulting from others' negligence outweighed the traditional belief that clear boundary lines ought to be maintained. So there was a loss of judicial confidence that certainty of the law's limits had to be maintained even at the cost of some arbitrariness or apparent injustice in the drawing of those lines. The result was, for a brief period, that the designers and providers of goods and services could be liable to third parties (with whom they had no contract) for the financial consequences if the goods or services turned out to be defective, and it could be shown that the designers or providers were at fault (in the sense that they had not exercised reasonable care and skill at the relevant time).

The background to this remarkable expansion in liability is found particularly in three House of Lords' decisions: *Hedley Byrne* v. *Heller & Partners*[28], *Dorset Yacht Co.* v. *The Home Office*[29] and *Anns* v. *Merton London*

28 [1963] 2 All ER 575.
29 [1970] AC 1004.

Borough Council[30]. These cases relaxed the degree of "proximity" which had to be shown between the claimant and the person liable, creating a climate which permitted purely economic losses to be recoverable in tort, rather than the traditionally limited forms of physical damage. The conveniently self limiting nature of physical damage, as a natural boundary, was abandoned in favour of the liberal criterion of "foreseeability". A liability could arise for negligence in tort merely because the loss sustained by some third party could be said to be foreseeable (though the courts reserved a somewhat residual category to create special exceptions if public policy demanded that there be no liability even though the loss was foreseeable).

The expansive mood of the judges culminated in the House of Lords' decision in *Junior Books Limited* v. *Veitchi Limited*[31]. A specialist supplier of goods and services (a nominated sub-contractor) was held to owe a duty to a third party (with whom there was no contract) to take care to avoid the financial losses that would flow from defects in the goods and services provided. The majority of the judges in this court expressly abandoned the 'floodgates' principle. They were more concerned to impose liability for the benefit of a claimant whom they thought deserving, than they were to preserve clarity and certainty as to where to limits of liability should lie. Lord Brandon dissented. He objected that the law of tortious negligence was not intended to provide claimants with rights which were properly only the province of contract. He was right. His dissent provoked, within just a few years, a new orthodoxy. The floodgates were back in place. A succession of appellate court decisions restored the traditional limits of *Donoghue* v. *Stevenson*, at least as far ordinary manufacturing and supply industries were concerned. It seems however that professional advisers continued to bear a heavier burden of liability. Paradoxically, the more limited nature of professionals' contractual obligations (being only to take care, rather than to warrant results) itself made negligence liability a natural characteristic of professional activity. The courts have found it difficult to resist extending that liability beyond the context of the contract to third parties who might also suffer losses resulting from professional negligence.

The new normal principles of liability

Leaving aside the professional advisers and specialist contractors whose expertise is relied upon by clients, it seems that ordinary contractors and suppliers of goods and services will benefit from the restriction on the range of claimants to whom they owe a tortious duty and from the limitation on the types of losses which will be recoverable. The normal requirements of liability in tortious negligence will be that there must be actual or apprehended damage to the plaintiff's person or property.

It will not, it seems, suffice if the only damage occurring is within property which the defendant had negligently designed or produced and the damage is attributable to that negligence (subject to the applications of the *D & F* complex structure approach). This is asserted despite the fact some cases

30 [1978] AC 728.
31 [1983] AC 520.

regard the *Junior Books* case as one of physical damage, to the surface of the floor (*cf.* its treatment in, *e.g. Simaan* v. *Pilkington*[32]). Difficulties will however arise in determining whether the defendant can be said to have caused damage to 'other' property if one product, or part, which he supplies causes damage to another he supplies with it.

The criterion of "other property"

In *Aswan Engineering Establishment Co* v. *Lupdine Ltd*[33], Lloyd LJ, with whom Fox LJ agreed, said:

> "The distinction between a defective product which renders the product itself less valuable, and a defective product which creates a danger to other property of the plaintiff, was the corner stone of Lord Brandon's dissenting speech in Junior Books. It is a distinction which is well established both in English and American law. Where the defect renders the property less valuable, the plaintiff's remedy (if any) lies in contract. Where it creates a danger to other property of the plaintiff, the remedy (if any) lies in tort, although it may also lie in contract if the manufacturer is also the seller, as in *Grant* v. *Australian Knitting Mills*."
>
> "*Junior Books* was the first case to cross the line, as it were, between tort and contract. That step was justified because the relationship between the parties was such that it could be regarded as equivalent to contract. In the great majority of cases the question whether the danger created is danger to other property of the plaintiff admitted of an obvious answer. The peculiarity of the present case is that the position is not so clear."

The problem was with plastic pails which collapsed when stacked in full sunshine on a Kuwaiti quayside. Their contents, a waterproofing compounding known as "Lupguard", were a total loss. But Aswan were buying Lupguard in pails; not Lupguard and pails. So, was there damage to other property? Lloyd LJ speculated on other cases. What if a defective car tyre, part of the original equipment, bursts and the car is damaged? Presumably the car is other property of the plaintiff, even though the tyre was a component part of the car. Say a bottle of wine is undrinkable because of a defect in the cork; is the wine other property, so as to enable an action against the cork manufacturer in tort? Suppose the electric motors in Muirhead had overheated and damaged the pumps. Would the plaintiff have recovered for physical damage to the pumps as well as to the lobsters? The provisional view was that in all these cases there was damage to other property of the plaintiff, so that the threshold of liability was crossed.

Whether liability would be established in any particular case was another matter. It was clear that much would also depend on the foreseeability of the damage, otherwise the loss would be held too remote anyway.

32 [1988] QB 758.
33 [1986] 2 Lloyd's Rep 347 at 360

The return to Donoghue, and the intermediate examination principle

A further requirement of normal negligence liability is that there must have been no reasonable opportunity for intermediate examination which would have enabled the plaintiff to be aware of the potential for harm before it occurred.

This return to the principal limitations of Lord Atkin's neighbour principle in *Donoghue* v. *Stevenson*[34] flows from the decisions of the Court of Appeal in *Muirhead* v. *Industrial Tank Specialities*[35] and *Simaan General Contracting Co.* v. *Pilkington Glass*[36] and of the House of Lords in *D & F Estates* v. *Church Commissioners*[37]. In *Donoghue* v. *Stevenson*, Lord MacMillan observed that the categories of negligence are never closed. It seems from the negative reaction of the courts in the late-1980's to the expansionist policy of the previous decade, that some categories can be closed, even where they have been open for some time. The trilogy of *Hedley Byrne, Dorset Yacht* and *Anns* v. *Merton* had suggested that negligence liability could arise in any circumstances so long as reasonably foreseeable loss was the result of a lack of reasonable care. By contrast, the House of Lords in *Hill* v. *Chief Constable of West Yorkshire*[38], following the restrictive views of the Privy Council in *Yuen Kun Yeu* v. *The Attorney General of Hong Kong*[39], required caution at the very least in any new extension of negligence liability beyond existing categories. The courts were required to pay particular regard to the categories of cases where liability was already established.

The position of professional advisers and other with specialist expertise: the reliance principle

The difficult question, somewhat unresolved, is whether the limits upon tortious liability imposed by the appellate courts in the late-1980's will have any effect in restricting the liabilities of professionals and others with specialist expertise. It could be said that the main emphases of the restrictive judicial policy leave the expansive attitude to professional negligence liability untouched.

Policy factors behind retrenchment

It appears that the courts' caution applies particularly to the following categories.

- public authorities;
- manufacturers supplying non-specialist mass retail markets;
- ordinary contractors whose expertise is not particularly specialist, as compared with their clients or the advisers whom their clients could reasonably be expected to employ;

34 [1932] AC 562.
35 [1985] 3 All ER 705.
36 [1988] 2 WLR 761.
37 [1988] 3 WLR 368.
38 [1988] 2 WLR 1049.
39 [1987] 3 WLR 776.

- any supplier of goods and services where the likely losses will be suffered by an indeterminate range of claimants for indeterminate amounts.

These four categories reflect various policy reasons for limiting the range of claimants to whom a duty in the tort of negligence is owed. They partly reflect a principle that wherever possible people should be encouraged by the legal system to look after their own interests and avoid losses, rather than assume that there will always be an opportunity to off-load the responsibility for that loss on to someone insured or able to pay. The four categories also reflect a reassertion of the "floodgates" principle: that some limit on claims has to be imposed to prevent the courts being flooded with claims. Hence the fundamental criterion for normal negligence liability is actual or apprehended physical damage (*i.e.* to person or property) which the victim could not reasonably have avoided.

This limitation (to damage or danger to person or property) of the kind of harm that is normally regarded as actionable in tort is regarded by some as explicable in more significant policy terms than the mere floodgates argument. Some see it as a natural expression of what "tort" connotes, as an actionable civil wrong. That is, the purpose of the law of tort is to offer protection against careless invasion by others of our personal safety or that of our property. For our wellbeing in those two respects is valued by the law sufficiently to require the imposition of involuntary duties to avoid those particular forms of harm. But, if we wish to protect our financial wellbeing then we must do so by securing the voluntary assumption by others of a duty so to save us from purely economic harm. The normal way to do that would be by contract, though such a duty might be voluntarily assumed in a special relationship less than, but akin to, contract.

When are economic losses recoverable in tort?

The courts draw an important distinction between financial losses which are consequent upon physical damage and claims which are for purely economic loss unrelated to physical damage. The reason for this is that the "apprehended or actual physical damage" criterion itself, as we have said, naturally places an acceptable limit on the range of possible claimants. The courts are therefore normally willing to countenance the recovery of economic losses resulting from the physical damage by that limited range of persons. These economic losses are themselves by definition also limited in range because they are contingent upon the physical damage. Assuming, as we have, that most claims framed in tort in respect of experts systems in law will be for financial losses which are not the result of physical damage, then we have to consider to what extent the law will allow such losses to be recovered after the restrictive decisions of the late-1980's.

We have seen that a renewed emphasis is being placed upon the closeness and directness of the relationship (proximity) between the defendant and the claimant, and upon the alternative opportunities to have avoided the loss. The difficult question for the courts is to define in what circumstances that proximity will be high enough to allow pure economic loss to be recovered without thereby opening the floodgates to other claims.

There is one well established category for the recovery of pure economic loss: that is, cases of professional advice which lead only to financial losses, where it is reasonable for the plaintiff to have relied on the special expertise held out by the adviser: see the case of *Hedley Byrne & Co.* v. *Heller & Partners*[40]. Three factors have expanded this realm of liability in the 25 years since its first recognition:

1. The tortious basis of action can be chosen by a victim of negligent professional advice, even though the victim also had a contract with the adviser (see *Esso Petroleum Co.* v. *Mardon*[41] (petrol companies advice to a potential tenant), *Batty* v. *Metropolitan Property Realisations*[42] (builder/developer's failure to investigate neighbouring ground conditions before building a house) and *Midland Bank Trust Co.* v. *Hett, Stubbs & Kemp*[43] (solicitors advice to client)). However, there are dicta of the Privy Council in *Tai Hing Cotton Mill Ltd* v. *Liu Chong Hing Bank Ltd*[44] indicating that their Lordships did not believe there was any advantage for the law's development in searching for liability in tort where the parties were in a contractual relationship. This was said to be particularly so in a commercial relationship. Their Lordships believed it correct in principle and necessary for the avoidance of confusion in the law to adhere to the contractual analysis: on principle because it was a relationship in which the parties had, subject to a few exceptions, the right to determine their obligations to each other, and for the avoidance of confusion because different consequences followed according to whether the liability arose from contract or tort, *e.g.* in the limitation of actions.
2. Liability has been extended to persons other than the immediate client of the adviser (see, *e.g.* the many house surveyor and valuer cases beginning with *Yianni* v. *Edwin Evans & Sons*[45] (mortgage lenders' valuing surveyor liable to house purchaser), and see *JEB Fasteners* v. *Marks Bloom & Co.*[46] (auditing accountants' liability to persons interested in the company)).
3. Professional advice may be too narrow a definition. Negligent professional acts or omissions, if advisory in nature, may be regarded as breaches of duty leading to recoverable pure economic loss: *Ross* v. *Caunters*[47] (liability of solicitor to a beneficiary under the client's will in respect of the drafting of the will).

The more recent cases have treated the *Hedley Byrne* principle as depending on a "voluntary assumption of responsibility", perhaps even "akin to contract", though in the House of Lords in *D & F* the governing criterion seemed to be "reliance".

Reliance on professionals

A remaining problem is whether the *Hedley Byrne* principle extends beyond the category of undoubted professionals acting in advisory capacity (such as

40 [1963] 2 All ER 575.
41 (1976) 2 Build LR 82.
42 [1978] QB 554.
43 [1979] Ch. 384.
44 [1986] AC 80.
45 [1982] QB 438.
46 [1983] 1 All ER 583.
47 [1980] Ch. 297.

lawyers, accountants, surveyors and valuers). There is even doubt as to whether an architect or consulting engineer owes this form of liability when acting in the traditional way as a consultant on a construction project: consider *e.g. Pirelli* v. *Faber (Oscar) & Partners*[48], *London Congregational Union* v. *Harriss*[49], *Pacific Construction* v. *Halcrow*[50] and *Salliss* v. *Calil*[51]. It seems unlikely therefore that such liability would be extended even further to parties who had specialist expertise but were not regarded as consultant professionals in a traditional institutional sense. This last group of potential defendants with specialist expertise would therefore be held liable in the tort of negligence for causing purely economic loss, unrelated to physical damage, only if they could be brought within what remains of the principles articulated by the majority in *Junior Books* v. *Veitchi*. It is very important to note that Lord Roskill actually found for *Junior Books* on quite precise and detailed reasons on the particular facts: he articulated what has come to be regarded as a checklist of eight factors highlighting the specialist expertise of the defendant sub-contractors in that case who were alone responsible for the product concerned and must have known that the owner of the factory in which they were working was relying on their skill and experience; the relationship between the parties was as close as it could be, short of actual contract. It has since doubted whether there is any useful purpose in any case citing the majority decision in *Junior Books* v. *Veitchi* (see *Simaan* (CA) and *D & F* (HL)): *i.e.* it is to be regarded as a decision entirely dependent upon its own particular facts. Certainly the strict limits on the application of the *Junior Books* majority decision are made very clear by the Court of Appeal in *Muirhead* v. *Industrial Tank Specialities*[52], *Simaan General Contracting* v. *Pilkington Glass*[53] and *Greater Notts Co-op* v. *Cementation Piling*[54], and the House of Lords in *D & F*.

The resolution of some of these difficulties may come from a more explicit recognition that the true distinguishing feature is between cases where a product (*i.e.* a thing, an artefact) is supplied or physical work is carried out, on the one hand, and, on the other hand, those cases where only advice is given. This would go a long way to explaining why professional advisers can owe duties to third parties in tort to avoid purely economic losses, whereas for all other categories of defendant only the victims of actual or apprehended physical damage can recover. The tort duty cannot be viewed in isolation from the contractual obligations that normally attach to the relevant category of defendant. In all those cases where a product is supplied or physical work is carried out, the normal form of contractual obligation will be one to achieve results: a performance obligation warranting quality or fitness for purpose. Those, however, who merely give advice will, even in contract (and in the absence of terms to the contrary), owe an obligation only to take reasonable care in the formulation and giving of the advice; they do not impliedly warrant that the advice will lead to successful results by action in reliance thereon. The adviser category therefore enjoys a reduced form of contractual liability which,

48 [1983] 2 AC 1.
49 [1986] 280 EG 1342.
50 (1988) 4 Const LJ 131.
51 (1987) 3 Const LJ 125.
52 [1985] QB 507.
53 [1988] 2 WLR 761.
54 [1988] 3 WLR 396.

by being framed as a duty to take care, is analogous to a tortious duty in negligence. Thus, third party victims of negligent professional advice will find it relatively easy to assert the view that a duty of care which the professional already owes to his client ought also to be owed to foreseeable categories of third party who might also rely on the advice. This is especially so because the form of the advice will often be a report which foreseeably can be passed on to third parties in circumstances where it must have been known to the original professional adviser that third parties would receive and act on its content. Contrast the position of a third party who is complaining of loss resulting from a product supplied to another or from physical work carried out for another. Here the essence of the complaint is likely to be that the product or the work has not met the performance objective expected (*e.g.* it is defective). Even if the third party victim can show reliance on the person responsible for the product or work by asserting that the victim purchased from another the property comprising or incorporating the product or work on the strength of the reputation or representations of the person responsible, there will be the answer that the original purchaser of the product or work had the contractual opportunity to bargain for performance obligations. Therefore the third party victim should have similarly sought contractual protection from his immediate vendor when taking over the product or work. There is no justification for his having rights in tort direct against the person responsible.

Why will the user allege negligence by framing an action in tort?

The obvious reason for framing an action in tort is that the claimant has no contract with the defendant. Of necessity all third party claims have thus to be grounded in tort. However, before the development of Hedley Byrne liability, the courts showed that a contract might be implied between two parties: see *Shanklin Pier Co.* v. *Detel Productions*[55]. So far as negligence liability is concerned, the appellate courts in the late 1980's turned the judicial clock back to a position very similar to that obtaining in the early 1950's. It might be therefore that more liberal judges will now be willing to use the implied collateral contract device as a way of enabling third parties to sue the parties responsible direct for defects in products.

There are also reasons why a user may wish to frame an action in the tort of negligence, even if there is a contract with the defendant. We have seen above that this notion of concurrent duties in contract and in tort flows from the decision of the Court of Appeal in *Esso Petroleum Co.* v. *Mardon*[56]. (See also *Batty* v. *Metropolitan Realisations Ltd*[57].) But the *Tai Hing* dicta now limit the scope for such concurrent duties outside the context of professional advice. To the extent that the courts continue to allow a duty in tort to be recognized even where there is a contract with the defendant, the advantages in so grounding the action in tort would be as follows:

- The claim in tort could extend the time limits within which the action could be started. This is because the rules on limitation of actions are different in tort than in contract.

55 [1951] 2 KB 854.
56 (1976) 2 Build LR 82.
57 [1978] QB 554.

- The difference in the basis for calculating damages, as between tort and contract, could work to the advantage of the claimant.
- There could be a moral or persuasive advantage in framing the action on the basis of tortious negligence. The breach by a defendant of such a duty imposed by law may invite greater judicial disapproval than a mere breach of contract. This might lead not only to judicial sympathy with the claimant but also presumptions that the contract ought not to exclude or restrict that negligence duty imposed by law (see *e.g.* Section 2 Unfair Contract Terms Act 1977).

What is reasonable care? How much care is needed to avoid being negligent?

The legal principles governing the standard of care required to avoid being found negligent in law were explained, for example, by Bingham LJ in *Eckersley* v. *Binnie & Partners and Others*[58]:

> "The law requires of a professional man that he live up in practice to the standard of the ordinary skilled man exercising and professing to have his special professional skills. He need not possess the highest expert skill; it is enough if he exercises the ordinary skill of an ordinary competent man exercising his particular art. So much is established by *Bolam* v. *Friern Hospital Management Committee*[59] which has been applied and approved time without number. 'No matter what profession it may be, the common law does not impose on those whose practise it any liability for damage resulting from what in the result turn out to have been errors of judgment, unless the error was such as no reasonable well-informed and competent member of that profession could have made' (*Saif Ali* v. *Sydney Mitchell & Co.*[60] *per* Lord Diplock).
>
> "From these general statements it follows that a professional man should command the corpus of knowledge which forms part of the professional equipment of the ordinary member of his profession. He should not lag behind other ordinarily assiduous and intelligent members of his profession in knowledge of new advances, discoveries and developments in his field. He should have such awareness as an ordinarily competent practitioner would have of the deficiencies in his knowledge and the limitations on his skill. He should be alert to the hazards and risks inherent in any professional task he undertakes to the extent that other ordinarily competent members of his profession would be alert. He must bring to any professional task he undertakes no less expertise, skill and care than any other ordinarily competent members of his profession would bring, but need bring no more. The standard is that of the reasonable average. The law does not require of a professional man that he be a paragon, combining the qualities of polymath and prophet.
>
> "In deciding whether a professional man has fallen short of the standards observed by ordinarily skilled and competent members of his profession, it is the standards prevailing at the time of acts or omissions which provide the relevant yardstick. He is not ... to be judged by the wisdom of hindsight. This of course means that knowledge of an event which happened later should not be applied when judging acts and/or

58 (1988) CILL 388.
59 [1957] 1 WLR 582.
60 [1980] AC 198 at 220D.

> omissions which took place before that event ...; ... it is necessary, if the defendant's conduct is to be fairly judged, that the making of [any] retrospective assessment should not of itself have the effect of magnifying the significance of the ... risk as it appeared or should reasonably have appeared to ordinarily competent practical man with a job to do at the time."

The notion, central to this formulation of the standard of care, that the defendant has the benefit of not being judged with the wisdom of hindsight is often the "state of the art" defence. It will be a defence to a charge of negligence to show that one acted reasonably having regard to the state of the art at the time. This is further qualified by allowing the state of the art to be defined in terms of what the ordinarily assiduous and intelligent member of that profession could reasonably have been expected to keep up with. In this latter respect there is an important difference between the state of the art defence in negligence law and the more narrowly framed "development risk" defence in product liability (at least as it is expressed in the European Directive: *cf.* the United Kingdom implementation'.

Does the degree of care depend on the cost of the service?

The relevance of the fee charged to the standard of care required was discussed by the judge in *Wimpey Construction (UK)* v. *D V Poole*[61]. It was argued that the Bolam test was not applicable if the client obtains and pays for someone with especially high skills. This had been considered, but not decided upon by Megarry J in *Duchess of Argyll* v. *Beuselinck*[62]: "If the client engages an expert, and doubtless expects to pay commensurate fees, is he not entitled to expect something more than the standard of the reasonably competent?" Megarry J's questions appears not to be have been further considered until Webster J in *Wimpey* v. *D V Poole*[63] rejected the submission. He held himself bound by the clear words of the *Bolam* test, as approved without qualification by the Privy Council in *Chin Keow* v. *Government of Malaysia*[64] and the House of Lords in *Whitehouse* v. *Jordan*[65]. Judge Newey went even further in *Governors of the Hospital for Sick Children* v. *McLaughlin & Harvey Plc and Others*[66]. He said that in a claim against a member of a profession for breach of contractual duty equivalent to a duty in negligence, what the plaintiff had to prove (to recover actual damages) was substantially the same as in negligence. The amount paid for the defendant's services was immaterial to whether he acted in breach of duty. This was, the judge said, perhaps particularly unfortunate for engineers, who generally were not well paid as compared with members of other professions.

It seems that there is more justification for taking the view that the level of the defendant's fees is irrelevant to the standard of care required where the claim is framed in tort by a third party. If, however, the claim is framed in contract, albeit alleging negligence by breach of a contractual duty to take care,

61 (1984) 128 SJ 969.
62 [1972] 2 Lloyd's Rep 172 at 183
63 (1984) 128 SJ 969.
64 [1967] 1 WLR 813.
65 [1981] 1 WLR 246.
66 (1987) CILL 372.

then one would have expected, as Megarry J suggested in the *Duchess of Argyll* case above, that the standard of care ought to be commensurate with the level of fee charged to the client. In contractual cases, the solution probably is that, whatever fee is charged, the contractual obligation of the professional is defined by default by the *Bolam* test, unless the parties provide otherwise in their contract, expressly or impliedly. There therefore could be an argument that the level of fee alone would be an indication that in a particular case the parties had impliedly intended that the high level of fee should carry a higher standard of care (in the sense of a higher contractual performance objective).

Even if the standard of care itself, in professional cases, is not variable by reference to the level of the defendant's fee, there are other ways in which the level of fee may nonetheless affect the degree of liability owed by the defendant. First, where a claim is framed in contract against the supplier of goods or services, the performance obligations owed by the supplier (as to the quality and/or fitness of the goods and services) will certainly depend upon the price charged for those goods or services. Secondly, even in tort claims the question of the cost of the service could be a material consideration. This is because the standard of care required of the defendant is only one of the three fundamental elements for the successful assertion of a claim in tortious negligence. To succeed, the claimant in tort has to establish (1) a duty of care owed to him, (2) breach of that duty, and (3) damage resulting from that breach. Earlier in this discussion there was outlined the circumstances in which a duty is owed, and what forms of loss will constitute actionable damage: in other words the first and third of these requirements. The second requirement, the breach of duty, is the facet determined by reference to the standard of care required of the defendant. Even if, therefore, the cost of the defendant's goods or services is irrelevant to the standard of care required, it may still be relevant to the extent of the duty owed. Ultimately, the question of whether a duty of care is owed in the law of tort depends on whether a court considers that it is just and reasonable that it should be so owed: see *Governors of the Peabody Donation Fund* v. *Sir Lindsay Parkinson & Co.*[67].

European Product Liability

The European Community Directive on Product Liability has been implemented by the United Kingdom Parliament in the Consumer Protection Act 1987, which came into force on 1st March 1988. Although the Government said, when the Act was published as a Bill, that this legislation does not apply to buildings, it is clear from a careful reading of the Act that the construction industry is indeed affected by it.

The main thrust of Part I of the Act is to make it easier for people to obtain compensation where they are injured by unsafe products. This new form of liability is a liability without fault. Lawyers call it strict liability. It is no defence to say that all reasonable care had been taken. It is most unusual for English law to extend strict liability (liability without fault) beyond contractual responsibilities. So this is a burdensome liability. And it is supplementary to existing liabilities. It does not displace ordinary negligence liability to third

67 [1985] AC 210.

parties but merely adds an alternative, easier access to compensation for the victim. Under the Directive, it is still necessary to prove the damage, the defect and the causal relationship between them. Rights of contribution between defendants who have caused the same damage are preserved, as is the principle of contributory negligence (which reduces damages payable in proportion to any blame on the part of the victim).

There are two defences which offer some relief to producers of buildings.

First, there is the "development risk" defence. This was framed very narrowly indeed in the European Community Directive: "That the state of scientific and technical knowledge at the time when [the producer] put the product into circulation was not such as to enable the existence of the defect to be discovered". This reference to all scientific and technical knowledge makes the defence as so framed much less easy to invoke than the normal "state of the art" defence applicable to ordinary negligence liability actions. However, the implementation of the "development risk" defence in the United Kingdom Act has arguably been framed too liberally for producers. Section 4(1)(*e*) of the 1987 Act provides that it shall be a defence "that the state of scientific and technical knowledge at the relevant time was not such that a producer of products of the same description as the product in question might be expected to have discovered the defect if it had existed in his products while they were under his control". This formulation seems much closer to the ordinary negligence test which may be summarised as "reasonable competence having regard to the scientific and technical knowledge available to the defendant at the relevant time". The United Kingdom Act has therefore been challenged by consumer organizations alleging that the United Kingdom is in breach of its treaty obligations by failing to implement faithfully the European Directive.

Secondly, it is a defence to show that the defect did not exist in the product at the time of supply.

There are other important limits on this form of liability which mitigate some of its impact. First, for the liability to arise, there has to be a defect in the product. But, for this purpose, the notion of defect is not related to quality or fitness for purpose in the usual sense. The criterion of defectiveness is a safety criterion. There is a defect if the product is not as safe as persons generally are entitled to expect. Secondly, the liability will arise only if a narrowly defined form of damage is suffered by the victim. This is death or personal injuries, or, damage to any item of property other than the defective product itself. The property damage actionable in this context is also subject to two further restrictive conditions: a lower threshold of value of the damage to the property (£275.00), to discourage small claims; and, a requirement that the property was in use by a private consumer.

So we may conclude in relation to product liability that even if a building, or parts of a building, are capable of being a product for the purposes of this new law, the liability will not arise simply because an occupier has found quality defects in the building itself. Still less is the new law of any relevance to quality and fitness defects in commercial properties.

How long can product liability exposure last? Victims will be able to start an action within three years from discovering the damage. This is directly analogous to the provisions of the Latent Damage Act 1986. However, there will also be a long stop period applicable to product liability claims. This is different to that introduced by the Latent Damage Act 1986 for ordinary negligence claims in three respects:

- The long stop period is only 10 years.
- It does not start from breach of duty, but rather from the time the product was supplied.
- It extinguishes the right, rather than merely barring the remedy (this is significant in relation to rights of contribution between defendants).

What are the practical implications for the management of this new form of product liability?

First, it depends upon how, and to whom, the builder is supplying his products. Contract documentation ought to be carefully reviewed in this light. There are provisions in the Consumer Protection Act 1987 which relieve builders from this liability in certain circumstances. The most important aspect of this is the major difference between those who supply goods comprised in land by the disposal of an interest in that land, and those who supply goods by carrying out building works. There are therefore product liability implications when decisions are taken as to whether the organization actually building is also in law the organization disposing of the product to clients. Other aspects of management of this liability include a careful review of the insurance implications. This is a no fault liability. So, it would not be covered by the ordinary professional indemnity cover which building designers would normally carry. It is not a "negligent act, error, or omission". Nor can the liability be controlled by ordinary disclaimers and exemption clauses. The Act prohibits producers and suppliers from simply contracting out of product liability. However, it should be recognised that there are other ways in law of achieving the same result. Once again these require a careful review of contractual and other documentation so that they may be redrafted in order to reduce the potential liabilities arising. One approach is to focus on the criterion of defectiveness: this depends on what persons generally are entitled to expect from the product. There is clearly scope here for the management of the liability by controlling expectations.

Legal controls on disclaimers and limitations of liability, and alternative avoidance mechanisms.

At common law, liability may be limited or disclaimed altogether by appropriately clear wording. Obviously this can be by contractual agreement. Duties can also be prevented from arising in tort (see, *e.g. Harris* v. *Wyre District Council*[68]; though *cf.* Section 13 of the Unfair Contract Terms Act 1977 which was not mentioned in that case).

However, certain statutes provide specific obligations and then purport to prevent any contracting out of that obligation. An instance we have just seen is the product liability provisions contained within the Consumer Protection Act 1987. Otherwise, the general legislative interference with freedom of contract

68 [1987] 1 EGLR 231.

in this area, imposing limits on parties' abilities to restrict or limit their legal liabilities, is contained in the Unfair Contract Terms Act 1977.

The title of the Unfair Contract Terms Act 1977 is something of a misnomer. It does not control terms because they are "unfair". Rather, it has specific provisions, applying in limited circumstances and mainly to exclusion and limitation of liability clauses. However it is not limited to contractual obligations and liabilities.

The effects of the provisions of the Act may be summarised as follows (leaving aside certain exceptions from the Act's application such as international supply contracts):

1. The Act applies, with few exceptions, only to "business liability".
2. Liability in negligence (which includes a contractual duty to exercise reasonable care and skill) causing death or personal injury cannot be excluded or restricted.
3. Consumers' (*i.e.* private persons dealing with businesses) rights against their immediate contractual suppliers, in respect of the description, quality and fitness for purpose of goods supplied, cannot be excluded or restricted.
4. Otherwise, liabilities for negligence and for misrepresentation and in respect of description, quality and fitness for purpose of goods, can be excluded or restricted but subject to a reasonableness test.
5. The only control on freedom of contract in respect of more general contractual obligations is to impose a reasonableness test (in favour of a consumer or a person whose contract is on the other party's written standard terms of business) on excluding or restricting liability for breach of contract, or on claiming to be entitled to render no contractual performance or a performance substantially different from that reasonably expected.

There are some guidelines for the application of the reasonableness test in supply of goods cases. Otherwise, there is a difficulty of predicting the effect of the reasonableness tests in this Act, in view of the policy of "minimum guidance by appellate courts" adopted by the House of Lords in *George Mitchell (Chesterhall) Limited* v. *Finney Lock Seeds*[69]. Lord Bridge expressed the House of Lord's view: that appellate courts should refrain from interference with trial judges' application of what is reasonable in the particular circumstances of a particular case. One general factor that has emerged is that clauses are likely to be found reasonable if they are the product of negotiation between interested parties "on both sides" of the industry concerned. (See the *George Mitchell* case above; *R W Green Ltd* v. *Cade Bros Farms*[70]; and *Walker* v. *Boyle*[71]).

The Act does not control indemnity clauses at all except as against persons dealing as private consumers (see Section 4.)

69 [1983] 2 AC 803.
70 [1978] 1 Lloyd's Rep 602.
71 [1982] 1 WLR 495.

Exemption clauses and third parties

Attempts to rely on exemption and limitation clauses against third parties are fraught with legal difficulty.

There are three possibilities:

1. by the use of agency law to find (or construct) a direct relationship based on the exclusion clause, with the third party (consider *The Eurymedon*[72]).
2. by creating a "circle of indemnities" (see *Gillespie* v. *Roy Bowles Transport*[73]). However, this approach is weakened by the danger of insolvency in the chain, or a mismatch in indemnity provisions.
3. There may be success in reliance on "consent" reasoning in the law of tort. Certainly, similar effects can be achieved by adequately framed "warning notices".

The House of Lords has addressed, but not provided an answer to, this third possibility both in *The Eurymedon*[74] and in *Junior Books* v. *Veitchi*[75]. There seems a curious judicial reluctance, particularly in the appellate courts, to grasp this nettle. (Lord Denning, by contrast, offered a solution when he was in the House of Lords as long ago as *Midland Silicones* v. *Scruttons*[76]; but his "consent" reasoning has been only partially taken up, and only in *Johnson Matthey* v. *Constantine Terminals.*[77])

The present dilemma is well illustrated by the refusal once again of the House of Lords to clarify this matter in *Leigh & Sillivan Ltd* v. *Aliakmon Shipping*[78].

For the construction industry it may be significant that the late Judge David Smout QC had already reached a simple conclusion similar to that of Robert Goff LJ in *Aliakmon*. Judge Smout's judgment in *Southern Water Authority* v. *Duvivier*[79] was delivered some months before, but was not cited in *Leigh & Sillivan* v. *Aliakmon Shipping*.

Limitation of Actions

The principle of the English law of limitation which therefore applied to latent damage cases until the coming into force of the Latent Damage Act 1986, is that a plaintiff must commence his action within a particular period beginning with the date of the accrual of his cause of action. So, the period for actions resulting from tortious negligence not involving personal injury or death is six years; and the cause of action accrues in such cases when the actual damage occurs whether or not it is yet discoverable.

The difficulty that arises from this normal rule is how, in law, to identify when the actionable form of damage occurred. The implication of recent cases restricting contractors' negligence liability to third parties is that what now constitutes sufficient harm to be actionable damage must be is more than mere

72 [1975] AC 154.
73 [1973] QB 400.
74 [1975] AC 154.
75 [1983] 1 AC 520.
76 [1962] AC 446.
77 [1976] 2 Lloyd's Rep 215.
78 [1986] 2 WLR 902.
79 (1984) CILL 90. (Later reported as *Southern Water Authority* v. *Carey* [1985] 2 All ER 1077.).

defects in the building itself. So, in the new restrictive era, a cause of action will not accrue normally until there is actual or apprehended physical damage to person or other property.

The result of the courts' narrowing liability in tort is the renewed importance of contractual lines of claims. It appears that the Latent Damage Act 1986 applies only to tortious negligence, and that it therefore leaves unaffected contractual limitation periods (even though breach of contract can cause latent damage). So, in contract cases, where the parties have not agreed any particular limitation period, the usual periods in the Limitation Act 1980 will continue to apply:

- 12 years from the relevant breach of contract, in cases of contracts under seal;
- 6 years from breach for simple contracts (*i.e.* not under seal).

Although the principle is that contractual causes of action accrue at the time of the breach of contract, a breach of a contractual duty would often be regarded as continuing at least until completion of the contract and in some cases even later.

A warranty as to fitness for purpose however is presumably not broken (depending on its terms) until it first becomes unfulfilled: The breach of contract would then be regarded as occurring at the date of the failure of the warranty, not at the time of any particular act or omission which may (*e.g.* during construction) have been the reason for the eventual failure of the warranty. On this view there is no conflict between normal statutory limitation periods and the periods of 60-year or building lifetime warranties. Rather, the limitation periods applicable to accrual of causes of action arising from breaches of contract operate in the normal way from the date of the breach upon the eventual first failure of the warranty. The same would apply to "duty of care" warranties, though the breach in those cases would, as in tort, arise at the time of the act or omission complained of, such as the failure to take reasonable care.

Parties to a contract have the freedom (subject to the Unfair Contract Terms Act 1977) to provide expressly for their own limitation period and so cut down the period of exposure that would otherwise apply under the 1980 Act. Also limitation periods can be extended beyond the statutory periods as they operate as defences which the defendant can agree not to plead.

Alternatively matching protection can be sought by a potential defendant from another by requiring an indemnity from that other. However, it should be noted that the way in which indemnities operate can give rise to very long periods of protection or exposure (depending on whether you are giving or receiving the indemnity). The call on an indemnity could extend well beyond the 15 year long stop period which, under the Latent Damage Act 1986, would bar the third party tort claim. This is because the right to sue on an indemnity accrues only when the loss indemnified has itself been established. Therefore, if a contracting party were successfully sued in tort 14 years after a breach of duty and the claim were the subject of an indemnity under seal the party granting the indemnity could be sued up to 26 years after the relevant breach of duty.

So far as negligence actions in the law of tort is concerned, the new time limits are laid down by the Latent Damage Act 1986. The new limitation timetable in the Act is:

- 15 years from breach of duty, if this expires first (the "long stop");
- Otherwise, whichever is the later of six years from accrual of the cause of action (occurrence of the damage) or three years from its discoverability.

These new limits apply only to negligence actions and, negligence appears to mean for this purpose only tortious negligence. Certainly, they do not apply to claims including damages for personal injuries; nor to cases of deliberate concealment. The point must be emphasised that all these periods start from different times and that the purpose of the 15 year long stop is that it may expire before the six year or three year period.

The 1986 Act also confers new rights on successive owners. A problem had arisen because in *Perry* v. *Tendring District Council*[80] it had been held, following *Pirelli*, that a successive owner of property already latently damaged on disposition to him had no right of action because he had no interest in the property when the damage occurred. The purpose of Section 3 of the 1986 Act is to cure this gap in the law. Despite the extremely convoluted drafting of Section 3, which does give rise to some legal difficulties, the intended effect in the end seems to be relatively simple: broadly speaking, a person acquiring an interest in property after the damage occurs but before knowledge of it has arisen is given a fresh cause of action which is treated by the statute as accruing to that new person as from the date of the original damage. So the new person is put broadly into the same position as the person who owned the property at the time the damage occurred, with an extension period running for 3 years from discovery, subject to the long stop.

The most novel aspect of the Act is its introduction of the so called "long stop". However a complicating feature is that the 15 year period is timed as from the date of the breach of duty. There is complex case law showing that some breaches of duty can be regarded as continuing or revived by later conduct (such as remedial works). A further difficulty is that past case law concerned with establishing a breach of duty is focussed more on the point that it had happened rather than when it happened. There are four important cases where the defendant's period of exposure to liability may extend beyond 15 years from breach of duty, because the long stop does not apply.

- Deliberate concealment;
- Rights of contribution;
- Claims under contactual indemnities;
- Property claims involving damages for personal injuries.

There was controversy in Parliament because the long stop would not protect builders in deliberate concealment cases. Deliberate concealment includes deliberate commission of a breach of duty in circumstances in which it is likely to be discovered for some time. In such a case, the limitation period will not even begin to run until the plaintiff has discovered the deliberate concealment (or could reasonably do so) there is some suggestion in recent case law that the courts may more readily impute "deliberate concealment" to a

80 (1984) 30 Build LR 118.

contractor than they would under the previous statutory wording of "fraudulent concealment".

Other aspects of managing liability to third parties

It appeared for a while, as a result of the decisions in *EDAC* v. *Moss*[81] and *Victoria University Manchester* v. *Wilson*[82] that the courts might impose extensive duties to warn on the various parties to the construction process. Hence, in *EDAC* v. *Moss* it was said that a contractor under an ordinary workmanship contract, who had undertaken no design obligation, could nevertheless owe a duty to warn the building owner and the architect of defects in the latter's design. However, these two decisions have been explained in the case of *University of Glasgow* v. *W Whitfield and John Laing Construction Ltd*[83] as depending upon a special relationship between the parties. Otherwise, it was said, they could not stand with more recent decisions. Furthermore the reference to a duty to warn the architect was to the architect as agent of the employer.

This latter context is one illustration of many where the ordinary neligence liabilities of a contractor will be extended if the contractor undertakes a special responsibility or induces reliance on his expertise in a special relationship with a particular party. Otherwise, the normal criterion of negligence liability is pitched by the law at a level of reasonableness consonant with the average competence of the defendant concerned. Furthermore, that competence is to judged by the standards prevailing at the time of the alleged negligence and not with the benefit of hindsight. In other words, builders are entitled to the benefit of the 'state of the art' defence. With regard to professional services, such as design, there are abundant dicta from the courts defining the standard of care required. It has been particularly well explained recently by Bingham LJ in the Court of Appeal in the *Abbeystead* case (*Eckersley* v. *Binnie & Partners*[84] (1988)) (quoted above).

However, contractors must recognize that this relatively low standard of care of the ordinarily competent practitioner applies only to obligations involving reasonable skill and care, such as the ordinary negligence responsibility (whether in contract or in tort) of a consulting architect or engineer in respect of design. If a contractor undertakes design along with his building obligations, it does not follow that in respect of that design a contractor will enjoy this low care-based form of liability. It is clear from the case law that such a design and build contractor may be held impliedly to have warranted the fitness for purpose of the design.

Two consequences follows:

(*a*)Contractual documentation must be reviewed very carefully to ensure that there is not a mismatch of obligation as between the contractual obligations of the builder to his customer on the one hand and that builder's rights on the other hand against outside designers who are commissioned for part of the design. Without proper contractual drafting the latter may be held only to owe

81 2 Con LR. 1
82 (1984) CILL 126.
83 (1988) CILL 416.
84 (1988) CILL 388.

a duty of reasonable skill and care, yet the builder may have a more onerous responsibility to the client.

(*b*)There are also implications for professional indemnity cover in relation to design activities. The case of *Wimpey* v. *Poole*[85] witnessed the spectacle of a contractor seeking to persuade the court that it had been negligent because it ought to be required to owe a higher standard of care than that of the ordinarily competent. Why should a contractor be arguing for a higher degree of responsibility on itself? The reason was that they were suing their own insurers on their P.I cover, having already carried out remedial works for the client. If, however, the defects which were remedied were not the result of care below that of the reasonable average, then it would not constitute negligence within the meaning of the P.I. policy.

Even though the courts are placing new restrictions on negligence liabilities of designers and builders, a decade or so of expanded liability has left a raised claims consciousness. Owners and tenants of buildings have become accustomed to holding builders directly responsible (even if they have no contract with them) for mere defects in the buildings which are not otherwise damaging or dangerous. As negligence liability recedes under a new judicial conservatism, owners and tenants are looking for new forms of legal protection. These are being expressed as duty of care letters and deeds, special warranties, and various forms of assignment or novation. They attempt to create either a direct additional responsibility from the builder to the beneficiary, or a transfer of the original clients' rights under the building contract to third party end users. Once again, considerable caution is needed in assessing contractual and other documentation associated with building works.

85 [1984] 2 Lloyd's Rep 499.

Departures in Contract 22

Professor M. P. Furmston

Synopsis

This paper, with some revisions since the Conference, gives particular consideration to rights and liabilities arising by implied terms in contract and quasi contract, as well as in the law of restitution and on the contract/tort boundary.

A.Implied Terms

Contract making is largely a mass production rather than a bespoke enterprise. Life is too short and management time too expensive to permit every contract to be negotiated from first principles. English law uses two main devices for the mass production process; the standard form contract and the Implied Term. Much of the other discussion in this book concerns developments of the standard forms. The main outlines of the existing law on Implied Terms as applied to building contracts are tolerably clear.[1] Sale of goods analogies are applied to the quality of materials so that in general the contractor is strictly liable if the materials are defective even though it is clearly in no way his fault. This is usually defensible because the contractor has a channelling function. Claims can be passed back up the line until they reach the manufacturer of the defective materials. On the other hand professionals are usually assumed to be under an implied duty only to act with reasonable care. There remain, however, a number of uncertainties or possible areas of development.

It is not wholly inconceivable that in some circumstances a professional might be held to warrant that his work is adequate and not merely of a reasonably careful standard. It is not necessarily absurd that if a professional is asked to design a building for a particular purpose he should be held liable if the building does not achieve that purpose without it being necessary to prove that he was negligent. This could be very important where the reason why the building is defective is the negligence of some other professional for whom the lead professional is not vicariously liable and who is not himself adequately insured or solvent. If it is arguable that a doctor may warrant that his

1 Regan (1987) 3 Const LJ 241.

operations will succeed then similar arguments cannot be dismissed in relation to construction industry professionals.[2]

There are already signs in the authorities that a contractor who takes on work of a design nature which has historically been done by an independent consultant professional may warrant that the work will succeed and not merely that reasonable care will have been taken.[3]

It is clear that in principle the implied terms can be excluded[4] though such an exclusion would now presumably be subject in some cases to the reasonableness test, under the Unfair Contract Terms Act 1977. This presents relatively little problem where the contract expressly says that the implied terms are excluded but this is in practice rather unusual in English building contracts. A much more difficult problem arises where it is suggested that the implied terms have been impliedly excluded because of the express terms as to the quality of the work. In *Young & Martin* v. *McManus Childs*[5] it was held that the implied terms as to the quality of the materials were not excluded by the requirement to use Somerset Thirteen Tiles. In this case, however, the Somerset Thirteen Tiles would in general have been perfectly adequate but the particular batch bought by the contractor was defective. Presumably the result may be different if it can be shown that all Somerset Thirteen Tiles would be inadequate. Certainly it would then be rather difficult to see how there could be a fitness for purpose obligation though perhaps the position as to merchantable quality is less clear.[6] Where the contract specifies that work is to be done in a particular way or that particular materials are to be used, the question arises whether that express obligation excludes the implied obligations or marches hand-in-hand with them. In some cases it must be arguable that the express requirement only excludes implied requirements *pro tanto*.

B. The Tort/Contract Borderline

A detailed discussion of the flowing and ebbing of Tort liability in relation to defective building is a matter for other chapters but we must say something here about the borderline between Contract and Tort liability. In *Bagot* v. *Stevens Scanlan*[7] Diplock LJ argued that on the same facts an architect could not be liable both in Contract and in Tort and that if he was in principle liable in Contract he was not liable in Tort. This would have come close to accepting the French notion of non-cumul but it has been widely assumed that this view cannot be sustained in the light of the leading judgment of Oliver J in *Midland Bank* v. *Hett, Stubbs & Kemp*[8] So in the leading case of *Pirelli* v. *Faber*[9] where the plaintiff clearly had a Contract claim which was statute-barred it was not thought worthwhile to argue that this was an obstacle to his having a Tort claim

2 See the contrasting views in *Thake* v. *Maurice* [1986] QB 644.
3 Support for this view can be found in *Greaves* v. *Baynham Meikle* [1970] 3 All ER 99 and *IBA* v. *EMI* (1980) 14 Build LR1.
4 *Gloucestershire* v. *Richardson* [1969] 1 AC 480.
5 [1969] 1 AC 454
6 See Atiyah in *Contract Law Today* (ed. Harrison & Tallon) at pp 30-3737.
7 [1966] 1 QB 197.
8 [1979] Ch 384.
9 [1983] 2 AC 1.

as well. It seems to have been generally assumed that the later cautionary words of Lord Scarman in the *Tai Hing case*[10] did not affect the possibility of overlapping Contract and Tort liability at least in relation to limitation. It is probably important to emphasize that in *Tai Hing* the Privy Council at first decided that there was no claim in Contract and was then refusing to extend the law of Tort in order to get round the absence of a claim in Contract. In the limitation cases there has always been a perfectly good Contract claim which could be enforced but for the limitation difficulty. So *Tai Hing* and *Pirelli* are similar in that in each case the Contract and Tort result is the same (limitation apart).

A separate, though no doubt related point, is the extent to which a party may have a Tort claim arising out of conduct in the course of negotiating a Contract. It is clear of course that there is a claim in deceit on appropriate facts and since *Esso* v. *Mardon*[11] that there is a claim in negligence where one party reasonably relies to the other's knowledge on that other's advice. In *Esso* v. *Mardon* the advice was followed by the conclusion of a contract between the parties. A question not yet litigated in England is whether negligent advice which is not followed by the conclusion of a contract between the negotiating parties but which causes loss in a different way may give rise to liability. Suppose, for instance, that a sub-contractor carelessly estimates for work and that the contractor relies on that estimate as part of his main contract tender only to find that when he is awarded the contract the sub-contractor has withdrawn his estimate because it was too low. It is clear that on such facts orthodox contract law says that the sub-contractor's estimate can be withdrawn at any time until it has been accepted. However there is an arguable tort case if the estimate was careless since the contractor might plausibly argue that he suffered loss not so much by relying on the sub-contractor actually contracting but on his relying on having estimated in a careful fashion. He might reasonably assume that if the sub-contractor withdraws another one can be found at much the same price. This line of reasoning was rejected in New Zealand in *Holman Construction* v. *Delta Timber*.[12]

C. Privity of Contract

English law is now almost alone in having a very rigid doctrine of Privity of Contract. A good many of the leading economic loss cases arise out of attempts to overcome the absence of Privity of Contract between the parties who nevertheless have a close relationship. The much debated case of *Junior Books* v. *Veitchi*[13] is a very good example.[14] Of course on the facts of that case it is not at all clear why the employer could not have sued the contractor who could in turn have sued the sub-contractor (presumably the contractor was either insolvent or for some other reason effectively immune from suit). This shows that in most cases the restrictive rules about assignment of liability mean that

10 [1986] AC 80.
11 [1976] QB 801.
12 [1972] NZLR 1081.
13 [1983] AC 520.
14 Though the case reached the House of Lords on Appeal from Scotland which does not have the English doctrine.

loss can be passed indirectly along the chain even though it cannot be the subject of a direct action. In this respect the very recent decision of the House of Lords in *D & F Estates*[15] appears to make the position of contractors and sub-contractors very different in Tort to what it is in Contract. It is clear that in a Contract claim it will be no answer at all for the contractor to say that he exercised reasonable care in the appointment of apparently competent sub-contractors. Clearly if the answer is different in Tort this may have very important consequences for the organization of the industry since it will pay contractors to sub-contract as much work as possible rather than to use their own workforce. There is a noticeable trend towards such "management only" contracts in any case.

Another important Privity problem is the extent to which guarantees are transferable, a matter of great interest to second-hand purchasers or lessees of buildings. Life appears to have been conducted on the basis that the NHBC guarantee is freely transferable to second purchasers but this seems very far from clear.[16]

D. Inchoate Contracts

It is of course very common for the parties to make a deal and then hand the matter over to the lawyers to convert it into lawyers' language. It is alas by no means infrequent for one party to repent of the transaction before the lawyers have completed their task. One important practical example of this is of course the practice of gazumping. No no doubt there are devices available to the skilled draughtsman such as conditional contracts which can overcome most of the problems if the lay client will co-operate! It is a matter for serious consideration whether the law should be more willing to recognise that parties have made three quarters or seven eighths of a contract. Empirical studies of negotiating practice suggest that where parties have made a series of negotiated agreements but have not yet completed the negotiations going back on what has been agreed is widely regarded as not acceptable (this is really the problem with gazumping). Apart from the draughtsman's potential to avoid these problems, courts have also developed useful techniques. In some cases, for instance, a collateral contract may be discovered. Perhaps the best modern example is *Harvela* v. *Royal Trust of Canada.*[17] Sometimes a letter of intent may give rise to legal liability as in *Turriff Construction* v. *Regalia*[18], though the opposite conclusion was reached on different facts in *British Steel Corporation* v. *Cleveland Bridge.*[19] In some cases it has been held that a person who has done work in a belief that the contract will come about may have a restitutionary claim. This was the analysis adopted by Robert Goff J in *British Steel* in a judgment which is very interesting but leaves many unresolved questions. Another example is *William Lacey (Hounslow) Ltd* v. *Davis.*[20]

15 [1988] 2 All ER 992.
16 *Kijowski* v. *New Capital Properties Ltd.* 15 Const LR 1.
17 [1986] AC 207.
18 (1971) 9 Build LR 29
19 [1984] 1 All ER 584.
20 [1957] 1 WLR 932.

E. Quasi-Contractual Developments

In certain circumstances a plaintiff who has done work does not have a contractual claim and may decide instead to pursue a quasi-contractual claim. Two particularly interesting decisions from other jurisdictions are worth discussing here. In the California case of *Boomer* v. *Muir*[21] Boomer was a sub-contractor of Muir who was engaged in constructing a large dam. The parties fell out and Boomer abandoned work some 18 months after the contract had been made. It was held by the court that he was justified in leaving the site because Muir's failure to supply materials as rapidly as Boomer needed them was a fundamental breach of the contract. It was held that on these facts Boomer could bring a quasi-contractual claim on a quantum meruit basis for the value of the services which he had in fact rendered up to the termination of the contract. Approaching the matter in this way the Californian court awarded Boomer $258,000 even though only some $20,000 was still due under the terms of the contract. (The reason for the discrepancy is of course that the contractual terms which Boomer had agreed provided for a rate of payment which was below market rates so that Boomer was better off because the contract had been broken than he would have been if the contract had been carried through to a successful conclusion). The difference in the figures is so large as to make one wonder whether the conclusion can be correct. It is worth noting, however, that in *Davis Contractors* v. *Fareham UDC*[22] it seems to have been assumed that if the contract had been frustrated the plaintiff would have been entitled to payment for finishing the houses on a quantum meruit basis. Clearly the plaintiff formulated his claim in this way because he expected to recover more on a quantum meruit basis than he would have recovered under the contract.[23]

In the very recent decision in the High Court of Australia in *Pavey & Matthews Pty Ltd* v. *Paul*[24], it was held that a plaintiff who could not enforce a building contract directly because the contract did not comply with a statutory requirement that building contracts be in writing, could nevertheless recover on a quantum meruit basis because the defendant had really accepted the benefits rendered by the plaintiff under the contract. The judgment of the High Court is marked by an elaborate examination of the historical basis of such claims. It is already clear that the decision will provoke a lively debate as to whether the decision is technically correct and also as to whether the result is or is not desirable.

21 24 P.2d 570 (1933).

22 [1956] AC 696.

23 The view that a plaintiff has a free choice between Contractual and Quasi-Contractual remedies is supported by *Planche* v. *Colburn* (1831) 8 Bing 14 but challenged by *Goff and Jones on Restitution* (3rd Ed.) pp. 465-468. Reference should also be made to the rather unsatisfactory Privy Council decision in *Lodder* v. *Slowey* [1904] AC 442.

24 [1987] 69 ALR 577.

23 Extending and Curtailing Liability

Anthony May

Synopsis

This paper as delivered at the Conference highlights instances by which a variety of drafting devices in construction contracts may extend or curtail what would otherwise be the general liabilities of a party. The implications of recent case law and statutory provisions are considered.

Introduction

In *Greater Nottingham Co-operative Society* v. *Cementation Piling and Foundation Ltd.*[1] Purchas LJ said that there was:

> "no precedent for the application of strict logic in treading the path leading from the basic principle established in *Donoghue* v. *Stevenson* towards the Pandora's Box of unbridled damages at the end of the path of foreseeability."

As with that topical but difficult subject, there is no strict logic in choosing from the Pandora's Box of possibilities the subjects that could be included in a paper on extending and curtailing contractual liability in the construction field. All such possibilities, however, have to be viewed against the basic rights and liabilities which would result from the simplest form of construction contract.

If I agree with you that you will build me a house in accordance with identified drawings and specifications prepared by my architect and that I will pay you £100,000 for doing so, we have an agreement technically complete in law. Depending on the precise terms of the specification, implied terms would probably flesh out the agreement to provide that the works will be carried out with good workmanship and with sound materials of their respective descriptions and, so far as the specification left the choice of materials to you, that they would be suitable for their purpose. You would not expect to be responsible for my architect's design. You would be obliged to carry out the works within a reasonable time.

1 [1988] 3 WLR 396.

In a sense, any sophistication of that contractually basic package would constitute extending or curtailing our rights and liabilities as, for instance, if there were provisions for:

- Payment by instalments;
- Completion within a stipulated time period;
- Extension of time;
- Remedying defects appearing after completion;
- A retention fund;
- Loss and expense;
- A final certificate

to mention but a few.

Indiscriminate dipping into a Pandora's box of possible contractual provisions is plainly unhelpful, and so I have chosen a selection of subjects for brief (sometimes very brief) discussion which have one or more features in common, in particular:

- provisions dealing with the time during which liabilities may subsist, and
- provisions which allocate or reallocate liabilities to persons who might not otherwise be under those liabilities.

The subjects which I have chosen are:

- Exclusion clauses
- Statutory Limitation of Actions
- Indemnities
- Defects Liability Clauses
- Liquidated Damages Clauses
- Final Certificate Clauses
- Liability for Sub-contractor's Design and Direct Warranties
- The Influence of Tortious Liabilities

Any one of these subjects could occupy the entire space available to me, so that trying to deal with all eight necessarily means that I shall do little more than skate over the surface. If that points a way for further more extensive consideration, my object will be achieved.

Exclusion Clauses

Clarity is the essence of successful contract drafting. I take the general subject of exclusion clauses first because the basic requirement of a successful exclusion clause is clarity and the principles of law which apply are touched on in some of my later subjects.

In the 1970's, there was a trend fostered by Lord Denning among others to apply what became known as the doctrine of fundamental breach to clauses purporting to exclude liability for breaches of contract. In its simplest form the doctrine said that, if a fundamental breach of contract amounting to repudiation was accepted by the innocent party that terminated the contract so that any exclusion clause which might otherwise have operated was destroyed also. The doctrine was buried by *Photo Production Ltd.* v. *Securicor Transport Ltd.*[2] in which it was held that a doctrine of fundamental breach (by virtue of which the termination of a contract brought the contract, and with it, any exclusion clause to an end) was not good law. The question whether and to what extent an exclusion clause was to be applied to any breach of contract was a matter of construction of the contract and normally when the parties were bargaining on equal terms they should be free to apportion risks as they thought fit.

Lord Diplock said (at 850E)

> "Parties are free to agree to whatever exclusion or modification of all types of obligation as they please within the limits that the agreement must retain the legal characteristics of a contract; and must not offend against the equitable rule against penalties ...",

and at 851B,

> "In commercial contracts negotiated between businessmen capable of looking after their own interests and of deciding how risks inherent in the performance of various kinds of contract can be most economically borne (generally by insurance), it is, in my view wrong to place a strained construction upon words in an exclusion clause which are clear and fairly susceptible of one meaning only even after due allowance has been made for the presumption in favour of the implied primary and secondary obligations."

Thus a clear exclusion provision susceptible of only one meaning is capable of being effective according to its terms. The bias of the judicial mind - using "bias" in an entirely uncritical sense - towards rigorous intellectual honesty on the one hand or sympathy for a deserving plaintiff on the other can, of course, produce varying results in practice.

There are statutory limitations in the Section 2 of the Unfair Contract Terms Act 1977 (which applies more widely to consumer contracts and contracts entered into on written standard terms of business) on the extent to which a person can exclude or restrict his liability for negligence. Negligence is defined in Section 1(1) of the Act to include the breach of "any obligation, arising from the express or implied terms of a contract, to take reasonable care to exercise reasonable skill in the performance of the contract". Such exclusion clauses are subject to the "requirement of reasonableness" (see Sections 2(2), 9 and 11 and Schedule 2). The statutory "Guidelines" for application of the reasonableness test include the relative strength of the parties' bargaining positions, a consideration which is perhaps subsumed in the passage from Lord Diplock quoted above. The extent to which Section 2(2) in conjunction with the "Guidelines" may operate to prevent reliance on an otherwise effective clause may be quite limited. In *Photo Production* v. *Securicor*, Lord Wilberforce said at 843C:

> "But since then [the decision in *Suisse Atlantique*[3]] Parliament has taken a hand: it has passed the Unfair Contract Terms Act 1977. This Act applies to consumer contracts and those based on standard terms and

2 [1980] AC 827.
3 [1967] 1 AC 361.

> enables exemption clauses to be applied with regard to what is just and reasonable. It is significant that Parliament refrained from legislating over the whole field of contract. After this Act, in commercial matters generally, when the parties are not of unequal bargaining power, and when risks are normally borne by insurance, not only is the case for judicial intervention undemonstrated, but there is everything to be said, and this seems to have been Parliament's intention, for leaving the parties free to apportion the risks as they think fit and for respecting their decisions."

For an interesting recent case on Section 2(2) of the 1977 Act, see *Harris* v. *Wyre Forest District Council*[4] where a disclaimer was held to negative a surveyor's duty of care so that there was no duty to which Section 2 of the Act could apply. However, some months after this paper was given, the House of Lords reversed this decision.

Statutory Limitation of Actions

Certain straightforward points are worth enumerating:

- The limitation period for claims for breach of simple contracts is six years and runs from the breach.
- The period for contracts under seal is 12 years, so that people wanting to extend potential liabilities should make their contracts under seal.
- Where there is bad building, breaches of contract normally occur at practical completion, but could arguably at least occur earlier when the relevant work is done. Contracts drafted to impose clear obligations arising at completion are desirable if the limitation period is to run its full period from then without complication or uncertainty.
- The limitation period for negligence claims is generally six years but, unlike claims for breach of contract, the period runs from the date when damage occurs. This is subject to the provisions of the Latent Damage Act 1986 which is outside the scope of this discussion. Recent attempts to overcome limitation difficulties by bringing essentially contractual claims as negligence claims may be severely hampered by a number of cases culminating in *D & F Estates* v. *Church Commissioners* (HL 14 July 1988). The clear message now is that the drafter of a contract should firmly resist any idea that deficiencies in the drafting can be cured by the panacea of a claim in negligence.
- The limitation period for an indemnity claim is six or 12 years (depending on whether the relevant agreement to indemnify is under seal or not) and runs from the date when the liability or loss indemnified against is established or incurred (see *R & H Green & Silley Weir Ltd.* v. *British Railways Board*[5]). Thus indemnities are potentially the longest surviving and most effective rights, and I return to this essential point later.
- For contribution claims there is a special two year limitation period normally starting from the date when the liability towards which contribution is sought is determined (see Section 10 of the Limitation Act 1980).

4 [1988] 2 WLR 1173. See also [1988] 2 AllER 514.
5 17 Build LR 94.

- Limitation defences have to be pleaded and a party is not obliged to make such a defence. If the defence is not taken, the court will not entertain it.
- Limitation periods can by agreement be curtailed or extended.

There being nothing in principle to prevent parties to a contract agreeing special contractual limitation periods, clauses providing, for instance, that claims will be barred if they are not notified within a stipulated period are capable of being effective. Since, however, such clauses potentially limit what would otherwise be expected rights or remedies, they will be strictly construed so that:

- The mere stipulation of time periods (without the explicit barring of claims made outside the period) may not be effective to bar the late claim. Notifying the claim in time has to be made a condition precedent to its success.
- Limiting or excluding claims for payment under the contract will not normally limit or exclude parallel claims for damages for breach of it. Many "loss and expense" claims can equally be made as claims for damages. Clause 26.6 of the 1980 Standard JCT Building Contract expressly preserves (as did Clause 24(2) of its 1963 predecessor) such parallel claims. If it is intended to limit or exclude these, precision and clarity are essential.

Indemnities

A contract of indemnity is an agreement by which one party agrees to make good a loss suffered by another. It normally denotes an agreement to undertake an independent obligation to indemnify as opposed to a collateral contract in the nature of a guarantee. Indemnities can cover wide-ranging areas of potential loss such as the consequences of injury to person or property, claims by third parties, losses consequential on the need to remedy defective work and so forth. The classes of loss need to be carefully spelt out, which is why indemnity clauses often, for safety's sake, contain a tedious string of near-synonyms. There can even be indemnities against the consequences of your own negligence (which could be understandable where you are paying the indemnifier to take out insurance or where the indemnifier is an insurer) but, to be effective, such an indemnity needs clear, express words (see, for example, *AMF International Ltd.* v. *Magnet Bowling Ltd.*[6]).

The most significant point, however, is that concerning limitation to which I have already referred. The limitation period for an indemnity claim runs from the date when the liability or loss indemnified against is established or incurred, and thus indemnities are potentially the longest surviving and most effective (or damaging, depending on your point of view) of rights.

Defects Liability Clauses

It is uncontroversial law (but not always appreciated by non-lawyers) that a defects liability provision will not normally operate as a limitation of liability.

6 [1968] 1 WLR 1028.

On the contrary, it extends the contractor's liability by making him liable not only for defective work appearing after completion, but also to do the making good himself. *Hancock* v. *B.W. Brazier (Anerley) Ltd.*[7] is one authority on this point - a case where an express liability on the builder for structural defects discovered within six months of completion did not exclude liability for defects discovered outside that period. It is, of course possible to draft a defects liability clause which does also limit liability, but that can only effectively be achieved by using clear words of explicit exclusion or limitation, and most standard form clauses do not set out to do this.

Liquidated Damages Clauses

Often colloquially referred to as "penalty clauses", that is precisely what they should not be. If the amount of agreed damages is not a genuine pre-estimate of likely loss, it will be held to be an unenforceable penalty (see *Dunlop Pneumatic Tyre Company Ltd.* v. *New Garage and Motor Company Ltd.*[8] in particular at p.86). The temptation to agree excessive sums in terrorem should thus be avoided.

It seems, however, that liquidated damages clauses may operate to limit liability, there being no principle of law that an agreement to pay liquidated damages is unenforceable if the agreed amount is unduly little. There have been varying academic views whether an employer, for instance, faced with a contractor in delay has a choice of operating a liquidated damages clause or ignoring it and claiming general damages in excess of the agreed amount. In principle this question should be a matter of construing the contract to determine whether the clause in question does in truth limit the contractor's liability, and different contracts could produce different answers.

In *Temloc Limited* v. *Errill Properties Limited and Others*[9] a JCT Standard Form of Building Contract 1980 Private Edition Without Quantities provided that, if the contractor failed to complete by the stipulated completion date, he should "pay or allow to the Employer ... a sum calculated at the rate stated in the Appendix as liquidated and ascertained damages". The relevant part of the Appendix under the item "liquidated and ascertained damages" was filled in as "£ nil" and the period over which payment was to be made was left blank. The contractor contended that these provisions meant that the liquidated damages were simply to be £ nil. The Court of Appeal held that the clause and the appendix stating that the sum was to be nil constituted "an exhaustive agreement as to the damages which are or are not to be payable by the contractor in the event of his failure to complete the works on time".

Although *Temloc* had the peculiarity that the stipulated amount was nil, it illustrates the possibility that liquidated damages clauses may be construed to limit the liability of the party in breach. Circumstances may also arise where a clause stipulating the payment of agreed damages for delay becomes inoperable. This most frequently happens where the employer has caused delay but the contract does not provide for an appropriate extension of time

7 [1966] 1 WLR 1317.
8 [1915] AC 79.
9 CA. 29 July 1987.

(see *Peak Construction (Liverpool) Ltd.* v. *McKinney Foundations Ltd*[10]). The employer can then resort to general damages (if he can prove them), but it is unclear whether those general damages could exceed the now defunct liquidated damages. (Cases on this subject are referred to in *Keating on Building Contracts* 4th Edition p.156 and see also the Supplement for that page.) It is thought that, since a party should not benefit from his own breach of contract - and the employer's delaying event will often be a breach - general damages ought not to be recoverable in these circumstances in excess of the former liquidated damages.

Agreeing compensation in advance does not have to be confined to damages for delay. It could extend to other contemplated breaches. Allied clauses are those which undisguisedly limit a party's liability to a quantified or quantifiable sum - as for instance £x or x% of the contract sum. There is nothing inherently objectionable in such provisions, but they need to be drafted with care to anticipate pitfalls arising from imprecision. They will generally be construed against the party relying on them and examples of problems to anticipate are:

(a)to define precisely the classes of breach which the limitation is to cover. If all classes of breach are intended, the use of the word "whatsoever" is more or less obligatory (see *Gillespie Brothers & Co. Ltd.* v. *Roy Bowles Transport Ltd.*[11]) and the express exclusion of liability for the consequences of the party's own negligence is highly desirable (see for example *Canada Steamship Lines Ltd.* v. *The King*[12]).

(b)to be sure that the sum of money to which liability is to be limited is surely quantifiable. If, for instance, it is to be x% of the contract sum, does this mean the contract sum at the outset of the contract, the amount finally payable at the end or something else?

Final Certificate Clauses

Standard Final Certificate Clauses are hybrid in the sense that they limit both the substance of continuing liabilities and the time within which other claims have to be made. Needless to say, the mere provision for something called a "final certificate" will have no limiting effect by itself. Provisions, however, that unless arbitration proceedings are started within a specified period a Final Certificate shall (subject to exceptions) be conclusive as to the sufficiency of the Works and the adequacy of payment can be effective (see for example *P & M Kaye Ltd* v. *Hosier & Dickenson Ltd.*[13] where there was an interesting division as to the extent to which the Final Certificate should be held to be conclusive in the circumstances of that case).

10 [1971] 69 KLGR 1.
11 [1973] 1 QB 400.
12 [1952] AC 192.
13 [1972] 1 WLR 146.

Sub-contractors' Design and Direct Warranties

There is, of course, an enormous number of matters which could be the subject of express inclusion or exclusion as risks or liabilities of one party or the other. Clauses can be drafted providing that the contractor shall be responsible for this or shall not be responsible for that. I choose sub-contractor design as an example which so often causes difficulty unless it is dealt with clearly.

The system of nominating sub-contractors is widely adopted even if it does not have unanimous approval by the theorists. Nominated sub-contractors are often specialists and are frequently expected to undertake elements of the specialist design. A mechanical engineering consultant will produce a specification and drawings showing what he may call the "design intent" and may expect the sub-contractor to work up the detailed design often by means of shop or installation drawings. The production of shop drawings is a process which hovers on the fringe between workmanship and design. Main contractors are habitually responsible for their sub-contractors' workmanship and materials including those of their nominated subcontractors. But most main contractors would not expect to undertake responsibility for any design let alone sub-contractor's design and many standard forms of main contract appear to be drafted on this basis. Yet specifications are often drafted so as to make the main contractor responsible for shop drawings and much confusion has been caused in consequence. The problem is not helped if the contract conditions provide that nothing in the Bills or Specification shall override or modify that which is contained in the conditions (see *Gleeson, MJ (Contractors) Ltd*. v. *Hillingdon*[14] and *English Industrial Estates* v. *Wimpey*[15] and compare and contrast Condition 12(1) of the 1963 JCT Standard Form with Condition 2.2 of the 1980 JCT Standard Form).

The general point which this example illustrates (but does not solve) is the need for foresight and extreme care both in original contract drafting and more especially when amending standard printed forms. Specially agreed provisions will usually be given preference to standard printed ones, but the moral is to leave no one in doubt. Sloppy drafting may be saved, but is not justified, by rules of construction.

Standard forms of direct sub-contractors' warranty are in common use and often include warranties by the sub-contractor to the employer direct that he has exercised or will exercise reasonable skill and care in the sub-contract design (insofar as he has undertaken it), the selection of sub-contract materials and the satisfaction of relevant performance specifications. Although such agreements are in principle capable of being effective, they are often difficult to enforce in factually complicated circumstances. Their possible further effects include:

1. a possible curtailing of what might (in ambiguous cases at least) otherwise be the main contractor's responsibilities;
2. the probable elimination of any direct claim by the employer against the sub-contractor in negligence other than an orthodox *Donoghue* v. *Stevenson*

14 [1970] 215 Estates Gazette 165.
15 [1973] 1 Lloyd's LR 118.

claim for physical impact damage (see *Greater Nottingham Co-operative Society* v. *Cementation Piling and Foundation Ltd.* (*supra*));

3. a correlative need for the employer to undertake certain direct payment obligations to the sub-contractor.

We do not need to go further to see that not only do extensions of this kind have wider ramifications than might at first appear, but that their inclusion tends towards the building of an increasingly unwieldy contractual edifice. We have travelled a long way from the simple contract with which we started. Sophistication and commercial good sense are not always found together.

Tortious Liabilities

Since this is the topic of the moment, I cannot resist mentioning it in closing.

Until recently, there were wide-ranging possibilities of extending contractual liabilities by bringing parallel claims in tort. The principal attraction was that claims in tort have a generally more favourable limitation period than claims for breach of contract. The plaintiffs in *Pirelli* v. *Oscar Faber & Partners*[16] sued their consulting engineers for negligence resulting in damage to a factory chimney which cracked. It was held that the cause of action accrued when the damage came into existence, not when it was discovered or should with reasonable diligence have been discovered. On the facts of that case, the plaintiffs were unsuccessful because it was held that their claim was statute barred. Had their claim been in contract only, limitation would have run from an even earlier date.

The tide which ran in favour of tortious claims has, however, turned and the very recent House of Lords decision of *D & F Estates* v. *Church Commissioners*[17] is but the latest in a series of decisions which have severely limited the scope of negligence claims. It is perhaps too early to judge what the effects of *D & F Estates* may be. Its effects may include that:

(*a*) *Junior Books Ltd.* v. *Veitchi Co. Ltd.*[18] is "unique" and "cannot be regarded as laying down any general principle" - this had been anticipated - but the dissenting speech of Lord Brandon enunciates principles of fundamental importance.

(b) *Anns* v. *Merton London Borough Council*[19] may become quite limited in its application.

(c) The tortious liability of the builder of a dangerously defective structure may only arise if the defect remains hidden until the defective structure causes personal injury or damage to property other than the structure itself. If the defect is discovered before any damage is done, the loss sustained by the owner of the structure, who has to repair or demolish it to avoid a potential source of danger to third parties, would seem to be irrecoverable pure economic loss.

(*d*) "Complex structures" may be different. Damage to one part of the structure may qualify to be treated as damage to "other property".

16 [1983] 2 AC 1.
17 HL 14 July 1988.
18 [1983] 1 AC 520.
19 [1978] AC 728.

(*e*) The equivalent of warranties of quality or fitness for purpose cannot arise other than by contract.
(*f*) Claims for breach of statutory duty may be differently treated.

Two other recent cases should be mentioned in this context - *Simaan General Contracting Company* v. *Pilkington Glass*[20] where Bingham LJ analysed the cases and concluded that, whereas a claim in negligence for economic loss alone was possible (*e.g.* as in *Hedley Byrne & Co. Ltd.* v. *Heller & Partners Ltd.*[21]), a claim for pure economic loss, unaccompanied by physical damage to property of which the plaintiff was owner or to which he could show possessory title, lay only where there was a special relationship which amounted to reliance by the plaintiff on the defendant; and *Greater Nottingham Co-operative Society* v. *Cementation Piling and Foundation Ltd.*[22] where it was held that a direct limited contract was inconsistent with any assumption of responsibility beyond that which had been expressly undertaken. This did not affect normal liability in tort but did negative the existence of the exceptional circumstances needed for liability for economic loss.

It now seems clear that an orthodox *Donoghue* v. *Stevenson* claim will not sustain a claim for pure economic loss. Claims for economic loss may be limited to (*a*) exceptional cases where, in the absence of a contract, a defendant has assumed responsibility *e.g.* for advice and (*b*) claims "truly consequential" upon actual physical injury to person or property (*e.g.* loss of earnings in personal injury claims or as in *Spartan Steel & Alloys Ltd.* v. *Martin & Co. (Contractors) Ltd.*[23]). It remains for debate whether commercial obligations assumed as part of a contractual chain can ever afford members of the chain claims in negligence against those with whom they are not in direct contract; and whether it remains the law that professional people owe their clients parallel obligations both in contract and tort (as *Esso Petroleum Co. Ltd.* v. *Mardon*[24] said they did, but as *Tai Hing Cotton Mill Ltd.* v. *Liu Chong Haing Bank Ltd.*[25] suggests they may not).

This brief and incomplete excursus into the highly complicated and uncertain field of negligence only emphasises that no reliance whatever should now be placed in expressing contractual obligations on the possibility of remedies outside the contract itself. Nor is it at all safe to suppose that any period of limitation other than the contractual period will apply.

20 [1988] 2 WLR 761.
21 [1964] AC 465.
22 CA 23 March 1988.
23 [1973] QB 27.
24 [1976] QB 810.
25 [1986] 1 AC 80.

24 Towards better Contracts - are we chasing our tails?

George Stringer

Synopsis

This paper as delivered at the Conference considers the likely practical opportunities to resolve some recurrent problems of liability, given the constraints on attempting consensus drafting of industry wide standard forms and the realities on the ground with shortages of labour, skills and materials in the marketplace. Practical examples are considered, such as the problems of nominated sub-contracts and the increasingly onerous expectations of consultants through duty of care deeds.

Introduction

This title (which I did not choose but which I happily adopt) is the final paper of this three-day Conference on Construction Contract Policy and the last of Session IV "Special Problems and Extra Contractual Matters".

I hope, therefore, that you, the organisers and my fellow speakers will forgive me if my paper questions the relevancy of many of our deliberations. You, the delegates, should know, however, that none of us who have been invited to give papers have met or discussed generally or seen our fellow contributors' papers so that I hope that our, no doubt differing views, will enliven the discussion following today's papers. The organisers of the Conference could not, however, have foreseen when they decided on the general theme of "Construction Contract Policy" and the specific titles for individual papers how much more important contractual relationship might become following the confirmation of previous judicial trends by the speeches of the House of Lords in *D & F Estates and Others* v. *Wates Limited*.[1]

I follow two and a half days of papers by Her Majesty's Judges, Her Majesty's Counsel and this morning alone two Professors of Law, three Professors having preceded them. I am a practising solicitor, specializing in Construction Law and the problems with which I am faced by my clients are less rarified than many we have debated together during this Conference. My clients, whether they be employers, their professional consultants, main contractors, managing contractors, sub-contractors, specialist or otherwise,

1 [1988] 3 WLR 368.

suppliers and manufacturers, are concerned in the main with the overheated economy in the construction industry generally and in the South-East in particular, the present and future shortage of skilled labour, the ever-extending periods for delivery of basic and fabricated materials, the "threat" of 1992 in terms of competitive labour and the opening of the Channel Tunnel in terms of the sucking in of imports.

In the recent report Building Britain 2001 published in May 1988 by the Centre for Strategic Studies in Construction of the University of Reading, "Building Contracts and Contractual Disputes" was but one of some 18 areas "for action if the building industry is to prosper". Some of these, such as the increasing fragmentation of the industry, the decline in the number of school leavers (and of the forecast rise in the total labour force of 912,000 between now and 1995, 761,000 are expected to be women), the decreasing training and therefore skills, latent defects and after-sales care are of more importance.

Towards better contracts? From whose point of view? All in the industry would say "the clients' of course" but would they mean it and how would such better contracts be achieved? In the building industry, presumably by the Joint Contracts Tribunal. The construction industry is a "cosy" fraternity and cosiness is perhaps nowhere better evidenced than in the production of its Standard Forms of Contract and the bodies of the "great and the good" it has created to monitor, oversee and generate these Standard Forms.

I say "perhaps nowhere better evidenced" because although I do not wish to deliver a polemic in an area overcharged with emotion, I believe the prime example of cosiness in the industry is the adoption and continual promotion of arbitration as the preferred method of dispute resolution and I shall return to this, briefly, when considering the industry's response to the growing demands of those who commission its products.

Any consideration of better forms of contract must proceed from an evaluation of what has been achieved thus far. I read in one of the journals last month that at the request of, I think, a publishing house, convinced, or having been convinced, that none of the present Standard Forms are satisfactory, because amongst other things they are too long, a team of four have been gathered together under the chairmanship of Dr Parris to produce "within months rather than years" a new, short Standard Form. Why? What is wrong with the JCT's Minor Building Works Agreement, or for that matter, despite its unfamiliar format and fashionable addiction to decimalisation, the Intermediate Form of Contract? In my opinion they serve their purpose well.

All of us here are interested in contracts and we and most of the industry's consultative bodies tend to concentrate on the main forms of Contract and the ever changing judicial pronouncements on these forms. In 1987, the United Kingdom construction industry consisted of more than 170,000 firms, 155,000 of which employed fewer than eight people. Many of these are indeed one-person firms. The number of individual holders of 714 Certificates in June 1987 was 400,000. It is true that the firms employing less than eight people accounted for only 27 per cent of total construction output but they are responsible for 44 per cent of all repairs and maintenance work. I suspect the majority, by number of contracts entered into by these firms, amounted at most to a written acceptance of an estimate.

The Joint Contracts Tribunal

My purpose is not to criticise a body of which I was once a Joint Secretary, incidentally just before Ian Duncan Wallace, writing in *The Quantity Surveyor*, delivered this characteristic broad side :

> "In fact the title 'Joint Contracts Tribunal' with its impressive judicial and official overtones, is misleading. It has no official or statutory origin or backing. It is not a tribunal at all in any ordinarily accepted sense of that word. It meets in secret and its affairs are conducted in secret. The local authority connection since 1963 appears in practice to have done nothing, any more than the architects have as 'founder-members' to arrest the remorseless tide of drafting an amendment against the employer's interest."

I simply question whether, on the evidence of the forms it has produced so far, the Tribunal is the body from which we can expect "better contracts". From the clients' point of view I doubt it. Historically the Tribunal consisted of representatives of the RIBA and the then NFBTE from 1931 until 1947 when, by invitation, the RICS nominated quantity surveyor members. Representatives of the then local authority associations joined the Tribunal to help produce, or some would say to lend some credence to, the 1963 Edition which, with all its faults and despite the strenuous efforts of the Tribunal and many of its constituent bodies, remains very popular.

In 1966 the Scottish Building Contracts Committee took what some of our friends north of the border believe was the retrograde step of joining the Tribunal and thus adopting the English system of main contract with nominated and domestic sub-contractors and suppliers. The Scots had a long tradition of direct trades contracting and it is ironic that under the latest "flavour of the year", *i.e.* construction management, direct contracting has become fashionable in England, or at least here in the South-East.

At the same time, CASEC and FASS, representing the specialist, *i.e.* would be nominated sub-contractors, joined the Tribunal.

To help with the 1980 Edition the Association of Consulting Engineers joined the Tribunal.

Until this time the Tribunal remained "cosy". To be nominated by one's constituent body, members have to be sufficiently senior in their profession or company, to have found the time to become reasonably prominent within the constituent body and to devote the time required to attend the meetings of the Tribunal and its sub-committees. Everyone had and still does have a common background, the construction industry professions. The NFBTE and now the BEC were represented in the main by surveying directors of main contractors, the local authorities were represented by their technical officers and occasionally their solicitors and the specialist sub-contractors were represented by engineers or again by surveying directors.

The main area of the industry unrepresented was the mass of non-public authority clients. True, the British Property Federation joined the Tribunal after 1980, but in 1983 published its own Manual of the BPF system and in 1984 joined with the Association of Consultant Architects to publish a joint form of Main Contract.

Private sector clients can be divided into three groups; owners, investors and property developers. The BPF represents investors and property developers but by far the largest group of those who commission buildings, are the owners, whose demands can range from a single house to a major out-of-town shopping centre. Probably the greatest changes in contractual relationships and procedures in the last two or three years have been introduced by private sector clients with sufficient patronage to get their own way. The emergence of the expert client is a fact with which all in the industry are going to have to live, it is a phenomenon which for the first time challenges the cosiness of the industry and this phenomenon, with design and build, is going to influence our industry more in the last decade of the century than any further standard forms.

To Nominate or not to Nominate?

There are many examples of the way in which the Tribunal, with the best will in the world, fails to realize that the industry cannot wait for its forms to catch up. It is quite understandable, the necessity for consensus amongst all its constituent bodies means that it can only act slowly. It is by its nature reactive though its reactions usually run counter to quite strongly expressed judicial criticism.

The Tribunal's devotion to nomination in its main forms of contract is only too apparent. Three cases, all admittedly on the 1963 Edition, have greatly weakened building owners' confidence in a system which can leave them so unprotected.

In the 1952 and 1957 Editions of the Standard Form the owners' interest was weakened by introducing first the main contractor's right to reasonable objection to proposed nomination (even to the eventual nomination of a firm whose name had been given in the main contractor's original tender information) and in 1957, and preserved ever since, the right under Clause 23(g) (now 25.4.7) to an extension of time "by reason of delay on the part of nominated sub-contractors or nominated suppliers which the Contractor has taken all practicable steps to avoid or reduce". In *Jarvis Limited* v. *Westminster City Council* in 1971[2], Lord Salmon said of Clause 23(g) :

> "Paragraph (g) is highly anomalous, it would appear to have been included in this form of contract without any regard to the manifest injustice and indeed, absurdity implicit in it ... it leaves the employers to bear the loss caused by a delay for which they are in no way to blame and allows the party at fault ... to escape from the liability they would otherwise justly have to bear ...".

In *Bickerton* v. *NW Metropolitan Hospital Board* in 1970[3] the House of Lords established that under the 1963 Edition, upon failure of a nominated sub-contractor, the architect must re-nominate and the employer must pay to the main contractor the additional cost of the second nominee's quote. No-one in the industry, or at least those represented on the Tribunal, appeared to think there was anything wrong in such a decision or seek in any way to correct it.

The Government took the decision to heart and to put matters beyond doubt added Clause 38(5) to GC/Wks/1 :

2 [1970] 1 WLR 637.
3 [1970] 1 WLR 607.

> "In the event of the termination of a sub-contract ... the Contractor shall, subject to the consent in writing of the Authority, either select another sub-contractor or supplier ... or himself undertake to complete the execution of that work ... and the Authority shall pay the Contractor the sum which would have been payable to him ... if termination of the said sub-contract had not occurred ...".

By contrast, the Tribunal absorbed the decision in *Bickerton* and instead of reversing it, some ten years later, confirmed its reasonableness in the greatly expanded Clause 35 of JCT 1980. Indeed, to an objective viewer, the whole elaborate machinery envisaged by Clause 35 of JCT 1980, together with NSC/1, NSC/2, 2(a), 3, 4 and 4(a), looks like the tail wagging the dog.

I will leave you to guess the name of the author of the following criticism :

> "In 1980 a totally new system of nomination was introduced in the entirely new JCT/RIBA Contract of that year, distinguished as a whole by a startling degree of incomprehensibility, obscuring almost entirely unchanged policies, and in the special context of nomination, by a bewildering separate code of nomination, the main purpose of which appears to have been to invest the actual nomination procedures with extraordinarily detailed mandatory tripartite intercommunications and notices between architect, main contractor and sub-contractor best calculated to prevent a successful perfected nomination ever taking place at all".

Two further cases, *Percy Bilton Limited* v. *GLC* in 1982[4] and *Fairclough Building Limited* v. *Rhuddlan Borough Council* in 1985[5] finally exhausted the patience of those employers with access to any specialist legal advice.

The then Director of CASEC, writing in *Building* in May 1980 said:

> "Although nomination has never been universally popular, it is still widely used ... in CASEC's eyes the worst development for all parties would be a drift away from nomination caused simply by fear and ignorance ..."

Even more prophetically he commented :

> "CASEC fears a backlash against nomination which could turn its achievements on the JCT into a Pyrrhic victory".

What has happened since 1980? The JCT has produced, in 1984, its Intermediate Form under which the title "nominated" disappears to be replaced by "named". Quite simply this is a rose by another name and has been recognized as such by any half-well advised employer. IFC 84 recognizes a distinction between a sub-contractor named in the original main contract tender documentation and one who is named later in an instruction as to the expenditure of a provisional sum. In the latter case, the main contractor can make a "reasonable objection". Once the named sub-contractor has been appointed, then the sub-contract cannot be terminated without the architect's consent and if such consent is given, the architect can (*a*) re-name, when, following the *Bickerton* principles, the main contractor is to be paid the new increased price and receive an extension of time or (*b*) tell the contractor to do

4 [1982] 1 WLR 794.
5 30 Build LR 26.

the work when the contractor is to be paid as if it was a variation, given an extension of time and direct loss and/or expense or (*c*) omit the work and have it executed by an "artist, tradesman or other", to adopt the old JCT expression, giving rise to claims for both extensions of time and direct loss and/or expense.

True, and adopting the decision in *Fairclough*, if course (*a*), *i.e.* re-naming, is adopted, IFC 84 provides at Clause 3.3.4(a) "there shall be excluded from the price of the second-named sub-contractor any amount included therein for the repair of defects in the work of the first-named sub-contractor". What does that mean? Few employers imagine that having excluded something from one computation, it will not turn up again under another heading.

Geoffrey Cutting's feared "backlash" has not been long in the coming. A number of standard form contracts produced since 1980 and innumerable one-off forms have sought to regain the old principle that the main contractor is responsible for carrying the commercial risk for all his sub-contractors and suppliers.

The Government Form, as we have seen, has been quite uncompromising and GC/Wks/1 Edition 2 has emphasized that in the event of termination against a nominated sub-contractor, the contractor shall either:

> "select another sub-contractor or supplier to undertake or complete the execution of the work ... or himself undertake or complete the execution of that work ... and the authority shall pay to the contractor the sum which would have been payable ... if termination had not occurred ..."

There is, however, an indication that even the Government may be prepared to drop its guard in that the draft GC/Wks/1 Edition 3 issued for consultation purposes also disposes of the title "nominated" in favour of "specified sub-contractor" but does allow the possibility, provided the main contractor has complied with at least five other clauses of the contract and the original sub-contractor is insolvent, that the Government may pay the amount of the claim.

Government, as we have seen, can look after itself and the Tribunal has since 1963 had on it representatives of the local authority associations though in April of this year these associations were recorded as saying :

> "The JCT system of nomination is now held in such low regard that to simply tinker with the commercial risks or procedural aspects would be to fail in the eyes of the construction industry generally".

Both the BPF system and the Association of Consulting Architects forms have sought to return to the original principle that main contractors are responsible for their sub-contractors and suppliers, whether nominated or not. Following the principle of the Government's Contracts and ignoring all the industry approved compromises inherent in JCT 1963, 1980 and IFC 1984, both the ACA and BPF Contracts provide that if a substitute sub-contractor has to be appointed, either at the outset or because of subsequent termination :

> No adjustment shall be made to the Contract Sum (or the Time Schedule) and the Contractor shall not be entitled to claim any damage, loss and/or expense arising out of or in accordance with any of the matters referred to in ..." this Clause, *i.e.* the obligation to select a substitute.

Neither the ACA nor the BPF/ACA forms have yet been widely used mainly, I suspect, because other methods of contracting have become more fashionable, but I have seen many one-offs which seek to eliminate nomination entirely and whatever expressions are used, "selected sub-contractors", "named sub-contractors", "Specified Sub-Contractors", "private sub-contractors" or JCT 1980's splendid introduction of the Dutch Auction under Clause 19, being "never less than 3 persons named in the list ... able and willing to carry out the relevant work". However named, all these are domestic sub-contractors with none of the privileges of direct access to the professional team, directed certification, direct payment in certain circumstances, rights of appeal to the architect on extensions of time, acceptance of sub-contract package practical completion, cessation of responsibility for damage after practical completion, possibility of early release of retention or protection against unfair set-off.

What has been the industry's reaction to the recent explosion of one-off forms and what are becoming standard amendments to Standard Forms? Not surprisingly :

> "Clients' representatives are misusing the IFC 84 Form to avoid the responsibilities of nomination ... the industry needs nomination, pre-tender naming of sub-contractors or detailed designs to price, not an imprecise mixture of the 'three'" - *Building*, 18th March 1988.
>
> "When Clauses 1 - 71 of the ICE Conditions of Contract are incorporated in a Contract they are best incorporated unaltered. The Clauses comprise closely inter-related conditions and any changes made in some may have unforeseen effects on others". - Guidance Note 2B ICE Conditions Standing Joint Committee.

The industry enjoys the status quo and even in a report such as Building 2001 which attempts to look forward to the next century we find;

> "While clients are increasingly demanding more customised contracts, the level of onerous and ad hoc amendment to Standard Forms is confusing to all the parties and tends to generate an adversarial approach which can and does lead to disputes".
> "Meddling with the Standard Forms is unhelpful and leads to disputes".

The Action Plan which concludes Building 2001 lists some 18 actions which are considered to be both essential and urgent. There is a Key Message for each action and in the case of building contracts and contractual disputes the Key Message is:

"Stop meddling with the Standard Forms of Contract".

It took the Joint Contracts Tribunal some 13 years of long and arduous negotiation to produce JCT 1980 reflecting the highest point which nomination has ever achieved. Unfortunately the industry had not waited, the "backlash" foreseen by Geoffrey Cutting occurred and I refer you again to the comments of the local authority association members of the Tribunal quoted above.

The Role of the Architect and Engineer

All the standard forms, JCT, ICE, IEE/IMechE in which the consultative bodies in the industry have invested so much time and money have one feature in common, the dual role of the lead consultant as designer and agent of his client and as the "fair" administrator of the construction contract :

> "The architect's primary professional responsibility is to act as the client's adviser and additionally to administer the building contract fairly between client and contractor" - RIBA Architects Appointment 1982.

> "If in the performance of his services the Consulting Engineer has a discretion exercisable as between the Client and the Contractor, the Consulting Engineer shall exercise his discretion fairly" - Clause 7 ACE Conditions of Engagement."

Contrast this with the preface to the BPF Manual 1983 explaining why the Federation considered a new system was needed :

> "Design consultants, in their training and in their practices, have distanced themselves from contractors in the marketplace. The traditional system, almost inevitably, causes them to administer the contract as if they were umpires independent of the client. Even more, the client has become separated from the contractor apart from paying his bill".

This is neither the time nor the occasion upon which to rehearse the history which led to the present position. Suffice it to say that until the latter years of the last century architects and engineers were often the developer/builders who directly employed teams of tradesmen who, as master builders, interpreted the design concept with great skill. Architects, like their tradesmen, had a thorough knowledge of the two basic materials and crafts, masonry and carpentry which were and remain essential to the construction of buildings.

The 20th century has seen the separation of the design and building processes, in large part engendered by the desire of the professional classes to distinguish themselves from trade. In all professions this has involved the self-imposition of codes of professional conduct which in the case of the construction professions has involved the voluntary acceptance of the role of "fair" administrator/umpire. In turn this has led, quite logically, to the unquestioned acceptance of arbitration as the means of resolving such disputes as remain after the contract administrator has done his best.

Even the BPF System which seeks to remove the responsibility of contract administration from the architect, splits those duties between the "Design Leader", a Client's Representative, a Supervisor, an Adjudicator and ultimately an Arbitrator.

Architects are not really very good at administering contracts. There are some notable exceptions but contract law administration and procedure plays a very small part in their academic training and whilst the solving of design problems is second nature to an architect, they are not at their best in coping with the ever more complex forms of contract which they are required to administer. Engineers are better at it, but then theirs is a much smaller industry by numbers of engineers, and civil engineering contractors and the vast majority of their work comes from the public sector.

In recent years architects, who have in any event relied upon the quantity surveyors for much of their advice about contract law and procedures, have become increasingly concerned about "contract supervision" in that they and their professional indemnity insurers have faced more and larger claims for alleged negligent failure to detect deficiencies in the workmanship of a by now always insolvent contractor. Further, and until very recently, the professions have been faced with liability, apparently unlimited in time and, in tort, to any number of future users, tenants, purchasers, mortgagees and pension fund investors who have later acquired interests in buildings which the professionals had designed.

Recent reversals in the apparently inexorable extension of the class of non-contracting parties to whom the construction professions have been held liable has resulted, in the last 12 months, in the growth of an entirely new contract drafting industry namely the production of Duty of Care Agreements under which, for no extra compensation, architects and engineers are required to acknowledge, under seal, that they owe duties of care to all those that I have instanced above and beyond them to their assignees.

Perhaps the one new Standard Form of Contract to which the professional institutions and their consultative bodies ought to be addressing their urgent attentions should be a series of standard Duty of Care Agreements as those currently being produced or drafted by solicitors who, though familiar with the property world and experienced in conveyancing, know nothing of the construction industry and appear to know nothing of the extent and availability of professional indemnity insurance for the construction professions.

Indeed the proliferation of these documents, which it would be professionally negligent of their originators not to seek, is currently a perfect example of allegedly "better contracts which result in chasing our own tails".

Frequently the draftsman seeks to impose the much stricter standard of care of "fitness for purpose" together with the requirement that the professional firms shall maintain professional indemnity insurance at some arbitrarily chosen figure for anything up to 15 years. Such requirements happily ignore the possibility that the professional firm may not continue for 15 years, may be quite unable to pay ever increasing premiums out of reduced fee income but most important of all, fail to appreciate that professional indemnity insurers give cover for negligent acts, errors and omissions not for breaches of contractual warranties of "fitness for purpose".

Will architects and engineers continue to fulfil the role of umpire? Under the standard form of contracts I think the answer must be yes because it is very much in the interests of main contractors that the architect, who is frequently an innocent abroad, should continue to shoulder this responsibility. Specialist contractors who hope to be nominated and who therefore look to the construction profesions for their introduction to the work will certainly seek to ensure that there is no reduction in the protections and rights of direct access, etc. which they are granted by Clause 35 of JCT 1980 and Clause 59 of the 5th Edition of the ICE Conditions.

Building 2001 forecast that :

> "The building professions are likely to change from large numbers of relatively small practices to the domination of a few very large

> consultancies. Such a development has already occurred over the last 10 years in the financial services sector and it is likely that major financial consultancies will take over many of the more progressive building professionals.".

Whilst it is true that the building professions may become dominated by a few very large consultancies, I have no doubt myself that there will continue to be large numbers of relatively small practices dealing the length and breadth of the country with those relatively unrepresented owners and dealing with the successors to the 155,000 contractors who currently employ less than eight people.

New Forms of Contracting

The publicity given recently to the launching of the JCT Management Contract documentation, which despite its distressing length is to be welcomed, may blind us to the fact that management contracting has been gaining steadily in strength for the last 20 years. It is the logical acceptance of the long term shifts in the structure of the industry such as the growth of specialist sub-contracting and of labour-only sub-contracting, the lack of public finance and new client attitudes to forms of contract and to project financing. In the last five years in the South-East generally and in Docklands and the City in particular, a further refinement has been the division between the developers core and shell and the subsequent purchasers' or tenants' fit-out, the former involving the basic construction, materials and skills and the latter involving ever more sophisticated specialist sub-contracting skills.

Management contracting involves an acceptance that what the better contractors are good at is managing projects, *i.e.* what you don't nominate they will sub-contract any way. The specialist sub-contractors would add as a gloss that what management contractors seem best at managing is sub-contractors' money. Indeed a 1987 analysis of the 1986 financial results of five major construction conglomorates commented :

> "Nevertheless, the basic model of a large U.K. construction group remains. Plenty of house building funded by what is clearly the real benefit of a large contracting business - the generation of cash quickly taken from clients and more slowly given to sub-contractors and suppliers".

Management contracting further recognises the increasing fragmentation of the industry during the last ten years. I have already instanced the huge growth in the number of small construction firms, many of which are specialists, supplying more, if not all, of the design of their work. Further, and despite the long maintained opposition of the unions, labour-only sub-contracting has won the day even if, as we have seen during the last few weeks at the new British Library, it can produce old-fashioned picketing.

I say that I welcome the JCT Management Form, which the Tribunal admits is "low risk", *i.e.* low risk for the management contractor not for the employer or the works contractors. It has, like JCT 1980, been long in gestation and like JCT 1980 may perhaps be too late. Its natural users would be the private sector developers and owners, those who have become expert clients, and they have moved on, or arguably backwards, to construction management.

Such expert clients have also attacked what I discern is the prime example of the cosiness in the construction industry. At the launching of the new JCT Arbitration Rules in July 1988 the Chairman of the Tribunal's speech stated :

> "The building industry and its clients or customers have always favoured resolving disputes by arbitration"

Where is the evidence for this assertion on behalf of clients and customers? How frequently were such clients consulted as to how they would prefer to resolve disputes.

Most construction management agreements and their accompanying documents, including the appointment of the design consultants eschew arbitration and either are silent on the matter or specifically state that disputes are to be resolved in the courts.

Construction management appears to work well on such huge projects as Broadgate and is or will be used for much of the redevelopment of Docklands, Kings Cross/St. Pancras, Paternoster Square and the Holborn Viaduct to Blackfriars redevelopment. The author of a three part series on Broadgate published in Building in April 1987 suggested that "chances are that, in a few years time, United Kingdom construction will be divided into two eras, pre and post-Broadgate" where on Phases 1 - 4 alone over 150 trade contractors have been involved.

The system, which puts each trade contractor into direct contractual relationship with the employer, certainly has its attractions to the specialist firms. Being paid direct by the owner avoids the absolute peril of main contractor insolvency and the constant problem of cash-flow under traditional or even management contracting.

The forms, however, are not simple. There is of course no "standard form" and those used (and constantly refined) are derived from United States precedents. Because of the involvement of the expert client, they are rarely so "low risk" as the JCT or most other management forms. Either within the construction management agreement itself or in a side document, and for an additonal fee, the construction manager is required to assume a responsibility for the workmanship and materials quality of each trade contractor's work. For this and other reasons, the Forms used are not simple nor are they single. Trade contracts are accompanied by warranties for design, frequently couched in the language of "fitness for purpose", together with performance bonds and parent company guarantees required in favour of both the employer and additionally in favour of the construction manager.

When things go well they go very well but if anything slips, the knock-on-effect on parallel and later trade contracts can be considerable and as all such forms permit the construction manager to apply set-off of "bona-fide" assessments, the effect on cash-flow to an allegedly defaulting trade contractor may be catastrophic.

Do management contracting and construction management produce better contracts, as distinct from forms? Owners and trade contractors seem to think so. The approval of a risk-free management contractor can be taken for granted. In that they acknowledge the way in which the building industry is now and will increasingly be organised, these methods, with their variants such as contractor led, designer led, design management and construct, with or without a guaranteed maximum price with savings shared between owner and contractor, will find increasing favour.

These "new fangled" methods of building used to be thought to be alright for the South-East which in 1986/87 attracted 42.4 per cent of the total new construction orders of mainland United Kingdom. They were not thought likely to be used elsewhere. The public sector, which in the past has been the single largest patron of the industry, used to elevate public accountability to such a level that innovation in design and shared commercial risk stood no chance. In the last seven years the public sector share of the market has reduced markedly and will reduce further. Recently the public sector has shown itself to be more flexible and has been prepared to experiment with design and build, management fee arrangements and most obviously in motorway repair contracts, with incentives, based upon performance.

Many building owners, particularly the major retailers who now operate and are building throughout the land, are introducing the methods of development, *i.e.* financing, design and management of construction, with which they experimented and which they have refined in the South-East.

I believe that the future of the industry will lie in management and design and construct forms and that they are better than the older methods enshrined in JCT 1980 which served the industry well when it happened to be organized in that way. They have had their day except, as I remind you, in that vast mass of work undertaken throughout the country by those contractors who employ less than eight people and in particular in the repair and maintenance side of the industry.

Are we chasing our own tails?

Are we chasing our tails and, if I may mix the metaphors, have we spent the last three days fiddling whilst Rome burns?

The South-East of England is today the world's leader in volume of construction. This is producing its own inflation, much greater than that of the industry generally or of the country. It is sucking in skilled contractors and labour from the rest of the United Kingdom and it is causing an increasing shortage of materials and components. It is distorting the industry but it is only a foretaste of what may happen in the future.

During the next five years there will be a dramatic reduction in the number of school leavers and I would remind you, that if the forecast is correct, only 151,000 of these school leavers will be male. Rightly or wrongly, the image of the construction industry has always been male but as these 151,000, even if they were all employable, will be the only pool of new labour available for all industry, commerce, the services, and the professions, how many will the construction industry attract? Clearly far less than it will need to stand still. Building sites are thought to be dirty, cold, wet, windy and unsafe. Although increasing numbers of works packages will be manufactured, fabricated and put together off-site and in factory conditions, the above image of the industry will be very difficult to change in the minds of school leavers.

Two reports were issued in August 1988 which have stressed the concern of the industry. The first a report on future skilled shortages by the National Engineering Construction Employers Association concerned with both onshore and off-shore work estimates that by 1993 the heavy engineering construction industry will suffer a shortfall of 9,000 man years of work, *i.e.* a shortage of 9,000 site manual workers skilled and unskilled during any 12 month period. This may be a somewhat nebulous statistic until it is realized that 33,500 man years are likely to be required and only 24,500 man years is likely to be available. The report concludes that :

> "Even the lowest figure in this range (a minimum shortage of 1,250 man years) would be high enough to set off an inflationary spiral as competition for labour destroyed the controls which the overtime and second tier provisions of the NAECI provide. This inflation and loss of control would, at the full turn of the economic cycle, make the U.K. a less desirable location for investment and cause demand for engineering construction labour to dwindle once more".

Secondly, lest we should think that the problems are all in the South-East, a report on the skill shortage problem in the construction industry in the North-West (in 1986/87 attracting 8.5 per cent of new construction orders) published in August by Network Manchester with the assistance of the BEC, reported shortages of bricklayers, joiners, plasterers, painters, plumbers, scaffolders, sheet metalworkers, stone masons and slaters.

In the 12 month period to December 1988, of 114 construction firms replying to Network Manchester's questionnaire, 68 expected to need more bricklayers, 87 more joiners and 30 to need more plasterers. Whether or not they are able to attract the labour, 65 per cent of the firms expressed themselves as dissatisfied with the standard of skill level among today's craftsmen.

One consequence of the sharply reducing number of school leavers will be a marked increase in the average age of the workforce. In the engineering construction industry the experience of most companies suggests that as employees reach 45 years of age and above, more and more tend to look for employment which does not involve them in working out in the open or on construction sites.

Over the past decade there has been a noticeable reduction in training caused by the down-turn in workload coupled with the increase in self-employment. Very few of the 155,000 firms employing less than 8 persons can afford to train apprentices. Traditionally, training has been based on the tried and test craft skills but the growing area of repair and maintenance requires multi-skill operations and re-training of the older existing workers will be essential.

In the field of materials procurement you will all have read some of the horror stories of recent months. In July one project manager reported that within one month toilet modules and air handling unit lead times had gone from nine to 36 weeks and electrical transformers from 16 to 50 weeks. For facing bricks the waiting period is now up to 6 months and for the cheaper bricks up to 12 months. Lifts are taking between nine and 12 months for delivery.

If we assume that the present boom will continue, then clearly the skills shortage, despite re-training and increased productivity, will become more obvious and the materials shortage, despite greater capital expenditure at home, will remain at best the same. If this assumption is correct then from where will the industry obtain the skilled workers and materials?

Before 1993, when Spanish and Portuguese labour will be freely available, we must expect a large influx of Danish, Dutch and German skilled sub-contractors and skilled labour, particularly in the electrical field. 1993 is also the year forecast for the opening of the Channel Tunnel and if, for example, bricks sell today in Belgium for 110 per 1,000 and after importation sell here for 180 per 1,000, then we should expect that any shortfall in domestic manufacture will readily be made up from the continent of Europe.

To overcome the reluctance for work on open sites, to achieve higher quality from fewer skilled workers and to raise productivity, as much as possible will have to be made off-site, in factory conditions. Prophecies are already coming true. Building 2001, recognizing that an increasing proportion of building work will be in the mechanical and electrical services field, forecast that:

> "Much greater modularisation of components will occur as one-off designing for specific uses is replaced by flexible servicing with short life plug-in components and frequent replacement in mind. Integrated services systems will require service installers with general skills. For example, traditional pipeworking skills will be superseded by fixing skills".

The Managing Director of HOW Engineering Services, interviewed in Building on 22 July of this year, said :

> "We are taking the skills off the site and putting them into factories ... at Broadgate we are sending all our pipework out to factories".

Whilst therefore we have devoted nearly 3 days to a detailed consideration of existing Forms and better Forms for the future, what will such labours avail us if there will be neither the workforce nor the materials and components to achieve the desired product.

25 Developments outside the Terms of Contract

This final session of papers given to the Conference widened the focus of discussion. It turned to a range of issues still bearing upon construction contract policy, but those largely arising alongside or outside the contract itself. The earlier sessions of the Conference had sought improved procedures and practice in the letting, administration and carrying out of construction contracts. The search for sound policies on allocation of risk, project management, and the control of quality, programme and payment, inevitably directed the earlier discussions towards the terms of the construction contract itself and the procedures for its administration. By contrast, the theme of this last session examined how construction contracts operate within a wider context of legal liabilities. The management of risk, quality and money has to provide for the obligations and liabilities imposed by the legal system itself upon the parties to the design and construction process.

The principal rights and obligations of those parties to the construction process are defined by the express terms of their contract - be it a main contract, sub-contract, supply contract, or consultation agreement. How then does the legal system impose additional rights and obligations beyond, or even despite, the express terms of the parties' contractual arrangements? Four principal sources are illuminated in these papers.

- Additional terms which are implied into the contract by judges or by statute (Papers 21, 22);
- Duties of care in the law of tort (all four papers);
- Statutory duties (papers 21, 23);
- Rights arising in the law of restitution, *e.g.* for a quantum meruit, because the parties have not in the event entered into a contractual relationship (Paper 22).

Sources of additional rights and obligations

These sources of additional rights and obligations provide a "default" background or context for the evaluation of a policy for drafting contracts. These would, by default, be the governing sources of law if the parties took no steps at all to express their relationship in legal terms. More usually these sources provide gap fillers in the contract or parallel rights and duties outside it, because the parties leave it open by their drafting for the general law of obligations to supplement their contractual framework. So, largely by default, one or more of the above four categories may bear upon any particular construction dispute.

The default position is in one sense almost bound to be reasonable. It would be odd if the law were consistently to produce allocations of risk that were unreasonable. However, what is reasonable for the generality of circumstances governed by the law of tort or restitution or statute, or by generally implied terms, is likely often to prove inappropriate or unacceptable to the commercial allocation of risks and responsibilities in a particular construction project. Parties involved in design and construction have therefore to consider whether the default position needs to be extended or curtailed. If it should prove that extensions or curtailments of the general law are consistently demanded by significant sectors of the construction industry, then the question arises: should some new standard form(s) of contract be prepared to cover those aspects of the default civil law position which are manifestly (or by experience) inappropriate to construction?

Themes in the papers

The above themes are reflected in the four papers given in this Session under the general heading of "Special Problems and Extra-contractual Matters". They begin with a detailed and broad ranging insight (Paper 21) into the additional liabilities that may attach beyond the expressed terms of the construction contract and into the policies that underly the imposition of such liabilities, with particular emphasis on how they may be managed. Then through a more particular consideration (Paper 22) of rights and liabilities arising by implied terms in contract as well as in the law of restitution and on the contract/tort boundary, we come to a third paper in which there is highlighted (Paper 23) instances by which a variety of drafting devices in construction contracts may extend or curtail what would otherwise be the general liabilities of a party. Finally careful consideration is given (Paper 24) to the likely practical opportunities to resolve some recurrent problems of liability, given the constraints on attempting consensus drafting of industry-wide standard forms and the realities on the ground with shortages of labour, skills and materials in the marketplace.

A recurrent theme in this final session is: how may extra-contractual and implied obligations be effectively managed, and can this be achieved by better contracts?

Management of liability: assuming a stable legal system

The management of liability involves two principal actors. The first actor comprises the parties themselves, with their autonomous contractual and other legal powers; the other principal actor is the legal system. Inevitably there is interaction between the two. However for the parties themselves to be effective in the management of their liabilities it is a pre-requisite that the legal system should offer a reasonable degree of predictability and stability in regard to the obligations which it requires.

In the three main sessions of the Conference which preceded this final session, the focus of the Conference had very much been upon the law of contract, and the ability of the parties under the English legal system to use the law of contract to achieve risk allocation and rights of control which are commercially appropriate to the bargains that they strike. The whole of that discussion, and the attainment of a policy for construction contracts, however, actually proceeds upon two vital assumptions about the law of contract:

The first assumption is that clear and unambiguous contractual provisions agreed between the parties will be treated as binding and enforceable by the courts.

The second assumption is that the many ancillary rules which comprise the law of contract (*e.g.* as to contract formation, interpretation, breach, discharge, damages, assignment, implied terms, etc) will remain relatively stable and unchanged at least for the contemplated period of the performance of the bargain that has been struck.

The reality of shifting judicial trends

The reality demonstrated by these papers is that such assumptions cannot reliably be made. It will be noticed from the papers given in this final session that predictability and stability have been markedly absent as characteristics of the law of tort in the 1970's and 1980's. And a false sense of security may be engendered by the contrast that in that particular period the law of contract has appeared remarkably quiescent and stable. For, it was not always so in the law of contract. The preceding two decades, the 1950's and the 1960's, witnessed similar judicial creativity and interventionism (with the pendulum of liability imposition swinging back and forth) in regard to the law of contract, much as more recently has been true of tortious negligence. For example, the courts invented and used to great effect the instrumental doctrine of fundamental breach to strike down exemption or limitation clauses of which they disapproved (a doctrine described in Paper 23); judges were singularly creative in inventing terms to be implied into contracts and were even prepared to imply the whole contract (as Paper 21 explains). Express oral warranties came readily to be regarded as automatically overriding printed or other standard terms within a contract even if the latter were clear and apparently intended to prevent any such result. The retail finance industry in particular found much of the risk allocation in its standard forms of contract overridden by judicial activism until Parliament put in place its statutory controls by the Unfair Contract Terms Act 1977. (The provisions of that Act are treated in Papers 21 and 22).

Legislative intervention

This last point illustrates another feature which has distorted the assumptions of stability and predictability. For, throughout this whole post-war period of four decades private law in England has increasingly been the subject of legislative intervention. Few instances of that intervention may be applauded for their clarity of drafting or achievement of a coherent policy. One exception stands out: the Defective Premises Act 1972 is a model of good drafting, at least when compared with the complex obscurity which besets most of the other principal pieces of legislation in this context, *e.g.* the Unfair Contract Terms Act 1977 and the Latent Damage Act 1986. Papers 21 and 23 seek to clarify these sources of new law, which much more than any standard form of construction contract deserve the label "farago of obscurity"[1]. The curious form of implementation of the European Product Liability Directive in the United Kingdom by the Consumer Protection Act 1987 is also examined in Paper 21.

Tortious negligence and economic loss.

Far above all other concerns for the construction industry has, however, been the impact upon contractual allocations of risk of the swinging pendulum of tortious negligence and economic loss. The importance of the subject speaks for itself: all four of these papers emphasise how the potentially wide implications of *Junior Books* v. *Veitchi*[2] were reversed by the trend of cases culminating in *D& F Estates* v. *Church Commissioners*[3]. Paper 21 examines the development in depth and detail, summing up the position thus:

> "... quality and fitness for purpose obligations would unarguably be the exclusive province of contract law were it not for a remarkable expansion in tortious liability for negligence in the decade or so from the mid-1970's to the mid-1980's. For a while, it appeared that the mere failure of a product to perform as well as the user reasonably expected could be redressed by a claim framed in tort. Appellate court decisions in the late 1980's however suggest a return to the traditional view that users who want rights to a certain level of quality, fitness for purpose, or freedom from defects in goods and services (which are not otherwise dangerous or damaging) must make their contract to that effect with whomsoever they wish to make responsible."

Paper 23 puts the point in this way: the drafters of contracts should resist any idea that the deficiencies of drafting can be cured by the panacea of a claim in negligence.

Beyond gap-filling to parallel obligations in two-party relationships

It will be seen from these papers that important though implied terms may be (see Papers 21 and 23) the general law has supplemented construction contracts not just by what the Americans call "gap fillers". There is a more wide-ranging legal issue of concern to construction. How far will rights and obligations in the general law subsist in parallel with the parties' contractual framework?

1 See *Peak* v. *McKinney* (1969) LGR 1.
2 [1983] AC 520.
3 [1988] 3 WLR 368.

Tortious liability for negligent mistatement (at least before the general retrenchment of the late 1980's) might even be asserted in respect of pre-contract negotiations (as Paper 22 speculates in respect of the *Holman* v. *Delta Timber* case[4]).

Paper 23 focusses on a number of examples: eg, how liabilities subsist despite so-called "defects liability period" clauses (the label "Defects Correction Period" in ICE Minor Works is so much better); how claims for breach may subsist in parallel to claims pursuant to express terms in the contract (a point that could be developed with great significance after *Crouch* v. *NRHA*[5] when comparing the powers of courts and arbitrators); how express provisions on damages for delay may be treated as an exhaustive definition of the parties' rights; and, how (as a result of the typically complex contract documentation in the construction industry) attempts to delimit obligations (*e.g.* as to design) may fail through inconsistent implications arising from the documents.

A vital but as yet unresolved problem in regard to parallel obligations is addressed by Papers 21 and 23: will the courts be less willing after the *Tai Hing*[6] decision in the Privy Council (and the implications of the *Cementation* case[7]) to allow tortious duties to be found between parties already in a contractual relationship. In Paper 22 the analysis of *Tai Hing* compared with *Pirelli* points to a possible underlying policy.

Obligations owed parallel to third parties: issues unresolved after D & F

Of fundamental importance to this session of the conference were the implications of the House of Lords decision in *D & F Estates* v. *Church Commissioners*[8]. Papers 21 and 23 stress the difficult issues left unresolved by the decision, especially: the scope of the "other property" and "complex structure" notions; whether the cost of averting danger is recoverable; what remains of *Anns* v. *Merton LBC*[9]; and, what scope there may be for actions framed in terms of breach of statutory duty for failure to comply with the Building Regulations.

Perhaps of greatest importance to the construction industry is the concern brought home in Papers 21 and 24: are consultant professionals (with such professional indemnity insurance as they can reasonably get) more at risk of third party negligence liability through the *Hedley Byrne* reliance principle preserved by *D & F?* Paper 24 points to the factors behind the differentiation of professional activities and the emerging pressures on professionals' duties of care.

An ultimate answer to parallel obligations is the re-emphasis of the contractual framework of allocation of risk.

This Conference was held in a period of significant transition in the general civil law. We have seen that the papers identify trends back from expansion of

4 1972 NZLR 1081.
5 [1984] 1 QB 644.
6 [1986] AC 80.
7 [1988] 3 WLR 396.
8 [1988] 3 WLR 368.
9 [1978] AC 728.

tort to re-emphasis of the contractual framework of risk. Clues are seen in such cases as those mentioned in Paper 23 *Temloc v. Errill*[10] and *Cementation* v. *Greater Notts Co-op*[11].

Soon after the Conference, two Court of Appeal decisions of considerable significance not only to the construction industry (from which both cases came) but also to the general law of tortious negligence, emphasized still more explicitly the determinative effect of the parties contractual framework in limiting parallel exposure to tortious liability: see *Pacific Associates* v. *Baxter*[12] and *Norwich CC* v. *Harvey*[13]

What policy response should address extra contractual factors?

In introducing Paper 21, Professor Capper argued strongly for clarity by effective legislation: a Defective Commercial Premises Act was called for. As for the alternative of more standard form drafting, Mr Stringer questioned cogently whether the issues could realistically be addressed and the problems ameliorated thereby: "stop messing about with the standard forms" was a cry being heard from the industry. But Mr Stringer did urge that consensus drafting was needed in one new form. There was need for a series of standard Duty of Care Agreements.

The nub of this session of the Conference is that the industry itself is beset by a market response to the legal system's attempt to manage tortious liability. The parties themselves as the other actor on the stage of liability management have become locked in a new but unproductive industry: the spiralling refinement of a multitude of contractual instruments intended, apparently, to fill the gap left by diminishing rights in tort: collectively they are labelled collateral warranties or duty of care deeds.

The doctrine of privity and defects of quality

There is a symmetry through the four papers comprising this last session of the Conference. It is expressed in a concern underlying all the papers that defects claims in the construction industry are more often about defects of quality rather than dangerous defects. Yet the doctrine of privity in English contract law, after the decision in *D & F Estates*, precludes third party claims in respect of the economic losses sustained in remedying defects of quality. *D & F* has halted the tide of bringing essentially contractual claims as negligence claims. The dominance of these themes, culminating in Paper 24, is exemplified by the concern of all the papers with the subject of nominated sub-contractors and the implications of *Junior Books* v. *Veitchi*[14].

10 39 BLR 30.
11 [1988] 3 WLR 396.
12 [1989] 2 AllER 159.
13 [1989] 1 AllER 1180.
14 [1983] AC 520.

One solution: channelling the risks

The realities of the market-place may themselves solve some of the legal problems presented in these papers. Paper 24 in conclusion points to developments in contractual practice which may also more effectively channel the legal risks. For, as Paper 21 points out, much of the present difficulty flows from a tradition of disparate lines of responsibility. So, Paper 24's predicted growth in Design and Construct and in Management contracting may have the side-effect of a better management of liability issues, though he is careful to differentiate major new building projects from small contractors operating particularly in repair and maintenance

The Present Alternative: Collateral Warranties and Duty of Care deeds

In recent years, the contract/tort boundary, focussed in these four papers, has been explored and redrawn through efforts to overcome Limitation Act defences that would otherwise statute-bar the claims (see *e.g.* Papers 21 and 23). As lines of suit in tort have been denied by the judges, they are being replaced by direct contractual lines of suit in the form of collateral warranties and duty of care deeds. These will raise new problems of definition in relation to limitation periods. But more significant will be the focus on new points of legal uncertainty: especially the relatively uncharted legal waters of the principles governing assignment (or transferability) of warranties (a topic suggested in Paper 22). The law on remoteness of damage in contract is likely to experience considerable refinement in the litigation that is bound to follow upon the testing of these contractual devices to preserve third parties' quality rights in the face of the doctrine of privity.

Part VI

Conclusions

Review and conference conclusions 26

Review of proceedings

Construction contracts have existed in their present form for the past 100 years or so. For most of this time they have been known to contain numerous difficulties and pitfalls which have periodically generated huge and costly disputes. The pace of development, both in the production of standard forms of contract and in the construction industry at large has accelerated markedly in recent years. That development cannot be regarded as likely to lead to any reduction in the extent of problems experienced in construction and in construction contracts in particular. The reverse is probably the case: the proliferation and increasing complexity of standard forms is generating larger, more complex and more costly disputes which ultimately may sap the vitality of the industry itself.

The aim of this Conference has been to examine policy for change. It was suggested at the outset, and the papers and debate have borne this out, that there presently exists no policy for change, although it is universally accepted that change is occurring and will continue to occur. It was suggested in the keynote speech of Sir Nicholas Lyell that an appropriate outcome for the Conference would be to embark on drafting a new form of contract. Other speakers have called for existing forms to be torn up and replaced by a new universally accepted form of contract. But this is not an option. Despite the recommendations of the Banwell committee in 1964, the proliferation of standard forms remains and will undoubtedly continue, and to draft another contract, whatever its aspirations and merits, is simply to add another form to the existing collection.

An appropriate outcome of this Conference is to present the broad conclusions which have been reached, carrying with them the opinion of those who contributed papers and of those who participated in the debate. Such conclusions may form a useful basis for determining the policy to be applied in any new standard form to be produced and in amendments to the existing standard forms. It would be unwarranted to say that the conclusions reached, which were by no means unanimous in all cases, must be adopted in any new drafting exercise. The matters debated should, however, be regarded as matters on which policy decisions need to be made; and those embarking on drafting standard forms in future should satisfy themselves that they are justified in adopting a policy which is at variance with the conclusions reached in the debates here.

A further reason for not embarking on the drafting of yet another standard form of contract is that no single form can now cover the whole field of construction work, in its many forms and varieties. Traditionally, standard forms for building and civil engineering (as well as for other forms of construction such as process plant) have evolved along different lines, often developed by different groups of professionals, and used almost exclusively in their own particular fields. One of the views repeatedly expressed during the Conference was that this proliferation was unnecessary and avoidable. One of the factors which originally led to the development of separate forms was the major differences that existed in the technical documentation relating to different areas of construction. Such differences are reconcilable and standardisation is a real possibility. Developments within the European Community have shown that this is so. Given such harmonization, there is no reason why standardization between different types of construction (and certainly between building and civil engineering) cannot be achieved.

However, there are now in existence much more important areas of division in which standardisation is undesirable as well as impracticable. This division relates to the variety of contract systems now available for construction work. At one extreme there is the traditional system whereby the whole of the physical work is undertaken by a main contractor, the employer providing the design through a separately employed professional. This is the system that has persisted for most of the last century. However, other systems now exist in which the provision of these services is arranged quite differently. These other systems include design and build contracts (in which the main contractor undertakes both design and construction), management contracts (in which the main contractor undertakes responsibilities of management rather than primary responsibility for the work) and project management (where the work is divided up into a series of separate packages). One indicator of the absence of policy in drawing up contracts for these different systems is the curious practice of using traditional standard forms as the model, and apparently making only the minimum amendments necessary to permit the new system to operate at all. The result has often been confusion about the true role of the parties involved in the new systems. More work is needed before acceptable standard forms can be drafted in these new areas, and the systems themselves are still undergoing changes. These are further reasons why a universal standard form of contract is not a practical possibility.

During the closing session of the Conference the debate widened to consider the question of future action on construction contracts arising out of the Conference. The view was strongly expressed that, whether or not new drafting was feasible, large commercial owners and public bodies could look after their own interests, and this was a further reason for not drafting a standard form of general application. However, there was a case for putting forward a new contract for "consumer" use, this being an area where the owners or clients had no influence and little choice, and where unplanned expenditure could be of relatively large significance. It is indeed curious that no such form presently exists in this field. It represents a large volume of construction work, although individual contracts will never be large enough to generate serious professional attention. There exist a number of statutory provisions[1] regulating the performance of such contracts. But there are many problems which can arise even with the comparatively modest scale of such work, and the interests of the parties involved would undoubtedly be served by having available a suitable standard form. This is a field in which the conclusions of this Conference may be aptly expressed. Accordingly, a standard form has been drawn up incorporating the opinions and debate of the Conference and the form is offered for use either by individuals or by any professional or trade body that wishes to adopt it. The form is contained at the end of this paper, accompanied by a brief commentary.

It has also been suggested that, in lieu of drafting a full construction contract, the Centre should consider drafting from time to time a series of model clauses with guidance notes, for consideration by persons involved in drafting contracts. This possibility will be kept under review.

This paper now turns to the conclusions to be drawn from the conference and the debate. They are set out in the form of recommendations for those embarking on the drafting or amendment of standard forms of construction contract.

Conclusions from the papers and debate

General Conclusions

Construction contracts must be workable and understandable by those who are to work with them. Over-sophistication and excessive length are self-defeating, if those whose primary object is to carry out the works are unable readily to understand the true effect of the contract.

The object to any contract should be to deal fairly with the interests of both parties, the terms of the contract being such as to avoid giving either party the opportunity to take unfair advantage of the other. Contracts should not encourage adversarial attitudes. The outcome of any contract should reflect the reasonable expectation of both parties. There should be mechanisms to ensure that the real risks are made apparent.

Contracts should define as clearly as possible the roles and responsibilities of the direct parties to the contract and also of any other parties who are given powers or duties under the contract, so that those parties and also the direct parties to the contract know where they stand.

Risks

All construction work involves risk. Many existing contracts approach the subject of risk in an obscure or oblique fashion, and there is no good reason for this. For example, risks are often dealt with purely in terms of describing claims that are available in particular circumstances. It is preferable to set out the risks which can be foreseen and to state plainly how they are apportioned

1 Defective Premises Act 1972; Supply of Goods and Services Act 1982.

between the parties. Risks need not be placed wholly on one party or the other; they may be shared in any manner that may be decided (for example, the contractor might accept half the risk of unforeseen ground conditions, so that he would recover half his additional cost).

The placing of risks should be reasonably consistent with the interest of the party in question in the work. It is usually inappropriate to place a large risk on a party who has little financial interest in the contract or in the particular risk.

Generally, each party should be given an incentive to avoid or reduce the incidence of risks. It is more efficient for a particular risk to be borne by the party who has the opportunity to control or reduce that risk. For example, it is usually the employer who has the opportunity of reducing the risk of unforeseen ground conditions, by carrying out further investigations of the site.

The contract should provide for all relevant risks, so as to avoid the incidence of unforeseen risk. Risks should be identified and, where they are to be borne by the contractor, the opportunity should be given to price the risk. Risks should be identified in broad, rather than narrow and detailed categories. Neither party should, in principle, accept a risk which amounts to a gamble. Large and uncontrollable risks should be covered by insurance, the cost of which would be provided for under the contract.

Where doubt exists as to the acceptability of particular risks, contractors may be invited to qualify their tender in regard to specific matters. In relation to risks being undertaken by the contractor, there should be a general duty on the employer to disclose information reasonably within his knowledge which is material to such risks.

Liabilities

The employer or client is entitled, generally, to be provided with a product that will conform to quality and fitness requirements, irrespective of fault. The employer must, however, be prepared to pay the proper cost, including the cost of cover against default. Generally, legal liability should be borne by those having sufficient interest and control of the relevant activities. The contract should identify as clearly as possible the liabilities being undertaken by all parties involved.

Design

If design services are to be provided by separately employed consultants, the employer should be conscious of the possible effects of seeking to reduce design costs. Statistically, design faults are more significant than other causes of defects. Design cost reduction can lead to over-conservative designs. It is preferable, if tenders were to be obtained for design work, for tenderers to specify their approach, so that the client knows what he is paying for.

In regard to the provision of design data, the extent of information provided at contract stage is frequently insufficient. Design discipline needs to be introduced, for example, by the provision of a certificate from the designer that the information provided is sufficient for tender purposes. The contractor has a right to expect full or sufficient information and the client cannot rely on tenderers to point out any such deficiency.

Management

The quality and quantity of management provided is crucial, whether under traditional forms of contract or under management contracts. The purpose of management is to ensure that effort is directed into the work being carried out, and not into conflict and disputes.

There is a conspicuous lack of adequate definition of management, both under construction contracts and under management agreements. Management needs to be defined, either in terms of the input to be provided or in terms of the performance to be achieved (or both). The objects of management should also be set out. Workable sanctions need to be provided to ensure that these obligations are complied with.

Where management is to be provided by contractors, the tasks to be undertaken need to be defined. Where management is being undertaken by an agent appointed by the client, consideration needs to be given to possible conflict between the management function and the independent or adjudication function of the agent.

Remedies and Sanctions

The contract should provide effective and efficient remedies against defects. Where Quality Assurance is employed, its effect should be recognized as being dependent upon the degree of enforcement. Guaranteed self-regulation is likely to be more effective than external regulation where enforcement cannot be guaranteed.

Effective sanctions against non-performance must include the ability to bring effective claims against all potentially liable parties. Certificates and other contractual devices which limit or exclude liability are generally unnecessary and undesirable.

So-called "defects liability clauses" should not be given undue prominence. They should be seen for what they are: an opportunity to the contractor to remedy his own breach of contract, and thereby to limit his liability. If something other than this is required, for example, genuine maintenance, a new type of clause should be drafted.

Supervision and Control

Partial supervision (for example by architects who do not provide regular supervision) is undesirable as a sole means of control. Alternatives to full time supervision should be considered. These include self-regulation by contractors, and the greater involvement of properly qualified clerks of works.

Any provisions relating to supervision should not remove the contractor's overall responsibility for the quality of the product. The supervisor should, however, have a discretion to sanction a departure from the contract, if the employer's interests were reasonably safeguarded.

Certification and Adjudication

Under traditional contracts, there is no reason why these functions cannot be performed by the employer's agent who is also providing design services. However, a distinction should be drawn where the agent undertakes a management role, where this may be inconsistent with acting independently. Any such management role must be clearly spelled out so as to highlight any possible inconsistency. In principle, no one should give decisions or adjudicate on matters in which they have an interest.

Where adjudication or settlement of disputes on an interim basis is necessary, and cannot be performed by the employer's agent, consideration should be given to providing for an adjudicator to be brought in to make a temporary decision, binding until completion. It is usually preferable for the adjudicator to be selected specially, and not appointed at the outset.

Payment Provisions

The contract should clarify the status of Bills of Quantities. If they are to be used for the purpose of pricing only, the employer should take responsibility for errors, for example, by giving a warranty that the Bills had been prepared with reasonable care.

Generally, a full and mutual disclosure of information is considered desirable, provided that adequate confidentiality can be maintained. The contractor should give a breakdown of his rates, and there should be no objection in principle to a disclosed loading of prices, for a legitimate purpose, such as covering against foreseen risks.

The pricing of extras should be dealt with in a flexible manner, giving alternative means of valuation, including the provision for quoting an all-inclusive price.

The use of stage payments, linked to progress rather than valuation, is a possible means of regulating the contractor's performance; but this poses difficulties which need to be overcome in drafting. The contract ought to spell out the employer's rights of set-off. Interest should be payable at a commercial rate on sums withheld, whether under a bona fide dispute or otherwise.

Claims

Provisions for additional payment should be specific and well-defined; and payment on vague or arbitrary grounds should not be included. Contracts should not permit additional payments arising out of the contractor's default. Where variations arise, the contract should make clear whether the valuation of those variations is to be inclusive of all additional cost.

In regard to claims generally, it should be possible to prefix certain items of cost, but it is generally unsatisfactory to attempt to fix the value of claims in advance. Regular reports on cost projections should be provided under the contract by the contractor. Notice provisions should be directed to ensuring the provision of timely information and warning the employer of additional cost. Notice provisions ought not to rule out genuine claims.

Time provisions

If fixed time limits are to be applied, machinery has to be incorporated to provide for extensions of time. Liquidated damages clauses are often difficult to operate in practice, and do not provide an effective means of regulating performance by the contractor. Alternatives which may be considered include bonus payments, on a sliding scale. Further, the contract should require performance with due diligence and expedition, which can give rise to a claim for damages in appropriate circumstances.

Better use can be made of programming technology. There are dangers in incorporating programmes into contracts, but the status and use of programmes can be developed much further. Regular reports on progress and delays should be required contractually; and these could be incorporated regularly into an updated programme in order to provide mutually accepted data regarding delays. Programming should be regarded as a key management tool of equal value to the contractor and the employer.

Pre-contract planning was also important, particularly in management contracts. Where delays occur and extensions are granted, the employer should have the option to order acceleration, and thereby to "buy back" lost time.

Disputes

The existing disputes mechanisms under contracts are grossly unsatisfactory in two respects. First, there is rarely adequate machinery to permit all potential parties to be brought before the same tribunal, whether in arbitration or in court. Secondly, the machinery for dealing with disputes frequently leads to procedures which are far too long and costly.

Conciliation is one alternative that should be considered. Consideration should also be given to limiting the matters that may be disputed under the contract. Where such provision is to be made, appropriate machinery is needed to obtain the decisions which are to be binding. The contract itself, however, ought to encourage the parties to seek to avoid both disputes and their consequences.

General conclusions

The companies and groups which make up the construction industry in the United Kingdom are becoming larger individually but correspondingly fewer in number. The role of the construction industry abroad is a matter of growing importance, particularly in relation to the European Community, which represents about one quarter of the total of the world's construction market. The influence of United Kingdom systems and forms of contract in particular are an important element in the performance of the United Kingdom construction industry abroad.

Within the United Kingdom, contract law and contracts are of increasing importance in the light of the decreasing role of tort. It remains unsatisfactory that there should be significant gaps in construction contracts, to be filled by implied terms, necessarily involving a degree of uncertainty. Furthermore, reliance on the accidents of litigation to resolve doubt and uncertainties under construction contracts is quite unacceptable. It is a matter for the policymakers and the draftsmen to decide what the contracts should contain, and then to produce clear and concise documents to put their decisions into effect.

The Consumer Construction Contract

The simple form of contract which follows embodies many of the principles debated at the conference, albeit applied to small-scale works. The form is offered for use by individual clients or for adoption by any professional or trade body, subject to acknowledgment.

Terms of Agreement between ______ (the client) and ______ (the contractor).

The Contractor having given a quotation or estimate which is dated ______ (or which is attached to this contract) and the client wishing to have carried out the work quoted or estimated for, the parties now agree as follows.

1. The Work to be Done
The contractor will carry out the work contained in the contractor's quotation or estimate and also any other work necessary to make the finished job reasonably fit for its purpose.

2. Details and Instructions
The contractor acknowledges that:
(a) he understands the nature of the work to be done and the purpose for which it is required;
(b) he will supply any further designs or details that may be needed;
(c) he can complete the work to be done without further instructions from the client.

3. Changes
Neither the client nor anyone else has authority to instruct a change in or addition to the work to be done. The work in this contract may be varied only if the parties agree in writing and also agree the change to be made in the price.

4. Time
The contractor must begin the work promptly, carry it out diligently and continuously (unless inappropriate to the work) and complete it within a reasonable period of time.

5. Undertaking
The contractor undertakes that all the work that he does will be performed:
(a) to a good standard of workmanship;
(b) using materials of good quality, and which are new unless stated otherwise in the quotation or estimate;
(c) so that the finished job will be reasonably fit for its purpose.

6. Payment

The client will pay to the contractor for the work the sum(s) of money quoted or estimated by the contractor which shall be regarded as fixed. The money is to be paid as follows:

(a) the contractor shall be paid the fixed installments at the stages set out below:

Sum	Stage of work
__________	_________________________
__________	_________________________
__________	_________________________

(b) at completion if the client reasonably thinks that he cannot tell whether the finished job is fit for its purpose without waiting, he may retain out of the final installment 5% of the total sum(s) payable for up to six weeks.

7. Risks

(*a*) Until the job is finished, all new and/or altered works are to be at the risk of the contractor and he shall keep them fully insured against all perils that are usually insurable by contractors. The contractor's tools, plant and unfixed materials are to be at his risk.

(*b*) All existing work and/or buildings are to be at the risk of the client and he shall keep them fully insured against all perils that are usually insurable by building owners.

(*c*) The contractor is to be responsible for and insure against claims brought by third parties arising out of the work.

8. Contract

This document contains the terms agreed between the parties. It is not to be varied except by a later document signed by the parties.

SIGNED by the client ....

SIGNED by the contractor ....

Notes on the form

This form represents the simplest and most rudimentary form of construction, which still gives rise to potential difficulties about precisely the same matters as lead to major disputes in large projects, namely, time, price and quality. Various aspects of consumer contracts are covered by statutory provisions[2] as well as the common law[3]. The most recent statutory intervention even restricts the enforcement of arbitration clauses[4]. However, these matters still leave the consumer substantially exposed in many respects where the only appropriate protection is a clear and preferably simple contract.

2 See reference 1.
3 *Hancock* v. *Brazier (Anerley)* Ltd. [1966] 1 WLR 1317.
4 Consumer Arbitration Agreements Act 1988.

The form set out is intended to be suitable for minor construction works being undertaken for private clients. The potential complications have been kept to an absolute minimum so that, for example, no provision is made for the intervention of a professional adviser. It is assumed that a private client has obtained a quotation or estimate and wishes to proceed on this basis alone. Even on this simplified basis, complications may arise. The following notes are intended to explain the drafting rather than the detailed working of the clauses.

Clause 1 : The work to be done

The problem which frequently arises, even with the benefit of professional advice, is that the work quoted for turns out to be insufficient to achieve the object intended. Where it has been left to the contractor to draw up the quotation or estimate, it is reasonable to expect him to take the risk that other work turns out to be necessary. A simple example of this would be the renewal of a roof. The contractor may quote for renewing the tiles or slates and felt, but the whole purpose may be defeated if (for example) the battens or other parts of the roof structure are not also renewed. The contractor under this form is obliged to carry out all such work as is necessary.

Clause 2 : Details and Instructions

In the absence of professional advice and direction, it is appropriate for the client to rely on the contractor himself to supply any missing details and to take the risk of any misunderstanding concerning the nature or purpose of the work.

Clause 3 : Changes

Disputes about changes are a most frequent source of dispute. Clients invariably underestimate the effect of changes on a contractor. This form requires the parties to fix the work at the outset. It may then be changed only by changing the contract, by a further agreement in writing which must also embody the agreed change to the price.

Clause 4 : Time

This in part repeats obligations provided under statutes, but also obliges the contractor to work diligently and continuously. These additional provisions are important in that they may give rise to a claim for damages in appropriate circumstances.

Clause 5 : Undertaking

These obligations also follow statutory and common law precedents[6]. There is, however, advantage in having such provisions written down and signed as the parties may not know the law. This clause, together with Clause 1, makes clear that both the original work and any other work found to be necessary, must be done to the same standard.

Clause 6 :The Price

This clause deals with three matters. First, the sums quoted or estimated are to be regarded as fixed, which is not always clear from contractors' quotations. Secondly, provision is made for stage or installment payments, which are to be specified in advance. Fixed payments can be of benefit in larger contracts as an alternative to measurement. Where proper valuation is not an option, it remains important that the contractor should be paid fairly, but not over-paid. The installments should correspond approximately with the size of the work-stages to which they relate, while reserving a reasonably substantial sum as an incentive to complete the work.

Thirdly, a simple provision is built in to give the client the possibility of holding a retention for a limited period of time. Where work is obviously finished and its quality is readily apparent, for example, simple maintenance or decorating, it may be inappropriate to hold any retention. Conversely, where work needs to be put to the test, for example, a renewed or repaired roof needs to be tested in wet weather, it may be appropriate to impose a retention.

Clause 7 : Risks

These clauses can be exceedingly long and complex, and simple contracts often omit any provision, leaving it a matter of doubt who is responsible for what, and a matter of chance what insurance is available. This simple clause follows standard practice by requiring each party to take responsibility for and insure those elements in which they have an immediate interest.

Clause 8 : Contract

This provision aims simply to prevent the contract being overriden by any terms contained in previous correspondence or documentation. In effect, the contractor's quotation or estimate will be incorporated so far as it describes the work and fixes a price, but not otherwise.

General Note

It will be noted that even with this simple form of contract, serious disputes are possible. For example, if it is found that additional work is needed to make

6 See references [1] and [3].

the job reasonably fit for its purpose, there may be differences as to the extent or nature of the additional work to be done. There are also many areas of possible dispute about the quality of the finished job and about the time taken: a contract to complete within a reasonable period of time necessarily involves the possibility of different interpretation by the parties.

These illustrations are a microcosm of the types of dispute which typically arise in major construction projects. Provision for and avoidance of disputes is a matter of balance between drafting precision and clarity or simplicity of language. This short form of contract illustrates one type of balance. There are many others.

The consumer form of contract seeks also to illustrate the possibilities of adopting simple direct drafting. Construction contracts usually adopt more legalistic language. There is no good reason for this, and the effect is often to create obscurity or even uncertainty behind the guise of legal precision. Direct simple language is always to be preferred provided that reasonable precision can be achieved.

Future Action

This Conference has started a debate which has led to a range of interim conclusions. Its initial aim was to examine policy for change and development in construction contracts. This Centre intends to keep under review such changes and developments, when they occur with the aim of:

(1) Identifying and acknowledging improvements in construction contract, practice;

(2) Examining the policy, whether stated or implict, which has directed the change or development, and comparing this critically to the conclusions and guidelines set out in this volume;

(3) Issuing guidance notes and model clauses embodying the best identified practices.

Index